THE VALOUR STILL

SHINES

THE FALLEN OF GRAVESHAM

THOSE LISTED ON THE GRAVESHAM MEMORIAL

WHO LOST THEIR LIVES IN THE GREAT WAR

We thank our two sponsors for ensuring the publication of the book –

Funded by
Gravesham Borough Council

St. John's Catholic School

Introduction

THE VALOUR STILL SHINES - The Fallen of Gravesham

As we commemorate 100 years since the start of World War one; we pay our respects to those that made the ultimate sacrifice; we remember those who fought and returned back to us changed from seeing the horrors of war and pray for those known unto god but who lay in unnamed graves.

Here is a local story of local heroes; individuals and families that played an important part in bringing the final victory.

The Great War affected our community; its impact is marked by all those names on the many war memorials around the Borough of Gravesham.

The students of St John's Catholic Comprehensive school have researched the lives of the soldiers listed on those memorials, so many of our local heroes were lost that it has taken three volumes of *THE VALOUR STILL SHINES*, to document them comprehensively.

Each soldier has a biography with pictures and where they are buried, the detail the students achieved here about the events; the people; and the acts of heroism help to build a historically accurate document; a picture of what it was like 100 years ago.

The quality of the research has made this an interesting and emotional read, you share the life journey of every hero and feel the effect the horror of going to war had on the people who were resident here in this place, and how they came be sent from our home town to fight for our freedom.

The Great War took the lives of 17 million people the loss is still felt today, the names in *THE VALOUR STILL SHINES* are familiar to us because they are Gravesham people, and members of the families still live locally and are our friends and neighbours.

As Mayor of the fine borough of Gravesham I was proud to be asked to foreword this superbly detailed account of World War One, I thank the writers for bringing the stories together, you can feel the respect and reverence as you read.

It is an important and detailed book of Local people connected by this one thing; by their acts and sacrifices it gave us the chance to live our lives in peace and freedom.

John Càller

Councillor John Càller
Mayor of Gravesham

Foreword

It is with great pleasure that I write the foreword to this first book, in a series of five, which tells the stories of so many brave young men whose names are recorded on memorials in Gravesham after giving their lives in the (First) 'Great' war. The sheer scale of that War is reflected in the number of names listed on the many Memorials in the Borough. The many Memorials bear the names of those who gave the 'greatest sacrifice'. It is with this in mind that this project commemorates the centenary of that conflict.

So many men are listed that no less than five volumes are planned to cover all the Memorials. This first book will focus on the memorial at Windmill Hill and hopefully allows young people today to put some context to the images that so often flick across their television screens or to the topics they are taught in their history lessons. This book will be the first of three, no less. that will cover all those listed on this Memorial.

Having just returned from France and a visit to the D-Day beaches I have been acutely reminded of the courage and bravery that was needed to fight the menace of Nazi Fascism. The invasion of Europe in June 1944 ranks among the greatest of all engagements. Surely, we will never allow future generations to forget what was given – some 60 million dead world wide of which half a million were British.

This book seeks to remember and humanise those who were lost locally and provide our current generation the opportunity to learn and remember. The names will no longer be just that, having faded from the memory. Now, we will have their story and images to bring them back to life.

I would like to congratulate and thank all those who have contributed to this book in any way. Not least the students from our school, the History Society and the Local History Students. I would also like to thank the many supporters and all who helped from the local community and especially the 'Gravesham CAN' funding for the £2,000 grant that allowed this project to be realised. Most of all, however, I would like to thank Mr Murphy. His passion for making sure these stories are remembered and passed on, his commitment to working with students and involve them in the historical research and his sheer hard work are truly inspirational.

Enjoy the book and look out for the volumes to follow.

Sean Maher

Head of School

REMEMBRANCE SUNDAY

As the years go by and we grow old
Will we ever understand
The love, the courage and passion
That was spent to save our land

Those brave men that we never knew
Who fought to give us freedom
Just doing what they were told to do
Not questioning rhyme or reason

Imagine the sound of battle
With their only home a trench
The fear, the grief, the heartache
The bodies, mud and stench

When the order came to move forward
The enemy to repel
Two by two they progressed
One by one they fell

Their bravery will always be remembered
Our history tells it well
Those courageous men of valour
Who rescued us from hell.

Sid Harris

Preface

THE VALOUR STILL SHINES - The Fallen of Gravesham

War Memorials, we all know they exist; maybe we think a bit more about them annually on November 11th. Other than that many see them as little more than a memorial with a list of names. Ninety odd years ago, that list meant a lot to family and friends, but with the passage of time, the meaning has faded.

There is a quote I read in a history book by Sarah Wise and attributed to an English historian, George Macaulay Trevelyan:

"The poetry of history lies in the quasi-miraculous fact that once, on this earth, once, on this familiar spot of ground, walked other men and women, as actual as we are today, thinking their own thoughts, swayed by their own passions, but now all gone, one generation vanishing into another... The Dead were, and are not. Their place knows them no more, and is ours today. Yet they were once as real as we, and we shall tomorrow be shadows like them."

It makes you stop and think; those lists of names were real people who lived lives just like us. They were born, lived and worked in the same houses, streets and workplaces we still know of today. They served and died, as did so many others from countries across the world. Many of them were old enough to have children and their descendants are still in our community today. I feel they deserve to have more than just a name carved, inlaid or cast into stone, bronze or wood.

I think this work by St John's History Society on Gravesham's War Memorial in Windmill Gardens is a fine example of historical research and a valuable resource for local people, descendants and Great War enthusiasts. But, more than that, it is a wonderful tribute to ordinary people, from all walks of life who answered their Country's call and left home to fight in a war that cost them everything.

Andy White

Andy White,
Local Historian

ERECTED
IN PROFOUND AND GRATEFUL
REMEMBRANCE OF THE MEN
OF GRAVESEND WHO FELL IN
THE GREAT WAR
1914 ~ 1919.

NOT ONCE OR TWICE IN OUR ROUGH ISLAND STORY
THE PATH OF DUTY WAS THE WAY TO GLORY.

IN GRATEFUL AND ENDURING
1939 ~ REMEMBRANCE ~ 1945
OF ALL THOSE MEMBERS OF THE ARMED
FORCES AND CIVILIANS OF THIS BOROUGH
WHO FELL IN THE SECOND WORLD WAR

IHS

INDEX

1st Battalion, The Queens Own, Royal West Kent Regiment, at Neuve Chapelle on October 28th, 1914; painting by Frank Hyde [1849-1937]. The officer in the picture is Major H.B.H. White, D.S.O. At the time of the action he was a Lieutenant.

A PRIVATE
OF THE GREAT WAR
NAME UNKNOWN
ROYAL WEST KENT REGIMENT
9TH APRIL 1917

KNOWN UNTO GOD

Ste Catherine Cemetery, Arras

MEMORIALS & CEMETERIES

The Great War of 1914-1918 was so terrible and inflicted such large numbers of casualties on all sides that when it was over it was believed by many to be "The War to end All Wars". By the end of four years of fighting from August 1914 to November 1918 many thousands of families around the world were affected by the tragedy of the wounding or loss of one of their own. Communities were depleted of many of their young men. Villages and towns in the regions where battles had raged were badly damaged or almost completely destroyed. Some villages on the battlefield areas of The Western Front in France simply disappeared.

Preserving the memory of the people involved in the fighting, those people who were forever to be scarred by their involvement in the First World War, and the places ravaged by the war, was at the heart of a desire in the 1920s to find a way to mark their participation in such a large-scale, world-changing event.

Memorials to the First World War are many and varied. Official and private memorials are to be found on the battlefields of the various theatres of that war and in the home nation of those who served from the many countries which were involved in it.

Added to these more formalised memorial sites there were all sorts of ideas put forward for commemorating the war and the people who fought in it, which resulted in a wide variety of memorials. There were official tokens of Remembrance in the form of memorial plaques issued to relatives of the fallen and commemorative "Peace" medals. Charitable care for ex-Servicemen was begun under the auspices of the Flanders Fields Memorial Poppy, internationally recognised these days as a symbol of Remembrance with its roots in the tragedy of the First World War. Memorial rolls of honour were put up in factories, sports clubs, railway stations, schools, universities and so on. Church windows were designed and dedicated to military units or individuals. Memorial buildings were constructed to provide "living memorials", for example, as community centres, places for rehabilitation or worship.

From the very first battles in the early weeks of the fighting on The Western Front the number of military dead was already in the tens of thousands. The French Army suffered particularly badly, with a figure of 80,000 dead out of 250,000 killed and wounded by the end of the First Battle of the Marne (September 5th to the 12th, 1914).

As the war progressed over four years the casualties at each battle, whether it was a large-scale offensive or a more localised attack, were often very high. This was mostly as a result of the destructive capabilities of the weapons being used and the type of warfare being waged at that time.

REGISTRATION OF THE WAR DEAD

The scale of casualties in the First World War was unprecedented. Thousands of soldiers were being buried on the battlefields in individual or communal graves by their comrades. They were often buried where they fell in action, or in a burial ground on or near the battlefield. A simple cross or marker might be put up to mark the location and give brief details of the individuals who had died. In the early weeks of the war the British Army had no official register to whom these battlefield burials

could be formally reported with a name and the location of the grave.

Those individuals who reached a hospital in a safe area behind the fighting lines and who died of their wounds would usually be buried in a cemetery near to the hospital. Often it would be in an existing town or village cemetery or in a specially created annexed burial plot. These burials could be registered and their locations marked.

The large numbers of dead also confronted the warring nations with the question of what the military authorities and official authorities should do about registering the burials of the dead. The families who had lost a loved one would naturally expect that a record of the soldier's grave would be kept for pilgrimage visits or for the body's repatriation.

As a result, official war graves registration services were established by many of the fighting nations during or after the First World War.

THE "MISSING"

The difficult task for the graves registration services was increased by the nature of the fighting on certain battlefronts, such as the Western Front. The characteristics of siege and trench warfare on this battlefront meant that fighting often moved back and forth over the same ground. Between battle actions the day to day survival in filthy holes or trenches dug in to the ground and the hazards of exploding artillery shells, snipers and grenades resulted in many casualties from sickness and wounds. Many casualties were lost in collapsed underground tunnelling operations to mine under enemy positions.

Conditions in the landscape often added to the number of casualties. Heavy, prolonged rain could turn the landscape into a sea of mud. Accounts by soldiers during the 1917 Battle of Passchendaele at Ypres tell of men drowning and disappearing in the waterlogged shell craters and deep mud.

Graves and burial grounds situated in the area of a battlefront were often damaged by subsequent fighting across the same location, resulting in the loss of the original marked graves. Some bodies simply could not be retrieved from underground.

Added to this, the technical developments in the weaponry used by all sides frequently caused such dreadful injuries that it was not possible to identify or even find a complete body for burial.

These factors were generally responsible for the high number of "missing" casualties on all sides and for the many thousands of graves for which the identity is described as "Unknown".

COMMEMORATING THE "MISSING"

The nations involved in the First World War have chosen to commemorate the missing in various ways. There may be an official tomb or coffins in which an "Unknown" burial has been selected to represent the thousands of unidentified war dead of that country. There may be memorial walls in military burial grounds with names carved in stone or etched in bronze. Or there may be monuments with many thousands of names in battle sites to commemorate the individuals who are known to have died in that area but who have no known grave.

It is usually the victors who have the opportunity to put up memorials to honour their military dead. There may be many military dead, known or missing, from some nations who will never have their memory carved in stone or etched in bronze. Indeed, the German war graves agency, the Volksbund Deutsche Kriegsgräber Fürsorge (VDK) considers that there are still possibly approximately 80,000 German soldiers who fell in action in Flanders and whose remains cannot be accounted for. There is a similar figure for British casualties whose remains have never been found. They are all still "missing" in Flanders.

GRAVESEND – THE 'WINDMILL HILL' MEMORIAL

It is none other than George Matthews Arnold, as quoted by F.A. Mansfield, who wrote of Windmill Hill - *This well-known eminence is destined before another century to become (as I believe) the centre of our town, and hence the greater importance of its becoming public property, and a standing and permanent public ornament ..* prophetic words!

Arnold was an author and philanthropist. Born in 1826 he was a solicitor. He was one of the original members of Christchurch, Gravesend before converting to Catholicism in 1858. He was eight times Mayor of Gravesend. His philanthropy was extensive and his generous bequests include the two statues of Queen Victoria in the town as well as land for the extension of the 'Prom' [Promenade] and the General Gordon Memorial Gardens. He was also responsible for the restoration of St Catherine's Church, Shorne, St Mary's Church, Denton and Dode Church, Luddesdown. His antiquities museum forms part of the collection of the county museum in Maidstone and he had published several books.

Prior to his death in 1908 he established a fund to set up a monument in the memory of William Tingey, the founder of the town hospital, which was erected in the year of his death.

The Tingey Memorial lies further up Windmill Hill, to the right and beyond the War Memorial.

The Memorial is on the slope of Windmill Hill.

The Hill was a popular spot for Victorian tourists, because of the Camera obscura installed in the old mill and for the tea gardens and other amusements. Visitors started coming in the late 18th Century. Windmill Hill could be accessed directly by visitors arriving at the Town Pier by boat. Access to the Hill was by the High Street and Windmill Street. Visitors to Gravesend peaked in the first half of the 19th Century, former agricultural and mill buildings converted as the hill was developed to cater for visitors

The hill was the site of a beacon as early as 1377, which was instituted by Richard II, and still in use two centuries later at the time of the Spanish Armada. By then the hill was known as 'Rouge Hill'. The hill was also referred to as 'Ruggen Hill on other occasions.

It was during the reign of Elizabeth I that the first windmill was placed on top the highest point in Gravesend, 179 feet above the high water mark of the River Thames. The hill has been the site of farms and four mills, remnants still survive.
The hill was named Windmill Hill in 1719 after the mills which stood on the summit. Two mills are known to have existed during the 18th Century. One mill burnt down in 1763, and a replacement erected in its place the following year was demolished in

Recreation facility –
The view from the top of the Hill, left and right, the bowling green behind the War Memorial.

1894. The last surviving windmill was destroyed by fire during *Mafeking Night* celebrations in 1900.

Windmill Hill was purchased in 1843 by the Corporation. In 1889 the lower slopes were acquired. The latter were terraced and turned into pleasure and sports' grounds being formally opened by the Lord Mayor of London in 1902.

During the Great War, in 1915, the first bombs dropped on Gravesend were in the immediate vicinity and this is marked by the small granite commemorative stones.

Continuing with Mansfield - *A suitable memorial in honour of these men stands in Windmill Gardens, having been erected by public subscription, and formally dedicated on Wednesday, January 11th, 1922. The unveiling of the Memorial was marked by a solemn and impressive service, in the presence of a large concourse of people. It was performed by General Horne, the distinguished soldier who invented the creeping barrage.*

The position of the Memorial is unique being located in Windmill Hill Gardens, which were tastefully laid out at the beginning of the present century, and which provides accommodation for bowls and lawn tennis, which attract many people to the site.

A further and eminently practical Memorial of the War is the bungalows erected in a picturesque situation at the junction of Cross-Lane and Meopham-Road (east side). The ground was given by Mr T. C. Colyer-Fergusson, J.P. of Wombell Hall, in memory of his son who was killed in the War.

The scheme is to be credited to Mrs. H. Huggins, J.P. The necessary money for the building of the bungalows has been raised by subscription, and largely by a series of Tipperary Fairs, and it is desired to obtain a reserve fund for the maintenance of the buildings in good repair. There are ten cottages, in which ten families are housed, each having a garden, with a central green, the occupants having been selected by a body of Trustees.

19

The entrance to the bungalows …

The Memorial boards at the entrance.

THE FIRST MEMORIAL, 1917

The First War Memorial was unveiled in November, 1917 and comprised of wooden boards listing the names of soldiers already killed in the war. The boards were mounted on the outside of the [old] Town Hall.

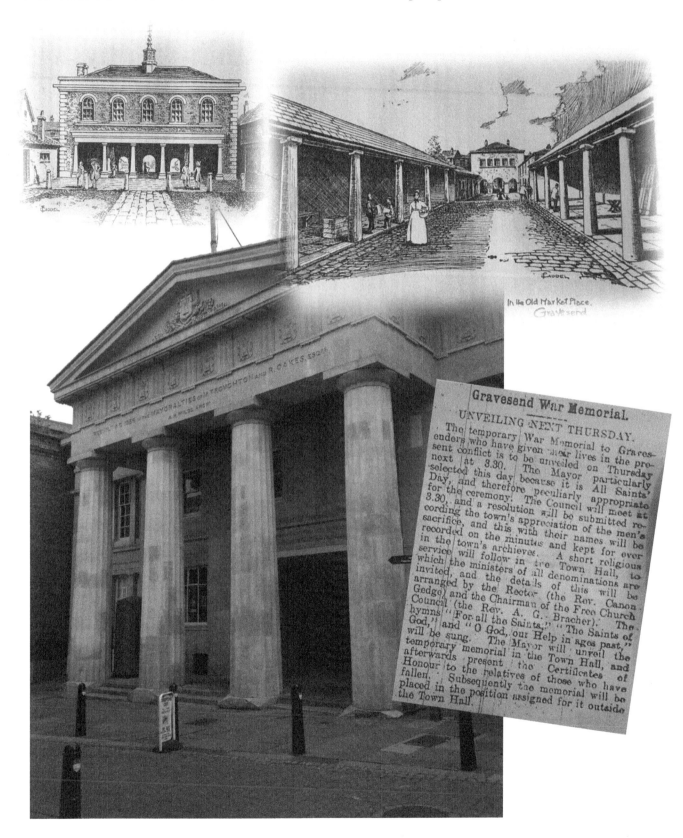

In the Old Market Place. Gravesend

Gravesend War Memorial.

UNVEILING NEXT THURSDAY.

The temporary War Memorial to Gravesenders who have given their lives in the present conflict is to be unveiled on Thursday next at 3.30. The Mayor particularly selected this day because it is All Saints' Day, and therefore peculiarly appropriate for the ceremony. The Council will meet at 3.30, and a resolution will be submitted recording the town's appreciation of the men's sacrifice, and this with their names will be recorded on the minutes and kept for ever in the town's archives. A short religious service will follow in the Town Hall, to which the ministers of all denominations are invited, and the details of this will be arranged by the Rector (the Rev. Canon Gedge) and the Chairman of the Free Church Council (the Rev. A. G. Bracher). The hymns "For all the Saints," "The Saints of God," and "O God, our Help in ages past," will be sung. The Mayor will unveil the temporary memorial in the Town Hall, and afterwards present the Certificates of Honour to the relatives of those who have fallen. Subsequently the memorial will be placed in the position assigned for it outside the Town Hall.

In Memory of the Fallen.

GRAVESEND'S WAR MEMORIAL UNVEILED.

A GATHERING OF SAD FACES.

The gathering which filled the Town Hall, Gravesend, on Thursday afternoon was a gathering of sad faces, indexes of sore and heavy hearts, for there was hardly one present who did not mourn the loss of a husband, a son, a father, or a sweetheart. The occasion was a special meeting of the Gravesend Town Council to place on record, in an official and formal manner, the sense of the town's appreciation of the sacrifices which have been made by the men who have fallen in the war, to unveil the temporary war memorial which is to be placed outside the Town Hall, so that passers-by may be reminded of the nobility of sacrifice and perchance breathe a prayer of gratitude for the fragrant memories which these brave men have left behind, and to present to a relative or representative of each fallen man a Certificate of Honour, to be treasured in the home alongside those other little treasures which have the personal interest of the dead attached to them. But if it was a gathering of sad faces and sore hearts, it was also a gathering in which the spirit of pride and resignation was predominant. "How can man die better than facing fearful odds?" asked Lord Macaulay in his story of Horatius, but no Roman soldier ever faced the fearful odds our men have faced in this grim war, in which all the instruments of the Devil have been commissioned by an unscrupulous enemy. They died nobly and they deserved this recognition at the hands of their grateful townsfolk.

The gathering was the most impressive we have attended in Gravesend, and the religious element in the proceedings was the happiest of inspirations. Everything was well arranged. The relatives of the men occupied seats facing the dais, on which were seated the members of the Council, and representatives of the Established and Free Churches, and below were placed the officials of the Council, with the Town Clerk in the centre. The members of the Council present were the Mayor (Alderman Huggins), Aldermen H. E. Davis, S. Walter, A. E. Enfield, W. H. Archer and F. Goldsmith, Councillors J. G. Prevost, W. E. Thomas, J. Fulljames, F. Cutton, W. E. Cunningham, W. Harrington, H. Hinkley, J. H. Austin, R. L. Priestley, J. Berrey and W. G. Wynn. The ritual of the ordinary Council meeting was observed—the announcement by the mace-bearer "The Mayor," the rising to the feet on the entry of his Worship, the placing of the "bauble" on the front of the Mayoral desk, and the declaration calling upon persons to attend the Court and the patriotic tag "God Save the King." Then the names of the members of the Council present were recorded, and the proceedings began with the singing of the hymn "For all the Saints" — appropriate for the occasion, which was All Saints' Day. Prayers were then offered by the Rev. Canon Gedge and the Rev. A. G. Bracher, after which the hymn "The Saints of God" was sung.

Following this came the business part of the meeting. The Town Clerk was called upon to read the following resolution:—

"That this Council, with heartfelt grief and yet with patriotic pride, desires to place upon the permanent records of the Borough the names of all those men of Gravesend who up to the present time have given their lives for their country and for the cause of justice and freedom for which this nation has waged and continues to wage war. That the Town Clerk be ordered accordingly to cause those names to be duly and honourably recorded upon the minutes of the Council. That his Worship the Mayor be asked to unveil the temporary memorial to the fallen men which is to be placed in front of the Town Hall, and to hand to their relatives now present the Certificates of Honour prepared and issued by the Town Council."

Alderman H. E. Davis: It is my duty, as senior Alderman, to move the resolution as read to you by our worthy Town Clerk. I assure you most sincerely every word in this resolution has my heartfelt sympathy. I need not say to you, friends, anything beyond the expressions in this resolution, but believe me it is the most sincere wish of the Council that those dear ones you have lost will be remembered to us on this tablet and not be forgotten. They have given their best—they have given their lives for their King and country.

Councillor Prevost: As senior Councillor it falls to my lot to second the resolution. As you read the resolution as printed it seems just to be a bare official statement, the same as will be inscribed on the minutes. But I want you to feel that although we give you the official part of the business we want you to know that here on the platform beats an ordinary human heart. I want you not only to recognise us as the official representatives of the town, but as human beings, who feel for you deeply from the bottom of our hearts. I should like to say that so far as we are concerned it is no scrap of paper we are offering you. We feel it is something you will be able to look upon in future years with satisfaction. Of course it is impossible for us to bring back to you your sweetheart, your husband, or your father. It is beyond us, and we know that for the rest of your lives you have got to try and bear your sorrow. You may be sure our hearts go out to you. Nothing we can do can assuage the grief you will feel for the rest of your lives, but we pray sincerely when you do look back you will feel that those loved ones who have given their lives for a good cause have followed the example of their Master, who gave His life for all of us, and I trust that not only you but we shall endeavour to serve our fellow men, so that when the time comes we shall hear what these loved ones of yours have heard, the words of the Master, "Well done, thou good and faithful servant."

The Mayor: Before I proceed to unveil this memorial I would just like to say a few words. In the first place the scheme for this temporary memorial and certificates of honour originated through two men. It was Alderman Enfield who proposed that the representatives of each man who had lost his life through this terrible war should be presented with a certificate of honour. I remember well when he proposed that resolution. I said I envied him because I had not thought of it myself. I think it was a splendid idea, and I am glad it has borne fruit. As regards the temporary memorial, it was Councillor Thomas who proposed that we should have a war shrine, but afterwards we thought we should like to have this temporary memorial instead. It is well-known to you that after the war is over—let us hope, in the providence of God, it will be soon—(applause)—there will be a permanent memorial erected in Gravesend worthy of our dear old town. I feel I cannot say a great deal about the nobility of the men who have laid down their lives, because that is too fresh in your minds and too sore a point with all of us, but we hope that their example will not be in vain, and that those who are left will follow up what they have done and lead our beloved country to a brilliant victory (applause). I should mention the generosity of Mr. H. Allen, who has done all the painting on this beautiful work of art free of charge (applause). We ought to thank him. Having in remembrance the

splendid work these men have done, how can we help in the good work? There are many ways in which we can help in carrying on this war, and one great point upon which we can help is being as economical and as saving as possible. You will see that toll of men. It can be replied to by us. Many sailors lose their lives in bringing foodstuffs to this country. In this way we may lessen the chance of the enemy in succeeding in his big attack by submarines. It behoves us to be as careful as possible and to save all we can, and so help the country in its hour of need. There are other ways, in charities, but I need say nothing about that, for Gravesend is proverbial for its charitable nature, and I hope that will continue after the war. We can also help in these terrible times of air raids by keeping up our courage and by not being downhearted in the way in which the Germans would wish us to be (applause). These raids are one of the parts of the German campaign of frightfulness in the hope of intimidating us into a peace. I am sure all Gravesend people will keep up their courage and do everything to prevent any panic. We in this hall will do all we can to emulate the magnificent example of these lads and, looking back, we then can all say "We have done our peace."

His Worship then unveiled the memorial, remarking that they would all agree with him as to its artistic merit.

The Town Clerk then read the names on the Roll of Honour, and as each was called a relative approached the dais and was handed the Certificate of Honour by the Mayor. This ceremony occupied upwards of an hour, and on its conclusion the hymn, "O God, our help in ages past," was sung, the Benediction was pronounced by the Rector, and the Nunc Dimittis was brought to a close by the singing of the National Anthem.

The CERTIFICATE OF HONOUR awarded to the next of kin of Thomas Allen. [Andrew Marshall].

Huggins,   Mayor.

Borough of Gravesend.

Unveiling of a Temporary : : Memorial to the Men of Gravesend who have fallen in the War, and Presentation of : : : : "Certificates of Honour" to the relatives of the men who have so : : : : : fallen. : : : : :

Record of the Proceedings

at a Special Meeting of Town Council held in the Town Hall on the Festival of All Saints', 1st November, 1917, at 3.30 p.m.

"Not once or twice in our rough island story
The path of duty was the way to glory."

H. H. BROWN, Town Clerk.

The programme for the unveiling on November 1st, 1917.
The programme lists the names of all those listed on the temporary Memorial.
[Courtesy Gravesend Library]

Names of the Gravesend Men who have lost their lives in the War, and whose Relatives received on the 1st November, 1917, a Certificate of Honour from the Gravesend Corporation.

Name.	Unit.
AMOS, JOSEPH H.	Pte., 6th Batt. R. W. K.
ASHDOWN, W. F.	Pte., 1st Border Regt.
ALLEN, HERBERT F.	Pte., 10th Batt. R.W.K.
ATKINS, FRANK STANLEY	Pte., 1st Batt. Coldstream Guards.
ACOTT, BERNARD	Pte., R.W.K.
ALLEN, WILLIAM F.	Lance-Corpl., 13th Royal Sussex.
ACWORTH, GORDON W.	Lieut., London Regt.
ALLSON, ERNEST H.	4th Officer, Merchant Service.
ALLEN, REGINALD P.	Rifleman, London Brigade.
ARCHER, EDWARD C.	Sapper, R.E.
ALLEN, THOMAS	Pte., R.W.K.
BARR, CECIL	Sapper, R.E.
BUCK, W. E. J.	A.B., R.N.
BAYLLON, G.	Pte., 2nd Batt. Scots Guards.
BOX, FRANK C.	Pte., 7th Buffs.
BETTS, JOHN C.	A.B., R.N.
BENSON, FREDERICK	2nd Steward, "Clan MacNaughton."
BENNETT, ROBERT Wm.	Gunner, R.W.K.
BURCHAM, FRED	Pte., 1st Batt. Buffs.
BARTLE, ERIC	Pte., 1st Infantry Brigade, C...
BOYD, CHARLES J.	Gunner, R.F.A.
BOORMAN, CYRIL	Trooper, West Kent Yeomanry.
BOWLER, H. LESLIE	Drummer, East Surreys.
BRADLEY, H. Wm.	Pte., R.W.K.
BRIDGLAND, NEVILLE LINTON	Lieut., 3rd E. Surreys.
BELL, ALBERT JOHN	Pte., 2nd Queen's R.W.K.
BIDDLECOMBE, PERCY	Pte., 24th Royal Fusiliers.
BUSH, F. G.	Storekeeper, R.N.
BARR, P. STANLEY	Corpl., 2nd Canadian Rifles.
BOX, PERCY T.	Storekeeper.
BROAD, PERCY A.	Pte., N.R. Guards.
BONFIELD, E.	Corpl., R.W.K.
BEAN, ALFRED HENRY	Seaman, R.N.R.
BURRILL, ALEC	Gunner, R.N.R.
BOTTING, H. A.	Pte., City of London R.F.
BROOMAN, ARTHUR FRANK	Pte., 1st Batt. R.W.K.
BRADY, G. W.	Bombardier, R.F.A.
BRITTEN, T.	Pte., 2nd Queen's R.W.S.
BARRETT, ERNEST JOSEPH	A.B., R.N.
BURLEY, T. G.	Lieut., R.F.A.
BOLDEN, Wm.	Pte., R.W.K.
CHAMBERS, ROBERT	Gunner, Motor M.G.S
CONGROVE, FRED	Petty Officer, R.N.
CHAPMAN, GEORGE Wm.	Pte., R.W.K.
CADIC, BERNARD FRANCIS	Captain, R.G.A
CADIC, LAURENCE WILLIAM	Captain, Essex Regt., M.C.
CREED, A. V.	Pte., 6th Batt. Norfolk Regt.
CORBY, J.	Pte., The Buffs
CROCKETT, A. J.	Sapper, R.F.R.E.
COLVILLE, S.	Petty Officer, R.N
CROTHALL, GEORGE	2nd Class Stoker
CLARKE, J. J.	Captain, Essex Regt.
CHRISTIAN, A.	Pte., R.W.K.
CALLAN, JAMES	R.N.D.
CHENNAL, JOHN	Lance-Corpl., R.M.L.I.
CRAVEN, JOHN HENRY	Lance-Corpl., R.D.F.
COSGROVE, LOUIS GEORGE	Pte., Durham L.I.
CORK, J.	Ship's Fireman.

24

The temporary Memorial Boards are currently housed inside the [old] Town Hall. Still in good condition the Boards remain as poignant as when erected if now very much out of the public view. [courtesy of Stephen Thompson & Dean Nelson]

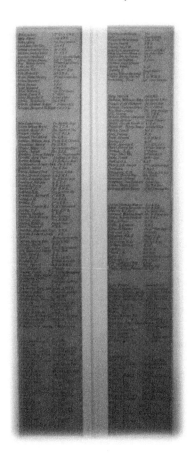

COMMEMORATING THE PEACE –

The 'official' Peace proclamation was on July 5th, 1919. The Mayor, James Berrey, performed the task at various points throughout the town with a huge throng in attendance at the Clock Tower where a Guard of Honour attended the proclamation there.

On the 6th there were thanksgiving services in the many and various churches in the town with the Mayor in attendance at St George's Church.

PEACE SOUVENIR, G.R.; Gravesend Library

Proclamation and Thanksgiving.

HISTORIC CEREMONIES AT GRAVESEND AND NORTHFLEET.

THE historic ceremony of proclaiming Peace to the inhabitants of Gravesend was performed on Saturday afternoon, July 5th. The Mayor, with members of the Corporation and other leading citizens, visited various parts of the town and officially informed large crowds that had assembled that we were once more at peace with Germany. The crowd was particularly large at the Clock Tower, although a little more enthusiasm might have been shown in the proceedings.

On Sunday there were Services of Thanksgiving at all the Churches, and crowded congregations seemed to be the general rule. The Mayor and Corporation attended St. George's Church, and there was a civic procession of a most representative character. At Northfleet in the afternoon a United Service took place in the Ebbs Fleet Pleasure Ground, and a big assemblage entered whole-heartedly into the ceremony. At Swanscombe and various other places also the citizens joined together in thanksgiving.

Proclaiming Peace at the Gravesend Clock Tower, on the 5th. July, 1919.

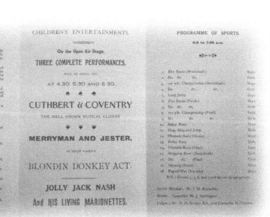

[images courtesy of
Gravesend Library]

A fortnight later a Children's Gala was held in the Paddock, Hillside; the impact of the Dublin Fusiliers is very evident – the Gala included the very typical sports' meeting in the form of an athletics' programme which again includes several typical Irish traditional events to include the 'hop, step and jump'.

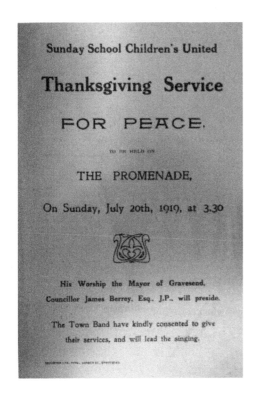

The Thanksgiving Service for Peace was held the following day, July 20th with the Mayor presiding. The event was held on the 'Prom'.

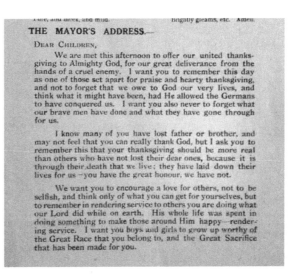

COMMEMORATING THE HEROES – short term

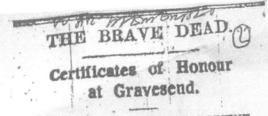

THE BRAVE DEAD.

Certificates of Honour at Gravesend.

FATHER OF V.C. WINNER PRESENT.

Yesterday (Thursday), at Gravesend Town Hall, more relatives of local men who have recently fallen in the war were presented by the Mayor with "Certificates of Honour" as small tokens of the borough's gratitude and pride.

This was the second ceremony of its kind, and the names on the "honour" list represented many branches and units of the fighting forces; the fallen also were drawn from all classes. The solemnity of the occasion was in a way intensified by the present critical stage of the war.

After two hymns (in which Mr. Howard Moss and choir assisted), and after prayers had been offered by the Rector (Canon Gedge) and Rev. A. G. Bracher, the following resolution was moved by Alderman H. E. Davis, C.C. (Deputy Mayor).

"That whereas this Council did on the 1st November, 1917, cause to be duly and honourably recorded on their minutes, and upon the Temporary Memorial now erected in front of the Town Hall, the names of those men who up to that date had fallen in the war. And whereas since then other Gravesend men have so fallen and the Council wish to do them the same honour. The Town Clerk be ordered to cause these additional names to be recorded in a like manner as heretofore, and that His Worship the Mayor be asked to hand to the relatives now present the Certificates of Honour prepared and issued by the Town Council."

In proposing the resolution, the Alderman said that from the innermost recess of his heart he sincerely hoped for a speedy and successful termination of this most terrible war. When that came their duty would be to look after those boys who returned, and to do their duty to the relatives of those who had fallen.

As senior Councillor, Councillor J. G. Provost seconded, and assured the bereaved of the Corporation's sympathy. Nothing they could say could bring back the touch of the vanished hand or the sound of the voice that was still. Those young fellows had died for us, and "greater love hath no man than this, that he lay down his life for his friends."

The Mayor said hearts were too full for them to say all they felt and thought. It was a memorable occasion and the certificates were presented in grateful thanks for the noble services which their fallen friends had rendered for those at home.

The certificates were then handed to the relatives by the Mayor, as the Town Clerk read out the names. Mr. T. C. Colyer Fergusson, J.P., of Wombwell Hall, Gravesend, was presented with one in memory of his son, the late Lieut. T. R. Colyer Fergusson, V.C., Northants Regiment.

The Benediction, followed by the National Anthem, brought the meeting to a close. Following is the list of Gravesend men

The temporary Memorial, dedicated on November 1st, 1917 listed the names of those local men who had died on active service up to that date. *Certificates of Honour* were given to the next of kin.

Six months later, in April 1918, the Council presented further Certificates of Honour to commemorate those who were killed or died on active service in the interim. Among those receiving a Certificate was Thomas Colyer-Fergusson, father of the Victoria Cross winner.

Despite the solemnity of the Memorial it would seem that some believed that the memory of those listed was not receiving the reverence due as the Chairman of the local Branch of National Federation of Discharged and Demobilised Sailors and Soldiers felt the need to write a letter to the press, below.

THE GRAVESEND WAR SHRINE.

TO THE EDITOR.

Sir,—I desire, on behalf of the Gravesend Branch of the National Federation of Discharged and Demobilised Sailors and Soldiers, to call attention to the War Shrine erected in High-street in memory of fallen heroes. To no one can this Shrine be so dear, except the immediate relations, of those fallen heroes, as to us. These fallen heroes were our comrades, and fought in the same battles as several of the members belonging to this Branch of the Federation. In a great many cases the Shrine is the only cemetery that fallen heroes have, and to all intents and purposes it is the official cemetery of all heroes belonging to Gravesend who have fallen in the Great War. A cemetery if only in this sense—the place where we hope the name of these heroes will live for ever. I therefore ask all citizens to pay the same amount of respect when passing or approaching this one spot in High-street, as they do when entering a cemetery, i.e., men refrain from smoking, both men and women speak in a subdued voice and their whole attitude be one of reverence. I particularly appeal to parents that they should make this Shrine an object lesson for their children so that they may imbibe the same spirit as shown by these fallen heroes—self-sacrifice and devotion to duty, these being two of the most essential qualities the rising generation should possess to make them fit to carry on the great ideals for which we have fought.

B. HARPER (Chairman).
Gravesend District Branch.

January 8th, 1919.

KM 18/1/19 [Andrew Marshall]

GR 20/4/18 [Andrew Marshall]

COMMEMORATING THE HEROES – long term

The interest generated in the proposed Memorial was quite something else in the immediate post War years. It is difficult now to appreciate and understand the controversy caused; the whole question of what a Memorial is, the purpose and the different types, the question of the design and designer, the composition, the location of the Memorial and finally the names to be listed, specifically whether Mayor's names should be on the Memorial! It all proved most controversial with the pages of the *GRAVESEND REPORTER* and the *KENT MESSENGER* of the period reporting on the several issues and printing letters from as far afield as Dublin!

The interest in the Memorial, the many suggestions, generated an interest that ensured major conversation on the subject that became quite vehement on occasion. The Council's efforts to elicit the public view included letters to the press and the sending out of circulars both of which generated interest, response and to an extent, ridicule.

In January, 1919 the first letters to the *REPORTER* on the question of the Memorial focused on the nature of the Memorial. 'Invicta' expressed an unusual concept in the issue of January 18th, right, when writing about the necessity of having *a little imagination*; in this case the suggestion was to build a New Town Hall on the Woodville Gardens site with the Memorial, in the shape of a stone cross being located here.

The *façade of old Town Hall* was to remain, it is suggested, with *an arcade of shops leading into the Market Place.*

Not surprisingly, this concept generated much favour as Sidney Kneale Kelley of Wellington Street, among others, supported the idea of a new facility, Town Hall and accompanying public buildings in the *REPORTER* of January 25th.

The support in this case was to promote the building of *suitable accommodation for concerts, meetings and other local gatherings.*

By April the focus moved to the rasing of funds for a Memorial. Concern was expressed over rival fund raining activities – in particular *Gratitude Week*. Gravesend apparently raised the sum of £326 with £226 of this from public subscription. Reverend Poole, St. James' Church, described the contribution as *a humiliating experience.*

border running along the case of the arcade. There are two main reasons why I suggest Woodville Gardens. First, it is already a place consecrated to the memory of the dead, as the tombstones testify (these could be removed to another place to make way for the proposed arcade), and, secondly, I believe that the gardens will in future approximate a little nearer to what will be the future centre of Gravesend. For the town is not likely to stand still, especially if the Deep Water Wharf becomes an accomplished fact. With the growth of the town will arise the need for a new Town Hall. Already there exists a crying need for a large hall, secure from the importunities of the picture palace speculator, for meetings, concerts, theatricals, and various local gatherings. In deciding the place for the memorial, let us have a little imagination as to what is likely to be needed in the future. Imagination tells me that the finest site for a new Town Hall is at the angle of Windmill-street and Wrotham-road, facing Woodville Gardens. Here in a central building could be accommodated all the municipal offices and departments, and this part of the town could be so improved that it could be made a really beautiful centre. Of course, the cautious public man will ask what is to be done with the present Town Hall. I should be inclined to leave the present facade where it is as an entrance to an arcade of shops on each side leading into the Market-place, and the police station and the space where the present war shrine is situate could be converted into handsome shops which would be a great improvement to the thoroughfare. If these sites and buildings were sold the proceeds would go a long way towards paying for a new Town Hall. If, however, the site were leased the ground rents would materially assist in paying principal and interest on the loan which would have to be raised for the suggested new hall.

INVICTA.

The debate rolled on but gradually the concept of a Memorial in stone appears to become acceptable to the majority. There was also a growing desire to have the Memorial in a central location which appeared to rule out Windmill Hill and associated Gardens.

R J Tall of Darnley Road expressed his views, REPORTER May 3rd, on the *building of utilitarian memorials* as *quite wrong* and *nothing more nor less than obtaining something on a false pretext*. The Memorial in his view should be *something in the nature of a dignified, appealing, outstanding feature, designed to perpetuate the memory of those who gave their lives.*

By now the public interest was such that the Mayor, James Berrey, wrote asking for opinion from the public on the most suitable location of the Memorial, *REPORTER*, May 24th, as the Council would be discussing that topic on the following Wednesday, 28th May.

THE GRAVESEND WAR MEMORIAL SITE.

To the Editor.

Sir,—I feel it is very important that we should be unanimous, if possible, as to the above, and as there are several most excellent and suitable sites suggested, I should like to give those who have lost their dear ones in the Great War an opportunity of giving their opinion on this important question. It will come before the Council on Wednesday next, when I am sure the members will gladly welcome an expression of opinion from those most interested in the matter. The following sites are suggested: (1) Windmill Hill (top); (2) Windmill Hill Gardens; (3) Woodville Gardens (Windmill-street); (4) Pelham-road. I shall be very pleased to receive the wishes and opinions of those who will kindly send them to me not later than Wednesday next, May 28th.—Yours faithfully,

JAMES BERREY (Mayor).

Town Hall, Gravesend.
May 21st, 1919.

The Gravesend Soldier, writing from France, whose letter was published in the *REPORTER* on January 3rd, 1920, was not at all pleased with the year's work done by the Council! He neither concurred with the proposed location – *a more out of the way spot could not be found* - Windmill Hill, nor with the proposed Memorial format, the stone cross – *a cheaper memorial could not be designed or a more plain one erected!*

The debate raged on!

THE WAR MEMORIAL.

To the Editor.

Sir,—Various pieces of conversation I have heard in the trains, recent remarks made at meetings, but more particularly a letter which appeared in your last week's issue by "A Resident," lead me to the conclusion that the proposed war memorial is in danger of losing its chief value. First of all, what is a war memorial? Surely it should be something in the nature of a dignified, appealing, outstanding feature, designed to perpetuate the memory of those who gave their lives in the great war! Its place should be at, or near to, the heart of the town, and its erection should be prompted by gratitude on the part of the living for the sacrifice made for them by those who have fought and fallen. The building of utilitarian memorials such as meeting halls, concert rooms, and such like, or of acquiring recreation and pleasure gardens, is quite wrong, and, to my mind, is nothing more nor less than obtaining something on a false pretext. If these things be essential for the public good, then by all means, obtain them through the proper channels, but not under the guise of the war memorial. Let us not have it said that our Gravesend memorial is "two for the living and one for the dead"; it must be all for the heroes, and for them alone.—Yours faithfully,

R. J. TALL.

36, Darnley-road.
23rd April, 1919.

THE PROPOSED WAR MEMORIAL.

To the Editor.

Sir,—In the "Reporter" of the 13th December I have just read with disgust and shame the proposed War Memorial for Gravesend.

In the first place it has taken the brains of thirteen persons three months to come to a decision to erect a cross upon Windmill Hill when such a proposal could have been found in a twelve years old schoolboy in ten minutes.

In the second place, a more out-of-the-way spot could not be found to hide it, not five persons out of five thousand, visiting Gravesend or passing through on business or pleasure ever will see it, and the Hill itself is only used by the inhabitants five months out of twelve in the year. It would be more public if erected in Bentley-street or the Old-road.

Thirdly, a cheaper memorial could not be designed or a more plain one erected; such memorials are erected in the smallest villages of England, and even on the Continent, the same is being built in villages of only one hundred inhabitants.

Upon the fourth thought, what a vast difference between the Queen Victoria's Jubilee Memorial in Milton-road (the Clock Tower) and the proposed War Memorial. With the best respects for the beloved Queen, I cannot erase from my mind her life of luxury and ease to the life of hell and suffering endured for five years by our men, and the agony of fatherless homes with their struggling widows and orphans, yet the Memorial Committee consider that they are not worth an equal or better public memorial.

The concept of a utilitarian Memorial was again mooted in the REPORTER in the Spring and early Summer – from water baths to providing funds for the Hospital which according, *REPORTER*, May 22nd, to Alderman Davis was making an appeal for an additional £2,000, to the provision of education for the children of the *fallen heroes,* E L Hudson, *REPORTER*, May 29th.

Alderman Davis' letter provoked quite a response – in favour and opposition to his ideas on the form the Memorial should take and location; the letters become quite fervent at times with opinion sharply divided.

However as the Memorial morphed into something quite different and the location finally was settled, that being the Gardens on Windmill Hill another altogether different controversy came to the fore – that of the inclusion of the names of Mayors on the Memorial. This was seen by many correspondents as being an affront to the names of those soldiers to be listed on the Memorial.

The Mayoral names would not subsequently be on the Memorial.

THE WAR MEMORIAL.

To the Editor.

Sir,—From what I can hear, we [illegible]e likely to have two names at least, prob[illegible]bly four[illegible] of past and present Mayors inscri[illegible]d on the War Memorial.

In the Market Hall last Tuesda[illegible] evening, at the Ratepayers' Association meeting called to support the candidatur[illegible] of Mrs. Doughty for the bye-election, the following written question was handed u[illegible]: "Was Mrs. Doughty in favour of the [illegible]ames of past and present Mayors being in[illegible]ribed on the War Memorial, or should it [illegible] for the heroes only who fell in the Great [illegible]ar"?

Mrs. Doughty's answer was "[illegible]." She was not in favour of any other na[illegible]es being on the memorial than of those de[illegible] fellows who fought and died for us. T[illegible]ere were between 500 and 600 residents as[illegible]mbled in the Market, and when Mrs. Dou[illegible]ty gave her answer she was cheered by o[illegible] and all. I did not hear one voice raised [illegible] protest against her views.

I, for one, Sir, and there are h[illegible]dreds of others, I am sure, in this dear o[illegible] town of ours, would raise a protest again[illegible] such an absurd procedure. We do not want a memorial to the living placed on [illegible]e stone, which we subscribed to, and whic[illegible] is to be dedicated to our glorious dead.

If the Mayors, past and present, are anxious for a memorial, I woul[illegible] suggest that a fund be raised (to which I would gladly subscribe) to erect a memo[illegible]ial in the Woodville Gardens, on which th[illegible]ir names and virtues could be inscribed. But as a subscriber I must appeal that [illegible]he War Memorial be kept sacred to the dead.

I understand that unless a strong protest is made immediately, the War Memorial Committee will allow t[illegible]o, if not more, names of Mayors to be inscribed. I would advise the R.P.A. and the associations of Discharged Soldiers and Sailors, to make their feelings felt on this subject.

I would suggest a petition be raised of subscribers to the Memorial Fu[illegible]d and a deputation be formed to wait o[illegible] the War Memorial Committee, and there [illegible]ace their views before them.

Hoping this letter will appe[illegible] to the other subscribers, and thanking you, Mr. Editor, for allowing this to appe[illegible] in your valued journal,—I remain, yours faithfully,

A SUBSC[illegible]IBER.

GR 27/11/20

Correspondence.

[It must be clearly understood that we do not hold ourselves responsible for opinions expressed in letters to the Editor.]

THE WAR MEMORIAL.

Sir,—May I be permitted, through the columns of your journal, to add my protest to that of "A Subscriber" against the proposed inscription on the memorial to our fallen soldiers.

I refer, of course, to the inclusion of the names of Mayors who, by chance, happen to have held office during or after the period of the war.

What have they done that their names should be perpetuated in this manner beside the immortal names of Our Glorious Dead?

Surely it would be the greatest presumption on the part of any living man to suggest that, whatever he may have done during the war, his sacrifice was as great as those who gave up everything worth while to fight and die for King and Country.

I look to the people of Gravesend to make their voices heard and resist this attempt by the living to usurp the honours of the dead. —Yours faithfully,

G. C. MUIRHEAD,
Capt., Corps of Military Accountants
(Late Lieut., Gordon Highlanders).

St. Andrew's Hotel, Dublin.
2nd December, 1920.

GR 11/12/20

THE COUNCIL –

It was never otherwise that the Memorial 'boards' at the [old] Town Hall were other than a temporary arrangement until such time as peace returned, victory was secure and the Council would focus on a suitable commemorative Memorial. The *REPORTER* noted on May 25th, 1918, right – some months before the Armistice – that The Works Committee recommended *that the Council take steps to erect a war memorial., and for that purpose empower the Works Committee with power to add to their number, to inaugurate a scheme which "should be worthy of the occasion", a prominent site in the district to be utilised and the War Office to be approached with a view to securing a suitable trophy.* The *trophy* never did materialise even if the Memorial did eventually do so after several twists and turns.

THE WAR MEMORIAL.

The Works Committee having considered a letter from the Secretary of the Factory Club Committee (Mr. W. H. Steadman), which had been referred to them by the Council, they now recommended that the Council take steps to erect a war memorial, and for that purpose empower the Works Committee with power to add to their number, to inaugurate a scheme which "should be worthy of the occasion," a prominent site in the district to be utilised and the War Office to be approached with a view to securing a suitable trophy.—Councillor Huntley, who had come in after the Works Committee minutes had been confirmed, objected to the course the Committee had taken. It should be a matter for the whole Council, he declared. — Councillor Veevers rose to his feet with a view of clearing the air, saying that the Works Committee were only going to do the preliminary work in connexion with the memorial, but Councillor Huntley objected more strongly to this, as he said that the preliminary work, that of inaugurating a scheme, was the most important point.— Councillor Davis sympathised with Councillor Huntley and agreed with what he had said.—Councillor Huntley was about to rise to his feet again when the Chairman intervened. "I am sorry, Councillor Huntley," he said. "The Works Committee's minutes have been passed, and I can allow no further discussion upon them. You can give notice for the next meeting if you like."—"Then I immediately give notice of motion," replied the Councillor. The discussion ceased after there had fallen from the lips of Councillor Davis the words: "A public matter—absolutely."

ROUND THE CLOCK TOWER.

LOCAL AND DISTRICT NOTES AND GOSSIP.

WAR MEMORIALS.

NOW that the war is virtually over and finis is almost written to the long but honourable roll of the mighty dead, public attention is being turned in the direction of perpetuating the memory of those who have fallen in the great conflict. This subject is likely to be in the forefront in Gravesend in the very near future. The Mayor has promised to call the Memorial Committee together, but we trust with our correspondent whose article appears in another column, that the personnel of that committee will be enlarged so that it will be representative of every part of the community. We believe the local branch of the Discharged and Demobilised Sailors' and Soldiers' Federation have already moved, and have asked for a place for a representative on the committee. With regard to the form the memorial shall take there will naturally be many views and suggestions. One suggestion, which takes a long view into the future, appears in an article in this issue, but we should like to hear other suggestions before we endorse any particular one. The only reservation we make—and we believe we are echoing the bulk of public opinion—is that the memorial should take the form of a monument which everybody can see, and which shall stand to the generations yet unborn as the symbol of the greatest self-sacrifice that the world has ever witnessed.

The New Year brought the whole question into the public domain very much through the press. The *REPORTER* of January 18th, 1919 commented on the recent Council meeting where a proposal was made to erect a memorial; there were concerns over the Committee entrusted with the task, what the remit was, where the memorial was to be sited and what the memorial should be. The Editorial, left, concurred with the correspondent.

The major issue it seems was location – the memorial needed to be in a central location where it would be seen by the largest number of people possible; such sites as Windmill Hill, Gardens and summit and the 'Prom' were deemed to be too far out of the way to be considered.

The question of architect was also a cause of concern but the celebrated Herbert Baker was mentioned. This renowned architect was born in Owletts, Cobham in June, 1862 and would actually die there in February, 1946. Among his more famous

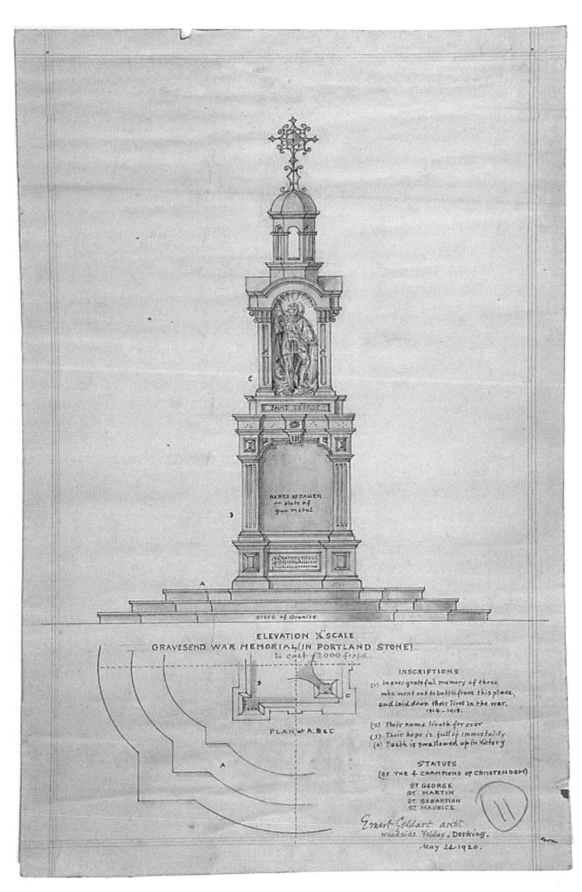

A submitted design for the Memorial by Ernest Geldart, dated May, 1920, above [courtesy Andrew Marshall].

creations was Tyne Cot Cemetery and both India House and South Africa House in London; he was also responsible for the Grace Gates at Lord's Cricket Ground, having presented the Marylebone Cricket Club with the celebrated Old Father Time weather vane. He worked for years in South Africa and India where his work was welcomed and well received. For one reason or another he would have no involvement with the memorial in Gravesend – perhaps he was all too aware of the sensitivities and passions that the memorial would arouse.

Before any Committee could deal with the issue it had to be created and a constitution agreed on as noted in the *REPORTER*, January 25th, right, and so the matter rumbled on.

THE PROPOSED WAR MEMORIAL.

The constitution of the committee to deal with this matter was discussed at some length, the present committee suggesting that outside members might be co-opted if thought fit. An application was received from the Gravesend Branch of the Discharged and Demobilised Sailors' and Soldiers' Federation asking for a representative, and Councillor Owen pleaded that the Mercantile Marine should also be represented. The present members were the Mayor, Aldermen Enfield and Goldsmith, Councillors Prevost, Thomas, Harrington and Fletcher, and it was agreed to add Aldermen Davis and Huggins and Councillors Fullames, Owen and Axcell, who were empowered to co-opt outside members if thought desirable.—A suggested site for the memorial was the triangle at the junction of Darnley and Pelham-roads, and Councillor Wynn expressed the view that the owner, Alderman Davis, might give the town that site for the purpose.

GRAVESEND'S

Permanent War Memorial.

PUBLIC MEETING SUGGESTED.

As a member of the committee deputed by the Town Council to make recommendations re the above, I shall be betraying no secrets dealing with the matter so far as it has gone at present. The committee is most anxious, not only to recommend a suitable memorial on a desirable site, but to have the assistance and advice of the townspeople as a whole, and particularly of the relatives of the brave men who have laid down their lives in the great struggle for freedom and right.

In a matter of this kind it is best to first decide upon the form the proposed memorial will take, and I think I am justified in saying that the general feeling is that a monument inscribed with the names of the fallen will be the most suitable and convenient method for the object desired, bearing in mind the amount of money likely to be available.

The next important question is, of course, the site, and the following have been suggested by people interested in the subject:—(1) The top of Windmill-hill; (2) the gardens at the bottom of the same; (3) the junction of Pelham and Darnley-road; (4) the promenade; (5) Woodville Gardens; (6) the land in front of the County School. In considering the above it will be found that each has certain objections as opposed to its advantages, and it is only by carefully weighing the pros and cons that we shall find the best spot for our purpose.

GR 29/3/19

The following month the *REPORTER* carried a lengthy article, left, by W J Harrington, a member of the Memorial Committee. He outlined the favoured option of the nature of the memorial and the various proposed sites and believed the matter to be so important as to require a public meeting be called so that the people of Gravesend would be able to express their opinions on the subject.

However there remained the thorny question of the cost with the Board believing that voluntary subscription was the only recourse, below.

The proposals for local war memorials vary in different districts. The provision of certain kinds of memorials (e.g., in the form of recreation grounds, or buildings to serve as libraries or hospitals) is ordinarily within the statutory powers of a local authority, who would in such cases, no doubt, proceed in the usual manner; but in other cases (e.g., where the provision of social clubs or village halls or institutions is suggested) sanction by the Board under the Act of 1887 would generally be required to authorize the expenditure. In the opinion of the Board a public appeal for voluntary subscriptions from the inhabitants should be made by the local authority before having recourse to the rates. It would also be desirable that the general opinion of the inhabitants of a district should be ascertained before the local authority commit themselves to any proposal involving large expenditure.

The War Memorial.

QUESTION OF SITE BEFORE TOWN COUNCIL.

The question of the site for the War Memorial came before the Gravesend Town Council on Wednesday, when the following Memorial report was received from the War Memorial Committee:—

The Town Clerk reported that the Rev. Canon Gedge, Rev. Father Kilmartin and the Rev. G. Sneesby had consented to act on the Committee.—The question of the site for the war memorial was again considered, and it was recommended that the memorial be placed on Windmill Hill.

Alderman Huggins moved that the words "and Windmill Hill Gardens," the final selection being left to the Committee," he added. He said there seemed to be a great deal of diversion of opinion as to whether Windmill Hill or Windmill Hill Gardens should be selected as the site for a memorial, and he considered under the circumstances that it would be the best thing to leave the decision to the Committee. He thought there was a large majority in favour of Windmill Hill, but a great deal depended on the character of the memorial.

Alderman Enfield seconded.

Councillor Harrington felt that the Council should have the opportunity of deciding on this very important matter. If the motion was passed it would not be possible to make any suggestions as to the alternative sites, as they would be investing the Committee with executive powers.

Councillor Porter thought in the interests of the Committee it was advisable that the Council should have the final selection, and that first of all it should be decided what form the memorial should take.

Councillor Hinkley referred to the form of the memorial, and thought if they would raise sufficient money they should follow the example of other towns and have some sort of institution. They did not want to erect stones that served no useful purpose.

FIRST LIST OF SUBSCRIPTIONS.

	£	s.	d.
His Worship the Mayor (Councillor J. A. Axcell)	25	0	0
Messrs. Russell's, Ltd.	500	0	0
Messrs. Imperial Paper Mills, Ltd.	210	0	0
Messrs. Charrington's, Ltd.	105	0	0
Messrs. Porter, Putt and Fletcher	50	0	0
Alderman H. E. Davis	25	0	0
A. Richardson, Esq., M.P.	21	0	0
C. E. Hatten, Esq.	21	0	0
Collection by Comrades of the Great War	19	12	0
Collection by Association of Discharged Sailors and Soldiers	15	1	9
Mr. and Mrs. E. A. S.	10	0	0
Gravesend Liberal Club	5	0	0
Mr. P. R. Davison	5	0	0
Mr. H. Mott	5	0	0
Mr. and Mrs. Bloxam	3	3	0
Mr. F. H. Simpkins	2	2	0
Mr. and Mrs. R. Doust	2	0	0
Anglo-Saxon Friendly Society, Brunswick Branch (No. 9)	1	1	0
W.M.S.	1	0	0
Councillor McGregor	10	10	0
Councillor Thomas	5	5	0
Alderman Walter		5	0
Alderman Huggins	2	2	0
Councillor Berrey	2	2	0
Councillor Catton		5	0
Councillor Harrington	2	2	0
Councillor Wynn	1	1	0
Councillor Priestley	1	1	0
Mr. W. J. Holland	2	2	0

By the end of May, Windmill Hill seemed to be the favoured site – if not yet finalised, *REPORTER*, May 31st, left, but the form of the memorial remained in question.

Finally, in December the Committee agreed that the memorial be sited in the Gardens, Windmill Hill, REPORTER, December 13th, below.

WAR MEMORIAL COMMITTEE.

It was recommended that the site for the Memorial be at the top of Windmill Hill. The votes were by order of the Committee as follows:— For — The Mayor, Aldermen Huggins and Prevost, Councillors Owen and Shade, Mr. J. Roche, the Rev. Sneesby, and Capt. Lane; against — Alderman Enfield, Councillors Fulljames, Harrington and Fletcher, and Mrs. Berrey. — Recommended that the Memorial take the form of a Cross with panels for the names of the fallen men, with fitting surroundings in accordance with the plan prepared by the Borough Surveyor.

There was some discussion concerning the site of the war memorial, and a majority expressed disapproval at the top of Windmill Hill being chosen. Eventually it was agreed by eleven votes against six that the memorial be erected in the Windmill Hill Gardens.

Decisions were finally being made. By May, 1920 a formal appeal was launched for funds and the list of subscribers was published in the *REPORTER* of May 28th, 1920.

AXCELL,   MAYOR.

BOROUGH OF GRAVESEND.

Gravesend War Memorial.

Town Clerk's Office,
Gravesend.

I NOW venture to make to the inhabitants of the Borough a formal and definite appeal for a donation to the above Memorial, and I regret the delay which has to a great extent been due to honest differences of opinion amongst those interested, differences I am glad to say now happily reconciled.

I may remind the Burgesses that it is now finally proposed that the Memorial shall take the form of a suitable and dignified monument to be erected in a prominent and easily accessible site in Windmill Hill Gardens, and any balance remaining will be applied in assisting dependants or relatives of fallen men.

The first list of subscriptions appears below, and I feel satisfied that, with such a beginning, we may look forward with confidence to a Memorial worthy of the Borough and, what is far more, in some slight degree worthy of the memory of the devoted band of sailors, soldiers, airmen, and merchant seamen who, in the Empire's hour of peril, laid down their lives for all that they held dear.

J. A. AXCELL, Mayor.

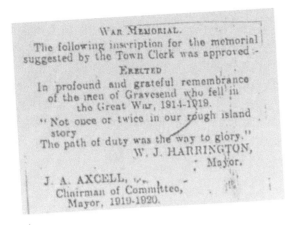

The final episode in the story came in November 1920 as the *REPORTER* of the 17th noted. Two important issues concerned the Committee in the meeting reported on – the inscription on the memorial and the *deletion of the names of the Mayor and the Chairman of the Committee from the inscription.*

Both were duly approved and so the names on the memorial would be those who had died as a result of the Great War.

The design that was chosen for the Memorial was one submitted by A. W. Doyle-Jones. *The Gravesend Reporter, below,* described

Councillor Ramsay moved the deletion of the names of the Mayor and the Chairman of the Committee from the inscription. He said he did so without any feeling of disrespect to the Mayor or Alderman Axcell. He felt that in such a case as this where a memorial of this character was concerned, no other names but those of the Glorious Dead should be on the memorial. He wanted to appeal to those two gentlemen to allow their names to be withdrawn, and in doing that he knew that he was voicing public opinion. If they would only withdraw he would promise to give them anything—he would place them on a scroll of honour in letters of gold. But they could not allow their names to go down to posterity with those men who had died for their country. He did not suggest that they wanted their names placed on the memorial as a cheap advertisement, because he thought they were above all that. Even although Alderman Axcell did work hard, it was his duty as Mayor to do so. If they allowed their names to go on, he looked upon it as nothing less than a sacrilege, and they would receive the scorn instead of the thanks of the populace of the town. He intended to fight tooth and nail for what the people wanted; he wanted no trouble, and he appealed to the Mayor and the Alderman to withdraw.

Councillor Hinkley, in seconding, said he was sorry that the whole matter had cropped up that evening. They all realised that it was about time that those poor boys who had given their lives for their country, were allowed to rest without the matter being continually raked up to allow someone to get some personal commendation. No names but those who had made the great sacrifice should be on the memorial.

Alderman Davis felt convinced that neither the Mayor or Alderman Axcell had acquiesced in their names being placed on the memorial without consideration. It had always been the custom to place at least the name of the Mayor on any new building or structure of this character that was erected, and he was sure the two gentlemen concerned would weigh up in their minds all that had been said, and come to a conclusion. At the same time he was sure they would all exonerate them from the motive of obtaining any cheap advertisement from this and occasion.

Councillor Cunningham suggested that the matter be referred back to the Committee for further consideration.

Alderman Prevost said an appeal had been made to the Mayor and Alderman Axcell, and it would place the members in a very awkward position to vote. He thought it should be left to their consciences to decide.

Councillor Ramsay and Councillor Hinkley agreed to accept the amendment to refer the matter back to the Committee, and this course was agreed to without further discussion.

the Memorial at length in the report of the unveiling in January, 1922. The life sized figure of Victory adorned the summit of the granite plinth on which the names of the 545 soldiers were listed.

THE UNVEILING

The Memorial was dedicated on Wednesday, January 11th, 1922.

The *REPORTER* of January 7th noted the event and the arrangements; it seems the Mayor and Councillors were to assemble at the Town Hall to walk together to Windmill Hill!

On conclusion of the ceremony it was back to the Town Hall on the High Street where *refreshments would be provided* – at least the return journey was downhill!

The route would in fact take the dignitaries past Woodville Gardens, the site of the current Municipal Buildings.

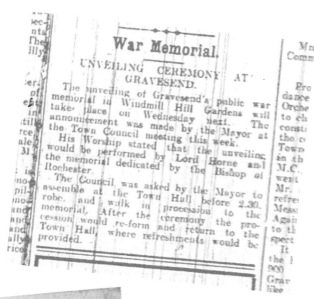

The programme issued on the occasion of the unveiling of the Memorial. [Gravesend Library]

SCRIPTURE READING by The Rev. G. Soonsby.   Revelations, Chapter 7, Verses 13-17.

---

13. And one of the elders answered, saying unto me, What are these which are arrayed in white robes? and whence came they?

14. And I said unto him, Sir, thou knowest. And he said to me, These are they which came out of great tribulation and have washed their robes, and made them white in the blood of the Lamb.

15. Therefore are they before the throne of God, and serve him day and night in his temple: and he that sitteth on the throne shall dwell among them.

16. They shall hunger no more, neither thirst any more; neither shall the sun light on them, nor any heat.

17. For the Lamb which is in the midst of the throne shall feed them, and shall lead them unto living fountains of waters: and God shall wipe away all tears from their eyes.

The Worshipful the Mayor (Councillor W. E. Thomas, J.P.) will ask General Lord Horne, G.C.B., K.C.M.G., A.D.C., to unveil the Memorial.

*   *   *

Lord Horne will reply and unveil the Memorial.

DESCRIPTION OF THE MEMORIAL.

*   *   *

The War Memorial consists of a bronze figure Emblematic of Victory bringing Peace. The figure is erected on a pedestal of granite, and on the pedestal are inscribed the names of the men who fell in the War, to the number of 543.

The Memorial was designed by Mr. F. W. Doyle-Jones, R.B.S. Its height over all is about 30 feet.

DEDICATION
By the Right Reverend The Lord Bishop of Rochester.

The Mayor will ask the Right Reverend the Lord Bishop of Rochester to dedicate the Memorial. His Worship using these words:

"In memory of all those of this Town who laid down their lives in the great cause for which they so bravely fought; for World Freedom and for International Righteousness, we have set up this Memorial which we now pray you to bless and dedicate to the Glory of God, and in thankful remembrance of their supreme sacrifice."

The Bishop will then dedicate the Memorial, using these words:

"In the faith of Jesus Christ we dedicate this Memorial to the Glory of God and to the undying memory of our brothers who gave their lives for us during the Great War. In the Name of the Father, and of the Son, and of the Holy Ghost." Amen.

THE LAST POST.

THE REVEILLE.

Roll of Honour.

A.

Acott, Bernard
Aitken, William Whiteley
Aitkin, Douglas G.
Albert, Thomas James
Allan, William Barclay
Allchin, Sidney Milton
Allen, Herbert F.
Allen, Thomas
Allen, William F.
Allen, Reginald P.
Alison, Ernest H.
Amos, J. H.
Amos, James
Anderson, Charles Henry

Andrus, Henry
Anual, James Alex. T.
Archer, Edward C.
Arnold, Bernard William
Ashdown, W. F.
Ashenden, Archibald Herbert
Ashenden, Stanley Rydar
Atkins, Frank Stanley

B.

Bailey, Herbert Sargant
Baker, Edward Charles
Banham, Frederick Stanley

Bare, Cecil L.
Barnes, William Henry
Barr, P. Stanley
Barrett, Ernest James
Bartle, Eric L.
Bayldon, G.
Bescon, Edward Jesse
Bean, Alfred Henry
Bell, Albert John
Belmore, William John
Bennett, George B.
Bennett, George
Bennett, Robert William
Bennett, Thomas Alfred
Benson, Frederick
Berridge, Victor Charles

Roll of Honour—continued.

Betts, John C.
Bavan, Franklin George
Biddlecombe, Percival
Bill, Rodney Edward
Bloomfield, Alfred
Blower, Walter C. L.
Bolden, William
Bone, Thomas
Bonfield, E.
Boorman, Cyril Adlington
Botting, H. A.
Bowden, Reginald Charles
Bowles, H. Leslie
Box, Frank C.
Box, Percy T.
Boyd, Charles J.
Bradbrook, Joseph William
Bradford, William
Bradley, Ernest Sidney
Bradley, H. William
Brady, G. W.
Brady, Joseph
Bridgland, Neville Linton
Brinkley, Thomas William
Britten, T.
Bread, Percy A.
Broad, Harold
Brooman, Arthur Frank

Brown, Sidney Frederick
Buck, W. R. J.
Buckmaster, Ernest John
Bull, George
Bureham, Fred
Burles, T. J.
Burles, William
Burrill, Alexander
Burville, John Thomas
Bush, F. G.
Butcher, Daniel
Byrne, Henry Robert

C.

Cadic, Bernard Francis
Cadic, Lawrence William (M.C.)
Callan, James
Carter, George Tristram
Chambers, Robert
Chapman, George William
Chibnall, John
Childs, Charles Edward
Childs, Frederick
Christian, A. R. (M.M.)
Church, Frederick V.

Clarke, Charles Watts Freelove
Clarke, Herbert V.
Clarke, J. J.
Clarke, Wildred Randall
Clifford, Edward
Colbourne, F. W.
Cole, Arthur
Cole, George
Collier, Harry Charles
Colville, S.
Colyer-Ferguson Riversdale (V.C.)
Connolly, John V. M.
Connolly, F.
Constant, Charles Frederick
Copper, Albert George
Coppins, Frederick John
Coppins, William
Coppins, Will James Thomas
Corby, J.
Cork, J.
Cosgrove, Fred
Cosgrove, Louis George
Cracknell, William H.
Craven, John Henry
Creamer, Alfred William
Creed, A. V.
Creed, C. E.

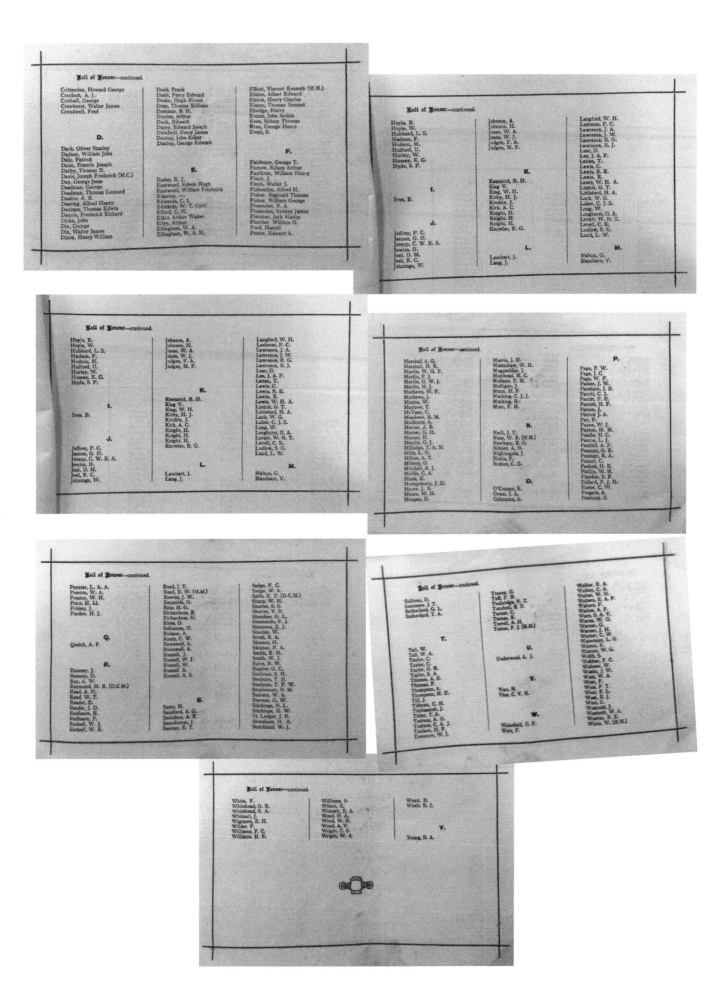

Roll of Honour—continued.

Crittenden, Howard George
Crockett, A. J.
Crothall, George
Crowhurst, Walter James
Crundwell, Fred

D.
Dack, Oliver Stanley
Dadson, William John
Daly, Patrick
Dann, Francis Joseph
Darby, Thomas N.
Davis, Joseph Frederick (M.C.)
Day, George Jesse
Deadman, George
Deadman, Thomas Leonard
Deakin, A. R.
Dearing, Alfred Henry
Denham, Thomas Edwin
Dennis, Frederick Richard
Dicks, John
Dix, George
Dix, Walter James
Dixon, Henry William

Dodd, Frank
Dodd, Percy Edward
Drake, Hugh Rivers
Dray, Thomas William
Dresman, R. H.
Dryden, Arthur
Duck, Edward
Duley, Edward Joseph
Dumbrill, Percy James
Dunlop, John Edgar
Dunlop, George Edward

E.
Eaden, E. J.
Eastwood, Edwin Hugh
Eastwood, William Frederick
Edgeley, —.
Edwards, C. L.
Edwards, W. T. Cyril
Elford, C. W.
Elkin, Arthur Walter
Riley, Arthur
Ellingham, W. A.
Ellingham, W. A. H.

Elliott, Vincent Kenneth (M.M.)
Elston, Albert Edward
Elston, Henry Charles
Elston, Thomas Samuel
Elvidge, Harry
Eves, John Archie
Eves, Sidney Thomas
Eves, George Henry
Evett, S.

F.
Fairbrass, George T.
Farrow, Sidney Arthur
Faulkner, William Henry
Finch, J.
Finch, Walter J.
Fishenden, Alfred H.
Fisher, Reginald Thomas
Fisher, William George
Fissenden, R. A.
Fissenden, Sydney James
Fletcher, Jack Haslip
Fletcher, William G.
Ford, Harold
Foster, Edward A.

Roll of Honour—continued.

Hoyle, E.
Hoyle, W.
Hubbard, L. S.
Hudson, F.
Hudson, H.
Hulford, U.
Hurley, W.
Hussey, E. G.
Hyde, S. P.

I.
Ives, B.

J.
Jeffrey, P. C.
Jenner, G. H.
Jessop, C. W. R. A.
Jewiss, H.
Joel, D. M.
Joel, R. C.
Johnings, W.

Johnson, A.
Johnson, H.
Jones, W. A.
Jones, W. J.
Judges, F. A.
Judges, M. F.

K.
Kennaird, R. H.
King V.
King, W. H.
Kirby, H. J.
Kirchin, J.
Kirk, A. G.
Knight, H.
Knight, H.
Knight, H.
Knowles, R. G.

L.
Lambert, J.
Lang, J.

Langford, W. H.
Lashmar, P. C.
Lawrence, J. A.
Lawrence, J. W.
Lawrence, R. G.
Lawrence, R. J.
Lear, D.
Lee, J. A. P.
Leitau, T.
Lewis, C.
Lewis, R. E.
Lewis, R.
Lewis, W. H. A.
Lintott, G. T.
Littleford, H. A.
Lock, W. G.
Loker, C. J. S.
Long, W.
Longhurst, G. A.
Lovatt, W. H. T.
Lovell, C. E.
Ludlow, S. G.
Lund, L. W.

M.
Malson, G.
Mandsam, V.

Roll of Honour—continued.

Marshall A. G.
Marshall, H. E.
Martin, W. H. F.
Martin, F.
Martin, G. W. J.
Martin, H. J.
Mathews, W. F.
Mathews, J.
Maxim, W.
Mayhew, T.
McVean, C.
Meadows, R. M.
Medhurst, A.
Mercer, A. R.
Mercer, G. H.
Merritt, G. J.
Milledge, T. A. N.
Mills, L. O.
Milton, A. T.
Milway, O.
Mitchell, A. J.
Mobbs, C. A.
Monk, E.
Montgomery, J. D.
Moore, J. A.
Moore, W. H.
Morgan, E.

Morris, J. H.
Mottashaw, W. H.
Muggeridge, J.
Muirhead, M. C.
Mullane, P. M.
Mulligan, J.
Munn, H. F.
Murking, C. J. J.
Murking, R.
Murr, F. H.

N.
Neill, J. T.
Ness, W. R. (M.M.)
Newbury, E. G.
Niblett, A. H.
Nightingale, J.
Noble, F.
Notton, C. G.

O.
O'Connor, E.
Oram, J. A.
Osbourne, A.

P.
Page, F. W.
Page, J. C.
Page, W. P.
Parker, J. W.
Parnham, J. R.
Parritt, C. J.
Parritt, F. E.
Parrott, H. F.
Parson, J.
Patrick, J. A.
Pay, F.
Payne, W. J.
Payton, H. M.
Peadle, H. C.
Pearce, L. J.
Penfold, A. F.
Penman, G. E.
Penman, R. A.
Pennel, C.
Perkett, H. R.
Phillip, W. H.
Playdon, S. F.
Pollard, F. J. H.
Porter, C. W.
Posgate, A.
Poulitney, S.

Roll of Honour—continued.

Poynter, L. A. A.
Preston, W. A.
Preston, W. H.
Price, H. Ll.
Prinley, J.
Purdon. H. J.

Q.
Quelch, A. F.

R.
Ramsey, J.
Ramsey, D.
Ray, A. W.
Raymond, H. B. (D.C.M.)
Read, A. H.
Read, W. T.
Reader, E.
Reader, J. D.
Redfearn, H.
Redfearn, F.
Redsull, W. J.
Redsull, W. E.

Reed, J. T.
Reed, E. W. (M.M.)
Reeves, J. W.
Reynolds, G.
Rice, H. G.
Richardson, R.
Richardson, H.
Rist, G.
Robinson, O.
Robson, A.
Route, C. W.
Rowsaell, A.
Rowsaell, A.
Russell, J.
Russell, W. J.
Russell, W. J.
Russell, A.
Russell, A. S.

S.
Sims, H.
Sandiford, A. G.
Saunders, A. E.
Saunderson, J.
Seamer, E. T.

Sedge, F. C.
Sedge, W. A.
Selfe, R. F. (D.C.M.)
Sharp, W. H.
Shorter, S. S.
Shorter, V. B.
Shrosbee, G. L.
Simmonds, F. J.
Simmons, E. J.
Sinclair, W.
Sivell, R. A.
Skinner, H.
Skinner, P. A.
Smith, R. H.
Smith, W. J.
Spice, W. W.
Stapley, G. C.
Stedman, S. H.
Stedman, T. H.
Stedman, T. P. W.
Stephenson, N. M.
Stevens, W. A.
Stevens, G. W.
Stickings, N. J.
Stickings, G. W.
St. Ledger, J. H.
Stoneham, H. A.
Strickland, W. J.

Roll of Honour—continued.

Sullivan, D.
Summers, J. T.
Sutherland, G. L.
Sutherland, T. A.

T.
Tait, W.
Tait, W. A.
Taylor, C.
Taylor, C.
Taylor, G. R.
Taylor, S. A.
Thomas, A. E.
Thomas, F.
Thompson, A.
Thompson, H. E.
Till, J.
Tillman, C. H.
Titchmarsh, J.
Titley, T. A.
Tooburn, A. G.
Toolatch, C. A. J.
Toolson, H. F.
Towncow, W. J.

Tracey, G.
Tuff, F. N.
Tunbridge, V. T.
Turnbull, R. D.
Turner, C.
Turner, E.
Turrell, A. H.
Tutton, F. J. (M.M.)

U.
Underwood, A. J.

V.
Vine, N.
Vine, C. V. N.

W.
Wakefield, G. F.
Weir, F.

Walker, R. A.
Walker, C. A.
Walter, W. H.
Walters, R. A. P.
Walters, F.
Walton, A. F.
Ware, S. A. V.
Warne, G.
Warner, G.
Warner, J. H.
Warner, C. W.
Waterman, L. G.
Waters, E.
Watson, W. G.
Webb, S.
Webber, F. C.
Webster, W.
Weeks, J. W.
West, W. A.
West, P.
West, P. T.
West, F. L.
West, E. J.
West, C.
Westcott, J.
Westcott, W. A.
Westor, E. E.
White, W. (M.M.)

Roll of Honour—continued.

White, F.
Whitehead, G. R.
Whitehead, S. A.
Whitnall, J.
Wigmore, R. H.
Wilder, F.
Williams, F. C.
Williams, H. E.

Williams, S.
Wilson, R.
Wimsett, E. A.
Wood, H. A.
Wood, W. N.
Wood, A. V.
Wright, C. S.
Wright, W. A.

Wyatt, B.
Wyatt, R. J.

Y.
Young, B. A.

Gravesend's War Memorial

UNVEILED BY GENERAL LORD HORNE.

IMPRESSIVE CEREMONY AT WINDMILL HILL GARDENS.

Gravesend's War Memorial, erected in Windmill Hill Gardens, is a fitting tribute to the gallant men of the Borough who gave up their lives in the War. Beautiful in design, skilfully executed, in harmony with its surroundings, it will preserve the names of local heroes and remind posterity that the men of Gravesend made the last great sacrifice for a high ideal—the bringing about of permanent peace.

The Memorial, which was designed by Mr. W. Doyle-Jones, R.B.S., consists of a life-like bronze figure, emblematic of Victory ringing Peace. The figure is erected on a plinth of fine-axed Peterhead granite, on the four sides of which are inscribed the names of 545 men who fell in the War. The cut letters are bronze-filled. The Memorial is about 30 feet high, and 20 tons of granite are used. The base is 11 feet by 10 feet. There is a setting of grey paving. Messrs. William Kirkpatrick, Ltd., Manchester Granite and Marble Works, were responsible for the erection.

On the side facing Clarence-place there is a shield containing symbolic emblems—the torch of patriotism enclosed in a wreath of bay laurel. Below are the words: "Erected in profound and grateful remembrance of the men of Gravesend who fell in the Great War, 1914-1919. Not once or twice in our rough Island story the path of duty was the way to glory."

The Borough Arms, with the inscription, Decus et Tutamen, appear on the side facing Windmill Hill.

The unveiling and dedication of the Memorial took place on Wednesday afternoon with a solemn and impressive service befitting the occasion. Gravesend was honoured by the presence of General Lord Horne, the distinguished soldier who displayed such brilliant qualities of leadership during the War, and who invented the creeping barrage.

THE PROCESSION.

Those taking an official part in the proceedings assembled at the Town Hall, at 2.30, where a procession was formed, which proceeded to Windmill Hill by way of High-street, Windmill-street and Clarence-place.

The order of the procession was: The Chief Constable; buglers of the Royal Engineers, non-corporate members of the Education Committee, Library Committee, Housing Committee, and the War Memorial Committee; the Borough Guardians; Borough Magistrates, officials of the Corporation; Councillors, Aldermen; Sir Alexander Richardson, M.P. and Col. d'Apice, D.S.O., Staff Officer, Thames and Medway Area; the Rev. Canon Gedge, M.A., and the Rev. G. Sneesby; the Right Rev. the Lord Bishop of Rochester, and the Bishop's Chaplain (the Rev. G. Griffiths); the Oar; Mace; His Worship the Mayor, General Lord Horne, G.C.B., K.C.M.G., A.D.C.; Captain Hewson, R.A., aide-de-camp to General Lord Horne; the Town Clerk and Clerk of the Peace.

In the meantime a large company had gathered in the Gardens, including the relatives of the fallen, and many ex-Service men. People were also congregated on Windmill Hill and round about. The surpliced choirs of the united Churches of Gravesend formed a semi-circle behind the Memorial, and were under the conductorship of Mr. Arthur Allen. The windows of houses in Clarence-place, and even the roofs, were vantage places for interested spectators.

On reaching the entrance to the Gardens the procession opened out and lined each side of the approach to the Memorial, and allowed the Mayor to pass through, the procession falling in behind from the end farthest away from the Memorial. Just before the arrival of the procession the united choir sang the grand old hymn, "O God, our Help in Ages Past."

The Mayor took up a position in front of the Memorial and facing Clarence-place. On his right he was supported by General Lord Horne, Col. d'Apice, Sir Alexander Richardson, M.P., Capt. Hewson, the Clerk of the Peace (Mr. H. L. Tatham). On the left were the Lord Bishop, the Chaplain, Canon Gedge, the Rev. G. Sneesby, Alderman J. A. Axcell, J.P., and the Town Clerk (Mr. H. H. Brown, B.A.). Immediately behind the buglers stood at attention. The Mace was placed, together with the Oar, on a Union Jack draped support in front of His Worship.

Lord Horne and Councillor W.E. Thomas, Mayor and H.H. Brown, Town Clerk at the unveiling. [TopFoto]

Horne, Col. d'Apice, Sir Alexander Richardson, M.P., Capt. Hewson, the Clerk of the Peace (Mr. H. L. Tatham). On the left were the Lord Bishop, the Chaplain, Canon Gedge, the Rev. G. Sneesby, Alderman J. A. Axcell, J.P., and the Town Clerk (Mr. H. H. Brown, B.A.). Immediately behind the buglers stood at attention. The Mace was placed, together with the Oar, on a Union Jack draped support in front of His Worship.

The robes and chain of the Mayor, the decorated officers, the clergy in their vestments, the men in khaki, with their bugles, made a splash of colour under the dull light of a leaden sky.

A guard of honour was formed by 110 members of the local branch of the British Legion, under the charge of Mr. Ben Russell and of Mr. R. Harper, whose interest in the welfare of ex-Service men is so well known.

The service had scarcely commenced when the threatening clouds deliquesced, but fortunately it was only a slight shower.

THE SERVICE.

The Rev. Canon Gedge said the opening sentences: The souls of the righteous are in the hand of God, and there shall no torment touch them. In the sight of the unwise they seemed to die; and their departure is taken for misery; and there going from us to be utter destruction; but they are in peace. Though they be punished in the sight of men, yet is their hope full of immortality. And having been a little chastised, they shall be greatly rewarded: for God proved them and found them worthy for Himself. As gold in the furnace hath He tried them, and received them as a burnt-offering. And in the time of their visitation they shall shine.

The hymn, "For all the Saints who from their labours rest," was feelingly sung by the Choir.

The Scripture reading, by the Rev. G. Sneesby, was Revelations, ch. 7, verses 13—17: And one of the elders answered, saying unto me, What are these which are arrayed in white robes, and whence came they? And I said unto him, Sir, thou knowest. And he said to me, These are they which came out of great tribulation, and have washed their robes, and made them white in the blood of the Lamb. Therefore are they before the throne of God, and serve Him day and night in His temple; and He that sitteth on the throne shall dwell among them. They shall hunger no more, neither thirst any more; neither shall the sun light on them, nor any heat. For the Lamb which is in the midst of the throne shall feed them, and shall lead them unto living fountains of waters; and God shall wipe away all tears from their eyes.

His Worship said: My Lord Horne, as Mayor of this loyal and ancient Borough of Gravesend, I ask you, as a brave and worthy soldier, to join with the citizens of this town in doing honour to Gravesend's glorious soldiers.

LORD HORNE'S ADDRESS.

In performing the ceremony the gallant soldier said: I unveil this memorial to the glory of God and in honoured memory of the men of Gravesend who gave their lives in the Great War.

Proceeding, he remarked: When 3½ years ago fighting ceased in Belgium and in France, the thoughts that were uppermost in the minds of all throughout the nation were feelings of relief from the strain, thankfulness for the victory, gratitude to the men who had given that victory, and pride in the endurance and determination that had been displayed by the manhood and womanhood of the British Empire. Those feelings of relief, thankfulness, gratitude and pride have found expression throughout the whole country, in every town, in every city, in every village and countryside; they have found expression in the erection of something in the way of a memorial to honour the memory, not only of those who served, but more especially of those who gave their lives. They were erected to the glory of God who gave us the victory, and in honour of the men who endured so much and who won that victory. And I can assure you that honour is due. Those who went through with the men whose names are written on this Memorial know what they did endure. Those who did not go through it would, perhaps, find it difficult to realise what the men were called on to perform during those four years of war. Standing here to-day no doubt there are many of those who were intimately connected with the men whose names are written on this beautiful Memorial. I take the opportunity of expressing, on the part of all of us, sympathy to those who have lost so much, and I hope that the honour paid to them throughout the country, and especially in this town, Gravesend, will bring some comfort to the stricken souls. Gravesend is a great and important town, and Gravesend has a record during the war worthy of its own importance. Situated, as you are, on the banks of the great River Thames, you have been intimately connected for centuries past with the life of the great Metropolis, and in all the life of the British Islands in general. During the war you sent many thousands of men to the Navy, Army, Mercantile Marine, to other branches of the Service, to munition factories, supply depôts, and other places throughout the country. Gravesend did her duty. Now you have put up this Memorial to the honour of your dead. I would remind you at the same time, although I daresay it is not necessary at Gravesend, that while we honour the dead, we must also remember the living. Many men throughout the country to-day would perhaps be almost better dead—crippled and handicapped in life; those are the men who helped to win the victory. I ask you to extend to them a hand of assistance. Remember that many of them, young boys, were handicapped in their entry into civilian life. They want more assistance; they have the first claim, I ask, and I wish you to remember that. Four years ago, over and over again, it was said in my hearing that nothing too much could be done for the men who fought for us. I do not hear that said to-day. I wish I did. Still, much can be done, and will be done, I feel sure in mentioning it here in Gravesend to-day I am echoing what is at the bottom of your hearts. I ask you, Sir, and the Corporation to do the best you can for the men. I ask the ex-Service men to show themselves worthy of the position they won during the war, and to put the same energy into the work that they did in the war. I ask the public generally to sympathise and help the men who did their duty. It is the duty of the rest to help them.

DEDICATION CEREMONY.

His Worship, addressing the Bishop, said: In the name of this town, I now ask you to dedicate this Memorial, in memory of the men of this town who laid down their lives in the great cause for which they so bravely fought for world freedom and international righteousness. We have erected this monument and we now pray you to give it your blessing, and to dedicate it to the Glory of God and in grateful remembrance of those who made the supreme sacrifice.

The dedication was in the following words: In the faith of Jesus Christ we dedicate this Memorial to the Glory of God, and to the undying memory of our brethren who gave their lives for us during the Great War. In the name of the Father, and of the Son, and of the Holy Ghost. Amen.

There was silence for a few moments, then orders were given in low but clear-cut tones, and the poignant notes of the bugles sounded out the "Last Post" and the "Reveille."

Alderman J. A. Axcell said: Mr. Mayor, as Chairman of the War Memorial Committee, I ask you now, on behalf of the subscribers to the same, to accept this splendid Memorial. I would like to ask you, in accepting this, always remember that the names of those heroes who are tabulated on that Memorial died in order that we might live.

The Mayor said: Alderman Axcell, on behalf of the Aldermen, Councillors and burgesses of this town, I gladly accept this Memorial, and I would like to take this opportunity, sir, to congratulate you and every member of your Committee, on the splendid result of their labour. Lord Horne of Gravesend are mindful of the noble service that you have rendered to-day. We have honoured, with ourselves, the memory of the brave men of Gravesend. We say that you are the right man to do this honour, because we recall that you, Sir, were at Mons, at the Marne when the world wondered, at Vimy Ridge, and also at Arras, and so as citizens to-day, we are honoured by your presence and your service. My Lord Bishop of Rochester, we of Gravesend are mindful of your service. You, by your presence, have added to the solemnity and the dignity of this memorable occasion. Citizens of Gravesend, this Memorial will remind us always of the dark days of the war. We have a record of which we may be proud. We recall our brave men and our brave women during the time that the Taubes and the Zeppelins were over our heads, when we were in the zone of battle, and the men and women of Gravesend did not flinch their duty and service. This Memorial will serve to remind us, and help us, to teach our children "Lest we forget."

Not once or twice in our rough island story Was the path of duty the way to glory.

This Memorial, with the figure surmounting the record of our glorious dead, preaches a message to-day of immortality, of hope and of reunion.

The hymn, "Peace, Perfect Peace," Benediction and the National Anthem concluded the impressive service.

The procession re-formed in the same order and returned to the Town Hall.

Immediately after the service a large number of beautiful floral emblems were placed round the base of the Memorial.

The Memorial was damaged during World War II; restorative work involved the dismantling and renovation. Work began in January, 1947 and was completed in June, 1949.

THE WAR MEMORIAL.

It is intended to restore as soon as possible the war memorial in Windmill Hill Gardens. The memorial was damaged by a bomb and was dismantled. The War Damage Commission will be asked to pay the cost of the re-instatement.

ROADS NAMED AFTER V.C.'s.

Councillor Howcroft suggested that three of the four new roads to be constructed adjoining Christian Fields-avenue should be named after local V.C.'s — Ferguson, Palmer, Harden. He also suggested the fourth should be named Hawkins-avenue, after the local hero of the "San Demetrio."

The suggestion will be considered by the Works Committee.

GR 4/1/47

GR 18/6/49

The Memorial remains the focus for Remembrance Day Services in the Borough to the present Day.

Situated in the gardens with the upper reaches of Windmill Hill as a background, the Memorial remains in a splendid situation.

Siting the Memorial in the gardens ensures more frequent visitors rather than if it had been sited on the summit.

The foliage furnishes an air of tranquillity to the situation.

There remains ample room for commemoration, more so than any other originally suggested sites.

[Image courtesy of Gravesend Library]

BRITISH LEGION
Gravesend, Northfleet and District.

GRAVESEND
War Memorial 1914-1918.
Destroyed by Enemy Action 1941. Restored and Re-dedicated in 1949.

Remembrance Sunday
ORDER OF SERVICE
AT THE WAR MEMORIAL
WINDMILL HILL GARDENS
ON SUNDAY, 9th NOVEMBER, 1952.
at 10.15 a.m.

Conducted by Rev. R. D. DAUNTON-FEAR, M.A., D.D., O.C.F.,
Rector and Rural Dean of Gravesend
and Rev. W. T. M. CLEWES, M.A.
Minister of Princes Street Congregational Church, Gravesend

GRAVESHAM BOROUGH COUNCIL 'BOOK OF REMEMBRANCE'

The 'Book of Rem-embrance' is housed in a display case in the Woodville Halls.

The book was dedicated on November 11th, 1999 in the presence of the Mayor, Councillor Joseph Jaggon.

The book is in the form of a diary with the pages being turned daily to correspond with the actual current day.

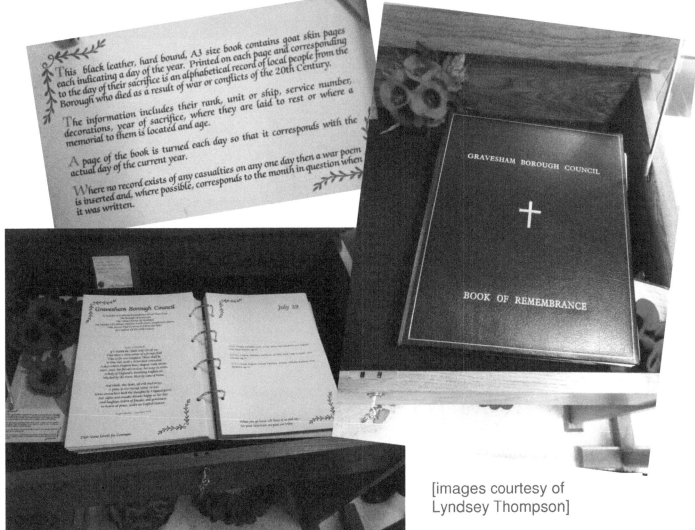

[images courtesy of Lyndsey Thompson]

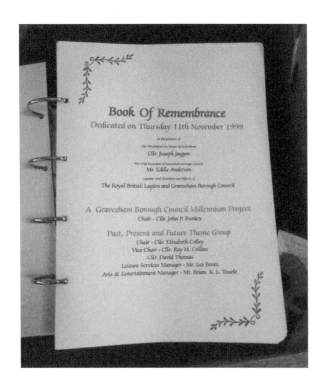

[images courtesy of
Lyndsey Thompson]

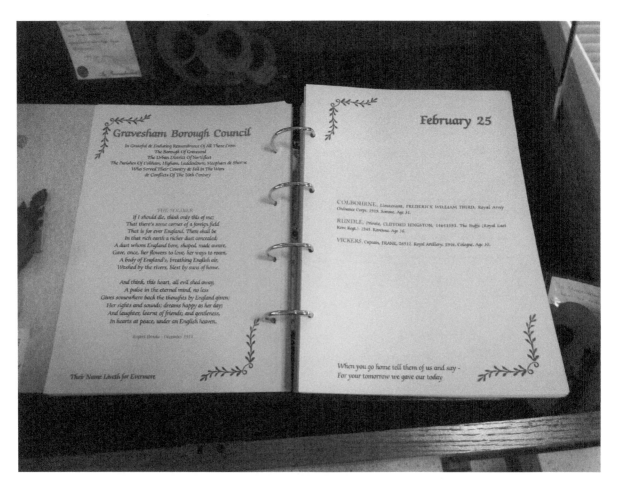

ROYAL WEST KENT RGT

&

THE ROYAL EAST KENT RGT

The majority of those listed on the Memorial served either with the Royal West Kent Regiment or the Royal East Kent Regiment.

A brief history of both Regiments follows.

ROYAL WEST KENT REGIMENT

The Queen's Own Royal West Kent Regiment was an infantry regiment of the Army from 1881 to 1961. It was formed as the Queen's Own (Royal West Kent Regiment) as part of the Childers Reforms by the amalgamation of the 50th (Queen's Own) Regiment of Foot and the 97th (Earl of Ulster's) Regiment of Foot. In January 1921, it was renamed the Royal West Kent Regiment (Queen's Own) and in April of the same year the Queen's Own Royal West Kent  Regiment. In 1961 it was amalgamated with the Buffs (Royal East Kent Regiment) to form the Queen's Own Buffs, The Royal Kent Regiment. It was popularly, and operationally, known as the "Royal West Kents."

When the regiment was formed, Kent was one of five counties (the others being Surrey, Staffordshire, Lancashire and Yorkshire) which was split to create more than one regiment. Kent was split into two areas, with those in West Kent forming the Queen's Own Royal West Kent Regiment, while those in East Kent becoming the Royal East Kent Regiment, The Buffs. The dividing line that separated the two regimental areas was east of the River Medway. The regiment's recruitment area covered both the towns and rural areas of West Kent and a number of London boroughs in the south-east of London.

The 1st Battalion took part in the Egypt Intervention in 1882. It then spent two years on garrison duty in Cyprus before being shipped to the Sudan and the Mahdist War. It spent the years up to the outbreak of the Great War on garrison duty, both at home and throughout the British Empire.

The 2nd Battalion was shipped to South Africa shortly after its formation, in the aftermath of the First Boer War. The following year, it was posted to Ireland and spent the remaining years of the 19th century in Britain, being sent back to South Africa for the Second Boer War. Its only action was a skirmish at Biddulphsberg, in the company of the 2nd Battalions of the Grenadier and Scots Guards. It then moved to the East, being stationed in Ceylon, Hong Kong, Singapore, Peshawar, and Multan before the outbreak of the Great War.

The 1st Battalion, which was in Dublin at the outbreak of war in August 1914, was one of the first units to be moved to France where it became part of the 13th Infantry Brigade in the 5th Infantry Division. Among its first major engagements were the Battle of Mons on August 23rd and Le Cateau three days later. In October the battalion made a heroic stand at Neuve Chapelle; being the only unit not to fall back. Out of 750 men, only 300 commanded by a Lieutenant and a Second Lieutenant survived. Apart from a brief period from December 1917 to April 1918, when it was moved with the 5th Division to Italy, the 1st Battalion was stationed on the Western Front for the duration of the war.

The 2nd Battalion was shipped from Multan to Mesopotamia, via Bombay, arriving in Basra in February 1915, where it was attached to the 12th Indian Brigade. Two Companies were attached to the 30th Brigade (part of the 6th (Poona) Division) and were captured in the Siege of Kut in April 1916. The remaining Companies were attached to 34th Brigade (part of 15th Indian Division), and were transferred to 17th Indian Division in August 1917. The Battalion remained in Mesopotamia for the duration of the war.

Most of the Territorial battalions spent the war on garrison duty, particularly in India and Egypt, relieving the Regular battalions for front-line service. However, the 2/4th Battalion took part in the Gallipoli Campaign and the 3/4th Battalion served as a Pioneer battalion in France. Several of the Service battalions of the New Army fought in France and Flanders and in the Italian Campaign. At Loos, the 8th Battalion lost all but one of its officers, and 550 men.

At the end of the war, the 1st Battalion was transferred back to India, where it took part (along with the Territorial 1/4th Battalion) in the Third Afghan War and the putting down of a Mahsud tribal rebellion in the Northwest Frontier in 1920. It spent the next few years in India, returning home to Britain in 1937.

The 2nd Battalion returned to India from Mesopotamia in 1919 and to Britain in 1921, briefly becoming part of the Army of Occupation in Germany - the British Army of the Rhine. It was stationed at various garrisons in Britain until 1937, when it moved to Palestine to aid suppression of the Arab revolt. In 1939, it was transferred to Malta.

The 1st Battalion was part of the 4th Infantry Division of the British Expeditionary Force in France in 1940, returning to Britain via Dunkirk. It remained in Britain until 1943, leaving to take part in the Tunisia Campaign, the Italian Campaign and the Greek Civil War that broke out after the German withdrawal in 1944.

The 2nd Battalion was part of the garrison of Malta during its protracted siege. It then formed part of the 234th Infantry Brigade in the abortive assault on the Italian held Dodecanese islands in 1943, being captured by the Germans on the island of Leros. (Kenneth Probert - one of the many soldiers captured - states that a British submarine took officers away before capture, leaving those left behind to serve in prisoner of war camps in Germany. These prisoners were transported in cattle trucks from Greece to Wernigerode in the Harz Mountains where they were forced to work in support of the German war effort). It was reconstituted in 1944 by re-designation of the 7th Battalion.

The 6th Battalion was part of the 78th *Battleaxe* Infantry Division and fought in the Tunisia Campaign notably helping to capture Longstop Hill in April 1943. The battalion was with the division throughout the Italian campaign.

The 9th Battalion was raised in 1940 converted to armour in 1942 as 162nd Regiment of the Royal Armoured Corps but retained its RWK cap badge on the black beret of the RAC.

Other hostilities-only battalions of the regiment fought in North Africa, notably at El Alamein and Alam el Halfa, and in Burma.

The 2nd Battalion was disbanded in 1948 (nominally being amalgamated with the 1st Battalion).

From 1951-1954, the sole remaining Battalion contributed to the security forces that successfully contained the Communist guerrilla uprising in Malaya. Less happily, it was involved in the militarily successful, but politically disastrous, occupation of the Suez Canal zone in 1956. It then took part in the campaign in Cyprus against EOKA guerrillas around 1958/59.

In 1959, it returned to Britain for the last time, being amalgamated in 1961 with the Buffs (Royal East Kent Regiment), to form the Queen's Own Buffs, Royal Kent Regiment.

A MAN OF KENT IN FLANDERS - Lady Elizabeth Butler

THE ROYAL EAST KENT REGIMENT

The Buffs (Royal East Kent Regiment), formerly the 3rd Regiment of Foot was an infantry regiment of the Army until 1961. It had a history dating back to 1572 and was one of the oldest regiments in the Army being third in order of precedence - ranked as the 3rd Regiment of the line. It provided distinguished service over a period of almost four hundred years accumulating one hundred and sixteen battle honours. Following a series of amalgamations since 1961 its lineage is today continued by the Princess of Wales's Royal Regiment.

The origins of the regiment lay in Thomas Morgan's Company of Foot, The London Trained Bands which was in existence from 1572 to 1648. In 1665 it was known as the 4th (The Holland Maritime) Regiment and by 1668 as the 4th (The Holland) Regiment. In 1688–1689 it was "4th The Lord High Admiral's Regiment" until 1751 it was named as other regiments after the Colonel Commanding being the 3rd (Howard's) Regiment of Foot from 1737 to 1743 at which point it became the 3rd Regiment of Foot, "Howard's Buffs".

From 1595 to 1665, the four regiments of the English Brigade served under Dutch command. In 1665, with the coming of the Second Anglo-Dutch War the British and Scotch Brigades were ordered to swear loyalty to the *Stadtholder*. Those who obeyed would be allowed to continue in Dutch service and those who disobeyed would be cashiered. Using his own funds, Sir George Downing, the English ambassador to the Netherlands, raised the Holland Regiment from the starving remnants of those who refused to sign. It was designated as the 4th Regiment of Foot.

In 1688 the Glorious Revolution deposed James II Stuart and seated William Henry, Prince of Orange-Nassau and Stadtholder of the United Netherlands, on the throne of Great Britain as William III of England. To reduce confusion between the Regent's Dutch Blue Guards regiment and the Stuart-era "Holland Regiment", the latter was renumbered the 3rd Regiment and had its title changed to The Lord Admiral's Regiment. Since Prince George of Denmark was Lord Admiral (and thus was its Honorary Colonel), it was also known as Prince George of Denmark's Regiment until his death in 1708.

The 1st (Regular) Battalion existed continuously from 1572 to 1961.

The 2nd (Regular) Battalion was intermittently raised in 1678–1679, 1756–1758, 1803–1815, and 1857–1949.

The Buffs obtained the name of "The Buffs" officially in 1744 while on campaign in the Low Countries. The 3rd Regiment was then under the command of Lieutenant-General *Thomas Howard*. At the same time, the 19th Regiment of Foot were commanded by their colonel, the Honourable Sir *Charles Howard*. In order to avoid confusion (because regiments were then named after their colonels, which would have made them both *Howard's Regiment of Foot*), the regiments took the colours of their facings as part of their names – the 19th Foot became the Green Howards, while the 3rd Foot became Howard's Buffs, eventually being shortened to simply *The Buffs*.

In between the campaigns of the Napoleonic Wars and India, "The Buffs" had a tour of service from 1821 until 1827 in New South Wales. For the duration of their service, The Buffs were divided into four detachments. The first was based in Sydney from 1821. The second arrived in Hobart in 1822. The third, entitled "The Buffs' Headquarters", arrived in Sydney in 1823. The fourth arrived in Sydney in 1824, but variously saw service throughout the colonies. The regiment reunited and was transferred to Calcutta in 1827.

In the Childers reforms of 1881 the East Kent Militia became the regiment's 3rd (Militia) Battalion (1881–1953) and its short-lived 4th (Militia) Battalion (1881–1888).

In 1881–1908 two Kent rifle volunteer corps were re-designated as the 1st Volunteer Battalion and 2nd (The Weald of Kent) Volunteer Battalion of the Buffs. With the creation of the Territorial Force (TF) in 1908 they became the regiment's 4th and 5th (TF) Battalions. In 1921 the TF was reformed as the Territorial Army (TA) and the two units were merged as the 4th/5th (TA) Battalion. The two battalions resumed separate existences on the doubling of the TA in 1939, but were again merged in 1947.

For service in World War I, nine battalions were raised:

- 2/4th (Territorial Force) Battalion [1914–1917]
- 3/4th (Territorial Force) Battalion [1915–1916]; 3/4th (Reserve) Btn [1916–1919]
- 2/5th (Territorial Force) Battalion [1914–1917]
- 3/5th (Territorial Force) Battalion [1915–1916]
- 6th (Service) Battalion [1914–1919]
- 7th (Service) Battalion [1914–1919]
- 8th (Service) Battalion [1914–1918]
- 9th (Service) Battalion [1914–1915]; 9th (Reserve) Battalion [1915–1916]
- 10th (Royal East Kent & West Kent Yeomanry) Battalion [1917–1918]

In 1956 the 410th (Kent) Coast Regiment (Royal Artillery) was disbanded and converted into infantry. It was then combined with elements of the 4th (Territorial Army) Battalion, The Buffs (Royal East Kent) Regiment to form the 5th (Territorial Army) Battalion of The Queen's Own Buffs, The Royal Kent Regiment and was the last separate unit to bear the distinct honours of The Buffs. In 1966 it became the 5th Battalion, The Queen's Regiment. In 1967 it merged with the 4th Battalion to become the 4th/5th (East Kent TAVR) Battalion, The Queen's Regiment.

In 1961 the "The Buffs", Royal East Kent Regiment was amalgamated with The Queen's Own Royal West Kent Regiment to form: The Queen's Own Buffs, The Royal Kent Regiment. In 1966, the The Queen's Own Buffs, The Royal Kent Regiment was amalgamated with the other three regiments of the Home Counties Brigade to form The Queen's Regiment. In 1992 the Queen's Regiment was amalgamated with the Royal Hampshire Regiment to form the Princess of Wales's Royal Regiment.

The Buffs was one of five regiments enjoying the Freedom of the City of London. This gave them the right to march through the City with drums beating, bayonets fixed, and colours flying. This is due to a Royal Warrant written in 1672 allowing them to raise volunteers "by beat of drum" in the City of London. Since recruiting parties paraded in full array accompanied by company or regimental musicians and marched with a colour, this right was given to the regiment as a whole.

A B C D E

ACOTT B.
AITKEN W. W.
AITKIN D. G.
A?OTT J.
AL?? W. D.
AL?G?N S. M.
ALLEN H. F.
ALLEN T.
ALLEN W. F.
ALLEN R. P.
ALLSON E. H.
AMOS J. A.
AMOS J.
ANDERSON C. A.
ANDRUS H.
ANNAL I. A. T
ARCHER E. C.
ARNOLD B. W.
ASHDOWN W. R.
ASHENDEN A. N.
ASHENDEN S. R.

ATKINS F. S.
BAILEY H. S.

FATHER IN THY GRACIOUS
KEEPING
LEAVE WE NOW

Tom Allen, Lapugnoy

Bernard Cecil Acott
Royal West Kent, 1st Battalion
Service No. S/8700 - Private

Bernard was born in Northfleet in 1895. His father William Thomas was a local man, born in 1857 in Northfleet and worked in the local Cement Works as a crane driver. Locomotives were used to carry the chalk from the quarry to the works and to carry the barrels of cement from the Factory to the dock. William married his wife Sarah who was eight years younger than her husband, in 1886. She was not a local woman, coming from Essex. The family lived at 24 London Road, Rosherville. The couple had seven surviving children; five boys, Herbert, born in 1887, Bruce, born in 1889, Bernard, Harold, born in 1897, Edward, born in 1904, and two daughters, Florence, born in 1892 and Beatrice, born in 1909. Bernard found employment on leaving school as a labourer at the Cable Works.

On the outbreak of war he enlisted and was posted with the 1st Battalion, Royal West Kent, service number S/8700. Bernard arrived in France on December 7th, 1914. On the evening of February 20th, 1915 the 1st R.W.K. took over the left section of 83rd Brigade's lines; this was to the south east of Zillebeke on the northern side of the railway line from Ypres to Comines, which here ran through a deep cutting. The trenches were in poor condition and the Germans had the advantage and were quite aggressive using mortars on a regular basis.

On February 22nd portions of the trench parapet were knocked down by heavy mortar fire. The Germans then turned machine guns on the gaps ensuring a torrid time for B Company in particular. There was no attempt at an assault. Throughout this and into March the 1st Battalion continued in this quarter being relieved and relieving every other day except for a period of rest at Ouderdom from March 11th through to the 14th. Sometimes it held the Zwarteleen sector, sometimes to the right of that, just north of the Ypres-Comines railway line. This sector contained a trench known as the International Trench because the Germans held the southern portion and the British the continuation northward, a situation which may well have given rise to the legend of the loophole through which the soldiers on either side took it in turns to fire at the other. Despite the lack of artillery support - the British guns were reduced to firing three rounds a day due to lack of ammunition, the 1st gradually wrested the ascendancy from the Germans, reducing sniper activity and returning the trenches to what they were meant to do.

At the end of March the 1st were withdrawn from this sector and rested at Vlamertinghe. The six weeks in this sector had seen 4 officers and 65 men killed among whom was Bernard, killed in action on March 8th.

He is buried in Tuileries CWGC Cemetery. The cemetery is on the outskirts of Ypres. With the Germans so close and in aggressive mood the situation was never quiet. The cemetery's name means "tile factory", as it was begun in the grounds of a tile works in 1915. The chimneys of the tile works were very visible and provided a means for the opposing side to calibrate their shells. This led to the cemetery itself being heavily shelled and the sites of most of the original graves were lost. Most of the gravestones are positioned around the edges of the otherwise empty-looking cemetery, and are marked "known to be buried in this cemetery", with the default additional phrase "Their glory shall not be blotted out", a line suggested by Rudyard Kipling.

Douglas Gordon Aitkin
Queen's Own Royal West Kent
Service No. 240826 - Private

Douglas was 22 years old when he died of wounds on October 20th, 1917. He is buried in Dozinghem CWGC Cemetery. He was born in 1894 in Gravesend and was the middle child of five surviving to Robert William and Emma Aitken. The family lived at 6 Milton Road. Robert was born in Gravesend 1863 and worked from home as a master tailor. Emma was two years his senior and was also a local. Prior to the Great War four of the children were still living at home – Wilfrid was a clerk with the Port of London Authority, Douglas, Winifred, born in 1896 and Marjorie born in 1898.

Douglas was a clerk with a local estate agent before enlisting at Dartford. Naturally, being from Gravesend he was with the 7th Battalion.

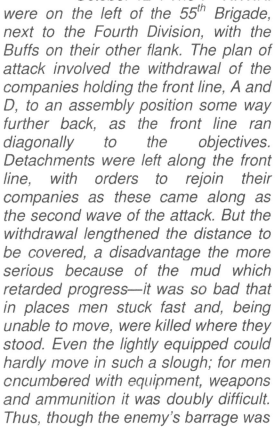

The Third Battle of Ypres had been underway since July 31st, 1917 and, by mid-October, it was drawing to a close as the British Army clawed its way through the mud up the Passchendaele Ridge. On the night of 10/11th, the West Kents moved into the front line in preparation for another major attack on the 12th. Eight British Divisions - nearly 140,000 men - would advance, with the West Kents attacking towards the village of Poelcapelle.

The Regimental History has this to say about 7th Battalion in October 1917:

Most unfavourable conditions, therefore, faced the Eighteenth Division when early in October it returned to the Salient to continue the attack, and to add to the handicaps the Brigade was called upon to attack at 24 hours' notice at a point quite different from that which it had expected to assault. The Division had been training to attack the main Passchendaele Ridge and had carried out several tactical exercises over a model of the ground till all ranks were familiar with their tasks. Actually it had to attack Poelcapelle and, on the night of October 10th/11th, the 53rd Brigade moved up to the front to relieve the Eleventh Division at that point. That division had attacked Poelcapelle on October 8th, and after losing heavily had captured part of the village, but the Northern end of it along the Staden road had remained in German hands.

The relief, which pouring rain, mud that surpassed all previous experience, and intense darkness, rendered exceptionally slow and difficult, had barely been completed before the time fixed for the attack of October 12th. The 7th R.W.K. were on the left of the 55th Brigade, next to the Fourth Division, with the Buffs on their other flank. The plan of attack involved the withdrawal of the companies holding the front line, A and D, to an assembly position some way further back, as the front line ran diagonally to the objectives. Detachments were left along the front line, with orders to rejoin their companies as these came along as the second wave of the attack. But the withdrawal lengthened the distance to be covered, a disadvantage the more serious because of the mud which retarded progress—it was so bad that in places men stuck fast and, being unable to move, were killed where they stood. Even the lightly equipped could hardly move in such a slough; for men encumbered with equipment, weapons and ammunition it was doubly difficult. Thus, though the enemy's barrage was not very effective, the battalion lost heavily from rifle and machine-gun fire before it cleared its own front line.

B Company, on the right, made fair progress at first and accounted for many of the enemy. Before long, they were held up by machine-gun fire from their right flank and from the Brewery, a strong point just east of the Staden road. All the officers became casualties, but Sergt. Tebbitt took command and carried on till, about 6.30 a.m., D reinforced the survivors of B. But even then the opposition was too strong to allow of much progress; casualties were heavy, and 2nd Lieut. Duffield, the only officer left with the two companies, reorganized them in a chain of posts just beyond the original line, and despite heavy fire maintained his ground successfully.

On the other flank C had found the barrage somewhat erratic, indeed several German machine-guns had escaped it and gave a great deal of trouble. The platoon on the flank, however, got on splendidly. When a machine-gun in a strong point threatened to hold it up, Pte. Ives rushed forward with a Lewis gun, and despite heavy fire knocked the machine-gun out, enabling the platoon to get on. Sergt. Hamblin, who had taken command on the fall of his officer, 2nd Lieut. Mitchell, led the platoon with so much determination and ability that it reached a strong point only just short of the battalion's objective and well ahead of the rest of the attack. This point it rushed successfully, capturing two officers and 50 men with a couple of machine-guns. From here the party, reduced by casualties to 16 men, became mixed up with the Household Battalion of the Fourth Division with whom they pushed on ahead.

The rest of C were less fortunate. A strong point at the Northern end of the village brought them to a standstill,

and though A came up to reinforce it was unable to carry the advance any further, nor could the 8th Suffolks of the 53rd Brigade achieve any more when they, too, pushed forward on the left. Finally, therefore, these two companies dug in a little in front of the line held before the attack ... but despite the gallantry and determination which the 7th had displayed it had achieved but little to compensate for very heavy losses. The weakness of the barrage and the great difficulties of getting forward over a water-logged stretch of mud there had been no time to reconnoitre were mainly responsible for the failure to accomplish more, but the battalion hung on all through the next day (October 13) and maintained its ground until that evening it was relieved by the 8th Suffolks.

But its cup was not yet full. When boarding lorries next day to withdraw to the back area, it had the misfortune to be attacked by German aeroplanes and suffered nearly 40 casualties in addition to those already incurred. These had been serious enough, just half the 600 men who had gone "over the top" were on the casualty list, along with 14 officers ... It was a sadly shattered remnant that was left of a battalion which had come up to the front in fine condition and fighting trim.

Among the wounded was Douglas who, sadly, would succumb to his wounds on October 20th. He is buried in Dozinghem Military Cemetery.

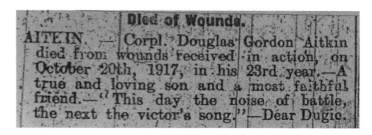

GR 3/11/17 [Andrew Marshall]

Mr. and Mrs. R. W. Aitken, of 9, Milton-road, Gravesend, have received the sorrowful news that their youngest son, Corpl. Douglas Gordon Aitken, Royal West Kent Regiment, has died from wounds in France. He was 22 years of age.

We hear that Mr. Tracey Robson is in hospital in England suffering from wounds.

GR 24/10/17 [Andrew Marshall]

GR 3/11/17 [Andrew Marshall]

Corpl. Douglas Gordon Aitkin, whose death from wounds received in action was recorded in our last issue, was a pupil of Wrotham-road Board School, where he received a good ground work under Mr. Miles (headmaster), who was like a father to all his boys, and who had a splendid influence over them. Finishing his education at the Modern School, under Mr. Waldegrave, he passed for the College of Preceptors in the Third Division, taking distinction in arithmetic, algebra and drawing; also in the second class, in which he took distinction in drawing. On leaving the Modern School, with a splendid character from his master (Mr. Waldegrave), he went to the office of Messrs. Glover and Homewood, where he stayed till he passed into the service of the Port of London Authority. He was an enthusiastic musician, like his brother Wilfrid, and he studied the 'cello, on which he was no mean performer. He was a member of the P.S.A. Band, and was also in request at local concerts. When war broke out he, with nine other fellow clerks, nobly responded to the call, joining up on his 20th birthday in the Royal West Kent Regiment on November 21st, 1914, and in 1915 he was sent to Bedford with a draft for the Dardanelles, but on being examined his eyesight failed him, and he was sent back as unfit. He embarked with a draft for France on September 12th of the present year, and was in action for the first time about October 18th. His parents received a letter saying he had been over the top and had got safely through. Shortly after they received a letter from the matron of the No. 4 C.C.S., saying their dear boy had been seriously wounded in the abdomen and back, and that he passed peacefully away on October 20th. His last words, when the matron told him she was writing to his mother, were "Give her my love." His life was an example to many, and it is interesting to record that he was the only man in his company who had any influence for good over the two worst characters in it. That he had a presentiment that he would never return was evident from facts which have come to his parents' knowledge, but he went fearlessly to the Front and died nobly.

Douglas Aitkin –
Dozinghem Military Cemetery, middle left and headstone, left,

HE NOBLY GAVE HIS LIFE
IN THE GREAT WORLD WAR

DEATH.

ACOTT.—Killed in action on March 8th in the trenches, Pte. Bernard Acott, "B" Co. Royal West Kent Regiment, aged 20 years.

GR 27/3/15 [Andrew Marshall]

Bernard Acott – Tuileries CWGC Cemetery

Chatham Naval Memorial, Panel 31 – Thomas Albert.

Gravesend Cemetery - William Aitken

Dearly Beloved Younger Son
L/Cpl WILLIAM WHITELY 731 7th Buffs
Who Nobly Made the Supreme Sacrifice
Passing
Out of the Sight of Men by the Faith of Duty
Near Arras May 3rd 1917, Wounded and
Missing
Aged 21 Years

Many of the inscriptions on the Arras Memorial are barely readable, William being among these.

William Whiteley Aitken
Royal East Kent, 7th Battalion
Service No. G/731 - Lance Corp.

Willie was born in 1896 in New Mills, Manchester. His father, William, was born in 1869 and came from Lanarkshire. He was a machine foreman at the Paper works and prior to the Great War he was a boarder with Walter and Mary Elliott at their residence at 28 Mayfield Road Northfleet. William's wife, Sarah Ellen and their three children lived at the family home in Whiteley Terrace, New Mills, Stockport. Sarah Ellen was born in Ripponden, Yorkshire in 1864. The couple married in 1889 and had three children – Thomas, born in 1891 who was an engineer, pattern maker, Margaret, born in 1894 and Willie.

The family moved several times as William sought employment, as a journeyman machinist. William it seems moved from place to place wherever he could find work. From Manchester and then Chester, Stockport and finally Northfleet where William worked in the Paper Works.

Willie was with the 7th (service) Battalion which was raised at Canterbury in September 1914 as part of Kitchener's Second New Army and joined 55th Brigade, 18th (Eastern) Division. The Division initially concentrated in the Colchester area but moved to Salisbury Plains in May 1915. The 7th proceeded to France on July 28th and concentrated near Flesselles.

In 1916 they were in action on the Somme in the Battle of Albert capturing their objectives near Montauban, The Battle of Bazentin Ridge including the capture of Trones Wood, The Battle of Delville Wood, The Battle of Thiepval Ridge, The Battle of the Ancre Heights playing a part in the capture of the Schwaben Redoubt and Regina Trench and The Battle of the Ancre. In 1917 they took part in the Operations of the Ancre. They fought during the German retreat to the Hindenburg Line and in the Third Battle of the Scarpe before moving to Flanders.

The 7th was part of 12th Division in the 3rd Battle of The Scarpe. As early as January 1917, the Division received notice that it would take part in an offensive at Arras. It moved to the front in that sector on January 14th. The task of the Division in the Arras attack was to capture the enemy's "Black Line" (forward position) then go on to the "Brown Line" - the Wancourt-Feuchy trench. The artillery bombardment opened on 4th April, and the infantry – many of whom had been able to approach the front line in the long tunnels and the subways reaching out from Arras itself, advanced behind a creeping barrage on the 9th.

Resistance was rapidly overcome; fine counter-battery work had stifled the German Guns. The leading troops quickly captured the Black Line. The 12th Division remained in position, as snow and sleet fell. The attack had been successful, making an advance on the Divisional front of some 4,000 yards at a cost of 2,018 casualties.

After a ten day rest the Division re-entered the Arras battlefield. On 28th April, formations north of 12th Division undertook an operation to capture Roeux but owing to heavy enemy shellfire and machine guns the attack fell back.

A larger effort – including the British Fifth, Third and First Armies – took place on May 3rd, with an artillery bombardment that began two days earlier. 12th Division's role was to make an advance of some 2,500 yards. A preliminary attack on the left by 36th Brigade in the early hours of 2nd May, including a gas barrage fired by Liens projectors. The main attack was of mixed fortune. Once again, German shellfire and heavy machine gun fire caused many casualties. Shellfire was heavy over the next few days and the uncertain position of the advanced troops meant that British artillery was cautious in replying on German trenches. The Division was relieved on 16th May having suffered a total 141 officers and 3,380 other ranks casualties.

William who had been promoted Lance Corporal was among those killed in action at the start of the 3rd Battle on May 3rd. his body was lost and he is commemorated on the Arras Memorial

GR 10/8/18. [Andrew Marshall]

Thomas James Albert
R.N.R. - Leading Trimmer
Service No. 363ST

Tom was born on August 17th, 1888 in Gravesend. His parents William and Ann Rose were both from Gravesend and were both born in 1867. The family moved to Grays and then to Tunbridge Wells before returning to Gravesend in 1911. William was a sweep and Ann found employment as a washer women. There were six children in the family – Thomas, who was the eldest, Rose, born in 1890, Joseph born in 1892, Minnie, born in 1901, Joshua, born in 1902, Jacob, born in 1904 and

LANCE-CORPL. W. W. AITKEN.

Mr. and Mrs. W. A. Aitken, of Alexandra Lodge, Lennox-road, have been in great suspense since May 3rd, 1917, concerning their son, Lance-Corpl. William Whiteley Aitken, of the 7th Buffs, who has been reported missing since that date. Notwithstanding every possible inquiry, no definite information could be obtained concerning him, but last week a letter was received from the War Office, "presuming" his death. The terrible suspense of the parents has thus to some extent been relieved, but they naturally cling to the hope that even yet it may transpire that he is still living. It appears the deceased had charge of a Lewis gun in the fighting somewhere about Chérisy in May of last year. The No. 2 on the gun saw him fall and heard him say something, but the din and roar of battle made it impossible for him to catch the words. That is the sum total of the information obtainable, and much sympathy will be felt for the parents in losing a devoted son in such tragic circumstances. At the age of 18 years he joined Kitchener's Army on September 7th, 1914, and went to the West Front in July, 1915. He took part in the Somme battle in 1916, and, as already stated, was in the battle of Arras in 1917, where, it would appear he was mortally wounded. The deceased was engaged at the Imperial Paper Mills West (where his father is manager) prior to joining up, and the only time he was home on leave was at Christmas, 1916. He was very popular with his numerous companions in civil life, and they feel that they have lost a valuable friend. He was at one time a teacher in the Wesleyan Sunday School (Wrotham-road), and attended the Wesleyan Church (Milton-road), where he was identified with the "Comrades." He was educated at the Secondary School, New Mills, Derbyshire. The parents are to be sincerely commiserated with, for they have also had the misfortune to lose an elder son (Thomas A. Aitken), who died about two years ago as a result of an accident at the Paper Mills, where he, too, was employed.

Lucy, born in 1905. The family lived at 13a Prince Street, Gravesend.

Thomas was initially employed as an errand boy in the Port. He married Elizabeth and the couple lived at 17 Wakefield Street, Gravesend prior to the Great War. With the Royal Naval Reserve he served as a Leading Trimmer on HM Whaler *Blackwhale*. There were 15 'Whalers' of this type in all. They were ordered on March 15th, 1915 and built by Smiths Docks Co. using designs provided by the Russian Government. They were originally numbered 1-15 and named later.

Blackwhale was number Z.5, Admiralty Number 868. The first of these 'Whalers' was launched in June, 1915. The expected manoeuvrability of these vessels made them suitable for anti-submarine escorts in coastal waters. However, their performance in heavy weather was poor and worse than comparable trawlers.

They were 125 feet long by 25 feet and were capable of 13 knots and were armed with one 12 pounder gun. The 'Whalers' served in three squadrons, one based at Stornaway, one at the Shetlands and one at Petershead or the Humber. *Blackwhale* was with the latter squadron between Peterhead, Aberdeenshire and the Humber.

Blackwhale was launched on June 28th, 1915. She struck a mine off Fife Ness on January 3rd, 1918 and sank

T. J. ALBERT (Leading Trimmer).

Thomas James Albert, husband of Mrs. Albert (née Lizzie Shuttlewood), 17, Wakefield-street, gave his life for King and country on January 3rd, 1918. He joined the R.N.R. Trawler Section in 1915, and for 2½ years served in H.M. "Whaler," and went down with her on January 3rd, "Somewhere in the North Sea." He was home on leave in December last year. Previous to the war he was employed by the Orient Company, in which he made several trips to the Colonies. He was well known and respected by all who knew him. Deceased was 30 years of age, and had been married 15 months.

GR 26/1/18 [Andrew Marshall]

with all hands aboard – there were no survivors. Thomas went down with the *Blackwhale* and his body was not recovered. He is commemorated on the Chatham Naval Memorial.

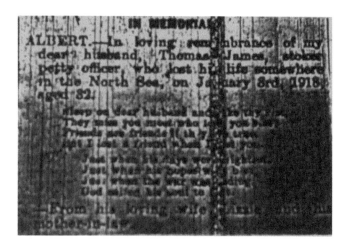

GR 26/1/18

William Barclay Allan
Merchant Navy
Service No. 748688

William was born in Lanark, Scotland in 1891. Shortly afterwards the family moved to Gravesend where his father William Lightfoot found employment as a hot water and sanitary engineer. William [father] was born in 1862 in Brixton and married Euphemia, seven years his junior, in 1889. She came from Belfast.

There were seven children surviving of nine born; William was the eldest with Edith born in 1895, Harold, born in 1897, Annie, born in 1900, Percy, born in 1901, Beatrice, born in 1904 and Mildred, born in 1905.

All but the eldest were born in Gravesend. William had a sister, Anna Jemima who was two years older than him. She was a spinster and a Headmistress in a L.C.C. school.

The family lived at 6 Portland Avenue.

On leaving school, William joined the Merchant Navy.

In June, 1916 he received his certificate as 2nd Mate at Tilbury.

William died of illness at Piraeus Hospital, Athens. At the time he was taken ill he was on *HMS Mesopotamia*.

Sidney Milton Allchin
Royal West Kent, 3rd Battalion
2nd Lieutenant

Sidney was born in 1898 and was one of two children born to Sidney and Minnie Allchin. He had an older sister, Muriel Milton who was three years older than him. The family lived at 39 Kent Road but originally lived in Hampstead, London. There Sidney senior worked for the Post Office; born in 1855 he was married to Minnie, who came from Gravesend, ten years his junior. They married in 1895. Sidney was in the years up to the Great War *retired, private means; hopeless, bed ridden invalid of about 35 years progression … without any pension* and by the time Sidney junior enlisted his father had died and the mother had moved to Sunny Hill Road, Bournemouth.

Boesinghe was, until July 1917, directly faced by the German front line on the east side of the Yser Canal; but in the Battle of Pilckem Ridge, begun on the 31st July, the British front was pushed forward. The Guards Division captured Artillery Wood, a copse on the north side of the railway line to Thourout, about half a mile east of the canal. Artillery Wood Cemetery is a little north of where the Wood was located. The cemetery was started by the Guards Division after the action on July 31st, and was used as a front-line cemetery until March 1918. It contained, at the time of the Armistice, 141 graves but it was then greatly enlarged by the concentration of 1,154 graves from the battlefields and small cemeteries around Boesinghe.

Sidney was with the 1st Battalion at Passchendaele in 1917. The 1st were involved in the third phase of the campaign; the Battles of Broodseinde and the 1st Battle of Poelcappelle, in early October and the 2nd Battle of Passchendaele, late October – mid November. Sidney was killed on December 12th, 1917.

He is buried in Artillery Wood Cemetery, being among the first of the 141 soldiers to be buried there.

> **Killed in Action.**
> ALLCHIN.—Killed in action on December 12th, 1917, Second-Lieut. Sidney M. Allchin, Royal West Kent Regiment, aged 19 years, the only and dearly loved son of the late Sidney Allchin and Mrs. Allchin, of 82, Sternhold-avenue, Streatham Hill, S.W., late of Hampstead and Gravesend.

GR 22/12/17 [Andrew Marshall]

Christened ***Herbert Francis Allen*** he signed up as ***Herbert Albert Allen***.

Herbert Albert Allen
Royal West Kent, 10th Battalion
Service No. G/11157 - Private

Herbert was born in the summer of 1890. His father James, born in 1866, was from Gravesend and his mother, Mary, three years younger than her

Gravesend Cemetery –

ALSO WILLIAM BARCLAY ALLAN
BORN JAN 21st 1891   DIED ON ACTIVE
SERVICE H.M.N.T. MESOPOTAMIA
NOV. 17th 1918
INTERRED BRITISH CEMETERY, PIREAUS,
GREECE.

William Barclay Allan, 1st Officer s.s. "Mesopotamia," whose portrait appears above, is the eldest son of Mr. W. L. Allan, ironmonger, 31, Queen-street, Gravesend. News has been received through the Admiralty that he died at Piraeus, Greece, on November 18th. On war breaking out he was in the merchant service abroad, and on returning home joined H.M.N.T., but on his last voyage he was transferred to H.M.M.T. and it is only this week that his whereabouts became known to his parents.

His ship had been to India and returned to th Mediterranean and so far as the information received by telegram from the Transport Officer at Piraeus states he died on arrival at that port of septicæmia. He was educated at Wrotham-road Schools, and afterwards went to Mr. Waldegrave's Modern School. On finishing there he went to London and studied for the Civil Service, but not being successful in gaining an appointment on his first examination his thoughts turned to the sea, and he was apprenticed. His father learns from his late employers, Messrs. Parker Hamilton, of Billiter-avenue, that they exceedingly regret his loss as he was such a promising young officer. His younger brother, Sec.-Lieut. Percy Allan, who won the Military Medal some time back, is also very ill in hospital in France. His parents have received this news from the War Office. His other brother, Corpl. H. J. Allan, R.E., is also in France. His many friends in Gravesend will regret to hear of the above young officer's death at the close of the war. He was 27 years old.

GR 7/12/18 [Andrew Marshall]

husband, came from Suffolk. There were seven surviving children in the family – Edith was the eldest, a year older than Herbert, Fred was a year younger, Hilda, born in 1894, Ethel, born in 1897, Dorothy, born in 1901 Victor, born in 1910. They lived at 12 Church Street. They took one boarder – William Hughes who was a marine store dealer. They subsequently moved to 8 Bath Street.

James worked on the docks as a labourer and Fred was a rag sorter. Herbert initially found employment working as an assistant in a Green Grocers'. He was a cellar man prior to enlisting with the 10th Battalion in mid-November 1915. He was 5 feet 5 inches tall, weighed 124lbs and had a chest measurement of 36 inches. He was described as being of fair physical development, but good enough for the Army nonetheless!

The 10th (Kent County) Battalion, The Royal West Kent Regiment was raised at Maidstone on May 3rd, 1915 by Lord Harris, Vice Lieutenant of Kent, at the request of the Army Council. After initial training close to home they joined 118th Brigade, 39th Division in July. In October they transferred to 123rd Brigade, 41st Division. They moved to Aldershot for final training in January 1916 and proceeded to France on May 4th, landing at Le Havre. The division concentrated between Hazebrouck and Bailleul.

The 10th moved to the Ypres salient and were sent to the trenches in Ploegsteert Wood on June 30th. The following day Herbert was badly wounded in the right leg and hip with gunshot wounds causing compound fractures.

He was immediately taken out of the war zone and sent back to England. On July 4th he was receiving medical treatment in the 1st Southern General Hospital, Birmingham. Further operations followed and after an amputation

of the right hip Herbert died from shock due to haemorrhage.

His body was removed to Gravesend and he is buried in the cemetery. The circumstances surrounding his funeral created some controversy.

The official confirmation of Herbert's death.

RWK 26/6
D4o

D4 4 R+E
War Office
Winchester House
S. James Square
London SW1

10 June 20

Reference: 20/30734

Reference attached, the particulars
recorded on as follows:-
No 11157. Private H. A. Allen
10th Batt. Royal West Kent
Died of wounds received in action
on the 21st of July 1916
at 1st Southern General Hospital
Birmingham
next of kin:- Mr J.J. Allen
8 Bath street
Gravesend.

Cols
No Records.

The list of personal items returned on Herbert's death.

GR 29/7/16 [Andrew Marshall]

DIED AFTER SIX OPERATIONS.—Pte. Herbert Francis Allen, son of Mr. and Mrs. J. J. Allen, 12, Church-street, has died from wounds, and was buried at Gravesend Cemetery on Wednesday. He was 25 years of age, and was for eleven years employed by Mrs. Arnold, West-street, while he was well known as a Wednesday football player and secretary of the "Jolly Boys Club" at the Prince Alfred Inn. He joined the 10th Batt. Royal West Kent Regiment on the 14th November 1915, and proceeded to the front on the 16th May last. He was wounded at La Bassée on the 30th June, and brought to England, where he became an inmate of the Dudley-road Hospital, Birmingham. Here six operations on his shattered thigh were carried out, but he succumbed under the last. His body was brought to Gravesend, and it was hoped to have the funeral on Wednesday with full military honours, but owing to the Suffolk Regiment band being engaged for the Tipperary Fête, Colonel Wallace was not able to send any more than a bearer and firing party. The Rev. Canon Gedge performed the interment. The mourners were his father and mother, Messrs. Fred and Victor Allen (brothers), Mrs. Loveridge, the Misses Ethel and Dolly Allen, and Mrs. Shuttlewood (sisters), Mr. Raynham (uncle), Mr. C. Raynham (cousin), Mr. J. Shuttlewood (brother-in-law), Mr. Hughes, Mr. W. Arnold, Mrs. Arnold, Mr. and Mrs. Shuttlewood, Mr. A. Shuttlewood, Mrs. Allen, Mr. and Mrs. A. Edgley, Mr. and Mrs. Pink and Mr. Cox, and Miss Dolly Perryment (London friends). Wreaths were sent by his parents, "Fred," "Ethel and Charley," "Dolly and Victor," "Louie and Jack," "Edie, Violet, and Lenny," "Billy," "Aunt Sarah," Cousin Bob, and family," Mr. and Mrs. Pressley and family, "Bert, Mrs. Arnold and the boy," Mrs. E. Gay. "Jack and Edie," Mr. and Mrs. Shuttlewood and a friend, Mr. and Mrs. Shuttlewood, jun., "From his chum, Johnny Ever, somewhere in France," Mr. and Mrs. Allen, Mr. and Mrs. and Arthur Bright, "Uncle Phil and family," Mr. and Mrs. H. Arnold, Mr. and Mrs. A. Edgely, "Willie Arnold and Albert Barnard," "Old friends and chums of the 'Prince Alfred,'" Dolly Scott, H. H. Librun, Mr. and Mrs. Pink, the station staff rest, Tilbury Dock, Mr. Cox, Mrs. Perryment and family, Mr. and Mrs. Beech, Miss G. Collins, Mr. and Mrs. J. Sutherland, Mr. and Mrs. Sutherland and family, Gunner H. Reader, K.R.G.A., and Miss Kate Sutherland, Mr. and Mrs. Lines, Neighbour and Friends, Mr. and Mrs. Colyer and family, "His friends," Herbert Rogers, Mrs. Healy, Mrs. Payne and family, Mrs. Taylor, Mr. W. Raven, etc. Mr. L. Solomon was the undertaker.

GR 12/8/16 [Andrew Marshall]

A fortnight ago we recorded the death and burial of Pte. Herbert Francis Allen, 10th R.W.K. Regt., son of Mr. and Mrs. J. J. Allen, 12, Church-street, who died in hospital after six operations consequent on wounds received at the front. It was his dying wish that his photograph and a letter from the Rev. E. Sayer Ellis, written from the 140th Field Ambulance, B.E.F., should be published in the "Reporter." The letter referred to states:—"As I saw your son last night you will be interested to hear how he was. He had been in rather a hot corner, and you have good reason to be thankful that he came through with his life. A shell burst near him, and his leg is badly fractured. The shock was naturally somewhat severe. He was showing splendid pluck when I saw him last, after the doctors had attended to him, and in a very short time he was put into a fine motor ambulance and went off to what is called a casualty clearing station. . . . He was keeping up his pluck in a quite sensible way that promises very well, so do not think that he is a lot worse than I am telling you. When a soldier is really rather badly hit I think it is best to tell his friends just how he is. Your boy's is a double fracture of the femur, and that makes a fellow feel bad. But by now I hope that the worst is past, and that he will be safely and comfortably in hospital at the base, or perhaps in England. . . Doubtless you are already very proud of your brave boy, but you have more reason than ever to be so now."

Military Honours.

To the Editor.

Sir,—In to-day's issue, and under local news, you report the sad death of Private Herbert Francis Allen, 10th Batt., Royal West Kents, after six operations through having his thigh shattered in France whilst fighting his country's battles. You also report the burial of this Gravesend hero at Gravesend cemetery on Wednesday last, and that Colonel Wallace, of the Suffolk Regt. was not able to send more than a bearer and firing party, and that owing to the Tipperary Fête being held at the Windmill Hill Gardens the band of the Suffolk Regt. could not be spared to play this Gravesend hero to his last resting place and afford him the full military honours which he, at the cost of his life, so bravely earned on the battlefields of France. Being well-known to myself and the waterside fraternity, a large circle of Private Allen's friends have requested me to ask you to allow me, on their behalf, to express their indignation at the authorities, both civic and military, of allowing an opportunity (and probably the only one) to pass of according full military honours to a brave and glorious Royal West Kent hero, now lying beneath his native soil. Surely the band could have been spared for one hour to assist in giving the last sacred rites to this Gravesend hero. How differently the East Ham authorities—civic, military and naval—were in giving Jack Cornwell his last sacred rites. I happened to be in East Ham this afternoon, and witnessed the homage paid to this brave "Chester" boy, which made me think how little we in Gravesend appreciate our Gravesend heroes. Surely the glorious deeds of the Royal West Kents recently should have been sufficient to have stirred the authorities to have paid every homage to Private Allen, when we had all that was left of him with us in his native town. I enclose words and music of a patriotic song dedicated to the memory of Jack Cornwell of H.M.S. "Chester."—Yours truly,

H. HINKLEY.

27, Brandon-street, Gravesend.
July 29th, 1916.

To the Editor.

Sir,—"Died after Six Operations." Pte. Herbert Francis Allen, 10th Batt., Royal West Kent Regt., gave his life for his country. Then I read in your report of his funeral: "It was hoped to have the funeral on Wednesday with full military honours, but owing to the Suffolk Regt. band being engaged for the Tipperary Fête, Col. Wallace was not able to send more than a bearer and firing party." Thus the amusement of a crowd of pleasure-seekers was of more importance than honour to a dead hero. The fête was in aid of disabled soldiers, but I wonder what the disabled friends of the late Pte. Allen will feel about it. In my opinion the fête could have waited until the dead had been honoured. Canon Gedge did his duty first and went to the fête afterwards, and the military band could have done the same. I hope the person responsible for this stupid act—as stupid as the error that consigned brave Travers Cornwell to a nameless grave—will go to the cemetery and do penance at the grave of a greater man—Pte. Herbert Francis Allen.—Yours faithfully,

INDIGNANT.

Gravesend.

Signing himself "Justice," a sergeant of the West Kents writes:—"In reference to what you have published in your paper of Private Allen, I myself do think it was absolutely disgraceful to think that this poor fellow was allowed to be buried in this style. Surely it is the last thing that could be done. As an old inhabitant of the borough, and a member of the West Kents, I deeply deplore the act."

Reginald Palmer Allen
London Rifles / Royal Irish Rifles
Service No. 5123 [LR] & 12/44607 [RIR] - Rifleman

Reginald was born in 1884 in Margate. His father, John Bonny, born in 1847, hailed from Biddenden. John was a manager of a grocer shop in Margate. His wife, Alice Stewart, born 1853, came from Bishop's Waltham. The couple married in 1876 and they had four surviving children; Alice, born in 1877, John, born in 1879 was the second oldest, Reginald and a younger sister, Marguerite, born in 1890. All the children were born in Margate.

Reginald found employment as a clerk at the Stock Exchange before enlisting with the 5th London Rifles. The 5th (City of London) Battalion (London Rifle Brigade) was formed in 1908. They wore black buttons and shoulder titles. Their headquarters was at Bunhill Road, and in August 1914 they were at their annual camp at Crowborough, in Sussex. They crossed to France in November 1914, joining the 11th Brigade, 4th Division, serving with them in the trenches at Ploegsteert. Men from the battalion took part in the Christmas Truce in December 1914. They took part in Second Ypres and in April-May 1915 they lost 16 officers and 392 men. Lance Sergeant D.W. Belcher was awarded the Victoria

Cross for bravery during this period. Due to the losses they formed a composite battalion with other London units until August 1915 when they became part of the 3rd Division. They served with them until the formation of the 56th (London) Division in March 1916 when they joined the 169th Brigade. They lost heavily at Gommecourt on July 1st, 1916, and fought again at Leuze Wood and Combles. In 1917 they were in the Battle of Arras and Third Ypres, and also took part in the Battle of Cambrai. By now Reginald was posted with the 11th Irish Rifles. The 11th (South Antrim) Battalion was raised in County Antrim September 1914. They joined the 108th Brigade, 36th (Ulster) Division at Clandeboye in December 1914. The Ulster Division was formed from the Ulster Volunteer Force in August and September 1914, a process complicated by the tension surrounding the issue of Home rule. In July 1915 they moved to Seaford, Sussex in England. They proceeded to France in the first week of October, landing at Boulogne. The 36th (Ulster) Division concentrated near Flesselles, north of Arras. With training and familiarisation, including periods in the trenches in the front line north of the River Ancre near Albert. On October 21st they moved to the area around Abbeville. The 36th Ulster Division took over the front line in the Spring. In 1916 the Division suffered heavily on the first day of the Battle of the Somme where they attacked at Thiepval. In

1917 They were in action at The Battle of Messines, capturing Wytschaete. They were then withdrawn from the front line.

But all too soon the 11th were 'back up the line' and on July 30th they were in position as support troops for the Lancashire units of the 55th Division who were among the units waiting to go over the top on the first day of Haig's hoped-for breakthrough. Being 'in support' was far from a cushy billet. It meant the drudgery of road making, carrying supplies and the rather more traumatic task of casualty clearing.

At first, it seemed that the advance would go according to plan - but then the rains came. Torrential downpours and the churning effects of thousands upon thousands of shells turned the battlefield into a morass.

For the next two weeks, the Ulster Division performed the twin duties of holding the British front line and acting as labourers. Throughout this period, German artillery observers kept their positions under a steady bombardment, constantly whittling away at the Division's strength. This shelling, coupled with living in the most miserable conditions were hardly the ideal preparations for a unit earmarked for the next major advance - the assault on the German lines at Langemarck.

It was in this period that Reginald was killed, On August 15th. He has no known grave and is commemorated on the Menin Gate. His probate was issued to his brother John Bonny Allen, Captain, A.S.C.

Killed in Action.

ALLEN.—Killed in action, August 15th, 1917, Reginald Palmer Allen, Rifleman, London Rifle Brigade (subsequently attached to Royal Irish Rifles), younger and dearly-loved son of Mr. and Mrs. John Bonny Allen, Homeleigh, Singlewell-road, Gravesend; served in Flanders, 1914-15-16 and 17.

GR 8/9/17 [Andrew Marshall]

Rifleman Reginald Palmer Allen, London Regiment, and subsequently attached to the Royal Irish Rifles, youngest son of Mr. and Mrs. John Bonny Allen, of Homeleigh, Singlewell Road. Gravesend, was killed in action on August 15th.

GR 15/9/17 [Andrew Marshall]

Sydney Allchin – Artillery Wood CWGC Cemetery

Herbert Allen – Gravesend Cemetery

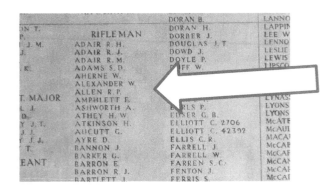

Reginald Allen – Menin Gate, Ypres

Royal Irish Rifles Memorial, Belfast

Thomas Allen

Royal West Kent
Service No. S/1095 - Private

Thomas was a career soldier with the 1st Battalion. He served on the Punjab Frontier, 1897-1898 and in South Africa.

He was born in late 1873. He was 5 foot 7 inches tall and weighed 145lbs. He had a chest measurement of 37½ inches, blue eyes and brown hair.

He married Clara Alice Eves in the summer of 1903. They lived at 1 Kempthorne Street. They had six children; Annie, born May 1905, James, born September 1906, Clara, born July 1908, Ellen, born June 1910, John, born June 1912 and Maisie, born September 1915.

He re-engaged for one year's service in the Royal West Kent Regiment Special Reserve on October 7th, 1914 at Gravesend.

The 1st Battalion were in action in The Battle of Mons and the subsequent retreat, The Battle of Le Cateau, The Battle of the Marne, The Battle of the Aisne, The Battles of La Bassee and

Messines and The First Battle of Ypres all of which he missed as he landed at Boulogne on April 23rd, 1915. He was posted with 'C' Company.

In 1915 the 1st were in action at The Second Battle of Ypres and the Capture of Hill 60. In the autumn 1915, many units were exchanged with units from the newly arrived volunteer 32nd Division, to stiffen the inexperienced Division, but the 1st West Kents remained with 5th Division. In March 1916 5th Division took over a section of front line between St Laurent Blangy and the southern edge of Vimy Ridge, near Arras. They moved south in July to reinforce The Somme and were in action at High Wood and The Battles of Guillemont, Flers-Courcelette, Morval Le Transloy. In October they moved to Festubert and remained there until March 1917 when they moved in preparation for the Battles of Arras. It was there that Thomas died of wounds, hematemesis, at 23 Casualty Clearing Station, Flanders, on March 27th, 1917. He is buried at Lapugnoy Military Cemetery, Pas de Calais.

GR 7/9/18 [Andrew Marshall]

The Borough of Gravesend
CERTIFICATE OF HONOUR
awarded in the memory of Tom
Allen and the envelope in which it
was delivered! [Andrew Marshall]

Memorial in St George's Church – Tom is listed
third name down.

[Courtesy of Neil Fisher, Church Warden]

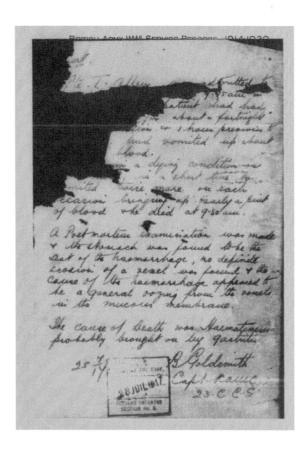

Thomas Allen – medical report, top left, articles returned, top right, Pension awarded, below left, and his headstone at Lapugnoy Military Cemetery, below right.

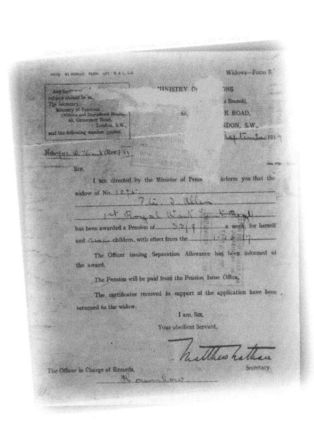

1914 1918

SOUTH AFRICAN MEMORIAL

ULSTER MEMORIAL

GLORY OF GOD

IN EVERLASTING MEMORY

ALLEN, Pte. T., S/1095. 1st Bn. Royal West
Kent Regt. 27th Mar., 1917. Age 42. Husband
of Clara Alice Allen, of 1, Kempthorne St.,
Greenwich, Kent. Served on the Punjab Frontier

WHO GAVE HIS LIFE IN THE GREAT WAR
THAT WE MIGHT LIVE
AND WHOSE NAME IS CARVED IN STONE
AT

AUSTRALIAN MEMORIAL

HIGHLAND MEMORIAL

YPRES
LOOS
ARRAS
BETHUNE
SAINT-QUENTIN
NEUVE EGLISE
BOUHLON WOOD
PÉRONNE
MONCHY
HEBUTERNE
WANCOURT
PASSCHENDAELE
BEAUMONT-HAMEL
CARNOY
THIEPVAL
SULLY-GRENAY
POZIERES
COURCELETTE
CROISILLES

CAMBRAI
LILLE
ALBERT
ARMENTIÈRES
LA BASSÉE
NEUVE CHAPELLE
TRONES WOOD
MONS
FRICOURT
GOMMECOURT
MAMETZ
HILL 60
DELVILLE WOOD
FLERS
ACHIET
HAVRINCOURT
VIMY RIDGE
BAILLEUL
GUILLEMONT

LAPUGNOY MILITARY CEMETERY - FRANCE

THIEPVAL - BRITISH MEMORIAL
In Memory of all British Troops who made the Supreme Sacrifice in FRANCE

73

Lapugnoy Military Cemetery –
Among the most tranquil and poignant
settings of all such cemeteries.

A Hero of Three Wars.

"Greater love hath no man than this: that he lay down his life for his friends." This may be said of many of our gallant heroes who are daily making the great sacrifice for those near and dear to them at home; also in the great struggle of democracy against the ghastly militarism of Prussia, the great principle of right against might, and the protection of the weak against brutal tyranny. Distinguished amongst those to whom the above quoted words apply one may name Thomas Allen, who died at a clearing station "somewhere in France," on March 27th, at the age of 43 years. Being local bred and born, it is felt it would be of interest to readers of the "Reporter" to know a little of his previous career, as he was particularly well known and respected. He joined the Army in November, 1889, in the Royal West Kents, 2nd Batt., leaving the army after completing 12 years and 8 months. During this time he served with distinction in India for seven years, gaining there the Punjaub Frontier Medal. After this he went through the South African War, gaining the King's and Queen's Medal with three clasps for engagements in Wittenbergen, Transvaal, and Cape Colony. On leaving the Army he was for six years employed at Russell's Brewery, during which time he not only bore a most exemplary character, but was immensely and deservedly popular with his workmates. Droll of a happy disposition, a good father and citizen, the first to help in any good cause, he will be sadly missed by many who enjoyed the pleasure of his acquaintance. While thus employed, the love of soldiering still strong within him, we find him for three years in our local Territorials. Soon after the outbreak of war he spontaneously joined up in the Royal West Kent's, October, 1914, went to France in April, 1915, his only furlough (seven days) being in January, 1916. He was engaged in Hill 60 and numerous other engagements. He leaves behind to mourn their loss a wife and six children. Great sympathy is naturally extended to his wife in her terrible loss and the great responsibility that lies before her; leaving her perhaps one great consoling thought (as with many others similarly placed) that her husband laid down his life for his King and country, and hearth and home. When he answers the last roll call may a fitting place be found him. He deserves it.—E.M.

Mrs. Allen has received the following letter from one of his comrades:—"I have been asked to write to you on behalf of some of my comrades, and I can assure you it is not a task I care about. It is with the deepest regret that I have to tell you of the death of poor Tom. It all happened so sudden that we were all surprised, as you know he was a very old comrade of mine, for we were in the same wars together and had seen both rough and good times. Often we have sat down and spoke about old times, even to the day before he died. He was such a jolly fellow, and he was one of the best, and we all miss him very much. The boys turned out and saw that he had a very rich funeral, and also placed two lovely wreaths upon his grave. Everything was carried out as it should have been. The minister who carried out the burial service has promised to write. He sympathises in the great loss for you, also for the six children. So I must now close, with deepest sympathy.—I remain, yours truly, S. Phillips."

GR 21/4/17 [Andrew Marshall]

William Farquhar Allen
Royal Sussex Regiment
Service No. SD/2604 – Lance Corp

William was born in Milton, Gravesend in 1892. He was the son of Edward John, a local man born in 1864 and Jane Maria, from Woolwich born in 1867. Edward was a pilot at Trinity House and worked on the Thames. The couple were married in 1888 and there were seven children in all of which six survived. William was the second child with the younger sisters being Doris, born in 1897 Clarissa, born in 1900 and Jean, born in 1908 – a younger brother, Harold was born in 1902. The family home was at 125 Milton Road but subsequently moved to number 10 The Avenue.

William was employed as a clerk in the Mercantile Marine Office prior to enlisting at Detling, joining the 13th Battalion, which was in the final phase of training.

In September 1914, Colonel Claude Lowther, the owner of Herstmonceux Castle and MP for the Eskdale constituency in Cumberland, received permission from the War Office to raise a Battalion of local men.

He set up recruitment offices all over Sussex, but principally in the seaside towns of Hastings, Bexhill, Eastbourne, Brighton, Worthing and Bognor. Recruitment started on September 9th and within two days 1100 men had volunteered. Originally designated the 9th Royal Sussex they later became the 11th, the first Southdown Battalion, a further two Battalions were raised by the end of the year, 12th and 13th. All original enlistments were given an "SD" (South Downs) prefix to their regimental number.

After further training at Detling, Kent and at Witley Camp in Surrey, they crossed to France via Southampton on 5th/6th March 1916, landing at Le Havre and proceeded to Fleurbaix, France, a front line sector, for instruction and further training.

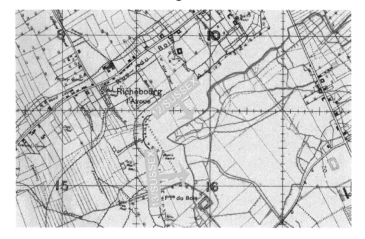

"Lowther's Lambs" suffered terrible casualties on June 30th, 1916. This was in a diversionary attack, a large scale raid launched by the 12th and 13th at a position called the Boar's Head, near Richebourg l'Avoue.

The Battle lasted over four hours and although initially the allied bombardment had successfully cut some of the wire, great parts of it remained intact. With smoke shells causing confusion, the attackers had to bunch together to get through the defences and this gave the Germans easy targets. When the front line was eventually breached, violent counter attacks pushed the British back. The cost to the three South Downs Battalions was terrible as in reality no ground was gained. The total casualties were 15 Officers and 364 other ranks killed or died of wounds and 21 Officers and 728 other ranks wounded. In total nearly 1,100. The fruitless attack that had no effect on the enemy's abilities to withstand the next day's assault on the Somme.

In August they moved down to the Somme and suffered terrible casualties on the Ancre, The Battle of Thiepval Ridge, The Battle of the Ancre Heights and the capture of Schwaben Redoubt and Stuff Trench as well as The Battle of the Ancre. Beaumont Hamel and Thiepval.

> **Killed in Action.**
> ALLEN.—On the 20th, in France, William Farquhar Allen, 13th Royal Sussex Regiment, dearly-loved son of Mr. and Mrs. Allen, 10, The Avenue, Gravesend, aged 24 years.

GR 30/9/16 [Andrew Marshall]
GR 30/9/16 [Andrew Marshall]

> Mr. and Mrs. E. J. Allen, of Lea Hurst, the Avenue, Gravesend, have received notification that their second son, Lance-Corpl. Allen, 13th Royal Sussex Regiment, was killed on the 27th September. Deceased, who was 24 years of age, was educated at the Gravesend County School and Grays College, and was on the headquarters staff of the Union of London and Smith's Bank. He joined the Army in December, 1914, and went to the front in March of this year. A letter from C.Q.M.S. Phillips, 13th Sussex, states that Lance-Corpl. Allen and a comrade were killed instantly by a shell in a village behind the trenches, and as Lance-Corpl. Allen had been C.Q.M.S. Phillips's deputy for some time his death was a great shock to him. He was exceedingly brave, and as a bomber went "over the top" five times in the Great Push. Both he and the Rev. J. Thom, C.F., who buried him in a British cemetery, pay high tributes to the deceased in letters they have written Mr. and Mrs. Allen.

William died of wounds received on the Somme on September 20th at 182nd Field Ambulance. He is buried at Bertrancourt CWGC Cemetery.

Ernest Henry Allson
Mercantile Marine – 4th Mate

Ernest was born in 1891, the son of Walter and Sarah Allson. He was married to Olive and the couple lived at 14 St James Avenue. He received his Certificate of Competency as 2nd Mate in February 1912 and that of 1st mate in May, 1913, both issued at Gravesend. His Certificate of

Gravesend Cemetery -

Reginald Allen –

LONDON RIFLE BRIGADE KILLED IN ACTION NEAR YPRES. AUG 15th 1917.

[Photograph – Andy White]

William Allen –

ALSO WILLIAM FARQUAHAR SECOND SON OF THE ABOVE WHO WAS KILLED IN ACTION SEPT 20th 1916 AGED 24 YEARS "WELL DONE THY GOOD AND FAITHFUL SERVANT".

[Photograph – Andy White]

Competency as master was issued in London in March, 1915.

By this time he was on the *SS Minnehaha*. The *Minnehaha* was the second of the four *Minne* class ships ordered by Bernard N. Baker in 1898 and built by Harland & Wolff, Belfast. She sailed on her maiden voyage from Belfast to New York on July 7th, 1900, making the return journey on August 11th, 1900 commenced her first voyage from London to New York. She is recorded as making a total of 160 voyages to New York between August 1900 and December 1915.

Captain John Robinson commanded *Minnehaha* until his retirement in 1907 and was replaced by Sydney Layland. As a new vessel *Minnehaha* had a narrow escape in channel fog when she almost collided with the South Eastern and Chatham packet *Lord Warden*. When she arrived in New York on September 18th, 1900, she struck and sank the New York Harbour Towing Company tug *American* in the North River, killing two of its crew. On December 27th, 1904, while she was at anchor off Gravesend *Minnehaha*'s stern was struck by the British steamer *John Sanderson*. Almost two years later, in October of 1906, *Minnehaha* rammed the Cunard Liner *Etruria* as both vessels attempted to leave New York harbour in fog. And in January of 1907 *Minnehaha* lost a propeller and had to complete her voyage with only one. And outbound on April 17, 1909, she grounded in the Gedney Channel, the dredged passage that forms the entrance to New York harbour, but was re-floated the following day.

Most famously of all however, the *Minnehaha* ran aground on the Scilly Isles in fog on April 18th, 1910. Landing the passengers was the first priority and they were welcomed so warmly by the locals that some resisted the line's

ATLANTIC TRANSPORT LINE
STEAMER MINNEHAHA
PASSING SHAKESPEARE'S CLIFF

attempt at removing them to the mainland to continue their journey. Once the passengers were safely ashore attention turned to the ship, which was first assumed to be a total loss. After 18 hours or so it was decided to remove the crew from the ship, leaving behind a skeleton crew of 20 or so men, mostly engineers. Cargo, which included pianolas, motor cars and of course cattle, was thrown overboard in an attempt to lighten the ship forward. Salvaged freight not spirited away by the islanders was later sold at auction on the mainland.

On May 11th the ship herself was successfully re-floated after three weeks aground, and two days later she steamed under her own power to Falmouth with an escort of salvage vessels. From there she went on to Southampton for repairs. Her damage proved not to be very serious and she was able to resume the London to New York service later that year.

The *Minnie* class ships were among the first to be fitted for wireless telegraphy. The *Minneapolis* was using her equipment by the beginning of April 1902 and her call letters were "MMA." On the fringe of range of the Marconi transmitter at Poldhu in England the *Minnehaha* relayed part of the midnight Marconi news service from *Titanic* the night before she sank. Unlike her sisters, the *Minnehaha* was

not requisitioned for use as a military transport during World War One but remained in company service. Sailing under the command of Frank H. Claret she maintained her regular and direct London/New York passenger/cargo service and was defensively armed. Passengers however, were few and the London-New York passenger service seems to have been terminated at the end of 1915. The *Minnehaha* continued sailing as a freighter, and became well-known as a carrier of munitions. In the summer of 1915 she survived a fire-bomb planted in New York by the German activist Erich Muenter after he had exploded a device in the Capitol building in Washington D.C. Meunter, who had been living underground under various aliases since his 1906 indictment for poisoning his wife, wanted the house of Morgan to stop financing war loans to the European allies and shipments of ammunition to them.

After leaving his fire bomb in New York he travelled to the younger J.P. Morgan's home on Long Island. The financier opened the door and managed to wrestle his assailant to the ground despite being shot. The butler then knocked Meunter out and called the police. Meunter later committed suicide in jail. Having been warned by wireless that there might be a device planted on his ship Captain Claret had the crew search the vessel. Nothing was found, but at 12:30 the bomb detonated. It caused considerable damage and started a fire that the crew could control but not extinguish, but miraculously it had been placed with harmless general cargo and did not detonate the many tons of high explosive on board.

The *Minnehaha* made 26 voyages from New York carrying munitions and sailing alone. Ironically she was in convoy with five other vessels when she was eventually torpedoed and sunk by *U48* 12 miles from Fastnet on September 7th, 1917. There were some 110 or so survivors which did not include Ernest who was listed as lost, drowned at sea. He is commemorated on the Tower Hill Memorial.

The *Minnehaha* lies some 12 miles south-east of Fastnet Rock, sitting upright, and mostly intact. The funnels and winches are clearly visible and portholes are still intact.

THE LATE Mr. E. H. ALLSON.

We regret to report the sad death of Mr. E. H. Allson, son of Mr. and Mrs. W. Allson, of 32, New-road, Gravesend, his ship having been sunk by enemy submarine on the 7th ult., and he unfortunately being reported drowned. It appears that he was in the act of getting the lifeboat, of which he was in charge, away after the ship had been struck, when the ship suddenly plunged and he was thrown forward, his head striking the side of the lifeboat, so that he fell unconscious into the sea. Undoubtedly if he had not received this blow he would have been among the rescued, for he was a strong swimmer and could have easily reached a raft or a piece of the wreckage, as so many others did. Mr. Allson had served about 2½ years on one of H.M. transports, and was married only 15 months ago to Miss Sunnucks, of Rosherville, and a fortnight later joined his ship, which was engaged in the Mediterranean. It was 13 months before he again returned home, suffering from chronic rheumatism, contracted during the time his ship was transporting to and from the Dardenelles, his being one of the first transports in the landing at Gallipoli. He was educated at the old Higher Grade School, and was a good athlete, being captain of the football team. He was only 26 years of age when he met his death, and undoubtedly had a good career before him, already having gained his master's ticket about three years ago.

GR 13/10/17 [Andrew Marshall]

GR 6/10/17 [Andrew Marshall]

On Active Service.

ALLSON. — On Sept. 7th, Ernest Henry Allson, dearly-loved son of Mr. and Mrs. W. Allson, 32, New-road, Gravesend, who lost his life in a recent shipping disaster, aged 26 years.

Tower Hill Memorial

80

James Amos
Royal West Kent, 6th Battalion
Service No. S/8545 - Lance Corp.

James was born in 1895 in Gravesend being one of nine children born to John, born 1854 in Rochester and Sarah, born in 1867, a local woman from Gravesend. There were eleven surviving children in the family – George, born in 1885, Charlotte, born 1887, [step children of John's] Arthur, born in 1889, Harriet, born in 1893, Joseph, born in 1891, James, Susan, born in 1898, Eugenia, born in 1901, Samuel, born a year later, Delia, born in 1906 and Frederick in 1909. The family lived at 4 Swan Yard.

Lance Corporal Amos was killed in action on November 30th, 1917. He has no known grave and is commemorated on the Cambrai Memorial, Louverval.

Joseph Herbert Amos
Royal West Kent, 6th Battalion
Service number – G/858 - Private

Joseph was born in early 1891, the elder brother of James Amos.

Joseph married Rachel Ann Hatton on May 11th, 1913 at Hoxton St Andrew, Hackney. The couple lived at 8 Ware Street, Shoreditch. At the time of the marriage he was an Able Seaman. They had two children – Francis, born in 1913 and Iris Rachel, born in 1915. He joined the 6th Battalion at Gravesend on August 31st, 1914. He was 5 feet 4 inches tall and weighed a mere 120lbs. He had a chest measurement of 36 inches. He had brown hair and brown eyes. Army life did not suit him as he twice was listed as absent – for seven days in September, 1914 and for six days in March, 1915. He travelled to London to see his family. He was already back in Aldershot by the time the Metropolitan

Police had called at the family home searching for him; Rachel had a card from Joseph which was postmarked – Aldershot - the day before. On January 21st, 1916 he was charged with using insubordinate language to his superior officer

The 6th (Service) Battalion, The Royal West Kent Regiment was raised at Maidstone on August 14th, 1914 as part of Kitchener's First New Army. They trained at Colchester and moved to Purfleet in September 1914. They spent the winter in billets in Hythe from December. They moved to Aldershot for final training in February 1915 and proceeded to France on June 1st, 1915 landing at Boulogne.

They concentrated near St Omer and by June 6th were in the Meteren-Steenwerck area. They underwent instruction from the more experienced 48th (South Midland) Division and took over a section of the front line at Ploegsteert Wood on June 23rd. They were in action in The Battle of Loos from September 30th, taking over the sector from Gun Trench to Hulluch Quarries consolidating the position, under heavy artillery fire. On the 8th they repelled a heavy German infantry attack and on the 13th took part in the Action of the Hohenzollern Redoubt, capturing Gun Trench and the south western face of the Hulluch Quarries. During this period at Loos, 117 officers

Bertrancourt Military Cemetery –
William Allen

Cambrai Memorial, Louverval –
James Amos

Joseph Amos – De Ruvigny entry [left] and
on Panel 96, Loos Memorial [below].

and 3,237 men of the Division were killed or wounded.

Joseph was among that casualty number, being killed in action on October 7th. He has no known grave and is remembered on the Loos Memorial.

Killed in Action.

AMOS.—On the 7th of October, 1915, Pte. Joseph Herbert Amos, of the Royal West Kents, killed in action. His home was at 4, Swan-yard, Gravesend.

GR 23/101/5 [Andrew Marshall]

Charles Henry Anderson
Mercantile Marine Reserve
Service No. 787481

Charles was born in 1881 and was with the Mercantile Marine Reserve in the Great War. He was a Leading Fireman on *HMS Eaglet.*

Charles was married to Alice Luff in December, 1916. They had one child, Winifred who was born in Gravesend in June, 1917. The family lived at 24 Southill Road.

Charles and Alice Ada.

Confirmation of widow's pension

HMS *Eagle* was a 74 gun third rate ship of the line of the Royal Navy. She was the first of many ships built for the Navy by Pitcher, Northfleet and was

launched February 27th, 1804. In 1830 she was reduced to a 50-gun ship, and became a training ship in 1860. The Mersey Division of the RNVR was established in the Customs House, Liverpool in 1904, before moving to HMS *Eagle*, at Brunswick Dock, in 1911. Mersey Division was mobilised in 1914 to form part of the Royal Naval

Division, serving at Gallipoli, and involved in the Battles of Vimy Ridge, Passchendaele and Cambrai.

To avoid confusion with a newer HMS *Eagle*, the frigate was renamed *HMS Eaglet* in 1919. The ship was destroyed in a fire in 1926, and replaced by the sloop HMS *Sir Bevis*, which was renamed *Eaglet*. The new *Eaglet* was berthed at Salthouse Dock.

Charles died from illness on February 28th, 1919 and is buried at the Eastern Civil Cemetery, Dundee.

Henry Andrus
New Zealand Medical Corps
Service number 3/163A - Corporal

Henry was born in 1871. His parents were Mordecai Francis, born in 1852 and Sarah Margaret, born in 1853. There were six children altogether in the family, all of whom were born in Gravesend, of which Henry was the second eldest. The family home was at 13 Somerset Street.

Henry immigrated to New Zealand and became an Estate Agent. He was married, to Marion, and the couple lived in Derwent Street, Island Bay, Wellington where Henry worked from. By the time of the Great War they had

moved to Newtown, Wellington retaining the offices at Derwent Street. Henry joined the army serving with the New Zealand Medical Corps. He was a driver with the Ambulance Service.

The duties of a Field Ambulance on service are many and varied but primarily focus on what the term suggests – removing wounded from the battlefield.

Early in August 1915, the Ambulance moved up through Nieppe to the dressing station at L'Ecole in La Rue de Messines, Armentieres. The activities of the Brigade in the sector were very marked, raining and trench work ensuring constant casualties.

In the middle of August the Ambulance entrained with the Division for the Somme, after having been relieved by the 1st/3rd Highland Field Ambulance, which had come direct from that region.

After a period of training at Allery, a quiet village in a beautiful farming district where harvesting was nearing completion, the unit followed the New Zealand Rifle Brigade through Picquigny, and marched to a bivouac behind Albert, whence it moved to Fricourt.

The New Zealand Division now took over a section of the battle-front, and the bearers of "A" and "C" Sections, under Major Martin, were detached to the No. 2 Field Ambulance and were the bearer-work of the Division.

It was at this time that Henry was wounded in the field - September 9th to be precise.

The Second Battle of Bapaume started on August 21st and continued through to September 3rd, 1918. The attack is often taken to be the turning point of the War on the Western Front and the beginning of the Hundred Days Offensive. On August 29th New Zealanders, after heavy fighting, occupied Bapaume having broken through, with the British 5th Division, the very strong Le Transloy–Loupart trench system and having overcome many other strong points around the town.

Casualties were mounting and the Ambulance Service was invariably in the thick of the fighting and with resultant fatalities, one of whom was Henry. He died from wounds on September 10th and is buried in Brookwood Military Cemetery.

ANDRUS.—On the 10th inst., at Weybridge, Corpl. Henry Andrus, of the New Zealand Expeditionary Force, Main Body, second son of Mr. and Mrs. M. F. Andrus, "Macknade," Darnley-road, Gravesend.— "R.I.P."

GR 14/9/18 [Andrew Marshall]

DEATH OF CORPL. H. ANDRUS.

It is with deep regret we have to record the death of Corpl. Henry Andrus, of the New Zealand Expeditionary Force (main body), the younger son of Mr. and Mrs. M. F. Andrus, 124, Darnley-road, Gravesend, with whom much sympathy will be felt. The deceased, who was in New Zealand at the outbreak of the war, was the first volunteer to join up at Wellington. He was engaged in the Gallipoli campaign, and was afterwards transferred to France, taking part in no less than 14 engagements. He was twice wounded. About a month ago he came to England, being located at Milton Barracks, whence he was removed to the New Zealand General Hospital, Weybridge. On Tuesday of this week he was about to visit friends in London, but while waiting at Weybridge station he collapsed and died on the platform. It is supposed that his heart was affected from a gas attack when in France. By the wish of the authorities the deceased was buried yesterday (Friday) with full military honours. The late Corpl. Andrus married Miss Shenton, a niece of Mr. Chaloner Shenton, an alderman and former Mayor of Winchester, and a relative of the late Hon. Sir George Shenton, eleven times Mayor of Perth, New Zealand, and president of the New Zealand Legislative Council. The Shentons are an old Winchester family, several of whom have occupied the position of Mayor of the ancient capital of England. Corpl. Andrus leaves one son, who is named after his maternal family, and who is serving in the New Zealand Expeditionary Force, and a daughter, who, with the widow, are residing at Wellington, New Zealand. It was only a few months ago that we received a visit from Corpl. Andrus and his son, when both were home on leave from France, and it is with peculiar sadness that we have now to record his death.

Our esteemed townsman, Mr. M. F. Andrus, has just been receiving visits from his son, Corpl. H. Andrus, of the New Zealand Forces, and his grandson, Pte. Kenneth Shenton Andrus, of the Otago Infantry, both of whom have been on furlough from the front. Corpl. Andrus went through the whole of the Gallipoli campaign, including the landing and the evacuation, and has seen service in France for the last 18 months. He was wounded in Gallipoli, but is now as fit as a fiddle, having returned to the front on Thursday. Pte. K. S. Andrus has been visiting his maternal relatives at Winchester—the Shentons, who are an old-established family in that ancient city, several members of which have occupied the position of premier Mayor of England. Two of his uncles are members of the City Council—Alderman Chaloner Shenton, Mayor 1906-7, and Councillor Percy Shenton. He is also related to the late Hon. Sir George Shenton, eleven times Mayor of Perth, Australia, and President of the Legislative Council of West Australia.

GR 22/9/17 [Andrew Marshall]

GR 14/9/18 [Andrew Marshall]

Henry Andrus – Brookwood Military Cemetery, above. Gouzeaucourt Military Cemetery – James Annal, below; Russian burials in the cemetery, lower image. [Courtesy Jean Horent]

James Alexander Annal

R.E. / Royal Garrison Artillery
Service No. 406543 [RE]; T6532 & 365523 [RGA] – Lance Corporal

James was born in Bowers Gifford, Essex in late 1898. His father, Alexander, born in 1872, was from Gravesend and his mother, Louisa, born in 1866, was from Berkshire. Alexander was a dock labourer and the couple lived in Billericay before moving to 48 Kempthorne Street. There were six children in the family; Clara, born in 1898, James, Alexander, born in 1901, Beatrice, born in 1904, Arthur, born in 1907 and Nellie, born in 1910.

He enlisted in the summer of 1916 with the Royal Engineers. He qualified as a signalman in March 1918 and was promoted Lance Corporal on June 9th, 1918. He was with 'D' Corps Signal Company, attached to 82nd Howitzer Battery, Royal Garrison Artillery. James was killed in action on October 3rd, 1918 and is buried at Gouzeaucourt New British CWGC Cemetery.

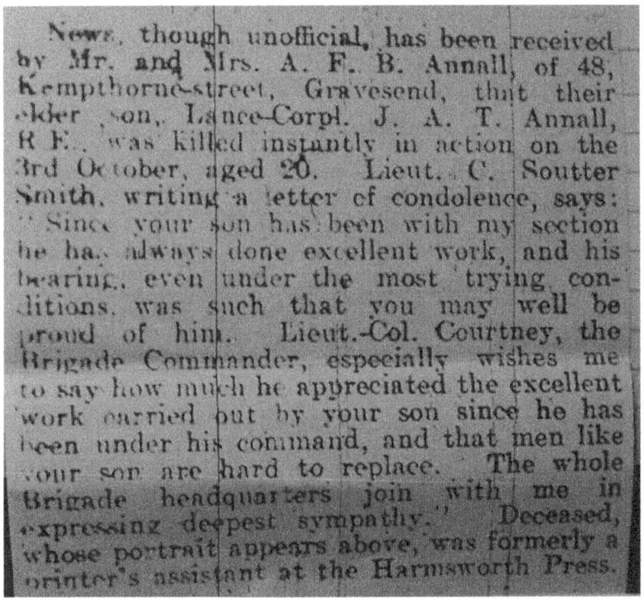

Gouzeaucourt is a large village 15 kilometres south west of Cambrai and 15 kilometres north-east of Peronne.

Gouzeaucourt village was captured by the 8th Division on the night of 12th-13th April 1917. It was lost on November 30th, 1917 in the German counterattack at the end of the Battle of Cambrai, and recaptured the same day by the 1st Irish Guards.

It was lost again on March 22nd 1918, attacked by the 38th (Welsh) Division on the following September 18th, and finally retaken by the 21st Division on October 8th.

The cemetery was begun in November 1917, taken over by the Germans in 1918, and used again by Commonwealth forces in September and October 1918, but the original burials are only 55 in number and include James. It was enlarged after the Armistice when graves were brought in from other cemeteries and from the battlefield of Cambrai.

The cemetery now contains 1,295 burials and commemorations of the First World War. 381 of the burials are unidentified but there are special memorials to 34 casualties known or believed to be buried among them.

News, though unofficial, has been received by Mr. and Mrs. A. F. B. Annall, of 48, Kempthorne-street, Gravesend, that their elder son, Lance-Corpl. J. A. T. Annall, R.E., was killed instantly in action on the 3rd October, aged 20. Lieut. C. Soutter Smith, writing a letter of condolence, says: "Since your son has been with my section he has always done excellent work, and his bearing, even under the most trying conditions, was such that you may well be proud of him. Lieut.-Col. Courtney, the Brigade Commander, especially wishes me to say how much he appreciated the excellent work carried out by your son since he has been under his command, and that men like your son are hard to replace. The whole Brigade headquarters join with me in expressing deepest sympathy." Deceased, whose portrait appears above, was formerly a printer's assistant at the Harmsworth Press.

GR 19/10/18 [Andrew Marshall]

Edward Charles Archer
1st/3rd Kent Field Company, R.E.
Service No. 1371 - Sapper

Edward was born in April 1899 in Milton. His father, Edward Thomas, born in 1875 was from Gravesend and his mother Mary Ann, born in 1873 was from Sutton Valence. Edward was a baker and ran the bakery from home. The couple were married in 1897 and had seven children; Dorothy was a year older than Edward with Walter born in 1903, Thirza, born 1906, Ronald, born in 1909, Mable, born 1910 and Kathleen, born in 1912. His father died just prior to the Great War. The family lived at 40 Bath Street and post war at 75 Havelock Road.

On leaving school he found employment as a baker with G Carter & Son, Gravesend but the excitement of war, the thrill and adventure got the better of him. He enlisted at Chatham on October 18th, 1914 giving his age as 17 years and 8 months old – two years older! He served with 1st/3rd Kent Field Company, Royal Engineers with the rank of driver. He was 5 feet 5 inches tall with chest measurement of 36 inches.

1st/3rd Kent were founded by Sir David Lionel Salomons (1851-1925) who resided at Broomhill, Southborough, Tunbridge Wells. He was the Honorary Colonel of the Kent Royal Engineers. He was a scientist and had interests in mechanics. He is quite remarkable in that he acquired the second car ever in England. He lectured in Electricity and had a great interest in transport. He organised the first motor show and was both a Magistrate and Mayor of Tunbridge Wells (1894). The first meal cooked with electricity was prepared at his home. After his son David 'Reggie' graduated from Cambridge in 1907,

the possibility of establishing a Royal Engineers Territorial Unit was investigated. This was not possible due to the existence of other RE units but it did not stop the formation of a Cadet Unit in Kent and this was raised and established in 1911. It was the fore runner of the 1st/3rd Company. David Salomons (Junior) became the officer commanding. Sir David Salomons paid for the conversion of an old gas works in Southborough and this became the drill hall for the new unit. In May 1914 the 1st/3rd Kent Fortress Royal Engineers came into being. They were initially responsible for the protection of the coastline, for searchlights and defence.

During the initial stage of the First World War the company remained at home and continued to train. They were converted to a Field Company from a Works Unit. The final stages of their training was in Woodlands Camp, Gillingham.

Royal Engineers were urgently required in the Dardanelles and the 1st/3rd were off to war. The company had a farewell dinner on October 11th 1915 and were cheered by crowds including their relatives as they left on Train Number 13. They went onto Devonport and boarded *H.M.T. Scotian*. They sailed to Malta landing on the 20th, remaining for two days taking on coal, before heading for Lemos Island, Mudros Bay. Orders were received that they were to proceed to Suvla Bay but this was then changed to Cape Helles.

With only two transports being available after leaving *H.M.S. Scotian*, they being H.M.S. Hythe and H.M.S. Redbreast, the company commanders tossed a coin to decide which vessel their respective companies would take, Captain Salomons won the toss and 1st/3rd Company took H.M.S. Hythe.

With a displacement of 509 tons, H.M.S. Hythe was a former cross-channel paddle-driven ferry built in 1905 for the South Eastern and Chatham Railway Company to work the Dover-Calais route. She had been requisitioned by the Admiralty in October 1914, and became a minesweeper with the Pennant No. M38. Armed with a couple of twelve pounder guns she was later based at Scapa Flow, but in 1915 she was sent to work on troop movements in the Dardanelles. By using shallow draught craft it was hoped that torpedoes would pass beneath.

Because the Hythe had no passenger accommodation a fabric awning was rigged on her deck to help protect the crowded deck from spray and the weather. Some 5 officers and 213 men boarded the Hythe plus 30 other personnel. The Hythe left Mudros at 4pm and had 50 miles to go to Cape Helles. It was travelling in a darkened state to avoid enemy bombardment. They were due to land and with forty minutes remaining of their journey the men donned their kit, drivers went to their vehicles, and the ship doused all her lights.

Within minutes the also lightless vessel H.M.S Sarnia was spotted which was steaming back empty to Mudros Bay from Cape Helles and on a collision course with H.M.S. Hythe. She had landed her cargo and troops and was leaving the Peninsula. Both ships were travelling in excess of 12 knots. Several attempts at a change of course by both ships, failed to avoid a collision. The Sarnia struck the Hythe on her port side. The force was so great that the Hythe stopped dead in the water. The foremast on the Hythe fell onto the fabric awning. The impact resulted in many fatalities on the deck. The gaping hole on her port resulted in sea water flooding in. She immediately began to sink and would go down in ten minutes flat.

There wasn't any coordinated rescue attempt – darkness and possible enemy attack. Captain Salomons and some 128 members – over half - of 1st/3rd Company were lost plus 15 other Army personnel and 11 crew from the Hythe. Among the casualties was Edward.

The disaster was compounded by the lack of life jackets and emergency lifeboats as well as poor organisation and could have been avoided by shipping following a set route inward and outward bound from Cape Helles.

Several memorials followed. In the Second World War a mobile canteen served troops in North Africa. On the side was the inscription "David R. Salomons 1885-1915". This was paid for by his sister Vera Bryce Salomons.

Between the wars the people of Southborough held a "Hythe Sunday". In church services they remembered the disaster on or near to October 28th. Edward is commemorated on the Helles Memorial.

News has been received of the death by drowning of Pte. Edward Charles Archer, son of Mr. E. T. Archer, 75, Havelock-road. Young Archer—he was only 17—joined up 12 months ago, and became attached to the 3rd Field Company, Kent (Fortress) R.E. He left England with his company a month ago for Galipoli. The troops were being transferred from one boat to another when there was a collision and one of the boats was practically cut in two. Several were drowned, including young Archer. He was very popular in Gravesend and among his company, and his parents are the recipients of many expressions of sympathy. A post card from him written on the day of the night on which he was drowned states:— "Dear mother,—I am quite well; write to me soon." His company commander, Capt. Solomon, son of Sir David Solomon is supposed to have gone down with him.

GR 13/11/15 [Andrew Marshall]

Bernard William Arnold
Royal Field Artillery
Captain

Bernard was born in 1895, the son of Bernard and Catherine Arnold. The family lived at 25 Clarence Place and later at Milton Hall. Bernard, born in 1862 in Gravesend was a solicitor. Catherine [Prendergast] was born in Cork in 1865 the daughter of James Prendergast and Mary Cotter. The couple had four children; Dolores, born in 1891, Bernard, Adrian, born in 1896 and Francis Xavier born in 1900. They had three servants, one a cook/governess, Mabel Brennan who was also from Cork.

Bernard attended Beaumont College. The estate lies by the River Thames on the historic highway from Staines to Windsor, near Runnymede. It was originally known as Remenham, after Hugo de Remenham, who held the land at the end of the 14th century. The estate then passed through different families until in the mid-eighteenth century it was acquired by Sophia, Duchess of Kent. In 1751 the Duke of Roxburghe purchased the land for his eldest son, the Marquis of Beaumont (then a boy at Eton College), and renamed it Beaumont. In 1786 Warren Hastings, the first Governor-General of India, acquired Beaumont Lodge at the cost of £12,000. He lived at Beaumont for three years. In 1789 the estate was sold to Henry Griffith, an Anglo-Indian, who had Henry Emlyn rebuild the house in 1790 as a nine-bay mansion with a substantial portico.

In 1805 the Beaumont property was bought for about £14,000 by Viscount Ashbrook, a friend of George IV. After his death in 1847, his widow continued to reside there until 1854, when she sold it to the Society of Jesus as a training college.

For seven years it housed Jesuit novices of the (then) English province and on October 10th, 1861 became a Catholic boarding school for boys, with the title of St. Stanislaus College, Beaumont, the dedication being to St. Stanislaus Kostka.

The 1901 census shows a John Lynch S.J. as headmaster. Resident at the date of the census were one other priest, three "clerks in minor orders" and a lay brother, 8 servants and 23 schoolboys including one American, one Canadian, one Mexican and two Spaniards; one of the latter was Luís Fernando de Orleans y Borbón, a Spanish royal prince.

Joseph M. Bampton S.J., rector 1901–1908, replaced the traditional Jesuit arrangement of close supervision of pupils by masters of discipline with the so-called "Captain" system, or government of boys by boys. Bampton's Captain system was adopted also at Stonyhurst and at sister Jesuit schools in France and Spain, and in 1906 Beaumont was admitted to the Headmasters' Conference. Beaumont thus became, along with Stonyhurst College in Lancashire and St Aloysius' College, Glasgow, one of three public schools maintained by the British Province of the Jesuits.

Bernard was studying engineering at University College, London on the outbreak of war. He tried to enlist in the Public Schools' Corps but was rejected due to his poor sight. He secured a commission with the R.F.A. however – 87th, Battery, 2nd Brigade. His younger brother Adrian was also with the R.F.A.

XII (Howitzer) Brigade comprised 43rd (Howitzer) Battery, 86th (Howitzer) Battery and 87th (Howitzer) Battery on the outbreak of the Great War. In May 1916, 87th went to 2nd Brigade. When the Brigade was broken up 87th went to 2nd Brigade with one section from each Battery going to form D Battery, 38th Brigade.

KM 13/4/18 [Andrew Marshall]

Captain B. W. Arnold
R.F.A. Killed in action. Second son of Mr. and Mrs. Arnold of Milton-next-Gravesend, Kent

Captain B. W. Arnold (Gravesend)
Royal Field Artillery.
KILLED IN ACTION.

A conspicuous act of gallantry cost Captain Bernard William Arnold, R.F.A. (second son of Mr. and Mrs. B. Arnold, Milton Hall, Gravesend), his life. It was on March 21st—the day of the great German attack in the Battle of Picardy—that he was laid low by a machine gun bullet while attempting successfully to save the guns. The position at the time was desperate, and every officer of his battery was killed, wounded, or is missing. No body of men could have fought more nobly. His Colonel writes: "It was essentially a soldier's death, and I cannot hope for a better one myself." It is a great sacrifice, but one which will illumine history. The Captain, who was 23 years of age, was a grandson of the late Alderman G. M. Arnold, J.P., D.L., of the Kent County Council, and who was eight times Mayor of Gravesend.

2nd Brigade, Royal Field Artillery initially served with 6th Division and proceded to France September 10th, 1914, landing at St Nazaire. They moved at once to the Aisne to reinforce the hard-pressed BEF. They moved north to Flanders and were in action at Hooge in 1915.

In 1916 they were again in action at Battle of Flers-Courcelette on The Somme, and again in The Battle of Morval and The Battle of Le Transloy,

in 1917 they were in action at Hill 70 and Cambrai. In 1918 they saw action in the Battle of St Quentin, The Battles of the Lys, The Advance in Flanders, Battles of the Hindenburg Line and The Pursuit to the Selle.

Bernard was promoted to acting Captain when on March 21st, 1918 he was killed on action. His Colonel wrote to the family of his death – *he was killed by a machine gun bullet while attempting successfully to save the guns of his battery. It was essentially a soldier's death, and I cannot hope for a better one myself. The Battery behaved magnificently. Every single one of the officers of his battery was killed or wounded or is missing.*

He is commemorated on the Arras Memorial.

Frederick William Ashdown
Border Regiment, 1st Battalion
Service No. 22618 - Private

Frederick was born in 1896 in Gravesend. His father died at the turn of the century. His mother Alice, born in 1858 in Northfleet was a dressmaker. She married Alfred Piper in 1901. He was born in 1877 and came from Dartford. He was a general labourer.

The couple lived at 14 Clarence Row. There were five children from her first marriage – Albert, born in 1888, Elsie, born in 1891, Florence, born in 1895,

Pte. F. W. Ashdown.

Frederick and Lily, born in 1898. Alice had one child from the second marriage – Edie, born in 1905.

Frederick worked in the cement works testing the cement for consistency and quality.

He enlisted with the 3rd, Royal West Kents, service number 8893 on February 9th, 1914. He was 5 feet 3 ½ inches tall and weighed a mere 109lbs. He had fair hair, grey eyes and had a fair complexion. Having been temporarily deemed to be unfit for service he re-joined the Royal West Kents – 6th Service Battalion on October 24th, service number 4174. His weight had gone up to 120lbs so he was obviously in a better state of health.

He had a somewhat carefree attitude to Army life as he was no sooner back in the colours and at Hythe than he was confined to Barracks for three days for being absent from parade in October and the following month received a 56 day sentence for disobeying an order.

He was posted to the 1st Battalion in February, 1915. He arrived in France on March 13th. Frederick was given a sentence of six days confined to quarters after going absent without leave for several hours on September 24th.

He was transferred to the 3rd Battalion, The Border Regiment on November 9th and on the 24th to the 1st Battalion. On the same day he embarked at Devonport for Suez, arriving on January 20th, 1916. He returned to France two months later, leaving Suez on March 11th and arriving in Marseilles on the 19th.

He was confined to Barracks for three days on the 21st for having a dirty rifle when on parade. On April 2nd the Battalion moved from Amplier to Acheux, billeting in woods there before moving on to Englebelmer the following day. The Battalion were involved in front line action throughout the month working on repairing communication links and repairing damage to trenches. Casualties were a constant feature of the front in this area and Frederick was among these.

He was killed in action on April 6th, 1916. He is buried in Auchonvillers Communal Cemetery

GR 31/8/18 [Andrew Marshall]

Archibald Herbert Ashenden
Royal Sussex Regiment, 7th Bn.
Service No. G/23693 - Serjeant

Archibald was born in late 1891. His parents were Herbert, born in 1865 and Susan, born in 1871. Herbert came from Meopham and was a Colporteur for the Metropolitan Tabernacle Colportage Assembly with Susan from Whitegate near Cork. She was a midwife. They married in 1891. There were three children in the family with Archibald being the eldest, Ronald two years younger and Gladys another three years younger. The family lived in Sheerness.

Archibald was an assistant school master. He married Eveline and the couple lived at 23 Cross Lane East.

He was a sergeant with the 7th Battalion, Royal Sussex Regiment. The 7th Battalion was the first Service Battalion of Lord Kitchener's New Army to be formed in the Royal Sussex Regimen. It began recruiting at Chichester on August 12th, 1914 when, *the scene for the following fortnight almost baffles description. A depot filled beyond capacity with recruits and more arriving every few hours... all joyfully expecting to be immediately issued with rifle and bayonet and sent to France."*

From Chichester the battalion moved to Sobroan Barracks at Colchester, where it became part of 26th Brigade, 12th (Eastern) Division. In October 1914 it moved again, to Shorncliffe, and in December to Folkestone, in billets. In March 1915 the battalion moved to Ramillies Barracks, Aldershot.

The 7th Battalion landed at Boulogne on May 31st / June 1st, 1915. The 7th were very much in the action from then through to November, 1918 to include the Battle of the Ancre in April 1918 and the Battle of Amiens from August 8th through to the 11th. Archibald was killed on the opening day – 8th. He is buried in Beacon CWGC Cemetery.

This part of the Somme did not see fighting until March 26th – 27th 1918, when the Third Army withdrew to a line between Albert and Sally-le-Sec ahead of the German advance. This line was held until July 4th, when it was advanced to Sailly-Laurette, and on August 8th, the first day of the Battle of Amiens, Sailly-Laurette and the road to Moriancourt were disengaged.

The cemetery (named from a brick beacon on the summit of the ridge a little southeast of the village) was made by the 18th Divison Burial Officer On August 15th when the 12th [East-

ern), 18th and 58th (London) Divisions attacked from the Ancre to the Somme and the Australian Corps beyond the Somme. At the Armistice, the original burials numbered 109, chiefly from the 12th Division, but it was then greatly increased when graves were brought in from the surrounding battlefields and some smaller burial grounds, including Sussex Cemetery, Sailly-Laurette, a half mile south east of Beacon Cemetery. It contained the graves of 44 soldiers mostly 7th Royal Sussex, all of whom fell on the 8th August; one being Archibald.

Sergt. A. H. Ashendon (whose portrait also appears), who was an assistant teacher at Cecil-road Council School for about two years, was killed in action in France on August 8th, 1918. He was a brother-in-law of Machine-Gunner Buckmaster, and was formerly in the R.W.K. Regt, but was later transferred to the Royal Sussex Regt. The sad news of his death was contained in an official communication received by his wife, Mrs. Ashenden, 4, Park-avenue, Gravesend, during the latter part of last week. No other details of his death have yet come to hand. Deceased joined the Forces in February, 1916, the same time as his brother-in-law, and for some time before he was sent to France performed the duties of Sergeant-instructor at Aldershot. Sent out to France in April of the present year he fell in action on August 8th, as stated above. His father and mother belonged to Sheerness, and the deceased himself was well-known in Gravesend scholastic circles owing to his connexion with Cecil-road Schools. He was 26 years of age, and leaves a wife and a little baby (the latter he has not seen). Much sympathy will be felt for the relatives bereaved.

GR 31/8/18 [Andrew Marshall]

GR 31/8/18 [Andrew Marshall]

Killed in Action.

ASHENDEN. — Sergt. A. H. Ashenden, R. Sussex Regt., beloved husband of Eveline Ashenden, 4, Park-avenue, Gravesend, aged 26 years, "Somewhere in France."

Frederick Ashdown –
Auchonvillers Communal
Cemetery and Archibald
Ashenden, Sailly-Laurette
Military Cemetery.

Stanley Ryder Ashenden
Royal West Kents, 7th Battalion
Service No. G/30568 - Private

Stanley was born in early 1899. His father Arthur, born in 1862 was self-employed as a florist and owned a garden nursery. Arthur married his wife Annie, born in 1866, in 1885. They lived at 97 Wrotham Road. There were six surviving children in the family; Hilda, born in 1891, Walter, born in 1895, Gladys, born in 1896, Stanley, Leslie, born in 1901 and Edgar born in 1905.

Stanley enlisted with the 7th (Service) Battalion, which was raised at Maidstone on September 5th, 1914 as part of Kitchener's Second New Army. After initial training, they moved to Colchester in April 1915 and then to Salisbury Plain in May for final training. They proceeded to France on the 27th of July, landing at Le Havre. In 1916 they were in action on The Somme - Albert capturing their objectives near Montauban, Bazentin Ridge including the capture of Trones Wood, Delville Wood, Thiepval Ridge, the Ancre Heights playing a part in the capture of the Schwaben Redoubt and The Battle of the Ancre.

In 1917 they took part in the Operations on the Ancre including Miraumont and the capture of Irles, and fought during The German retreat to the Hindenburg Line and in The Third Battle of the Scarpe.

Moving to Flanders they were in action on Pilkem Ridge and Langemarck and The First and Second Battle of Passchendaele. In February 1918 they transferred to 53rd Brigade still with 18th (Eastern) Division. They saw action at St Quentin, the Avre, Villers-Brettoneux, Amiens and Albert where the Division captured the Tara and Usna Hills and again captured Trones Wood. They fought in The Second Battle of Bapaume, at Epehy, St Quentin Canal and the Battles of the Selle. By November, 1918, German resistance was falling away.

At dawn on November 4th, 17 British and 11 French divisions headed a new attack – the Battle of the Sambre was under way.

The first barrier to the northern attack was the 60 to 70 foot wide Sambre Canal and the flooded ground around it. German guns quickly ranged the attackers with the loss of 1,150 men in the crossing, including celebrated war poet Wilfred Owen and Stanley. Even after the crossing the German forces defended in depth amid the small villages and fields, and it was not until midday that a 2-mile-deep by 15-mile-wide breach was secured. The advance continued and the battle objectives were reached. This resulted in a bridgehead almost fifty miles long being made, to a depth of two to three miles deep. But among the many casualties was Stanley.

Stanley lies in Montay-Neuville Road CWGC Cemetery. This cemetery was made by the 23rd Brigade, Royal Garrison Artillery, October 1918. It contained originally 111 graves, but after the Armistice it was increased when graves were brought in from the battlefields nearby, and from certain small cemeteries, including HECQ British Cemetery. Originally on the western edge of the village, the cemetery contained the graves of 25 soldiers who fell in October and November 1918, one of whom was Stanley.

Frank Stanley Atkins
Coldstream Guards, 1st Battalion
Service No. 12608 - Private

Frank was born on July 30th, 1892 in Gravesend. His father William was born in 1866 in Acton and his mother Elizabeth [Hollwey] was born in 1862

Gravesend Cemetery –

KILLED IN ACTION IN FRANCE 4ᵗʰ NOVr 1918 AGED 19 YEARS

Stanley Ryder Ashenden

Montay-Neuville Road CWGC Cemetery, Le Cateau –

MISSED BY ALL AT HOME

in Chilcompton, Bath. They were married in 1889 and were in New York when their first son Henry was born the year after. Back in Gravesend shortly afterwards William opened a nursery – the Cross Lane Nursery – and a greengrocer shop. The couple had a further six children – Frank, Dorothy, born in 1891, Kathleen, born in 1895, Ada, born in 1897, Evalina, born in 1899 and Edwin, born in 1902.

Frank was educated at Christ Church School and entered the service of the P & O Steamship Company on leaving school. He joined the Garrison Artillery in 1910 and enlisted in the Coldstream Guards on September 15th, 1914.

According to the Commonwealth War Graves' site Frank was killed in action on February 17th, 1915. However *De Ruvigney's Roll of Honour* notes that *he was killed at Cunichy on 25 Jan. 1915.* The report added that *he was buried where he fell, 500 yards from Cuinchy Church, and a cross marks the spot.*

The report concluded that *he was spoken of as a keen soldier, who never failed to do his duty.*

Cuinchy is a village astride the La Bassée Canal and is referred to by Robert Graves in his classic memoir *Goodbye To All That* –

Cuinchy bred rats. They came up from the canal, fed on the plentiful corpses, and multiplied exceedingly...

The British sector was to the east of Cuinchy: the front line ran 800 yards to the east of the village. The line here formed a salient; from the canal it ran towards the railway triangle, which was in German hands, and then back to the main road.

In late January 1915 the British front line was occupied by the British 2nd Division, one of whose brigades was the 4th (Guards) Brigade, which comprised 2/Grenadier Guards, 2/Coldstream Guards, 3/Coldstream Guards, 1/Irish Guards as well as the 1/1 Hertfordshire Regiment, which was a territorial battalion.

The war diary for the 1/Coldstream Guards describes the last few days in January:

23rd January CAMBRIN: The Battalion left CAMBRIN and went into the trenches at CUINCHY, relieving the London Scottish – trenches had not been completed. Communication trenches bad and some trenches full of water – heavy rain all night.

24th January CUINCHY: The Germans shelled the position most of the day with their heavy guns – most of the fire being directed on PONT FIXE. Impossible for working parties to be utilized on improving the trenches.

On January 25th the 1/Coldstream Guards were in the trenches when, at 7.30am, a number of mines were exploded and the Germans attacked. The defenders were forced back into a keep among the brickstacks until relieved that night by the 1st Guards Brigade. The war diary describes the day:

25th January CUINCHY: About 7am a German deserter came in and reported an attack imminent. The German attack commenced by the explosion of a mine in the trench held by No 4 Coy under Capt Campbell. The first line of trenches were consequently rushed by the Germans. No 1 Coy on the embankment by the La Bassée Canal held its ground and No 2 Coy under Lt Viscount Acheson held on to the keep and Brickstacks and repelled the German attacks. The Scots Guards on our immediate right shared a similar fate but were able to maintain a stand at the Brickfields. Reinforcements of London Scottish, Black Watch and Cameron Highlanders were sent up and a counter attack was made but it was found impossible to dislodge the Germans from the front trenches they had taken.

The German attack of January 25th is described in some detail by Rudyard Kipling in *The Irish Guards in the Great War, Volume 1.*

Their work was interrupted by another "Kaiser-battle," obediently planned to celebrate the All Highest's birthday. It began on the 25th January with a demonstration along the whole flat front from Festubert to Vermelles. ... Owing to the mud, the [Cuinchy] salient was lightly manned by half a battalion of the Scots Guards and half a battalion of the Coldstream. Their trenches were wiped out by the artillery attack and their line fell back, perhaps half a mile, to a partially prepared position among the brick-fields and railway lines between the Aire-La Bassée Canal and the La Bassée-Béthune road.

Here fighting continued with reinforcements and counter-attacks knee deep in mud till the enemy were checked and a none too stable defence made good between a mess of German communication trenches and a keep or redoubt held by the British among the huge brick-stacks by the railway. So far as the [Irish Guards] Battalion was concerned, this phase of the affair seems to have led to no more than two or three days' standing-to in readiness to support with the rest of the Brigade, and taking what odd shells fell to their share.

Frank is commemorated on the Le Touret Memorial. The Memorial is located at the east end of Le Touret Cemetery on the south side of the Bethune-Armentieres road.

Some 13,400 soldiers are commemorated on the Memorial; these are the soldiers who were killed in this sector of the Front from October 1914 to the eve of the Battle of Loos in late September 1915 and who have no known grave.

Private Frank Stanley Atkins, of the 1st Battalion Coldstream Guards, was killed in action at Cuincy between Bethune and Le Basse, on the 25th ult. He was only 22 years of age, and was the second son of Mr. and Mrs. Edward Atkins, of Cross-lane Nursery, Gravesend. He only joined Lord Kitchener's Army on the 15th September, after having served seven years at the P. and O. Co's. office at Tilbury Docks, where his loss is much regretted by his colleagues. Mr. Atkins has now lost two sons at the Front, and we understand that his eldest son is on his way home with the second contingent from Australia, and through all this tragedy Mr. Atkins states that one of his great regrets is that he cannot go to the Front himself. Both Mr. and Mrs. Atkins are bearing their great sorrow in a patriotic spirit.

GR 27/2/15 [Andrew Marshall]

ATKINS.—On January 25th, killed in action at Cuinchy, between Bethune and La Bassee, Frank Stanley Atkins, in his 22nd year.

GR 27/2/15 [Andrew Marshall]

the North Sea, 22 Sept. 1914.

ATKINS, FRANK STANLEY, Private, No. 12608, 1st Battn. Coldstream Guards, 2nd s. of William Edward Atkins, of Gravesend, co. Kent, Nurseryman and Florist, by his wife, Elizabeth Hollwey, dau. of William Hollwey, of Chilcompton, Bath; b. Gravesend, 30 July, 1892; educ. Christ Church School there, and then entered the service of the P. & O. Steamship Co. He joined the Garrison Artillery at the age of eighteen, and on the declaration of war enlisted in the Coldstreams, 15 Sept. 1914, and was killed at Cuinchy on 25 Jan. 1915, in his first action. He was buried where he fell, 500 yards from Cuinchy Church, and a cross marks the spot. He was spoken of as a keen soldier, who never failed to do his duty.

ATKINS, JAMES, A.B. (R.F.R.B. 3510).

Frank's biography in De Ruvigny

Le Touret Memorial

Frank Atkins

Gravesend Cemetery –

**KILLED IN ACTION
25th JAN 1915. AGED 22 YEARS**

[Photograph – Andy White]

A B C D E

BAILEY H.S.
BAKER E.C.
BANHAM F.S.
BARE C.L.
BARNES W.H.
BARR P.S.
BARRETT E.J.
BARTLE E.L.
BAYLDON G.
BEACON E.J.
BEAN A.H.
BELL A.J.
BELMORE W.J.
BENNETT G.B.
BENNETT G.
BENNETT R.W.
BENNETT T.A.
BENSON F.
BERRIDGE W.C.
BETTS J.C.

BEVAN F.G.
BIDDLECOMBE F.
BILL R.E.
BLOOMFIELD A.
BLUNDERFIELD W.C.
BLOWER W.C.L.
BOLDEN W.
BONE T.
BONFIELD E.
BOORMAN C.A.
BOREHAM F.
BOTTING W.A.
BOWDEN R.C.
BOWLER W.H.
BOX F.C.
BOX P.T.
BOYD C.J.
BRABROOK .W.
BRADFORD W.
BRADLEY C.A.

BRADY G.W.
BRADY J.
BRIDGLAND W.L.
BRINKLEY T.W.
BRITTEN T.
BROAD P.A.
BROAD G.
BROOMAN A.F.
BROWN S.F.
BUCKWELL .
BUCKMASTER E.J.
BULL E.
BURLES T.J.
BURLES W.
BURRILL A.W.
BURRILL J.T.
BUSH F.O.
BUTCHER D.
BYRNE W.R.

IN PROUD AND LOVING MEMORY
OF MY DEAR BROTHER
NEVER SHALL HIS MEMORY FADE

Herbert Bowler –
Brown's Road Cemetery

Herbert Stigant Bailey
Royal West Kent – Lance Corporal
Service No. 242479

Herbert was born in early 1899. He was the son of George and Mabel Bailey of 'Wichens', 3 Essex Road. George, born in 1869 was a plumber by profession. He married Mabel who was five years younger in 1896. They had three surviving children; Cyril, born in 1897 was the eldest, Herbert was the middle child and Norman the youngest was born in 1907.

He was a Lance Corporal with the 10th Battalion. The 10th (Kent County) Battalion, The Royal West Kent Regiment was raised at Maidstone on May 3rd, 1915 by Lord Harris, Vice Lieutenant of Kent, at the request of the Army Council. After initial training close to home they joined 118th Brigade, 39th Division in July. In October they transferred to 123rd Brigade, 41st Division. Herbert joined the 10th in the Ypres salient. In 1917 they fought during The Battle of Messines, The Battle of Pilckem Ridge, The Battle of the Menin Road and took part in the Operations on the Flanders coast. In November the Division was ordered to Italy, moving by train to Mantua. The Division took the front line near the River Piave, north west of Treviso. In February they were summoned back to France and departed from Campo San Piero, travelling by train to concentrate near Doullens and Mondicourt. They were in action during The Battle of St Quentin, The Battle of Bapaume and The Battle of Arras before moving to Flanders for The Battles of the Lys. They were in action during the Final Advance in Flanders, at Courtrai and Ooteghem with the village of Heestert being taken on October 23rd. Herbert was among the casualties and lies buried in Heestert CWGC Cemetery.

Lance-Corpl. H. S. Bailey, R.W.K Regt., whose death in action on October 24th was recorded in our obituary column last week, was the son of Mr. and Mrs. H. Bailey, of Wickens, Essex-road. Deceased joined the Army at the age of 15½ years, was discharged for a time, and then rejoined at the age of 18. According to the letter received from Lieut. A. M. Razzle, death was instantaneous. Immediately prior to his death the deceased had been recommended for decoration by the same officer for "very good work in face of very heavy machine gun fire."

GR 16/11/18 [Andrew Marshall]

Held by the Germans throughout the war, the village of Heestert fell late October 1918. The cemetery was started around February 1919 by farmers of the commune, acting under instructions from the local Burgomaster; they concentrated the graves of British and German battlefield burials from their farms. In 1920; the graves were reorganised and the German graves were placed at the south end of the rows, and later that year three British graves were brought in from Moen Churchyard.

Charles Edward Baker
Norfolk Regiment, 1st Battalion
Service No. 41490 – Private

Charles was born in Gravesend in 1899 to William and Helena Baker of 13 Minerva Cottages. William was born in Plaistow in 1864. He was a confectioner and ran his own business. Helena came from Lambeth and was two years older than her husband. The couple married in 1885 and had five children – James, born in 1890, Edward, Albert, born in 1902, Millie, born in 1905 and Frederick, born in 1908.

Charles enlisted in Maidstone and was duly posted to the 1st Battalion, The Norfolk Regiment. It was in Holywood, Belfast serving with 15th Brigade, 5th

Division, when war broke out in August 1914. They proceeded to France, landing at Le Havre in mid-August. They were in action in The Battle of Mons and the subsequent retreat, The Battle of Le Cateau, The Battle of the Marne, The Battle of the Aisne, The Battles of La Bassee and Messines and The First Battle of Ypres. Between March 3rd and April 7th, 1915 they were attached with 15th Brigade to 28th Division in in exchange for 83rd Brigade in order to familiarise the newly arrived troops with the Western Front. In 1915 they were in action at The Second Battle of Ypres and the Capture of Hill 60. In March 1916 5th Division took over a section of front line between St Laurent Blangy and the southern edge of Vimy Ridge, near Arras. They moved south in July to reinforce The Somme and were in action at, High Wood, The Battle of Guillemont, The Battle of Flers-Courcelette, The Battle of Morval and The Battle of Le Transloy. In October they moved to Festubertand remained there until March 1917 when they moved in preparation for the Battles of Arras. On 7 September 1917 the 5th Division moved out of the line for a period of rest before, being sent to Flanders where they were in action during the Third Battle of Ypres. 5th Division was sent to Italy and took up positions in the line along the River Piave in late January 1918. They were recalled to France to assist with the German Advance in late March 1918 and were in action during the Battles of the Lys. On August 14th the 5th Division was withdrawn for two weeks rest. Then moved to The Somme where they were more or less in continuous action over the old battlegrounds until late October 1918 and saw action in the Battles of the Hindenburg Line and the Final Advance in Picardy.

Charles was killed in action on August 23rd, 1918. He is buried in Achiet-Grand Communal Cemetery Extension. Achiet-le-Grand is 19 km south of Arras.

Achiet-le-Grand was occupied by the 7th Bedfords on March 17th, 1917, lost on March 25th, 1918 after a defence by the 1st/6th Manchesters, and recaptured on August 23rd, 1918. From April 1917 to March 1918, the village was occupied by the 45th and 49th Casualty Clearing Stations. Achiet station was an allied railhead. The communal cemetery and extension were used by Commonwealth medical units from April 1917 to March 1918. The extension was also used by the Germans to a small extent in March and April 1918, and again by Commonwealth troops in August 1918. After the Armistice 645 graves, mainly of 1916 and March and August 1918, were brought in from the battlefields around Achiet and from various small burial grounds. The Communal Cemetery contains four Commonwealth burials of the War.

The Extension contains 1,424 burials and commemorations of the First World War. 200 of the burials are unidentified but there are special memorials to eight casualties known or believed to be buried among them.

Frederick Banham
South Wales Borderers, 1st Btn
Service No. 18389 - Private

Frederick was born in Ramsgate. He enlisted with the South Wales Borderers, 1st Battalion in Newport, Monmouthshire.

1st Battalion, The South Wales Borderers were in Bordon serving with 3rd Brigade, 1st Division when war was declared in August 1914. They proceeded to France, landing at Le

Herbert Bailey –
Heestert CWGC
Cemetery

Achiet-le-Grand Communal Extension
Cemetery –
Charles Edward Baker

Havre on August 13th, 1914 and fought on the Western Front throughout the war, taking part in most of the major actions. In 1914 they were involved in The Battle of Mons and the subsequent retreat, including the recapture of Gheluvelt at the height of the crisis on October 31st, alongside the 2nd Worcesters. They were in action at The Battle of the Marne, The Battle of the Aisne, the First Battle of Ypres and the Winter Operations of 1914-15. In 1915 they were in action during The Battle of Aubers and The Battle of Loos. In 1916 they were in action in the Battles of the Somme.

Frank was killed in action on July 25th, 1916. He has no known grave and is commemorated on the Thiepval Monument.

Cecil Louis Bare
R.E. - Sapper
Service No. 13732

Cecil was born in late 1887. The Bare family lived at Crayland House, London Road in Swanscombe. His parents were James, born in 1855 and Louisa, born in 1858. James was an engine fitter at the Cement Works. There were four children in the family with Cecil having an older brother, William and two younger brothers, Ernest, born in 1894 and Stewart, born in 1900. William was born in 1884 and followed his father as an engine fitter.

Cecil subsequently moved to Cliffe, near Hoo before enlisting in the army. He was boarding with Joseph and Louisa Sacre at 7 Winifred Terrace. He also was an engine fitter and worked for a company manufacturing explosives.

On April 29th, 1914 he married Nellie Rose Perry, a spinster some four years his younger. They were married

in Chobham, Surrey. He, by now, was again living in Swanscombe.

Cecil was a sapper with the 59th [R.E.] Field Company. They served with the 5th Division providing engineer support to that formation which would include the construction of field defence, wiring, trench digging, and construction of strong points amongst other things.

He arrived in France on August 18th, 1914. 59th Field Company, The Royal Engineers served with 5th Division. 5th Division arrived in France with the BEF in mid-August 1914. They were in action in The Battle of Mons and the subsequent retreat, The Battle of Le Cateau, The Battle of the Marne, The Battle of the Aisne, The Battles of La Bassee and Messines and The First Battle of Ypres.

In the retreat from Mons – August 23rd to the 26th - the engineer field units were engaged in demolishing railway and road bridges. At Le Cateau- August 26th - 59th Field Company had its first experience of infantry fighting.

After the breakthrough – The Battle of the Marne, September 6th – 12th, and the subsequent advance to river Aisne the field engineers were engaged in repairing and constructing bridges over the rivers as the troops advanced. In the lead up to the 1st Battle of Ypres – October 14th to November 22nd - engineer field units were billeted close behind the support line, they spent their days collecting materials and their nights carrying them forward to construct entanglements and other defences.

As autumn passed, the battle of Ypres died down and the Royal Engineers were employed without respite on improving the trenches, repairing roads, improving billets, and manufacturing all kinds of trench stores, makeshift bombs, grenades, periscopes and mortars. Nearly every field company had a bomb factory. But by now Cecil had paid the full price – he was killed in action on November 18th. He has no known grave and is commemorated on the Menin Gate, Ypres.

GR 16/11/18 [Andrew Marshall]

William Henry Barnes
Royal Field Artillery, 40th Battery
Service No. 67131 – Lance B'dier
William was born in Northfleet in 1894 the son of William and Selina Barnes. William was born in 1865 and was a coal dealer. Selina was five years younger and came from Swanscombe. There were eight children in the family – Kate, born in 1889, Selina, born in 1892, William, George, born in 1906, Frederick, born in 1899, Lilian, born in 1901, Bertie, born in 1903, and Alfred, born in 1905. Selina became a widow shortly after the birth of Alfred and worked as a laundress to support the family. William enlisted with the 40th Battery in Woolwich.

GR 29/7/16 [Andrew Marshall]

Lance Bombardier Barnes died of wounds on October 17th, 1917. He is buried at Busigny Communal Cemetery Extension. Busigny is 10 km south-west of Le Cateau. Busigny was captured by the 30th American Division and British cavalry on October 9th, 1918, in the Battle of Cambrai, and in the course of the next two months the 48th, 37th and 12th Casualty Clearing Stations came to the village. The majority of burials were made from these three hospitals.

The cemetery extension was begun in October 1918, and used until February 1919. After the Armistice it was enlarged when graves were brought from a wide area between Cambrai and Guise. Busigny Communal Cemetery Extension contains 670 First World War burials, 64 of them unidentified.

Percival Stanley St.John Barr
2nd Canadian Mounted Rifles
Service No. 107077 - Corporal
Percival was born on May 7th, 1882 in Wandsworth, London. His parents were George and Charlotte Barr. George, born in 1862 was the rector of Holy Trinity, Milton in 1891. The church was demolished in 1963. Charlotte was born in 1863. They had three children, Beatrice born in 1889, Gertrude, born a year later and Percival. The family lived at 3 The Grove.

Percival married Grace Tertia Gregory in 1915 in Eltham, Kent. They lived at The Rectory, Longhope in Gloucestershire before moving to Victoria, British Columbia [Canada].

The 2nd Canadian Mounted Rifles Battalion initially recruited in Victoria and Vernon, British Columbia and was mobilised in Victoria. Percival himself

Thiepval Memorial –
Frederick Banham

Menin Gate – Cecil Bare

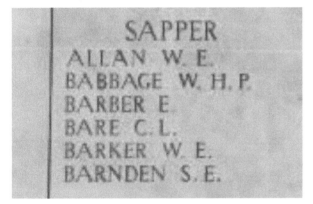

William Barnes –
Busigny Communal Cemetery

enlisted with the Battalion on December 8th, 1914 in Victoria, British Columbia having already some military service with the London Imperial Yeomanry. He was 5 foot 6½ inches tall, of fresh complexion with blue eyes and brown hair. He had tattoos on both arms – bullfish and snake on the right and a scroll on the left.

The 2nd Canadian Mounted Rifles Battalion, (known also as 2nd Battalion, CMR or simply 2 CMR) was authorized on November 7th, 1914 as the 2nd Regiment, Canadian Mounted Rifles, CEF, and embarked for Great Britain on June 12th, 1915. It disembarked in France on September 22nd, 1915 as part of the 1st Canadian Mounted Rifles Brigade with Percival being in 'A' Squadron.

On January 1st, 1916 it was converted to infantry, amalgamated with 'B Squadron' and the headquarters staff of the 3rd Regiment, Canadian Mounted Rifles, C.E.F. and re-designated the 2nd Canadian Mounted Rifles Battalion, CEF. It fought as part of the 8th Canadian Infantry Brigade, 3rd Canadian Division in France and Flanders until the end of the war.

He died of wounds on July 9th, 1916 and is buried in Ypres Reservoir Cemetery. His army record notes that he was *killed in action. This non-commissioned officer was shaving in the bath room of the Infantry Barracks, Ypres, when a shell exploded in the street, some splinters of it coming through the window and wounding him in the back and head. The pieces entering his back were believed to have pierced his lung. He walked into the Dressing Station in the barracks but while his wounds were being dressed, he collapsed and died a few minutes later.*

Bertie Barrett
Royal West Kent – 7th Battalion
Service No. G/3232 - Private

Bertie was the son of Francis and Emma Barrett of 32 Gordon Road, the family subsequently moving to 15 Beresford Road, Rosherville. Francis, born in 1847 was from Gravesend and was a barge builder by profession – the barges being built for the Cement Works at Swanscombe. There were eleven children in the family with Bertie being born in 1892.

The 7th (Service) Battalion, The Royal West Kent Regiment was raised at Maidstone on September 5th, 1914 as part of Kitchener's Second New Army and joined 55th Brigade, 18th (Eastern) Division. After initial training near home, they moved to Colchester in April 1915 and then to Salisbury Plain in May for final training. They proceeded to France on July 27th, 1915 landing at Le Havre the Division concentrating near Flesselles. In 1916 they were in action on The Somme in The Battle of Albert capturing their objectives near Montauban, The Battle of Bazentin Ridge including the capture of Trones Wood, The Battle of Delville Wood, The Battle of Thiepval Ridge, The Battle of the Ancre Heights playing a part in the capture of the Schwaben Redoubt and Regina Trench and The Battle of the Ancre but it was at The Battle of Thiepval Ridge that Bertie was killed in action on September 29th. The battle was the first large offensive mounted by the Reserve Army of Lieutenant General Hubert Gough and was intended to benefit from the Fourth Army attack at Morval by starting 24 hours afterwards. Thiepval Ridge was well fortified and the German defenders fought with great determination, while the British co-ordination of infantry and artillery declined after the first day, due to confused fighting in the maze of trenches, dug-outs and shell-craters. The final British objectives were not reached until the Battle of the Ancre Heights (October 1st – November 11th). Bertie is commemorated on the Thiepval Memorial.

Killed in Action.

Mr. F. Barrett, of 15, Beresford-road, Rosherville, has received the sad news that youngest son, Pte. Bert Barrett, of the 7th Batt. of the R.W.K., was killed in action on September 29th. He would have been 24 years of age in November. He answered his country's call on September 14th, 1914, an dleft for Cranee August 25th, 1915. He had just received his first class proficiency pay and two years conduct stripes. Pte. Barrett was in Trônes Wood with the West Kents' where he lost all his effects. The following letter has been sent to Mr. Barrett from Lieut. V. L. Johnson : "As his platoon officer I lost in him one of the bravest of men, who died gloriously for the love of his King and country, and beg you to accept my sincere sympathy in your great loss. He suffered no pain, death being instantaneous, thank God!" Mr. Barrett has three other sons serving their King, two being in the Royal Navy and one in the Buffs; the last-named was wounded in France in March, 1915, an dis now again at the front.

GR 28/10/16 [Andrew Marshall]
GR 21/10/16 [Andrew Marshall]

Killed in Action.

BARRETT.—Killed in action on the 29th September, Private Bert Barrett, 7th R.W.K. Regiment, aged 23, the youngest son of Mr. F. Barrett, 15, Beresford-road, Rosherville. "Greater love hath no man than this that he giveth his life for his friends."

Ernest Joseph Barrett
Royal Navy
Service No. 207439

Ernest was an elder brother of Bertie, being born in 1882.

He enlisted in the Royal Navy and served on board *HMS Vanguard*.

The ninth HMS *Vanguard* of the British Royal Navy was a *St. Vincent*-class battleship, an enhancement of the "dreadnought" design built by Vickers at Barrow-in-Furness. She was designed and built during the Anglo-German naval race and spent her life in the British Home Fleet.

At the outbreak of World War I, *Vanguard* joined the First Battle Squadron at Scapa Flow, and fought in the Battle of Jutland as part of the Fourth Battle Squadron. As one of twenty-four dreadnoughts in Jellicoe's Battle Fleet, she did not suffer any damage or casualties.

Just before midnight on July 9th,1917 at Scapa Flow, *Vanguard* suffered an explosion, probably caused by an unnoticed stokehold fire heating cordite stored against an adjacent bulkhead in one of the two magazines which served the amidships gun turrets 'P' and 'Q'. She sank almost

The above photograph is of Ernest Joseph Barrett, A.B., who was lost on H.M.S. "Vanguard." He was the son of Mr. F. J. Barrett, of 15, Beresford-road, Rosherville. The sad news was received from the Admiralty on the 13th inst. Deceased had been in H.M. Navy for 17 years, and had been on the "Vanguard" for about four years. Mr. Barrett has already lost another son in the war, Private Bert Barrett, of the West Kents, killed in action on September 29th, 1916. There are two other sons serving—one in the Navy, A. Barrett, Chief Petty Officer, at present stationed at Chatham, who has the Long Service and Good Conduct Medal, the South African War Medal, the Distinguished Service Medal (which was awarded him in December, 1915), as well as the Royal Society's Bronze Medal for saving life. The other son is Private G. Barrett, of The Buffs, now in France, who has been once wounded.

GR 28/7/17 [Andrew Marshall]

instantly, killing an estimated 804 men; there were only two survivors. Ernest was among the casualties.

In terms of loss of life, the destruction of the *Vanguard* remains the most catastrophic accidental explosion in the history of the UK, and one of the worst accidental losses of the Royal Navy.

Ernest is commemorated on the Chatham Naval Memorial and on the Gravesend War Memorial.

On Active Service.

BARRETT.—Ernest Joseph, A.B., aged 35 years, lost his life on H.M.S. "Vanguard" when blown up, July 9th, 1917; son of Mr. F. J. Barrett, of 15, Beresford-road, Rosherville.—"In the midst of life we are in death."

GR 21/7/17 [Andrew Marshall]

Eric Leslie Bartle
Eastern Ontario Reg – 2nd Battalion
Service No. 7605 – Private

Eric was born in Tamworth on February 10th, 1893 to Theophilus and Eliza Bartle. Theophilus was born in Tamworth in 1852. The couple married in 1873 and had six children – Gertrude, born in 1874, Florence, born in 1877, Bernard, born in 1880, Elsie, born in 1884, Constance, born in 1886 and Eric. Theophilus died in 1900 and Eliza remarried in 1906, moving to Gravesend.

He enlisted on September 22nd, 1914 at Valcartier, Québec with the Eastern Ontario Regiment.

The 2nd Battalion (Eastern Ontario Regiment), C.E.F. was created in response to the First World War. The battalion comprised local militia in many regions of Ontario (and even from Quebec City) Local militia gathered at Valcartier, in August 1914 and became part of the 2nd Battalion.

The battalion boarded the S.S. *Cassandra* from Quebec City on September 22nd, 1914, but sailed only as far as the Gaspé Basin, where more troops were collected. The battalion finally left the Gaspé Basin on 3 October as part of a convoy of at least 30 other ships, carrying a combined 32,000 Canadian soldiers, which would be the first of the Canadian infantry contributions to the war.

Bertie Barrett – Thiepval Memorial

Chatham Naval Memorial –
Ernest Barrett

Ypres Reservoir Cemetery –
Percy Barr

The *Cassandra* landed at Plymouth on October 25th, where the battalion disembarked and began rigorous training for the European battlefield.

On February 8th, 1915, the battalion was mobilized for war. They sailed out of England aboard the S.S. *Blackwell*, bound for France. The battalion's first taste of battle came later that month, on February 19th, when they entered the trench system at Armentières.

Their first battle was the Second Battle of Ypres, in April 1915. When the battalion pulled out of the battle, on April 29th, the final count included 6 officers and 68 other ranks killed, 4 officers and 158 other ranks wounded, and 5 officers and 302 other ranks missing, for a combined loss of 543 men.

Among those killed on April 26th was Eric. He lies in New Irish Farm Cemetery.

George Bayldon

Scots Guards, 3rd Battalion

Service No. 6134 - Private

George was born in Headingley in 1885. His father John was born in Kirkstall in 1848. He was a foreman confectioner in a factory. George's mother Martha was also from Kirkstall and was born in 1851. They had seven children – William, born in 1876, Jane, born in 1888, Martha, born in 1881, Richard, born in 1903, George, Henry, born in 1888 and Mary, born in 1890. The family lived at 5 Belmont Place, Leeds.

George worked in a public house prior to enlisting with the Scots Guards on July 17th, 1905 in London. He was 5 feet 10 inches tall and weighed 131lbs. He had a fresh complexion, grey eyes and light brown hair.

GR 19/6/15 [Andrew Marshall]

We regret to announce that Private Eric Leslie Bartle, son of Mrs. Salmon, of Edinburgh House, Pelham-road, Gravesend, has been killed in action. He came over with the Canadian troops. We may mention that he was a former pupil at the Modern School.

"The Evening Examiner," Peterborough (Ontario), on Friday, May 14th, stated: —

"Private Eric Leslie Bartle.—'The Big Chief' of No. 3 Company—the company which heads the 57th honour roll—was the sobriquet applied by his comrades to Eric Leslie Bartle, who is mentioned in to-day's list of missing. Private Bartle was a big boy of 20 years. His home was at Gravesend (Kent); he was an only son. Prior to the outbreak of the war he was employed as a machinist in the G.C. Electrical Works. The Militia made a strong appeal to him, and he was one of those who helped make No. 3 a crack company. He had lived in this country about two years."

The above-mentioned list refers to the casualty list issued after the battle of Langemarck, in which the Canadians were so heavily engaged about the end of April.

MR. G. BAYLDON.

He married Ann Mary Faulkner in St George's, Hannover Square in 1909. The couple had three children – George, born May 24th, 1911 in Leeds, John Francis, born on March 11th, 1913 in Gravesend and Elsie, born July 18th, 1915 in Gravesend.

He was with the 2nd Battalion until transferred to the 1st in January, 1911. His service in Egypt in 1910 and 1911 saw him struck down with severe gastritis and typhoid.

He was transferred to the Army Reserve in June, 1912 before re-joining to complete a further twelve months' service and in June, 1913 was again in the Army Reserve. Back in civilian life George was employed as a postman from March, 1913 – number 54571 – in Gravesend.

George was mobilised on August 5th, 1914 and transferred to the 2nd Battalion on the 26th before joining the 3rd Battalion on November 1st.

2nd Battalion, The Scots Guards were based at the Tower of London when war was declared in August 1914. In September they joined 20th Brigade, 7th Division, who were concentrating in the New Forest in Hampshire. The Division landed at Zeebrugge in the first week of October 1914, to assist in the defence of Antwerp, they arrived too late to prevent the fall of the city and took up defensive positions at important bridges and junctions to aid in the retreat of the Belgian army. The 7th Division then became the first British Troops to entrench in front of Ypres, suffering extremely heavy losses in the The First Battle of Ypres.

George's injuries incurred at Ypres ensured the transfer to the 3rd Reserve Battalion and on August 27th, 1915 he was discharged as deemed no longer physically fit for war service. He died on February 17th, 1916.

We deeply regret to report the death of Mr. G. Bayldon, late 2nd Battalion Scots Guards, who died at his residence, 12, William-street, Gravesend, on Thursday last. The deceased, who hailed from Leeds, Yorkshire, had had a fair share of military service. After serving in Egypt with his battalion he left the Army on Reserve, and for two years was employed at the Gravesend General Post Office. On war breaking out he was called up to the Colours again, and the 2nd Battalion Scots Guards (to which he belonged and went to the Front with) were attached to the famous 7th Division, and saw much fighting. Unfortunately he was wounded in the right arm at Ypres, which, with exposure, etc., caused him to be invalided out of the Army. Since that time he has been employed as electrical storekeeper at the Northfleet Engineering Works, where he made hosts of friends, who deeply regret his loss.

The remains were interred at Gravesend Cemetery, on Wednesday, with full military honours. The brass band of the Gloucestershire Regiment were in attendance, and played appropriate music throughout the ceremony, and the firing party who led the way performed the last rites for a soldier by firing three volleys over the grave to the sound of the "Last Post" by the buglers. The whole scene was most impressive, and thus another hero was laid to rest.

The chief mourners at the funeral were :—

First carriage: Widow and Brother, Mrs. Wilson (sister), Miss Bayldon (sister, Leeds).

Second carriage: Mrs. Griffiths (cousin, London), Mr. C. Franks, Mr. R. Offin, Mr. Walkling, Mr. Hembrey.

The Postmaster of Gravesend was present at the graveside, with a goodly number of postmen, to show their respect for an old comrade.

Deceased was interred in the Roman Catholic section of the Cemetery, the service being taken by Rev. L. J. Bourdelot.

Appended is a list of the wreaths:—

To my dear Husband, from his sorrowing Wife.

To our dear Daddy, from his Little Ones.

To my dear Brother, from his Sisters.

Gravesend Cemetery –

**ERIC
KILLED IN ACTION 1915
AGED 19 YEARS**

[Photograph – Andy White]

Eric Bartle

New Irish Farm Cemetery –

**IN LOVING MEMORY
OF DEAR ERIC**

116

Edward Jesse Beacon
Royal Navy - Stoker, 1st Class
Service No. SS/103253

Edward was born in Gravesend to William and Susan Beacon of 7 West Side Place on May 24th, 1878. [Naval Records record his birth as being 1883 but his birth is registered in Gravesend in 1878] The couple both born in 1859 had two children, Walter and Edward. William was a general labourer.

Prior to entering the Royal Navy he was a fireman on board the *SS Otway*. She was an ocean liner owned by the Orient Line, built by Fairfield Shipbuilding and Engineering Company of Glasgow, and launched in 1909. He served on *HMS Ettrick* during World War 1.

HMS Ettrick was a Palmer Type River Class Destroyer ordered by the Royal Navy under the 1901 – 1902 Naval Estimates. Named after the Ettrick Water in the Scottish Borders area south of Edinburgh, she was the first ship to carry the name in the Navy.

In early 1914 she joined the 9th Destroyer Flotilla based at Chatham. The 9th Flotilla was a Patrol Flotilla tasked with anti-submarine and counter mining patrols in the Firth of Forth area. By September 1914, she was deployed to Portsmouth and the Dover Patrol. Here she provided anti-submarine, counter mining patrols and defended the Dover Barrage.

In August 1915 with the amalgamation of the 7th and 9th Flotillas, she was assigned to the 1st Destroyer Flotilla when it was redeployed to Portsmouth in November 1916. She was equipped with depth charges for employment in anti-submarine patrols, escorting of merchant ships and defending the Dover Barrage. In the spring of 1917 as the convoy system was being introduced the 1st Flotilla was employed in convoy escort duties for the English Channel for the remainder of the war.

On July 7th, 1917 she was torpedoed by *UC-61*, 15 miles South by West of Beachy Head in the English Channel with the loss of 49 officers and men.

She lost her bows and was towed back to port and not repaired. She was hulked until the end of the War.

Edward was among those lost, his body was not recovered and he is commemorated on the Chatham Naval Memorial.

Alfred Henry Bean
Mercantile Marine - Seaman

Alfred was born in 1900 the son of Henry George and Annie Bean of 62 Suffolk Road. George was born in 1872 and was Gravesend born. He worked in a local public house as a cellar-man. Annie, who was a year younger, came from Tunbridge Wells. They married in 1899 and Alfred was the eldest of their three children – Rose, born in 1905 and Reginald, born in 1909 were the other two.

Alfred joined the Mercantile Marine and was with Ernest Allson among the casualties when the *SS Minnehaha* sank on September 7th, 1917.

Alfred is commemorated on the Tower Hill Memorial.

GR 15/9/17 [Andrew Marshall]

Albert John Bell
Royal West Kent Regiment, 2nd Bn
Service No. L/9937

Albert was born in Deal in 1892. His parents were Arthur and Esther Bell. Arthur was born in Norfolk in 1860 and joined the Navy at a young age. Esther was also from Norfolk, being born in 1868. They married in 1890 and lived in Walmer having ten children in all – Arthur, born in 1891, Albert, Henrietta, born in 1894, Ambrose, born in 1896, Alfred, born in 1898, Alice, born in 1899, Albina, born in 1900, Ada, born in 1904, Lilian, born in 1906 and Walter, born in 1910.

On leaving the navy around the turn of the century, Arthur moved the family to 79 Wrotham Road. With Esther being the shop manager, Arthur put his naval experience to good use and set himself up as a boot maker. Albert found employment in the family business on leaving school.

Albert enlisted in August, 1914 with the 2nd Battalion, Royal West Kents. The 2nd Battalion moved to Multan [Mooltan], India in August, 1914 and he arrived in Basra with the 2nd, being part of the Mesopotamia Expeditionary Force, on February 6th, 1915. Here it came under command of 12th Indian Brigade. Two Companies were attached to the 30th Brigade in the 6th (Poona) Division in November 1915 and became besieged at Kut-al-Amara, where they were captured on April 29th, 1916. The remaining Companies were attached to 34th Brigade which was part of 15th Indian Division, transferring to 17th Indian Division in August. 1917.

Albert died of wounds on July 28th, 1915. He lies in Basra War Cemetery.

118

Chatham Naval Memorial –
Edward Beacon.

Basra Memorial

Gravesend Cemetery – Alfred Bean

TORPEDOED ..... SEPt 7th 1917 IN HIS 17TH YEAR

Tower Hill Memorial; *SS Minnehaha –* Alfred was one of four Gravesend men who died as a result of the loss of the ship.

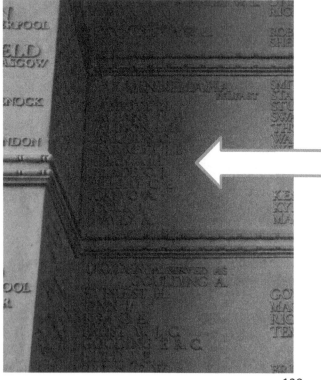

General sympathy is extended to Mr. and Mrs. Bell, Wrotham-road, on the death of their son, Albert John, in the Persian Gulf. The young soldier belonged to the 2nd Batt. Royal West Kent Regiment, and had been in the Army for two years. He was stationed in India when war broke out, and was immediately drafted to the sphere of action in which he was wounded, and where he died a soldier's death. Young Bell was most popular in the town, and the news of his death has been received with feelings of extreme sorrow.

GR 21/8/15 [Andrew Marshall]

During the First World War, Basra was occupied by the 6th (Poona) Division in November 1914, from which date the town became the base of the Mesopotamian Expeditionary Force. A number of cemeteries were used by the MEF in and around Basra; Makina Masul Old Cemetery was used from 1914 to 1916 and the Makina Masul New Extension was begun alongside the old cemetery in August 1917. These two sites, enlarged when more than 1,000 graves were brought in from other burial grounds, now form Basra War Cemetery.

The cemetery now contains 2,551 burials of the First World War, 74 of them unidentified. The headstones marking these graves were removed in 1935 when it was discovered that salts in the soil were causing them to deteriorate. The names of those buried in the graves affected are now recorded on a screen wall.

Killed in Action.

BELL.—On July 28th, Albert John Bell, aged 22, 2nd Battalion R.W.K. Regiment, Indian Expeditionary Force, second and dearly-beloved son of Mr. and Mrs. Bell, of Wrotham-road, Gravesend, who died from wounds received in action in Persian Gulf.

GR 21/8/15 [AM]   GR 5/8/16 [AM]

IN MEMORIAM.

BELL.—In loving memory of our dear son, Albert John, 2nd Battalion R.W.K., wounded at Mesopotamia July 24th, died July 28th, 1915, aged 22 years. From Father and Mother, Brothers and Sisters. "Gone, but not forgotten."

William John Belmore
Mercantile Marine

William was born in 1868 in Gravesend. His father, Horace John, was a barman, born in 1842 in Kirkady, Scotland. His mother, Mary, was born the same year in Clerkenwell. She became a shopkeeper in Stone Street after being widowed in 1890.

William lived at 232 Old Road West with his wife Emily. She was born in 1876 and came from New Cross, London. The couple married in 1895 and had three surviving children – William, born in 1897, Beatrice, born in 1906 and Harry, born in 1907.

He was a painter with the Mercantile Marine. He served on *H.M.S. Orama*. *Orama* was one of the latest additions to the Orient Line before the outbreak of War and was commissioned as an Armed Merchant Cruiser on September 3rd, 1914, when she was employed in searching for enemy raiders in the South Atlantic. On November 11th, she sighted the German *S.S. Novarra*, which was carrying munitions and stores for the enemy raiders, and sank her by gunfire. Towards the end of November she was sent to the Falkland Islands in charge of the colliers for Vice-Admiral Sir Doveton Sturdee's Squadron. After the Battle of the Falklands the ship was ordered to the West Coast of South America with *HMS Kent* to search for the German raider *Prinz Eitel Friedrich*. She was present at the sinking of the German light cruiser Dresden at the Island of Juan Ferdananz on March 14th, 1915. She was then employed on convoy duties in the North Atlantic and was torpedoed and sunk by *U-62* on October 19th, 1917.

U-62 was commissioned on December 30th, 1916 under the command of

Captain Ernst Hashagen. He enjoyed two spells as captain of U-62; December 1916 to December 1917 [when Otto Wiebalck assumed captaincy] and again from March until November 1918.

In 9 patrols *U-62* sank 47 ships with a total of 123,294 tons with a further 5 ships damaged with a total of 16,483 tons. On November 22nd, 1918 she surrendered eventually being broken up in 1919.

William died on active service on May 22nd, 1918.

GR 8/6/18 [Andrew Marshall]

George Bennett
Royal Marine Light Infantry
Service No. CH/8200

George was born in 1872 in Wrotham. He was the adopted son of George and Maria Bennett of 18 Newman Road, Perry Street. George [father] was born in 1854 and was a farm labourer. Maria was born in 1858. Both came from Wrotham.

George [son] was a general labourer before enlisting with the Royal Marine Light Infantry in Chatham. He served on board *H.M.S. Cressy*.

Cressy, named after the 1346 Battle of Crécy, was laid down by Fairfield Shipbuilding, Govan, in 1898 and launched a year later. She was an armoured cruiser. She was commissioned for service on the China Station and subsequently assigned to the North America and West Indies Station from 1907 through 1909 and placed in reserve upon her return home.

The ship was assigned to the 7th Cruiser Squadron shortly after the outbreak of war. The squadron was tasked with patrolling the Broad

We deeply regret to record the death P.O. William John Belmore, who contract malaria and pneumonia, and died at B mont-road Military Hospital, Liverpool, May 22nd. His wife and four children l at 232, Old road West, Gravesend, and n sympathy will be felt for them in t terrible ss. The body was brought hom and on Monday afternoon was buried w full military honours at the Cemetery. firing party attended from the Barrac Deceased who was 49 years of age, jo the Merchant Service at the outbreak war, and for some time had been on board vessel which was recently torpedoed so after it late Liverpool, and it was then th he contracted malaria, and had to be tak to the hospital. One son of the deceased it at present in Salonica. At the fune the mourners present were: Wife, so daughter, Mrs. Smith, and Mr. and Mr Lear (friends). Wreaths were sent fr the following: His heartbroken Wife a Children; Son (in Salonica): Moth Mother-in-law (E. Watts); his Brothers the R.A.O.B.; 27th Mess H.M.S. "Eaglet Messmates and men, Naval Barracks, Par lane, Liverpool; Mr. and Mrs. Howell a father; Mr. and Mrs. Robert Box; Mrs. Edwards; Mrs. Smith and family; Four his workmates of the Orient Co.; and M and Mrs. Penfold. The Rev., V. S. Tur

Fourteens of the North Sea in support of a force of destroyers and submarines based at Harwich which protected the eastern end of the Channel. During the Battle of Heligoland Bight on August 28th, the ship was part of Cruiser Force 'C', in reserve off the Dutch coast, and saw no action.

On the morning of September 22nd, *Cressy* and her sisters, *Aboukir* and *Hogue*, were on patrol without any escorting destroyers as these had been forced to seek shelter from the bad weather. The three were steaming in line 2,000 yards apart at a speed of 10 knots. They were not expecting a submarine attack, but had lookouts posted and one gun manned on each side to attack any submarines sighted.

U-9, commanded by Otto Weddigen, had been ordered to attack British transports at Ostend, but had been forced to dive and take shelter from the storm. On surfacing, she spotted the ships and moved to attack. She fired one torpedo at 06:20 at *Aboukir* which struck on the starboard side; the captain thought he had struck a mine and ordered the other two ships to close to transfer his wounded men. *Aboukir* quickly began listing and cap-sized around 06:55.

As *Hogue* approached her sinking sister, her captain, Wilmot Nicholson, realised that it had been a submarine attack and signalled *Cressy* to look for a periscope although his ship continued to close on *Aboukir* as her crew threw overboard anything that would float to aid the survivors in the water. Having stopped and lowered all her boats, *Hogue* was struck by two torpedoes around 06:55. The sudden weight loss of the two torpedoes caused *U-9* to surface and *Hogue*'s gunners opened fire without effect and the submarine submerged again. The cruiser capsized and sank at 07:15.

Cressy attempted to ram the submarine, but did not succeed and resumed her rescue efforts until she was torpedoed at 07:20. Weddigen had fired two torpedoes from his stern tubes, but only one hit. *U-9* had to manoeuvre to bring her bow around with her last torpedo and fired it at a range of about 550 yards at 07:30. The torpedo struck on the port side and ruptured several boilers. *Cressy* took on a heavy list and then capsized before sinking at 07:55.

From all three ships 837 men were rescued and 62 officers and 1,397 enlisted men lost: 560 of those lost were from *Cressy*. George was among those killed.

GR 16/12/16 [Andrew Marshall]

He has no known grave and is commemorated on the Chatham Naval Memorial.

In 1954 the British government sold the salvage rights to all three ships to a German company and they were subsequently sold again to a Dutch company which began salvaging the wrecks' metal in 2011.

CRESSY SINKING, by Henry Reuterdahl

George Benjamin Bennett
Northumberland Fusil'rs, 1st/5th Bn
Service No. 6506 - Private

George was born in 1896 in Gravesend. His parents were George and Matilda Maud Bennett of 7 Garden Road, Perry Street. George was born in 1873 and came from Wrotham. He worked at the cement works in Swanscombe as a general labourer. Matilda was born in 1873 and came from Bermondsey. She was in the employ of Thomas Colyer-Fergusson of Ightham Mote. The couple were married in 1895 and had seven surviving children – George, Charles, born in 1899, Alice, born in 1901, Violet, born in 1903, William, born in 1905, Ellen, born in 1907 and Joy, born in 1909.

George worked on a milk round prior to enlisting with the 1/5th Battalion, Northumberland Fusiliers. This was a territorial battalion and was based in Walker when war broke out in August, 1914. After training they proceeded to France in April, 1915, to join the 149th

William Belmore – Gravesend
Cemetery Memorial

George Bennett – Chatham Naval
Memorial, right, De Ruvigny
entry, above and *HMS Cressy,* below.

server at St. Clement's Parish Church, Ilford, and was for some time secretary of the Young Men's Guild.

BENNETT, GEORGE, Private, R.M.L.I. (R.F.R., B. 838), H.M.S. Cressy; lost in action in the North Sea, 22 Sept. 1914.

BENNETT, HUGH DONALD, Lieut., Royal Naval Reserve, H.M.S. Cressy, 4th s. of the late George Bennett, of Little

Brigade, 50th (Northumbrian) Division. They took part in the Second Battles of Ypres in 1915 and in 1916 the Battle of the Somme.

The Battle of the Ancre, November 13th – 18th, was the final large British attack of the Battle of the Somme in 1916, before the winter weather forced a pause in British attacks until the New Year.

The attack was the largest in the British sector since September and had a seven-day preliminary bombard-ment, which was twice as heavy as that of July 1st. Beaumont Hamel, St. Pierre Divion and Beaucourt were captured, which threatened the German hold on Serre further north. Four German divisions had to be relieved due to the number of casualties suffered and over 7,000 German troops were taken prisoner.

In II Corps, the 39th Division completed the capture of the *Schwaben* Redoubt, which took until 11pm. In V Corps the 37th Division relieved the 63rd Division and linked with the 51st Division to the north. Bombing attacks began up Beaucourt Trench towards Munich Trench, which reached the 51st Division around 10am. Patrols to Muck and Railway trenches found them empty. Companies of the 51st and 2nd Divisions attacked at 9am and were caught in their barrage, some troops reaching Frankfort Trench then returning to New Munich Trench. A 2nd Division attack with two battalions of the 37th Division lost direction in the mist and fell back to Wagon Road with many casualties, while a third battalion strengthened the left flank by building a strong point in the Quadrilateral,

near the top of Redan Ridge, as two tanks in support bogged down early George was killed in action on November 15th, 1916 on the Wancourt Ridge. It was a cold and overcast day with snow to fall on the 18th.

George's mother Matilda related the story that George appeared at the foot of her bed at the moment he was killed that night, November 15th. It was a deeply upsetting apparition for the family, remembered well throughout her long life by Violet who was 13 years old at the time. It is a story passed down through the years to the present generation of family descendants.

Matilda would decorate All Saints' Church with flags and plaques as a memorial to honour her dead son. The death of George would have a lasting impact on the family.

The grief was compounded by the death of Riv Colyer-Fergusson in July, 1917. The two families had a shared sorrow and grief and supported each other through the following months and years.

George has no known grave and is commemorated on the Thiepval Monument.

Robert William Bennett
Royal West Kent Rgt, 10th Bn
Service No. G/6863 - Private

Robert was born in 1897, the son of Robert and Jane Bennett of 5 Lower Range Road, Denton. Robert was born 1875 in Minster. Jane [Cryer] was born in 1876 and came from Deptford. Robert was a coal porter. The couple had three surviving children – Robert,

Daisy, born in 1907 and Mary, born in 1909.

Robert joined the 10th Battalion which landed in France on May 4th, 1916. The 39th Division of which they were a part were concentrated between Hazebrouck and Bailleul. The following year they were engaged in the Battles of Flers-Courcelette and the Battle of the Transloy Ridges on the Somme.

The Battle of Flers-Courcelette was in mid-September and marked the introduction of tanks into warfare. It also marked the debut of the Canadian and New Zealand Divisions on the Somme Battlefield.

Robert was killed in action on September 13th, in the opening phases of the Battle. He has no known grave and is commemorated on the Thiepval Monument.

Thomas Alfred Bennett
Royal West Kent, 1st/4th Battalion
Service No. 5005 - Private

Thomas was born in 1887 in Wrotham. His parents were George and Maria Bennett. George was born in 1865 and worked as a farm labourer. Maria was

Mr. and Mrs. R. Bennett, of 5, Lower Range-road, Denton, have received information of the loss of their only son, Pte. Robert Bennett, R.W.K. Regt., who was killed in action on the 12th September. Deceased, who joined the Army in May last year, only celebrated his nineteenth birthday in August. The bereaved parents have received a letter from Mr. F. A. Tennyson Smith, Lewis gun officer, Royal West Kent Regt., in which he says:—"I cannot properly express my proper feelings, as yours must be greater than mine, but, believe me, I feel Bennett's death very much. He has been with me for over a year now as a Lewis gunner. He has been one of the most willing men with me. He was No. 1 of the gun—that is, he was in charge of the gun. On Tuesday morning, 12th, he was carrying the gun to a new position. A German sniper saw him, and he was shot through the head. His death was absolutely instantaneous. We buried him, and I have let the Battalion orderly room know the position of grave. It hurts me to write to you like this, but I want to express my deepest sympathy with you in your grief."

GR 7/1016 [Andrew Marshall]

born in 1867. They were both born in Wrotham. There were seven children in the family – George, born 1884, John, born 1886, William, born 1888, Jenny, born 1891, Frederick, born 1893, Thomas, born 1898 and Ada, born 1900. The family moved following George's employment – Wrotham to Fawkham [1885] to Dartford [1887] and finally to Northfleet [1892].

126

Thomas married Dora Cousens in early 1911. Dora was born in 1890 in Northfleet. They lived at 12 Carters Road, Perry Street and had two children – Lillian, born March, 1914 and Queenie, born September, 1916. Thomas was a bricklayer before enlisting.

Thomas joined the 1st/4th when it was formed in September 1914 from men of the 4th who volunteered for overseas service. On October 30th it moved to India where it remained for the duration of the war. The Battalion transferred to the Jubbulpore Brigade in the 5th [Mhow] Division of the Indian Army.

Local Casualties.

News has been received that Private Thomas Alfred Bennett, the son of Mr. and Mrs. George Bennett, of 18, Newman's-road, Perry Street, and the husband of Mrs. Dora Bennett, of 12, Carter's-road, Perry Street, was accidentally drowned at Jubbelpore, India, on the 28th of last month, after serving 13 months in the West Kent Regiment in India. The sad news was received by cablegram on the 31st July, and the official news from the War Office on Saturday, but no details are to hand. Before joining up Mr. Bennett was employed at the I.P.M., and had been in the Army since May, 1916. He died at the early age of 30, and leaves a widow and three children to mourn their loss. A portrait of the deceased had not arrived at the time of going to press, and it will therefore appear next week.

GR 11/8/17 [Andrew Marshall]
GR 11/8/17 [Andrew Marshall]

On Active Service.

BENNETT.—Thomas Alfred Bennett, Pte. in R.W.K., who was accidentally drowned at Jubbulpore, India, on July 28th, aged 30 years.

Thomas died on July 28th, 1917 and is buried in Jubbulpore Cantonment Cemetery.

Fred Joseph Benson
Mercantile Marine Reserve
Service No. 39775 - 2nd Steward

Fred was born in Gravesend in 1877, the son of Frederick and Anna Benson. Frederick was born in Bradwell, Essex in 1844. He was a dock labourer in Tilbury. Anna was also born in 1844 and came from Purfleet. They had six children, all born in Gravesend – Frederick, Emma, born in 1879, Hannah, born in 1883, Maud, born in 1885, Ellen, born in 1886 and Jessie, born in 1889.

He married Florence Amy Tunstall in Gravesend in 1902. Florence was born in Gravesend in 1878. They had one child – Peggy Winifred who was born in September, 1909. The family lived at 66 Windmill Street.

Fred served as a second steward and storekeeper on the *HMS Clan McNaughton. HMS Clan McNaughton* was a 4985 ton passenger cargo vessel, built in 1911 and requisitioned November 1914 from the Clan Line Steamers Ltd, Glasgow, becoming an Armed Merchant Vessel. It is thought that Clan McNaughton foundered in a severe gale off the north coast of Ireland. Last heard from on February 3rd, 1915, wreckage was later found in the area and *Clan McNaughton* was presumed sunk with the 281 strong crew.

There is some speculation that as she had a new crew who were generally unfamiliar with the vessel, and that the armaments added to the deck destabilised her making the *McNaughton* vulnerable to such severe weather as was found on the day she lost contact.

Fred was among the dead. His body was not recovered and he is commemorated on the Plymouth Naval Memorial.

Thiepval Monument – George Bennett, right, and Robert Benett, below.

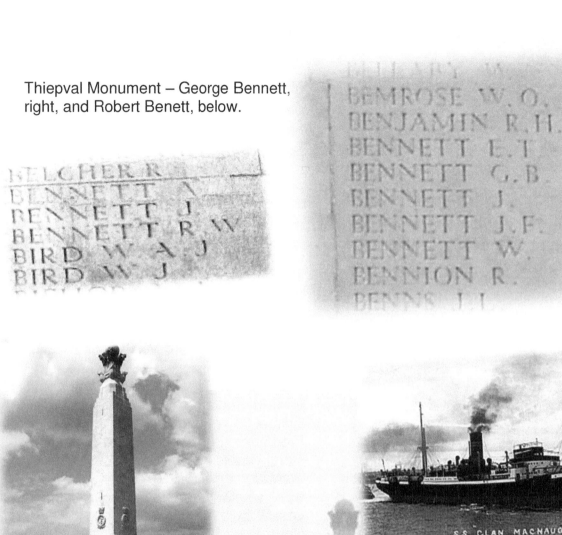

S.S. CLAN MACNAUGHTON.

Plymouth Naval Memorial – Fred Benson and Victor Berridge.
Fred, a 2nd Steward, was 'lost' when HMS Clan McNaughton foundered.

Victor Charles Berridge
Mercantile Marine
Service No. 881783 - Fireman

Victor was born in Gravesend in 1898. His father Thomas was born in 1869 in Sri Lanka. He was a seaman and travelled the world. His mother Annie was also born in 1869 and in Higham. They married in 1893 and had five children – Hilda, born in 1895, Dorothy, born in 1896, Florence, born in 1897, Victor and Ruby, born in 1905. The family home was at 27 Augustine Road.

Victor was a fireman with the Mercantile Marine Reserve. He was 5 feet 7 inches tall and weighed 150lbs.

Among the ships he served on was *H.M.S. Minnehaha* in July 1917 when he made the trans-Atlantic crossing...

He was killed in action when the ship on which he was serving, *R.F.A. Industry* was sunk in the Irish Sea near the Strangford Light Buoy by *UB92* on October 18th, 1918.

Victor's body was not recovered for burial and he is commemorated on the Plymouth Naval Memorial.

Lost at Sea.

BERRIDGE.—In ever loving memory of our darling Vic, only son of Frank and through the sinking of H.M.S. "———" by enemy action, on October 18th. —From Mum and Dad.

BERRIDGE.—In ever loving memory of our dear brother, Vic, lost at sea on October 18th 1918.—From Hilda, Florrie, Ruby and Frank.—"Till me meet again."

BERRIDGE.—In ever loving memory of our dear Brother Vic, aged 20 years, lost at sea, October 18th, 1918. — From his loving Sister and Brother (Dorrie and Sam).

GR 2/11/18 [Andrew Marshall]
GR 29/1/16 [Andrew Marshall]

Killed in Action.

BETTS.—On December 24th, 1915, killed in action, John Charles Betts, A.B., R.N.D., the only devoted son of the late John Betts and of Mrs. Adams, 2½, Clarence-street, at the early age of nineteen years. Sadly missed by all.

Charles Betts
Royal Naval Volunteer Reserve
Service No. Z/2452

John was born in 1896 in Gravesend. His father John was born in Gravesend in 1870 and was a shoe laster. His mother Alice was born in 1871 and was a dressmaker. They had two children – Clare born in 1893 and John. The family lived at 2 Eden Place. His father John died in September 1898 and his mother remarried. Her second husband was Charles Henry Adams. The marriage was in Gravesend in June 1899. They had four surviving children and the family of eight – the two children from the first marriage and the four from the second – lived at 2 and 4 Clarence Street. He was a shop assistant prior to the War. John enlisted on June 14th, 1915 and was drafted for the M.E.F. on October 25th that year. He was with the Hawke Battalion, Royal Naval Division from December 2nd. Hawke Battalion was part of 1st Brigade, Royal Naval

129

Division founded by the First Lord of the Admiralty, Winston Spencer Churchill, in late August 1914.

In October 1914 a large number of men of Hawke Battalion were either captured by the Germans or crossed into Holland and interned for the duration, as they retreated from Antwerp. A new Hawke Battalion was raised, 'D' Company was formed by volunteers from the 'Public Schools Battalion.' They remained in England when the RND sailed for the Dardanelles, finally re-joining the RND at Cape Helles on May 30th, 1915. The Hawke Battalion saw action at Gallipoli, from May 1915 to January 1916.

Able Seaman Betts was killed in action on December 24th, 1915. He has no known grave and is commemorated on the Helles memorial.

GR 19/2/16 [Andrew Marshall]

Franklin Beven is incorrectly listed as *F G Bevan* on the Memorial.

Franklin George Beven
East Yorkshire Regiment, 10th Bn
Service No. 30337 - Private

Franklin was born in Gravesend in 1899 to George and Sarah Beven.

George was born in 1872 in Gravesend. he was a sanitary dustman. Sarah was born in 1876 and was from High Halstow. The couple had four children – Franklin, Frederic, born in 1902, Hettie, born in 1904 and Richard, born in 1906.

Franklin was a sanitary labourer before enlisting on April 25th, 1917 with the 9th Battalion. He was mobilised on June 11th in Maidstone and posted to the 10th Battalion. He was 5 feet 6 inches tall and weighed 113lbs.

The 10th Battalion, The East Yorkshire Regiment was known as the Hull Commercials and was raised in Hull on August 29th, 1914 by Lord Nunburnholme and the East Riding TF Association. In May 1915 The Battalion joined the 92nd Brigade, 31st Division moving to Penkridge Bank Camp near Rugeley, the later to Ripon and Hurdcott Camp near Salisbury.

In December 1915 they set sail for Alexandria in Egypt to defend the Suez Canal. In March 1916 the 31st Division left Port Said aboard *HMT Briton* bound for Marseilles in France, a journey which took 5 days. They travelled by train to Pont Remy, a few miles south east of Abbeville and

130

marched to Bertrancourt arriving on March 29th, 1916.

Not long after arriving on the Western Front they took over a stretch of the front line opposite the village of Serre at the northern most end of The Somme suffering very heavy casualties as the battle was launched. In 1917 they were in action in the Battle of Arras and in 1918 they fought at St Quentin, Bapaume and Arras before moving north to counter the German Spring Offensive on the Lys.

Frankiln arrived in France on April 2nd, 1918. He was reported missing on the 12th and regarded as killed in action. He has no known grave and is commemorated on the Ploegsteert memorial.

GR 4/1/19 [Andrew Marshall]

Percy Biddlecombe

Royal East Kent & Royal Fusiliers – City of London Regiment - Private Service No. L/ 10661 & G/61608

Percy was born in Southampton, in 1898 the son of William and Gertrude Biddlecombe of 17 Bligh Street. William was born in 1864 in Southampton and was a general labourer. There were six children in the family – Albert, born in 1896, Percy, James, born in 1900, George, born in 1904, Louisa, born in 1911 and Charles, born in 1913. He and his elder brother Albert, two years his senior, attended the County Industrial School at Kingsnorth, Ashford. The school was built in 1875 as a result of the Industrial Schools' Act of 1872 at a cost of about £10,000 with an administration block and infirmary added in 1882 at a further cost of £7,000. It was certified in October 1875, for the reception of 200 boys. Boys received an education in addition to working on the school farm. The justices bought musical instruments in 1877 and employed a music teacher. It was that which enabled Albert to become a musician.

Prior to enlisting Percy worked in the local dairy obviously benefitting from his education at Kingsnorth. He joined the 24th (2nd Sportsman's) Battalion, The Royal Fusiliers (City of London Regiment) which was raised at the Hotel Cecil in the Strand, London, on the 25th of September 1914 by Mrs E. Cunliffe-Owen.

In June 1915 they joined 99th Brigade, 33rd Division at Clipstone camp near Mansfield. In August they moved to Salisbury Plain for final training and firing practice. By the 21st of November the 33rd Division had concentrated near Morbecque.

On the 25th of November, 1915 The Battalion transferred to 2nd Division as part of an exchange to strengthen the inexperienced 33rd Division. They took part in the Winter Operations 1914-15 and in 1915 saw action at The Battle of Festubert and The Battle of Loos.

Frederick Benson

Gravesend Cemetery –

IN
SACRED MEMORY OF
FREDERICK
JOSEPH BENSON
THEIR SON-IN-LAW
WHO WAS LOST BY THE
FOUNDERING OF H.M.S.
CLAN MACNAUGHTON
FEB 3rd 1915

[Photograph – Andy White]

Franklin Beven –
Ploegsteert Memorial

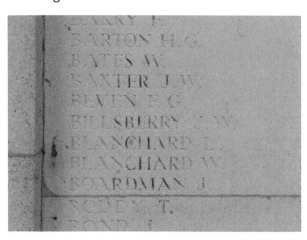

In 1916 they fought in the Battles of the Somme and the Operations on the Ancre. In 1917 they were in action during the German retreat to the Hindenburg Line, the Battles of Arras and The Battle of Cambrai.

Percy was killed in action on November 15th, 1917 and is buried in Regina Trench CWGC Cemetery.

Mr. and Mrs. Biddlecombe, of 17, Bligh-road, Gravesend, have received the sad news of the death of their son, Percy. In the letter from the officer in charge of Royal Fusiliers, "Somewhere in France," a very high and favourable opinion is given of his career as a soldier. Though only 19 years of age, he voluntarily enlisted some 13 months ago, and was soon in the fighting line, defending his country, in which he took a great deal of interest. Previous to joining the Colours he was employed at the I.P. works, where he was held in high esteem by all with whom he came in contact.

Rodney Edward Bill
R.G.A., 38th Heavy Battery
Service No. 1034 – 2nd Lieutenant

Rodney was born in Gravesend on January 1st, 1886. His father Edward was born in 1852 in Kington, Herefordshire. He was a tobacconist and hairdresser, the shop being at 66 High Street. His mother Lucinda [Humphreys] also came from Kington and was born in 1851. They married in 1871. There were four children in the family – Harold, born in 1882, Isobel, born in 1883, Rodney and Mary, born in 1888. The family lived at Radnor Lodge, Cobham Road.

Rodney was educated at Margate College and became a bank clerk on leaving school. He enlisted on the outbreak of War in August 1914 with the West Kent Yeomanry, service number 1034 before joining the Royal Garrison Artillery, 38th Heavy Battery.

38th Heavy Battery, Royal Garrison Artillery was raised as part of 38th Division, but left before the Division proceeded to France, and joined XLII Heavy Artillery Group.

He arrived in Egypt on September 23rd, 1915 and served in Gallipoli. On return to England which was not without excitement – the ship he was on was torpedoed – he trained for a commission. He was gazetted 2nd Lieutenant, R.G.A., on August 4th, 1917.

He arrived in France in November. He was killed in action near Arras while on patrol duty on August 26th, 1918. He is buried in Cabaret-Rouge Cemetery, Souchez.

Souchez is 3.5km north of Arras. Caberet Rouge was a small, red-bricked, red-tiled café that stood close to this site in the early days of the War. The café was destroyed by shellfire in March 1915 but it gave its unusual name to this sector and to a communication trench that led troops up the front-line. Commonwealth soldiers began burying their fallen comrades here in March 1916. The cemetery was used mostly by the 47th (London) Division and the Canadian Corps until August 1917 and by different fighting units until September 1918. It was greatly enlarged in the years after the war when as many as 7,000 graves were concentrated here from over 100 other cemeteries in the area. For much of the twentieth century, Cabaret Rouge served as an 'open cemeteries' at which the remains of fallen servicemen newly discovered in the region were buried. Today the cemetery contains over 7,650 burials of the First World War, over half of which remain unidentified. GR 14/9/18

Killed in Action.
BILL.—Killed in action on August 26th, in his 30th year, Rodney Edward, 2nd Lieut., R.G.A., the youngest dearly loved and loving son of Mr. and Mrs. E. W. Bill, of Gravesend. Laid to rest in the Military Cemetery, Abberville, France. "His duty to King and country well done."

Note the discrepancy in date of death –
CWGC has November 15th, 1917;
The headstone records January, 1918.

Percy Biddlecombe

Gravesend Cemetery –

IN LOVING MEMORY

ALSO PERCY, SON, KILLED IN ACTION JAN 1918

[Photograph – Andy White]

Regina Trench Military Cemetery

Rodney Bill -
Cabaret-Rouge Cemetery, Souchez

Alfred Bloomfield
Royal West Kent, 6th Battalion
Service No. G/10564 - Private

Alfred was born in 1879 in Cooling the son of George and Susannah Bloomfield of 1 New Cottages, Cooling. Both George and Susan came from Norfolk with George being born in 1836 and Susan in 1838. George was a farm labourer. There were seven children in the family – Arthur, born in 1868, Harry, born in 1870, Harriet, born in 1877, Alfred, born in 1879, Ellen, born in 1881, Ernest, born in 1883 and Elizabeth, born in 1885.

Alfred married Olive Rose Randall in September, 1901. She was born in 1881 in Cliffe. The couple had four children – Ellen, born in 1903, William, born in 1905, Doris, born in Strood in December 1911 and Alfred, born in Strood in September, 1916. Sadly Doris died in March, 1912. Alfred, their third surviving child, was born the month after his father was killed in action on the Somme and into the third day of the great Battle.

The family home was at Church Cottages before they moved to 12 Augustine Road, Gravesend.

Alfred was a farm labourer, like his father, enlisting at Maidstone on November 4th, 1915 with the Royal West Kent Regiment.

The 6th (Service) Battalion, The Royal West Kent Regiment was raised at Maidstone on August 14th, 1914 as part of Kitchener's First New Army. They trained at Colchester and moved to Purfleet in September 1914 they spent the winter in billets in Hythe from December. They moved to Aldershot for final training in February 1915 and proceeded to France on June 1st, 1915 landing at Boulogne.

On January 19th, 1916 they began a period of training in Open Warfare at Busnes, then moved back into the front line at Loos on February 12th. In June they moved to Flesselles and carried out a training exercise. They moved to Baizieux on June 30th and went into the reserve at Hencourt and Millencourt by mid-morning on the 1st of July. They relieved the 8th Division at Ovillers-la-Boisselle that night and attacked at 3.15 the following morning with mixed success.

Alfred was killed in action on July 3rd, 1916. He has no known grave and is commemorated on the Thiepval Monument.

Walter Charles Lucas Blower
Canadian Pioneers
Service No. 103159

Walter was born in Henley on the 13th of June, 1876 the son of Edward and Emma Blower. There were four children in the family – Ellen, born in 1861, Emma, born in 1868, John, born in 1874 and Walter.

He was a ship's steward in the Merchant Service and enlisted on October 14th, 1915 in Victoria British Columbia giving his sister Emma Smith as his next of kin. She lived at 3 Norfolk Road. He was 5 feet 7 inches with blue eyes and black hair and had a dark complexion.

The 67th Battalion (Western Scots) were commanded by Lieutenant-Colonel Lorne Ross, formerly of the 50th Regiment Gordon Highlanders. The Gordons were one of four Highland regiments that made up the famed 16th Battalion (The Canadian Scottish). Ross, then a Major, was seriously wounded during the 2nd Battle of Ypres in April 1915 and was on leave in Canada when he was offered a promotion and the job of raising a new battalion. He accepted the offer. On August 15th, when the

Alfred Bloomfield –
Thiepval Memorial, left.

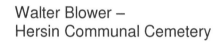

Walter Blower –
Hersin Communal Cemetery

battalion was officially authorised, the response was swift and by October the battalion was over strength at 1063 men and officers.

The Western Scots took up residence at Willows Camp and immediately began drilling in preparation for the visit of H.R.H The Duke of Connaught, above right. On Friday September 17th over 1350 officers and men, along with nearly 700 cadets and Boy Scouts, were reviewed by the Governor-General. Assembled under sunny skies were the 5th Canadian Royal Garrison Artillery, the Independent Squadron of B.C. Horse, the 50th Regiment Gordon Highlanders and the 88th Regiment Victoria Fusiliers, the No. 1 Army Service Corps and nearly 700 members of the 67th Overseas Battalion Western Scots.

With the royal spectacle over the Western Scots began an arduous training regime. Lt-Col. Ross stressed practical skills - trench making, engineering, bombing and physical fitness.

On Friday March 24th, 1916 the 67th Battalion Western Scots were given an enthusiastic send off by the people of Victoria as they boarded the Princess steamers, the first leg of their long journey to the Western Front. Awaiting the troops in Halifax was the *RMS Olympic*, the largest British-built liner in the world and older sister of *Titantic*. It had just arrived from Liverpool to ferry its first contingent across the ocean. The 67th Battalion, along with troops from the 59th, 61st and 71st among other battalions, arrived in Liverpool on April 11th.

The 67th became the 4th on April 1st, 1917 but the day before William was killed in action. He was buried at Hersin Communal Cemetery. Hersin is a village about 5 kilometres south of Bethune. The extension to Hersin Communal Cemetery was begun by French troops, who made over 100 burials, and was taken over by Commonwealth troops and field ambulances in March 1916. It was in use until October 1918.

Victor Charles Blunderfield
Royal Engineers – Sapper
Service No. 541632

Victor was one of 13 children, nine surviving to Robert and Rosetta Blunderfield of 4 New Street. Robert was born in 1861 in Gravesend and was a house painter; Rosetta was also from Gravesend being born in 1864. Victor was the third youngest in the family, born in 1895. By the outbreak of war Robert had died and Rosetta had remarried and was now resident at 2 The Terrace. Victor was a baker's assistant prior to enlisting.

Victor, in the image above, was with 527th [Durham] Field Company. 2nd Durham Field Company, The Royal Engineers joined 5th Division in September 1915. In March 1916 5th Division took over a section of front line between St Laurent Blangy and the southern edge of Vimy Ridge, near Arras. They moved south in July to reinforce The Somme and were constantly in action. In October they moved to Festubertand and remained there until March 1917 when they moved in preparation for the Battles of Arras. In 1917 they were renamed 527th (2nd Durham) Field Company. In September 1917 they moved out of the line for a period of rest before, being sent to Flanders where they were in action during the Third Battle of Ypres. In late January 1918 they were in Italy until recalled to France to assist with the German Advance in March 1918. Then moved to The Somme sector in August and it was here that Victor was killed on August 23rd, 1918

He is buried at Foncquevillers. In 1915 and 1916 the Allied front line ran between Foncquevillers and Gommecourt. The cemetery was begun by French troops, and taken over by Commonweatlh forces. The cemetery was used again from March to August 1918, when the German offensive pushed back the front line.

Walter Bolden
Royal West Kent, 11th Battalion
Service No. G/18786 - Private

Walter was born in 1884 in Stebbing, Essex. He and his wife Matilda lived with her parents Richard and Rebecca Killick in Caterham, Surrey. In addition to the two married couples there were another six children of the Killick family living in the five room house. Walter and Matilda had three children – Winifred, born in 1912, Edith, born in 1913 and Walter, born in 1915.

Walter was a farm labourer before enlisting in Caterham with the Royal Fusiliers, service number 41132.

He subsequently served with the 11th Battalion. The 11th (Lewisham) Battalion, The Royal West Kent Regiment was raised at Lewisham on May 5th, 1915 by the Mayor and a

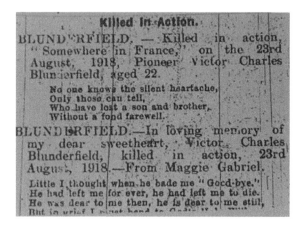

GR 21/9/18 [Andrew Marshall]

local committee. They proceeded to France on May 3rd, 1916 and the division concentrated between Hazebrouck and Bailleul. In 1916 they were in action on the Somme. In 1917 they fought during The Battle of Messines and The Battle of Pilckem Ridge.

Walter was killed in action on July 7th, 1917. He is buried in Tyne Cot Cemetery.

The cemetery lies on a broad rise in the landscape which overlooks the surrounding countryside. As such, it was strategically important to both sides fighting in the area. The area

138

was captured by the 3rd Australian Division and the New Zealand Division, on October 4th, 1917 and two days later a cemetery for British and Canadian war dead was begun. The cemetery was recaptured by German forces on April 13th, 1918 and was finally liberated by Belgian forces on September 28th.

After the Armistice in November 1918, the cemetery was greatly enlarged from its original 343 graves by concentrating graves from the battlefields, smaller cemeteries nearby and from Langemark.

The Cross of Sacrifice that marks many CWGC cemeteries was built on top of a German pill box, purportedly on the suggestion of George VI, in the centre of the cemetery, who visited the cemetery in 1922 as it neared completion. The King's visit, described in the poem *The King's Pilgrimage*, included a speech in which he said -

We can truly say that the whole circuit of the Earth is girdled with the graves of our dead. In the course of my pilgrimage, I have many times asked myself whether there can be more potent advocates of peace upon Earth through the years to come, than this massed multitude of silent witnesses to the desolation of war.

Thomas Bone

Royal West Kent, 2nd Battalion
Service No. L/8571 - Private

Thomas was born in early 1889, the son of George and Mary Bone of 2A Bentley Street, Gravesend, originally living at 2 Brewhouse Terrace, Gravesend. George was born in 1852 in Swanscombe. He was a general labourer. Mary was also born in 1852 and was from Gravesend. They married in 1873 and there were six children in the family – William, born in 1880, Pat, born in 1885, Benjamin,

born in 1886, Henry, born in 1892, Thomas and Edward, born in 1884.

Thomas was a career soldier and in the years prior to the Great War was stationed in India with the 2nd Battalion, Royal West Kent Regiment.

In August 1914 Thomas was in Multan (Mooltan), India with the Battalion. The Battalion moved to Mesopotamia, arriving in Basra on February 6th, 1915 where it came under command of 12th Indian Brigade. Two Companies were attached to the 30th Brigade in the 6th (Poona) Division in November 1915 and became besieged at Kut-al-Amara, where they were captured on April 29th, 1916. The remaining Companies were attached to 34th Brigade which was part of 15th Indian Division, transferring to 17th Indian Division in August 1917. The Battalion remained in Mesopotamia throughout the war.

Thomas died on October 23rd, 1916 and is buried in Baghdad [North Gate] CWGC Cemetery. In 1914, Baghdad was the headquarters of the Turkish Army in Mesopotamia. It was the ultimate objective of the Indian Expeditionary Force 'D' and the goal of the force besieged and captured at Kut in 1916. The city fell in March 1917, but the position was not fully consolidated until the end of April. It had by that time become the Expeditionary Force's advanced base, with two stationary hospitals and three casualty clearing stations.

The North Gate Cemetery was begun In April 1917 and has been enlarged since 1918 by graves brought in from other burial grounds in Baghdad and northern Iraq, and from battlefields and cemeteries in Anatolia. At present, 4,160 Commonwealth casualties of the War are commemorated in the cemetery, many on special memorials. Unidentified burials from this period number 2,729.

Foncquevillers Military Cemetery-
Victor Blunderfield

Gravesend Cemetery - Thomas Bone

[Photograph – Andy White]

Walter Bolden –Tyne Cot

Edward William Bonfield
Royal West Kent, 1st Battalion
Service No. L/9080 – Lance Corp.

Edward was born in Rochester in September, 1890. His father, William, a stone mason by profession, was born in 1862 and his mother, Elizabeth was born a year later. There were five children in the family; Florence, born in 1885, Frederick, born in 1887, Emma, born in 1889, Edward and Alfred, born in 1896. The family were from Rochester and subsequently lived at 49 Peppercroft Street.

Prior to enlisting in the Royal West Kents he was an assistant in a greengrocer's shop in Rochester. It was there he enlisted in October 1908 and was initially posted to the 3rd Battalion. He was 5 feet 4 inches tall and weighed 116lbs; he had grey eyes, light brown hair and was of fair complexion.

1st Battalion, The Royal West Kent Regiment was based in Dublin with 13th Brigade, 5th Division when war was declared in August 1914. They proceeded to France landing at Le Havre on the 15th. They were in action in The Battle of Mons and the subsequent retreat, The Battle of Le Cateau, The Battle of the Marne, The Battle of the Aisne, The Battles of La Bassee and Messines and The First Battle of Ypres.

He was promoted Lance Corporal with the 1st Battalion on August 21st, 1914.

He was killed in action on August 24th, the Battle of Mons and is commemorated on the La Ferte Souis-Jouarre Memorial. The Memorial commemorates 3,740 officers and men of the British Expeditionary Force (BEF) who fell at the battles of Mons, Le Cateau, the Marne and the Aisne between the end of August and early October 1914 and have no known graves.

Cyril Addlington Boorman
West Kent Yeomanry
Service No. 801

Cyril was born in 1891 the son of Frederick William and Ellen Beatrice Boorman of 'Maycroft', Wrotham Road. Both were from Gravesend with Frederick being born in 1861 and Ellen some three years his younger. Frederick was a solicitor. Cyril was their only child.

After school Cyril became an engineer. He was with the West Kent Yeomanry - Household Cavalry and Cavalry of the Line – which subsequently became part of the Imperial Camel Corps. The Imperial Camel Corps was raised in early 1916, from troops who had served at Gallipoli. Each Battalion was made up of 4 companies - each with 6 officers and 169 other ranks. The Imperial Camel Corps provided a mounted infantry role, although it was intended that the troops should go into action dismounted.

Three of the Corps' four battalions were drawn from Australian and New Zealand light horse, which had suffered very high attrition at Gallipoli. The 2nd Battalion however was composed from the remnants of the various British Yeomanry regiments who had fought there.

As a force composed largely of antipodeans the Corps had a reputation from the start for disrespect for authority, Although losses were still high, the Camel Corps were successful in their role throughout 1917, particularly at the Battle of Maghdaba and the third Battle of Gaza. In May 1918 many troops were redeployed from Palestine to the Western Front, the 2nd Battalion was not formally disbanded until May 1919, and continued in a patrolling role up to the end of the War.

The redundant camels were given to Major T.E. Lawrence, Lawrence of Arabia.

Cyril died on March 3rd, 1915 and is buried in Gravesend Cemetery.

THE LATE TROOPER C. A. BOORMAN.

MILITARY FUNERAL AT GRAVESEND.

The pathetic circumstances attending the death of Trooper C. A. Boorman, of the West Kent Yeomanry, alluded to in our last issue, have called forth a wide expression of sorrow and sympathy. The funeral, which took place with military honours at Gravesend on Saturday afternoon, was not only attended by large crowds, but on the line of route the blinds of houses and business establishments were lowered as marks of respect. The coffin, which was borne on a gun carriage, was covered with the Union Jack, and at its head was placed a floral crown, composed of violets and lilies of the valley—a beautiful symbolical tribute from the bereaved parents. The cortege was headed by a contingent of seventeen members of "B" Squadron, West Kent Yeomanry, under the command of Lieut. the Hon. A. Mills, and there followed 35 men of the Kent R.G.A. and 35 members of the Gravesend Volunteer Corps (under the command of Mr. C. P. Taylor), of which the father of the deceased is a member. The mourners were as follows:

First Carriage—Mr. and Mrs. F. W. Boorman (parents), Mr. and Mrs. J. H. Wyatt (uncle and aunt). Second Carriage—Mr. Frank Boorman, Mr. J. Adlington, Mr. Horatio Sandford (uncles); Mr. Horatio Sandford, jun. (cousin). Third Carriage—Mr. A. H. Burton, Mr. A. Beamish, Mr. Stanley Boorman, Mr. Wilfred Wyatt (cousins). Fourth Carriage—Dr. J. Dawson Hartley, Rev. Canon Gedge, Rev. J. T. Jones, Nurse Toogood. Fifth Carriage—Miss M. Travis, Mr. A. Henderson.

Amongst those also present either at the church or the graveside were: Lieut. May, Lieut. Stephenson, and Lieut. Ellison (old school colleagues of the deceased), Dr. Parker (Headmaster, King's School, Rochester), Messrs. H. E. May, H. Stephenson, Alex. Walker, E. Lovell, E. W. Lovell, Mrs. West, Mrs. Bergemann; etc.

The first portion of the service was held at St. George's Church. As the cortege entered, the hymn, "Rock of Ages" (a favourite of the deceased) was sung. Rev. J. D. Gedge read the opening sentences of the service, and the Rector (Canon G. L. Gedge) read the lesson. The Dead March ("Saul") was played by Mr. Moss as the coffin was removed. At the graveside the Rector officiated, assisted by the Rev. J. T. Jones. Finally, a trumpeter from the deceased's regiment sounded "Lights-Out."

Wreaths were received as follow:—A crown, to our own darling boy, from Father and Mother; Dear Cyril, with fond love, from Grandma; In ever loving memory, from Uncle Jack and Auntie Al.; In affectionate remembrance, from Wilfred; In loving remembrance, from Auntie Lizzie and Uncle Raish; In affectionate remembrance, from Frank and Edy; In loving remembrance, from Cousin Raish and Cousin Kenneth; In loving memory, from Auntie Ada and Uncle Jack; In loving memory, from Uncle Albert, Auntie Alice and Stanley; With loving memory, from Jessie; In loving memory, from Auntie Louie, Kath and Maddie; In loving memory of dear Cyril, from Auntie Martha, Arthur and Doris; With deepest sympathy, from Harold and Jean; In loving remembrance, from Mabel and Will; With deepest sympathy, from Mrs. C. R. Bullard; With heartfelt sympathy, from Connie and George, Norah and Farley; In affectionate remembrance, from Harry and Lizzie and family; With loving sympathy, from Tom and Emmie; In remembrance, from Hilda and Aubrey; With love and deepest sympathy, from Lill and Marjorie; With deepest sympathy, from his Comrades in No. 3 Troop, "B" Squadron, W.K.Y.; With deepest sympathy, from Norman A. Simes, Roland F. West, Edgar A. Whitfield, Leonard S. Molz, Douglas A. Smith, Rodney E. Bill, Darold B. Aylen and Harold V. Miall, his Gravesend friends in the West Kent Yeomanry; "He died that others might live," from the Gloucester Regt. (Milton Barracks); With deepest sympathy, from the Helpers of the Soldiers' Social Institute; In loving memory of our young master ("Peace, perfect peace"), from Minnie and Edith; With deepest sympathy, from J. and A. Henderson; With deepest sympathy, from the Churchwardens and Sidesmen of St. George's Parish Church; With deepest sympathy, from the Old Roffensian Society; With sincere sympathy, from the Members of the Gravesend Cricket Club; With sympathy, from the Gravesend Rowing Club; With deepest sympathy, from the Members of the Gravesend Tradesmen's Association; With deepest sympathy, from Friends at the Electricity Works; With deepest sympathy, from Mr. and Mrs. Spiers and family; With loving sympathy, from Effie; With kindest condolence and sympathy, Mr. J. Adlington Mason and family; With deepest sympathy, from Will and Kate; In remembrance and with deepest regret, from Ronald West; With deepest sympathy, from Dr. and Mrs. J. Dawson Hartley; With sincere sympathy, from Mr. H. D. Stephenson and family; With deepest and heartfelt sympathy ("Until the day breaks and the shadows flee away"), from Captain and Mrs. A. Larking; With sincere sympathy, from Mr. and Mrs. George Brooker; In deepest sympathy, from Mr. R. Weaver and Miss Weaver; With deepest sympathy, from Mr. and Mrs. Hugh Peckham; With deepest sympathy, from Florrie and her Mother; With deepest sympathy, from Mr. and Mrs. Thos. Schultz and family; With deepest sympathy, from Mr. and Mrs. Bulford and family; With deepest sympathy, from Mrs. W. T. Wildish and family; With very deep sympathy, from Mr. and Mrs. Henry E. Porter and family; With deepest sympathy, from Canon Gedge and family; In kind remembrance, from Dr. and Mrs. R. E. Inman and all at Gads Hill; With deepest sympathy and sincere respect, from Mr. R. French and family; With deepest sympathy, from Mr. and Mrs. Wm. French; ...... sympathy, from Mr. and Mrs.

KM 13/3/15 [Andrew Marshall]

GR 6/3/15 [Andrew Marshall]

KM 6/3/15 [Andrew Marshall]

The Imperial Camel Corps Memorial is situated in the Victoria Embankment Gardens, London.

Trooper C. A. Boorman, Gravesend.

Great sympathy will be extended to Mr. F. W. and Mrs. Boorman, of "Maycroft," Gravesend, in the irreparable loss they have sustained by the death of their only son, Cyril Adlington Boorman. He was only 23 years of age, and passed away on Wednesday, after an illness of five days' duration. The circumstances are peculiarly sad. A smart young fellow, who won the hearts of all his friends he was until the outbreak of the war following the profession of an engineer, in which he promised to carve out a career of distinction. Studying at the Finsbury Technical School, he had already attained his A.M.I.C.E., and few had greater prospects of success. When the national call to military duty came in August, he was attached for service to the "B" Squadron, West Kent Yeomanry, which he joined a couple of years back. For seven months, therefore, he had been serving with the county yeomen at Sturry and Fordwych, near Canterbury. A few days ago business called him home for a short stay, and it was while here that symptoms of an illness developed which proved so tragically fatal. If it is consolation to his parents in the hour of trial, Gravesend, which knew him so well, and held him in such regard, as well as his comrades in the West Kent Yeomanry, share keenly and fully the sorrow occasioned by the fact that such a bright young life should close so abruptly, Cyril Boorman's scholastic days were chiefly spent at King's School, Rochester, where he was a King's scholar, and he matriculated at London University. Both in his school days and after he was a keen cricketer and footballer, and often played for the Gravesend C.C.

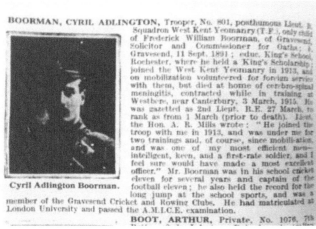

BOORMAN, CYRIL ADLINGTON, Trooper, No. 801, posthumous Lieut. B Squadron West Kent Yeomanry (T.F.), only child of Frederick William Boorman, of Gravesend, Solicitor and Commissioner for Oaths; b. Gravesend, 11 Sept. 1891; educ. King's School, Rochester, where he held a King's Scholarship; joined the West Kent Yeomanry in 1913, and on mobilization volunteered for foreign service with them, but died at home of cerebro-spinal meningitis, contracted while in training at Westbere, near Canterbury, 3 March, 1915. He was gazetted as 2nd Lieut. R.E. 27 March, to rank as from 1 March (prior to death). Lieut. the Hon. A. R. Mills wrote: "He joined the troop with me in 1913, and was under me for two trainings and, of course, since mobilisation, and was one of my most efficient men—intelligent, keen, and a first-rate soldier, and I feel sure would have made a most excellent officer." Mr. Boorman was in his school cricket eleven for several years and captain of the football eleven; he also held the record for the long jump at the school sports, and was a member of the Gravesend Cricket and Rowing Clubs. He had matriculated at London University and passed the A.M.I.C.E. examination.

Cyril Adlington Boorman.

BOOT, ARTHUR, Private, No. 1076, 7th

An **F Boreham** is listed on the Windmill Hill Memorial; this is an error in transcribing as the soldier is one **Frederick Burcham**.

Frederick Burcham
'The Buffs', 1st Battalion
Service No. L/6937 - Private

Frederick was born in 1884 in Gravesend, the son of Henry and Sophia Burcham. Oddly both parents were born in 1858 and both died in 1896, Sophia in the spring and Henry in early summer. Henry was a labourer at the Cement Works. The couple had children – Nellie, born in 1876 and Bertie, born in 1886. The family lived at 35 Wycliffe Road, Northfleet.

Frederick was a wire maker before becoming a carman. He enlisted with the 2nd Battalion, 'The Buffs' on September 1st, 1902. He was 5 feet 8 inches tall and weighed 123lbs. He had hazel coloured eyes, brown hair and of a fresh complexion. He had a mermaid tattooed on his left forearm and a sailor on his right forearm.

On January 3rd, 1903 he signed papers to extend his service to complete eight years with the Colours.

His army career was punctuated with minor offences – a half dozen or so every year! These ranged from being improperly dressed on parade to irregular conduct on parade to quitting his fatigue without permission, absent from tattoo, not complying with orders, hesitating to comply with an order, gambling in the barracks and being drunk.

On December 9th, 1907 he qualified as a baker. He transferred to the 1st Class Army Reserve on August 31st, 1910 listing his civilian occupation as a baker. By now he had qualified as a first class in musketry and had been a range warden in North Africa for two months.

He re-engaged on June 30th, 1914 in Gravesend. The Royal East Kent Regiment (The Buffs) were in Fermoy, County Cork, when war broke out in August 1914. They were mobilsed with 16th Brigade and returned to England, where 6th Division concentrated near Cambridge for training. They proceeded to France on September 10th, 1914, landing at St Nazaire and marched to the Aisne to reinforce the hard-pressed BEF. They moved north to Flanders and were in action at Hooge in 1915.

During the First World War, Hooge was the site of a château which was used as the Divisional Headquarters for the area. The staff at the château, from the 1st and 2nd Divisions were all killed when the château was shelled on October 31st, 1914.

> **HOW HE FOUND THE "REPORTER."**
>
> Pte. F. Burcham, who is serving with the 1st Batt. of the Buffs at the front, writes to the Editor saying: "Seeing several letters from my fellow-town's lads in your valuable paper, I thought I would just like to send a line or two to you. First, I will explain how I first saw your paper since I have been in France. I sailed on the 6th September on the "Minneapolis" and the Battalion has seen some lively times since then. On Christmas morning while billeting in a barn I happened to see one of our fellows reading a paper and on looking closely I saw it was the 'Reporter.' Well, you may be sure how pleased I was to see the old paper. I soon became acquainted with the fellow who happened to be a townsman. Well, Sir, I am proud to be a native of Gravesend and also proud to be fighting for my King and country. Last night we were in the reserve trenches and we could hear the Germans singing, but we fellows know we are winners, because the strain of being hungry and ill-clothed is telling on the Germans, who seem to me to be losing heart. Still my advice to the young fellows of Gravesend is 'Roll up and join and help us to avenge Scarborough.' I wish you, Sir, and all your staff, a Merry Christmas, and I soon hope to be in Gravesend again."

GR 2/1/15 [Andrew Marshall]

German forces attacked the château between May 24th and June 3rd, 1915, and, despite the detonation of a British mine by the 3rd Division, leaving a massive crater, took control of the château and the surrounding area on July 30th. The château and the crater (craters being strategically important in relatively flat countryside) were taken by the 6th Division on August 9th.

Frederick died from wounds on August 10th. He is buried in Railway Dugouts Burial Ground [Transport Farm].

Gravesend Private Killed.

We regret to record the death in action of Pte. Frederick Burcham, of 2, John's Cottages, John-street, Gravesend, who belonged to the 1st Battalion of the Buffs. He was thirty-one years of age, and had also served in the South African War. He had altogether served in South Africa some five years, and nine years in other parts. A particularly sad feature was the fact that the deceased had intended obtaining leave shortly to visit Gravesend to be married.

Writing to the deceased's brother Second-Lieut. Brock states: " It is with the very greatest regret that I write to inform you of the death of your brother—No. 6,937, Pte. Frederick Burcham. He was hit just before dawn on Tuesday, August 10th, by a piece of shell, which very mercifully rendered his death absolutely instantaneous and painless. . . . . Tell all that he died bravely in action near Ypres and was buried where he fell. I have been his platoon commander for about two months and I am very glad to be able to tell you that he was one of my very best men; always most cheerful and brave and always ready to volunteer for any work that was especially dangerous or difficult. In fact I am personally deeply sorry that he should have been among those who were killed in the recent fighting in which our Battalion has been engaged, and I can assure you that England has lost one of its best soldiers in Frederick Burcham. All his comrades too are I know very much affected by his death, as his steady cheerfulness and manly good nature made him very popular among them."

GR 11/9/15 [Andrew Marshall]

Railway Dugouts Cemetery is located 2 km south-east of Ypres. Railway Dugouts Cemetery is 2km west of Zillebeke village, where the railway runs on an embankment overlooking a small farmstead, which was known to the troops as Transport Farm. The site of the cemetery was screened by slightly rising ground to the east, and burials began there in April 1915. They continued until the Armistice, especially in 1916 and 1917, when Advanced Dressing Stations were placed in the dugouts and the farm. They were made in small groups, without any definite arrangement and in the summer of 1917 a considerable number were obliterated by shell fire before they could be marked. The names "Railway Dugouts" and "Transport Farm" were both used for the cemetery.

At the time of the Armistice, more than 1,700 graves in the cemetery were known and marked. Other graves were then brought in from the battlefields and small cemeteries in the vicinity, and a number of the known graves destroyed by artillery fire are specially commemorated.

The cemetery now contains 2,459 Commonwealth burials and commemorations of the First World War.

Frederick's brother, Herbert [Bertie] also enlisted, serving with the R.A.O.C. He was in correspondence with the Records' Office to ensure receipt of Frederick's medals.

S/9003 Private Bertie Burcham was stationed post war at the Advance Base Depot, Baghdad.

Henry Alfred Botting
Royal Fusiliers, 2nd/3rd Battalion
Service No. 252764

Henry was born in early 1877 the son of George Parker and Mary Ann Botting. Both were born in Gravesend, George in 1850 and Mary in 1854. George was a house painter. There were three children in the family – Henry, Nellie, born in 1879 and Katie, born in 1885.

Henry was a gardener and prior to enlisting he lived with his sister, Nellie, and her family – she was married to Walter Longford. They lived at 10 Brandon Street.

He served with the 3rd [City of London] Battalion, Royal Fusiliers.

He was killed in action on May 15th, 1917. He has no known grave and is commemorated on the Arras Memorial.

Cyril Boorman
– Gravesend Cemetery

In Loving Memory of
CYRIL ADLINGTON BOORMAN
Died on Active Service 3rd March
1915 Aged 22

Frederick Burcham –
Railway Dugouts Cemetery; note the
'unknown soldier' headstones on
either side.

Reginald Charles Bowden
Royal West Kent, 1st Battalion
Service No. G/4859 - Private

Reginald was born in 1891 in Bayswater. His father Frederick was born in 1855 in Paddington. His wife Rachel was from Gravesend being born in 1867. The couple married in 1884 and had seven children – Maud, born in 1889, Reginald, Delia, born in 1893, Lily, born in 1895, May, born in 1900, Vera, born in 1904 and Charles born in 1909. Frederick was a cabinet maker. The family moved from Paddington around the turn of the century and lived at 222 High Street.

Reginald was a cook on leaving school and subsequently became a cellarman. He was now living at the Basin Tavern, Tilbury. He enlisted on December 3rd, 1914 at Warley in Essex. He was 5 feet 8½ inches tall and weighed 198lbs!

He arrived with his Regiment in France on April 7th, 1915. On May 5th the Battalion had to hurry back to Zillebeke where they had withdrawn from on April 30th. A successful German attack to take Hill 60 had proved successful and the Dorsets driven off. But the Battalion was unable to retake the position and when it became clear there was no chance of a successful attack the Battalion was withdrawn just before daylight on May 6th to support trenches at Larch Wood,

Reginald, however, was already a casualty, being killed in action the day before, on May 5th. He was posted as missing, presumed dead. He has no known grave and is commemorated on the Menin Gate.

Herbert Leslie Bowler
East Surrey, 1st Battalion
Service No. 9496 - Private

Herbert was born in Agra, India in December, 1893. His father Joseph was a sergeant stationed there. His mother was Alice Amelia Smith. The couple were married in Allahabad, Bengal in October 1887. Joseph was born in 1860 and died in Agra, on April 1st, 1893. Alice remarried the following year, February 1894. She married John Wright in Agra. There were 4 children from the first marriage and one from the second. The family on return from India lived at 10 Mayfield Road.

He enlisted at Kingston on March 23rd, 1908 when 14 years old in the Royal Army Medical Corps. He was 4 feet 10 inches tall and weighed a mere 98lbs. He had grey eyes, brown hair and had a fresh complexion and was deemed fit for service. He learned to play the bugle and then became the Regimental drummer.

He did not settle well to the discipline of Army life as he was on no less than a dozen charges between March, 1909 and November, 1912. The charges varied from not sounding reveille [awkward when one is the bugler!] due to being in bed, missing lessons [bugling/drumming], insolence and being drunk. The total days confinement to Barracks in this period comes to over 70 days!

In November 1911 he was raised to

the rank of private having attained the required age. But army life was still not fully to his liking; in September 1912 he was insolent to an N.C.O. and compounded the action by resisting his escort – the sentence was 12 days confinement to Barracks. Two months later and with the Regiment in Dublin he was found drunk in the Barracks at 9.30pm when on duty – sentenced to 14 days confinement to Barracks. In July 1914 he was found drunk and creating a disturbance in Merginstown and resisted the escort – sentence being 14 days confinement to Barracks and a fine of 2/6.

His initial training was in Jersey where he remained until November, 1908. Then it was on to Plymouth until September 1910. He was stationed in Kinsale until September 1912 and then on to Dublin.

He arrived with his Regiment in France on August 13th but he was soon in trouble. On September 23rd, 1914 he was sentenced to three months Field Punishment No. 1 for absenting himself without leave when on active service. On October 12th he was sentenced to 21 days Field Punishment No. 1 for using obscene and threatening language to an N.C.O. The Battalion war diary records the events of October 20th as follows – *the Battalion crossed the canal at 8.45am and marched along a very winding road passing several Dragoon regiments, followed by two regiments of Alpine Chasseurs who warned them of two companies of German infantry close ahead. The Battalion soon engaged them and halted their advance. The Battalion Machine Gun Section knocked out three machine guns and every effort made by the enemy to retrieve them was frustrated by accurate fire. D Company and the Machine Gun Section held an orchard and farm buildings astride the road with the Battalion left line extended in open country. The left of the line made a small advance but were checked by enfilade fire and retired. The Battalion entrenched and strengthened its position during the afternoon. Shortly after dark the enemy attacked but were driven off. The rest of the night passed quietly. Casualties for the day were one officer killed [2/Lt A Thompson], five other ranks killed and sixteen wounded.*

Among the *five dead* was Herbert. He is buried in Brown's Road Military Cemetery.

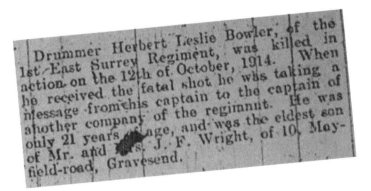

Drummer Herbert Leslie Bowler, of the 1st East Surrey Regiment, was killed in action on the 12th of October, 1914. When he received the fatal shot he was taking a message from his captain to the captain of another company of the regiment. He was only 21 years of age, and was the eldest son of Mr. and Mrs. J. F. Wright, of 10 Mayfield-road, Gravesend.

GR 8/11/14 [Andrew Marshall]

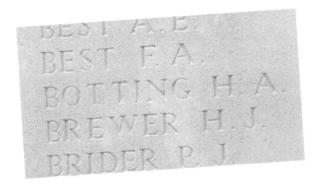

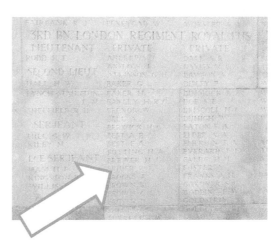

Henry Botting – Arras Memorial, above and Reginal Bowden, Menin Gate, below.

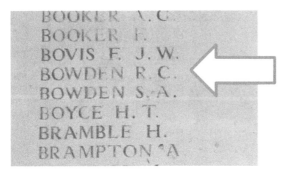

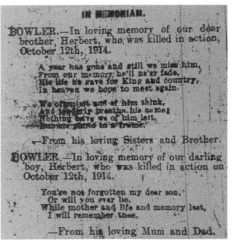

GR 9/10/15 [Andrew Marshall]

Herbert Bowler – Brown's Road Cemetery

Frank Charles Box
East Kent Regiment, 7th Battalion
Service No. G/734 - Private

Frank was born in Gravesend in 1895. His father, Thomas was born in 1864 and was a self-employed builder. Frank had four sisters, Amelia, born 1890, Ellen, born 1892, Ada, born in 1900 and Gertrude, born in 1904 and a brother, George, born in 1902. The family lived at 6 Pelham Road.

Frank enlisted in London on September 7th, 1914. He was posted to Canterbury the following day to join the 7th Battalion, the 'Buffs'. He was 5 feet 9½ inches tall and weighed 138 lbs. He had a healthy complexion at his medical, hazel eyes and fair hair and was deemed 'fit' for the army.

7th (Service) Battalion, The Royal East Kent Regiment (The Buffs) was raised at Canterbury in September 1914 as part of Kitchener's Second New Army and joined 55th Brigade, 18th (Eastern) Division. The Division initially concentrated in the Colchester area but moved to Salisbury Plain in May 1915. They proceeded to France in July and concentrated near Flesselles. In late December 1915 he suffered from bronchitis, not returning to his Battalion until January 6th. He was wounded in action less than a month later on February 5th, succumbing to his wounds on the 12th at 5th Casualty Clearing Station.

GR 19/2/16 [Andrew Marshall]

Many will regret to hear that this war has robbed the town of another promising young man, Frank Charles, the elder son of Mr. T. W. Box, builder, of 6, Pelham-road South. In September, 1914, he enlisted, at the age of 19, in the 7th Buffs, and was transferred to the M.G. Section, in which he acted as scout. In July, 1915, they went to France, and since then they have been taking their share in the trenches. From a report sent to his father by Lieut. J. G. Whitfield, on the night prior to February 1st, it appears the Germans shelled successfully the trench, putting the gun out of action, wrecking the emplacement, and killing the corporal. Frank's duty was to report, and to do so he had to cross ground which was subjected to a perfectly hellish shell-fire. This he managed to do safely, but on the return journey he was wounded severely by two pieces of shell. Fortunately he was quickly attended to, and within two hours he was on his way to the clearing hospital. The officer said the wounds were deep; but there was no cause for anxiety. On the 4th Frank sent a field post-card to say he was in hospital doing well. This was received on the 7th, together with the letter from his lieutenant, which seemed to confirm the hope of recovery. However, on the 6th a sister of the hospital wrote saying he was seriously ill, on the 8th he was no better, and on the 10th that he was worse. Then, on Sunday, the following telegram was received: "Regret to inform you No. 734, Private F. Box, 7th Buffs, died 12th February, at 5th Casualty Clearing Station. Attest Hounslow."

Universal sympathy will be felt with Mr. Box in his loss, for Frank was only 20 years of age. Educated at St. James's Church Schools and the Technical Institute, he was well-known to many, and especially to the members of the Wesleyan Comrades. He was fond of sport, and though injured at football was at it again when well. In this respect, it is worth recording the statement made about him by his officer. "He is a splendid boy, one of my best. His drums, Lee and Aitken, are terribly cut up and we all miss him. I only hope that when he is back on duty that he will be sent to this regiment." Alas, his fighting days are o'er, but, like many more, he has travelled to that land where his talents will be exercised in building up a new kingdom, and his life lived where sorrow, pain and the horrors of war will be forgotten in the enjoyment of endless peace.

He is buried at Corbie Communal Cemetery. Corbie is a small town 15 kilometres east of Amiens.

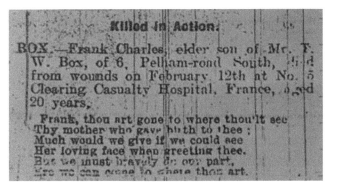

Killed in Action.

BOX.—Frank Charles, elder son of Mr. T. W. Box, of 6, Pelham-road South, died from wounds on February 12th at No. 5 Clearing Casualty Hospital, France, aged 20 years.

Frank, thou art gone to where thou'lt see
Thy mother who gave birth to thee;
Much would we give if we could see
Her loving face when greeting thee.
But we must bravely do our part,
Ere we can come to where thou art.

GR 19/216 [Andrew Marshall]

Corbie was about 20 kilometres behind the front when Commonwealth forces took over the line from Berles-au-Bois southward to the Somme in July 1915. The town immediately became a medical centre, with Numbers 5 and 21 Casualty Clearing Stations based at La Neuville, the suburb across the Ancre, until October 1916 and April 1917 respectively. The communal cemetery was used for burials until May 1916, when the plot set aside was filled and the extension opened. The majority of the graves in the extension are of officers and men who died of wounds in the 1916 Battle of the Somme. The remainder relate to the fighting of 1918. The communal cemetery contains 249 First World War burials, the extension 918.

Percy Tufnel Box
Mercantile Marine – Linen Keeper

Percy was born in 1890 in Gravesend. he was the son of William and Lizzie Box of 8 Warwick Terrace, Singlewell Road. William was born in 1859 in Gravesend. He was a commercial traveller by trade. Lizzie was also from Gravesend and was a year younger than her husband. The couple had three surviving children – Frank, born in 1886, Percy and Martin, born in 1893. Lizzie died at the turn of the century and William remarried; he and his second wife Ethel, born in 1880, were married in 1906. There were three children from this marriage – Russell, born in 1907, Winifred, born in 1908 and Douglas, born in 1910.

Percy was a linen keeper in the Mercantile Marine and in early 1916 was a crew member on the *S.S. Maloja*.

Maloja was one of P&O's M-class passenger liners, the first of which had been RMS *Moldavia* which was completed in 1903. Harland and Wolff Ltd built *Maloja*, completing her in 1911. She had capacity for 670 passengers plus a quantity of cargo. At 1500hrs Saturday, February 26th, 1916 *Maloja* sailed from Tilbury for Bombay carrying 122 passengers and a general cargo. Her passengers were a mixture of military and government personnel, and civilians including women and children. Following normal P&O practice, her complement of 301 comprised British officers and Lascar crew.

On the morning of the 27th *Maloja* approached the Strait of Dover at full speed and overtook a Canadian collier, *Empress of Fort William*. Under wartime conditions each ship would have to be examined by a patrol boat before being allowed to proceed.

The *UC-6* had recently mined the strait. At about 1030hrs *Maloja* was about 2 nautical miles off Dover when she struck one of *UC-6*'s mines. There was a large explosion, and the bulkheads of the second saloon were blown in. *Empress of Fort William* was still in sight and immediately went full ahead to assist, but while still a nautical mile astern the collier also struck one of *UC-6*'s mines and began to sink.

Gravesend Cemetery –

**ALSO FRANK SON OF THE ABOVE
WHO DIED OF WOUNDS FEB 11th 1916
AGED 20 YEARS
BURIED AT CORBIE, FRANCE**

[Photograph – Andy White]

Frank Box

Corbie Communal
Cemetery

As a precaution against enemy attack, *Maloja* was steaming with her lifeboats already swung out on their davits so that they could be lowered more quickly. Her Master, Captain C.D. Irving, RNR, immediately had her engines stopped and then put astern to stop her so that her boats could be lowered. She also sounded her whistle as a signal to prepare to abandon ship.

Irving then tried to order her engines be stopped again for the ship to be evacuated, but flooding in her engine room prevented the engines from being stopped and she started to make way astern at about 8 to 9 knots. She also developed a list to starboard which steepened to 75 degrees.

Passengers started to board the starboard lifeboats but the ship's speed and list prevented all but three or four of them from being launched.

Small vessels headed to assist her including the Port of Dover tugs *Lady Brassey* and *Lady Crundall*, trawlers, Dredgers and a destroyer. As *Maloja* steamed mid astern and unable to stop, the rescue vessels were unable to get alongside to take off survivors. A heavy sea was running and the hundreds who crowded her decks could only don a lifejacket, jump overboard and try to swim clear. A number of her rafts either were launched or floated clear, and some of her survivors managed to board them. *Maloja* sank 24 minutes after being mined, followed by *Empress of Fort William* which sank about 40 minutes after being mined.

Many of the deaths were from hypothermia, either in the water or after being rescued. Most of the people who survived were recovered from the water. The small vessels taking part in the rescue took many of the survivors to the hospital ships *Dieppe* and *St David*.

Others were brought ashore and Royal Navy ambulances took them to the Lord Warden Hotel. Survivors were later taken by special train to London Victoria.

At about 11.30am vessels started to bring bodies ashore. The chief constable of Kent took charge of the dead and designated the Market Hall below Dover Museums a temporary mortuary. 45 bodies were recovered but about another 100 people were unaccounted for.

Percy was among those whose body was lost at sea. He is commemorated on the Tower Hill Memorial.

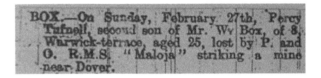

BOX.—On Sunday, February 27th, Percy Tufnell, second son of Mr. W. Box, of 8, Warwick-terrace, aged 25, lost by P. and O. R.M.S. "Maloja" striking a mine near Dover.

GR 11/3/16 [Andrew Marshall]

Tower Hill Memorial

153

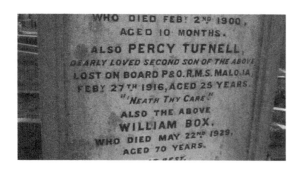

Gravesend Cemetery –

ALSO PERCY TUFNELL
DEARLY BELOVED SECOND SON
OF THE ABOVE
LOST ON BOARD P & O. R.M.S.
MALOJA
FEBy 27th 1916, AGES 25 YEARS
"Neath Thy Care"

[Photograph – Andy White]

Percy Box –
Tower Hill Memorial

154

Charles John Boyd
Royal Field Artillery, 51st Battery
Service No. 45691 - Gunner

Charles was born in 1887 in Gravesend. His father Charles was born in Gravesend in 1865 and worked as a barge hand. His mother Clara was born in 1867 and was also from Gravesend. The couple had six children – Charles, Frank, born in 1889, Oscar, born in 1891, Elsie, born in 1896, Eva, born in 1898 and John, born in 1904. The family lived at 17 Raphael Road, Milton.

Charles enlisted with the Royal Field Artillery prior to the Great War and was with the 76th Battery as a gunner prior to joining the 51st Battery.

The basic unit of the Royal Artillery was the Battery. At the outbreak of World War I, a field artillery brigade consisted of a headquarters (4 officers, 37 other ranks), three batteries (5 and 193 each), and a brigade ammunition column (4 and 154) had a total strength just under 800 so was broadly comparable to an infantry battalion (just over 1,000) or a cavalry regiment (about 550).

XXXIX Brigade, Royal Field Artillery was originally formed with 46th, 51st and 54th Batteries, and attached to 1st Infantry Division. In August 1914, it mobilised and was sent to the Continent with the Expeditionary Force, where it saw service with 1st Division throughout the war.

Charles died of wounds on November 20th, 1914. He is buried at Poperinghe Old Military Cemetery.

GR 26/12/14 [Andrew Marshall]

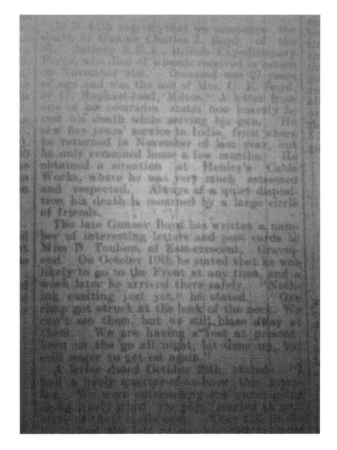

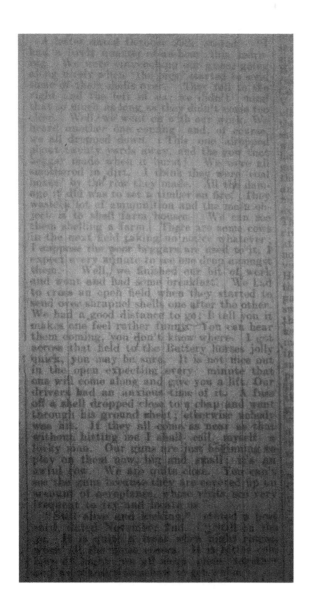

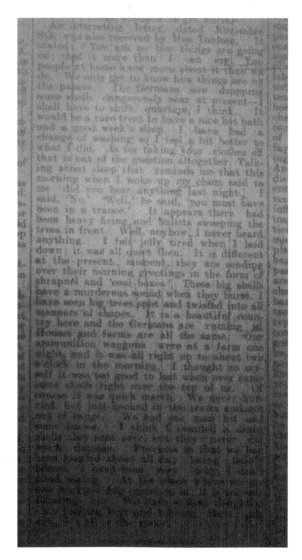

Joseph William Bradbrook
R.E., Inland Water Transport
Service No. 196938 - 2nd Corp.

Joseph was born in 1885 in Gravesend. His father Arthur was born in 1847 in Essex. He worked at the cement works as a labourer. His mother Elizabeth was born in 1843 and was from Gravesend. They had three children – Elizabeth, born in 1885, Sarah, born in 1892 and Joseph. The family originally lived at 29 Garden Road. On the death of Elizabeth [mother] both Arthur and Joseph subsequently lived with Elizabeth [daughter] and her husband Frederick Allen. They married in 1900 and had three children. The family home was at 33 Cutmore Street.

Joseph worked as a fireman with the Orient Line. He married prior to the Great War and he and Edith lived at 42 Cutmore Road. They had one child, a daughter, Alice who was born in 1914.

Joseph enlisted with the Royal Engineers, Inland Water Transport. He was sent to the Middle East where he drowned on March 11th, 1918. He is buried in Basra War Cemetery.

Acting-Lance-Corpl. Joseph William Bradbrooke, of the Inland Water Transport, Royal Engineers, was drowned in the Persian Gulf on March 11th, information having just been received by his wife, Mrs. E. Bradbrooke, 42, Cutmore-street, Gravesend. Before the war he was employed at the I.P.M. as a stoker, and he enlisted 16th August, 1916. He was sent out to Mesopotamia, and had been working on the River Tigris with the water transport.

GR 30/3/18 [Andrew Marshall]

William Edward Bradford
Royal Naval Reserve
Service No. 2302/SD
William was born in Gravesend on August 29th, 1881 the son of Edward and Harriet Bradford. the couple married in 1872 and had eight surviving children. The family lived at 15 Church Street and prior to enlisting with the Royal Naval Reserve William was an able seaman with the Merchant Service.

William married Mary Annie Maddern in mid-1918. The couple lived at St Peter's Hill, Newlyn in Cornwall. Their daughter Beatrice was born in June the following year.

William was a deckhand on *H.M. Motor Launch 570.* He died on November 11th, 1918 and is buried in Paul Cemetery, Penzance.

GR 30/11/18 [Andrew Marshall]

Able Seaman William Bradford, whose portrait above will be recognised by many Gravesenders, died at Newlyn, Cornwall, one hour after the armistice was signed, and we are sorry to add, only about a month after he had been married. Son of Mrs. Bradford, 21, Arthur-street, and educated at Church-street School, the deceased grew up to be esteemed by many in the neighbourhood. For some time he led a seafaring life, and then in May, 1915, joined the Navy, afterwards spending an exciting time off the Cornish coast, chasing German U-boats. Many a time he narrowly escaped with his life, and, had he lived, he might have told many thrilling tales. The funeral took place at Newlyn with naval honours.

Ernest and *William Bradley*, whose biographies now follow, were brothers.

Ernest Sydney Bradley
Coldstream Guards, 1st Battalion
Service No. 21020 - Private
Ernest was born in 1894 in Greenhithe. His father William was born in 1863 in Stone. He worked at the cement works as a labourer. His wife Elizabeth [Stevens] was also from Stone being born in 1860. They were married in 1885 and lived at 28 Victoria Road. They had seven children – Henry, born in 1887, Arthur, born in 1888, Albert, born in 1892, Ernest, Doris, born in 1897, Leonard, born in 1900 and Nellie, born in 1902.

Elizabeth's brother, John, was a boarder. The level of employment in the area was high at the time to judge by the fact that all found employment either as labourers in the cement works or on the docks or as in the case of Ernest, worked as a milkman.

The Battle of Cambrai was fought between November 20th – December 7th, 1917). Cambrai, was a key supply point for the German *Siegfried Stellung* (part of the Hindenburg Line) and the nearby Bourlon Ridge would be an excellent gain from which to threaten the rear of the German line to the north. The operation was to include an experimental artillery action. Major General Tudor suggested trying out new artillery-infantry techniques on his sector of the front. During preparations, J. F. C. Fuller, a staff officer with the Royal Tank Corps was in the process of looking for a place to use tanks as raiding parties. General Julian Byng decided to incorporate them into the attack.

Despite the initial success of the Mark IV tanks at Cambrai, German artillery and infantry defences exposed the frailties of their armour and the vehicles became mostly ineffective after the first day. The battle was largely an artillery-infantry engagement that achieved surprise and technical superiority against strong fortifications but weak German infantry and artillery defences, which were quickly reinforced. The attack demonstrated that the Hindenburg Line could be penetrated and showed the value of new artillery and infantry methods, such as sound ranging and infiltration tactics that would later play a vital part during the Hundred Days Offensive. However there were little territorial gains in this Battle.

The final effort to capture the key Bourlon Ridge was on November 27th by the 62nd Division aided by 30 tanks. Early success was soon reversed by a German counterattack. The British now held a salient roughly 11 by 9.5km with its front along the crest of the ridge. On November 28th, the offensive was stopped and orders given to lay wire and dig in. The Germans were quick to concentrate artillery on the new British positions. That day alone more than 16,000 shells were fired into the wood

Ernest was killed in action on November 27th, 1917. Hs body was lost and he is commemorated on the Cambrai Memorial, Louveral.

GR 28/9/18 [Andrew Marshall]

Charles Boyd - Poperinghe Old Military Cemetery.

Louveral –
Ernest Bradley

William Henry Bradley
Royal West Kent, 1st Battalion
Service No. L/8123 - Private

Henry was born in Greenhithe in 1887. He was the eldest of the seven children born to William and Elizabeth Bradley and the elder brother of Ernest.

News has reached Gravesend this week of the death of another of the borough's soldier sons. In the memorable fighting at Mons, in the early stages of the titanic struggle in France, Private Henry William Bradley, of Victoria road, Perry Street, fell mortally wounded when fighting with his regiment, the Royal West Kents. Born in Greenhithe 28 years ago, Private Bradley at the age of six years removed with his parents to Gravesend, in which locality he had since lived. He was an old scholar of High-street Council Schools, at Northfleet, and it was only a week or two ago that his name was added to that school's lengthy roll of honour. Private Bradley had served under the colours seven years and had been a Reservist for two years, at the time of the opening of hostilities he being an employee of the Imperial Paper Mills. His parents only received one postcard from their son all the time he was away, and on that he wrote that he was quite well. He took a keen interest in the sports of the town, and he will be missed by a large circle of friends.

GR 31/10/14 [Andrew Marshall]

Henry was an assistant in a grocery shop before enlisting in Maidstone with the 1st Battalion. The 1st Battalion, which was in Dublin at the outbreak of war, was one of the first units to be moved to France where it became part of the 13th Infantry Brigade in the 5th Infantry Division. Among its first major engagements were the Battle of Mons on August 23rd and Le Cateau three days later. In October the battalion made a heroic stand at Neuve Chapelle, being the only unit not to fall back. Out of 750 men, only 300 commanded by a Lieutenant and a 2nd Lieutenant survived.

Henry was killed in action on August 24th, 1914. He is buried at Hautrage Military Cemetery.

Joseph Brady

Royal Field Artillery, 80th Battery
Service No. 65732 - Bombardier

Joseph was born in 1894 in Redhill, Surrey. He was the son of Mark and Marion Brady of 27 Edwin Street. Mark was born in Chatham in 1859 and was a commercial traveller. His grandfather William came from Ireland being born in 1798. Marion was born in Edenbridge in 1863. The couple married in 1893 and had three boys – Joseph, Bernard, born in 1897 and Charles, born in 1902. The family lived at 19 Lord Street.

Joseph joined the 13th, Battalion, Dorset Regiment and was a drummer. However, when he enlists with the Royal Field Artillery on the outbreak of war in 1914 it is as George William and not Joseph! It seems he departed the 13th Battalion without permission!

Siege Batteries RGA were equipped with heavy howitzers, sending large calibre high explosive shells in high trajectory, plunging fire. The usual armaments were 6 inch, 8 inch and 9.2 inch howitzers, although some had huge rail or road mounted 12 inch howitzers. As British artillery tactics developed, the Siege Batteries were most often employed in destroying or neutralising the enemy artillery, as well as putting destructive fire down on strongpoints, dumps, store, roads and railways behind enemy lines.

The 80th arrived in France on April 19th, 1916. They were equipped with 2 12 inch road howitzers.

Bombardier Brady was killed in action on April 21st, 1917. He is buried in Lievin Communal Cemetery Extension. Lievin lies some 3.5km west of Lens and was captured by the Canadian Corps in April 1917. The majority of the soldiers buried here fell in April 1917, but others were killed as early as January 1915, and as late as October 1918.

There are now nearly 700, 1914-18 and a small number of 1939-45 war casualties commemorated in this site.

Mrs. Brady of 27, Edwin-street, has received official news that her son, Bombardier G. W. Brady, R.F.A. has been killed in action "Somewhere in France," on the 21st of April. He had served three years in the Regular Army, and came out in May, 1914, being called up again at the outbreak of war. Starting at the Battle of Mons, Bombardier Brady had been in all the big battles, and had only had seven days' leave about 12 months ago. In our issue of June 5th, 1915, was published a letter from the deceased to his mother, giving short descriptions of the battles he had been in during the first ten months of the war. He said then that he had been very lucky, and he was "still dodging 'em," and his motto was "Always keep smiling." Unfortunately his young life has been given up, but his mother has the one consolation that he sacrificed his life for others and his country. The following letter has been received by Mrs. Brady from Major H. E. O. B. Traill:— "Your son was doing his duty with the battery-in-action when he and two of his comrades were killed by a shell. He was killed instantly and had no suffering. I have commanded this battery for two years, and had a very high opinion of him. Please accept the sincere sympathy of myself and all his comrades-in-the-battery."

GR 2/5/17 [Andrew Marshall]

161

The Gallant Gunner

TEN MONTHS OF FIGHTING.

GRAVESEND MAN WRITES HOME.

Gunner G. W. Bradie, R.F.A., writes an interesting letter to his mother, who lives at 27, Edwin-street, Gravesend. He states: "I am still in the best of health, and will let you know what I have passed through since leaving the old town last August. I have had some narrow escapes, but Britishers never lose heart. 'Always keep smiling' is our motto. The first shot I heard fired on active service was at Mons, on August 23rd. Little we dreamed of what was coming off on that bright Sunday morning when we dug our guns in by the side of that Belgium coal pit. It got so hot that about 11.30 the following morning we started to make a road over the railway lines, ready to take our guns over, and withdrew from there about 12, mid-day, on to the grand retreat. Talk about get out and get under, well, it wasn't in it. From there we went to the (never to be forgotten) Le Cateau, and after some hard fighting for nine and a half hours, we had to 'hip,' for as fast as we shot the Germans down others came on us as thick as ever.

GR 6/5/17 [Andrew Marshall]

LINE AFTER LINE

of them. For a fortnight we were doing rearguard. That is the fifth division. When we arrived at a village about twenty kilometres from Paris, we were reinforced, and turned round on the enemy, who had to retire, the same as we did from Mons. And we got our own back, I can tell you. One of their heavy batteries had a commanding position, and held us up, along with dozens of other batteries and battalions, for a day, until our aeroplane located their position, reported it to a Major in the eighth brigade, and I think it was the 37th Howitzer Battery, got four direct hits on them. 'It was good-bye to them.' We saw them lying by their guns when we passed that way next morning. Later we saw a sight that is too awful for words. We went to —— to relieve a battery, but they didn't need us, as the Lancers had come to their assistance and had charged the 'Allemands.' There was nothing but dead and wounded lying about, including horses. I have been very lucky. 'Keep dodging 'em,' as they say.

ON THE MARNE.

"We took part in the fighting on the Marne. The first day we were crowned by a German battery that drove us out of action for a few hours, but we soon gave them as good as we received. At La Bassee, the place of horrors, we saw a good deal of scrapping during October 11th and 22nd. The firing almost made us deaf. With our guns we practically annihilated one German regiment. Then our right section's two guns picked up a position, under darkness, two hundred yards behind our infantry, with their French neighbours. The officer, two sergeants, and we ten gunners shook hands with the other four detachments before going up. We had a lively time of it. What with bullets and shells, there wasn't a man amongst us who expected to see daylight again. But we managed to scrape through all right. Shortly afterwards our 'friend,' the Kaiser, wished to try the strength of his renowned Huns against us—the contemptible little Army. So we made a move to ——, to give them

A WARM RECEPTION.

We remained there two months, after which we went to the Yser. Here we did not stop long. It was a very quiet shop. We were then relieved, and came back to our division, after spending a month or so here. We then proceeded to the well-known slaughter-house—Ypres. The town is in ruins. We took part in the operations of Hill 60 on the evening of April 11th, when the West Kents led the charge which took it out of Germans' hands. The Cheshires' Colonel praised our Battery up for the assistance we rendered him. They have poisoned us and the French with stink bombs and hose pipes, like firemen, from their first line trenches. We have respirators given us now to save us from the agony. Since we have been here, we have had four guns smashed up, one man killed, and ten wounded. All told, since the beginning, I am sorry to say we have had ten killed, and eighty wounded. There have been six D.C. medals and two commissions granted, and four men are recommended for the St. George's Cross."

William Bradley –
Hautrage Military Cemetery and the
De Ruvigny entry.

Lieven Communal Cemetery Extension
– the CWGC section, left, is down the
pathway, through the entrance, above.

Neville Linton Bridgland
East Surrey Reg, 3rd Battalion
Lieutenant

Neville was born in Gravesend on August 9th, 1894, the eldest son of Loftus and Annie Bridgland. The couple married in 1893 and lived at 'The Cedars', 100 Darnley Road. Loftus, born in 1867 was from Bearsted and was a land agent and surveyor. Annie, born in 1872 was from Gravesend. Neville had a younger brother, Cecil born in 1897 and a younger sister, Grace, born in 1900.

Neville attended the King's School, Rochester where he attained distinction as a cricketer. He was a member of the 1st XI from 1909 to 1912 inclusive. In playing St Lawrence College, Ramsgate he scored 110 runs, not out, out of 201 for one wicket in ninety minutes in partnership with his brother. He was also on the School's football 1st XI team. He maintained his sporting prowess in the army; in June 1914 at Shorncliffe, he scored 300 runs in eight innings at an average of just over 37.

He was gazetted to the Special Reserve of Officers as 2nd Lieutenant, 3rd East Surrey Regiment in November 1912, undertaking his six month's probationary training in Dublin with the 1st Battalion. He was confirmed his rank in April 1913 and promoted Lieutenant in March 1914.

On September 11th he took a draft of the 1st Battalion to France. The 1st Battalion were in action at Mons and the subsequent retreat, the Battles of Le Cateau, the Marne, the Aisne and La Bassee.

He was killed in action on October 22nd, 1914 at Lorgies, near La Basée and was buried in the garden of a house in the village. The church and churchyard were under the fire of German artillery at the time.

He now lies buried at Pont-du-Hem CWGC Cemetery, La Gorgue. The cemetery was begun in July 1915 in an apple orchard and used until April 1918 by fighting units and Field Ambulances. Burials from 20 locations and cemeteries were buried here after the Armistice.

Mr. and Mrs. L. F. Bridgland have the deepest sympathy in the unfortunate death of their eldest son, Lieut. Neville L. Bridgland, who has been killed in action at the Front. Educated at King's School, Rochester, he joined the O.T.C. attached to the School. On leaving school he attached himself to the Reserve of Officers. He received his commission as sub-lieutenant on November 2nd, 1912, being attached to the East Surrey Regiment, in connection with which he received his first six months' training in Dublin. Last May he was called up again for training in the Reserve, and on the 28th March last he was promoted to the rank of full lieutenant. When the war broke out the Reserve of Officers was mobilised, and Lieut. Bridgland joined his regiment at Dover on the 11th September, and went to the Front, being killed in action on the 22nd October.

Very popular among his many friends at Gravesend, it is extremely sad that a brilliant young officer should have had his career so prematurely cut short; for, we understand, he was only 20 years of age. He was a well-known cricketer and a most successful bat, having scored many hundreds of runs on the Bat and Ball, Gravesend, as well as for his school and for his regiment. There is no doubt he had a most promising future before him.

His untimely death is all the more pathetic when it is known that his last words to his mother on taking leave of her were these: "If I never come back you will know I have done my little bit."

The deceased's brother, Cecil Bridgland (18), is serving in the same regiment, and is expecting to go to the Front.

Mr. and Mrs. Bridgland received the following telegram on Wednesday evening:—

Buckingham Palace.
O.H.M.S.

To L. F. L. Bridgland, Esq.,
The Cedars, Darnley-road,
Gravesend.

The King and Queen deeply regret the loss you and the Army have sustained by the death of your son in the service of his country. Their Majesties truly sympathise with you in your sorrow.
(Signed) Private Secretary.

They have also been the recipients of many letters of sympathy from friends, far and near.

The appended verses by Laurence Binyon, appearing in the London "Standard," have been forwarded to the bereaved parents in the hope, no doubt, that they will prove some solace to them:—

They went with songs of battle, they were young,
Straight of limb, true of eye, steady and aglow.
They were staunch to the end against odds uncounted,
They fell with their faces to the foe.

They shall not grow old as we that are left grow old,
Age shall not weary them or the years condemn,
At the going down of the sun, in the morning
We shall remember them.

As the stars that shall be bright when we are dust,
Moving in marches upon the Heavenly plain,
As the stars that are starry in the time of our darkness
To the end, to the end they remain.

serred. We miss him sorely, and it is small consolation to us to know that he greatly decreased the number of our enemies when we think of how he met his end at the hands of a sniper."

BRIDGLAND, NEVILLE LINTON, Lieut., 3rd (Reserve), attd. 1st (31st Foot), Battn. The East Surrey Regt., s. of Loftus Frederick Linton Bridgland, of The Cedars, Gravesend; b. Gravesend, co. Kent, 9 Aug. 1894; educ. King's School, Rochester: was gazetted 2nd Lieut. Special Reserve of Officers, 3rd East Surrey Regt. in Nov. 1912, being promoted Lieut. in March, 1914; served with the Expeditionary Force in France and Flanders from 11 Sept. 1914, attached to the 1st Battn., and was killed in action at Lorgies, near La Bassée, 22 Oct. following. Buried in the garden of a house there.

BRIEN, JAMES, Private, No. 29, 10th (Service) Battn. The Highland Light Infantry, s. of James Brien, of Church Street, Kilcock, co. Kildare, late 2nd Royal Dublin Fusiliers (who served in the South African War): b. Kilcock

Pont-du-Hem Cemetery –
Neville Bridgland

King's School, Rochester.

The following account of the activities of King's School, Rochester, is taken from last week's "Sportsman." Since its publication the School has lost another of its gallant alumni at the Front. Lieut. Neville Bridgland (East Surrey Regiment), son of Mr. L. Bridgland, of The Cedars, Darnley-road, Gravesend, was killed in action last week. Both he and his brother, who is also in the East Surreys, were prominent members of the School elevens, both in cricket and football, and were well-known as cricketers after leaving school. Lieut. Neville Bridgland was at the School from January, 1906, to July, 1912, and had only passed his 20th birthday. His manly and modest bearing, and his kindly and straightforward character, won him the goodwill and respect of all who knew him, and his death has cast a gloom over the School.

"There is an old-time rivalry between King's, Canterbury, and King's, Rochester, as to which is the older foundation, and both can bring cumulative evidence to prove their point. Both supply a good number of Old Boys to the Services, the propinquity of Chatham, and the matches they play against the garrison and other regiments no doubt having a considerable influence on the Roffensians. There are many of them at the Front now, and E. O. Cruikshank, who was captain of cricket only three years ago, and played for the Young Surrey Amateurs in the same year, met a gallant death in action a few weeks ago. Nearly all those who have been prominent in school athletics during the last few years are serving their country now, and Northcott, a very promising boy bowler, was the youngest officer on the 'Fearless', in the Heligoland Bight scrap. As in all schools football has given place to 'O.T.C.' work to a large extent, and recruits came in so well this term that there are only five eligible boys who are not in the Corps, and one of these is lame. A bugle band has been started, as the Corps has to march two or three miles out for a really good ground, and was to make its first appearance last Thursday."

GR 31/10/14 [Andrew Marshall]

Thomas William Brinkley
Royal Navy - Chief Shipwright
Service No. 342780

Thomas was born at Dunwick in Suffolk on April 26th, 1878. He was the son of Walter, born in 1843 and Jane Ann Brinkley, born in 1839 of 204 Old Road West. They had six children – Eliza, born in 1870, Bessie and Mary Ann, born in 1873, Edith, born in 1876 and Rose, born in 1884 still living at the family home at the start of the Great War. Edith was a teacher with her two sisters being dressmakers.

Thomas followed his father into the Royal Navy and rose to the rank of Chief Shipwright. H.M.S. *Raglan* was an *Abercrombie* class monitor, the first class of big gun monitors to be commissioned for the Royal Navy during the First World War. When Lord Fisher returned to the Admiralty as First Sea Lord on October 30th, 1914 he and others foresaw the need for coast bombardment vessels to harass Germans on the Belgian coast, in order to frustrate their making naval use of it. All battleships were required either in the Grand Fleet or on patrol duties, so a new class of ship, with a shallow draught for inshore work and a requisite small number of big guns was specified.

By coincidence, in November, 1914 Charles M. Schwab, president of the Bethlehem Steel Company paid a call at the Admiralty to try to sell armaments. It transpired that he had eight 14-inch guns of the latest pattern which had been ordered by the Greeks for the battleship Salamis then building in Germany. Now that the British had commenced their blockade of Germany, the guns could not be delivered and Schwab, when asked what he had available, offered the now spare guns for sale.

Speed of design and construction was paramount. Contracts for the guns, their mountings and ammo were discussed in November. A meeting was held at the Admiralty with shipbuilders was held on the 11th to discuss the allocation of construction. A hull form was finalised a week later and in December the first of the monitors, designated M.3 was laid down at Harland and Wolff's yard at Govan, Glasgow. Lot No. 476, laid down as M.3, was given the name Robert E. Lee in February, 1915 - the names of the four ships of the class being American Civil War Generals to reflect the guns background. The monitor was launched in April, 1915, her guns having crossed the Atlantic in February. Due to U.S. Neutrality laws and the outcry the namings caused, the names were changed and Robert E. Lee, the last to be completed, had commissioned as M.3 under Captain Cecil Dacre Stavely Raikes. In June M.3 became Lord Raglan and later that month, became simply *Raglan.*

Equipped with Harland and Wolff engines, Raglan achieved the best trial speed of any of the monitors, whose anti-torpedo bulges and poor hull form slowed them considerably. They were promptly sent into action to the Dardanelles, *Raglan* being despatched in June in tow of the old protected cruiser *Diana.* She arrived in late July and went straight into action, supporting the Suvla Bay landings. Unfortunately, on one shoot, one of Raglan's guns fired prematurely and the shell exploded in the British lines, inflicting losses. Her gunnery officer at the Dardanelles was Lieutenant Arthur John Power, later Admiral of the Fleet. Continually supporting the troops with gunfire, in October *Raglan* embarked a R.N.A.S. Short 166 aircraft designed specifically for shipboard use, to help spot the shooting of the monitors firing on Gallipoli town. With the commencement of the evacuation from the peninsula, Raglan, due to a rather bad shooting record was kept in reserve with other ships at Imbros in case the withdrawal from Helles in the new year of 1916 should go awry. On January 7th the Turks launched a heavy attack on the British lines and all available ships were moved up to lend fire support. The evacuation of the position was eventually completed on the night of 8th/9th January with the loss of one man.

Raglan and her sister-ship Abercrombie were the only two of her class kept in the Eastern Mediterranean, and Raglan was employed regularly, bombarding Smyrna and the west coast of Turkey in February and March, 1916 before being sent to the Salonika front to bombard Bulgaria, setting afire crops. In May, Commander Henry Franklin Chevallier, Viscount Broome, the nephew of Earl Kitchener, took command, while the ship was undergoing a refit at Malta. She participated throughout the rest of 1916 and 1917 in lying off Imbros watching for Goeben and Breslau, and being engaged in supporting the Allied offensives in Salonika, at Stavros, and in Palestine, when she bombarded Deir Seneid in Gaza and Askalon.

Following her support off Palestine, on December 26th Raglan returned to Imbros, where with the small monitor M.28 she formed the Second Detached Squadron of the Ægean Squadron, again keeping watch for the German/Turkish ships from the Black Sea.

In the early morning of the January 20th, 1918, the battle cruiser Goeben and her consort cruiser Breslau sneaked out of the straits in the mist of the Sunday morning.

Goeben hit a mine, but the damage was not serious and the two ships proceeded towards Imbros to destroy whatever ships were anchored there. There ought to have been a Lord Nelson class battleship there but Agamemnon was stationed at Mudros 25 miles away and Lord Nelson was at Salonika with the Admiral. A little after half seven, Raglan sighted the two German ships and at 07:35 signalled "GOBLO" by wireless, the code that the breakout of the two ships had occurred. She then started exchanging fire with Breslau, each correcting their aim until they began to hit each other with medium calibre fire. However, the German's fourth salvo hit the spotting top and killed the Gunnery Officer and wounded Broome. The 14-inch gun was reloaded and ready to go into local control when a hit from Goeben pierced the tall armoured barbette and killed a number of the gun crew, having detonated the ready use charges. The First Lieutenant, who had been in the turret, came out, saw the carnage and unable to see the C.O. ordered the ship to be abandoned at anchor.

The Germans then closed to 4,000 yards and after several hits detonated the 12-pdr magazine, which sank her bow-first at 08:15 in 40 feet of water, leaving her foremast and spotting top jutting from the water. Unfortunately, 127 men from Raglan were killed while 93 survived; among those lost was Thomas.

The small monitor M.28 had also been sunk in the onslaught, but soon after the action Breslau hit a mine to the east of Imbros and went under. Goeben was also mined again and was forced to beach herself on the Turkish shore, where she effectively became a non-combatant.

Thomas is commemorated on the Chatham Naval Memorial.

Gravesend Cemetery –
Thomas Brinkley.
His father Walter Hallett
Brinley died on June 24th,
1922 and also served in the
Royal Navy.

Chatham Naval Memorial,
Panel 29 –
Tom Brinkley

Thomas Britten

Royal West Surrey, 2nd Battalion
Service No. G/3687 - Private

Thomas was born in Gravesend in 1892. His father, Henry was born in 1853 in Shoreditch and was a cabinet maker. He married Julia Murphy in 1877. She was born in 1860 in Islington. They had six children – Eliza, born in 1879, Gemma, born in 1880, Winifred, born in 1884, Alfred, born in 1887, Mary, born in 1889. His wife predeceased leaving Henry and Thomas boarding with Clara Ashdown, herself a widow, at 19 Brunswick Retreat.

Thomas was a labourer in a brewery prior to his enlistment in Gravesend on November 10th, 1914. He was 5 feet 3½ inches tall and weighed 108lbs. he was with the Royal West Kent Regiment, service number 4361 prior to being with the 2nd Battalion, Royal West Surrey. 2nd Battalion, were in Pretoria when war broke out in August 1914. They returned to England, landing on the 19th of September 1914. They joined 22nd Brigade, 7th Division who were concentrating in the New Forest, Hampshire. They landed at Zeebrugge on October 6th, 1914, to assist in the defence of Antwerp, they arrived too late to prevent the fall of the city and took up defensive positions at important bridges and junctions to aid in the retreat of the Belgian army. The 7th Division then became the first British Troops to entrench in front of Ypres, suffering extremely heavy losses in the The First Battle of Ypres. By February 1915 the Division had been reinforced to fighting strength and they were in action at The Battle of Neuve Chapelle, The Battle of Aubers, The Battle of Festubert, The second action of Givenchy and The Battle of Loos.

The Battle of Festubert – 15th – 25th May 1915 - was an attack by the British army in the Artois. The battle was the first British attempt at attrition. The attack was made by the First Army under Sir Douglas Haig against a German salient between Neuve Chapelle to the north and the village of Festubert to the south. The assault was planned along a 3-mile front and would initially be made, mainly, by Indian troops. This would be the first British army night attack of the war.

The battle was preceded by a 60 hour bombardment by 433 artillery pieces that fired about 100,000 shells. This bombardment failed to significantly damage the front line defences of the German Sixth Army, but the initial advance made some progress in good weather. The attack was renewed on May 16th but by May 19th the British 2nd and 7th divisions had to be withdrawn due to heavy losses. The Canadian Division, assisted by the 51st (Highland) Division, renewed the advance but this made little progress in the face of German artillery fire. The British forces then entrenched themselves at the new front line in conditions of heavy rain. The Germans now brought up more reserves to reinforce their lines. Festubert was subsequently captured. The offensive had resulted in a 3km advance at a cost of 16,648 casualties, among whom was Thomas. He has no known grave and is commemorated on the Le Touret Memorial. Winifred Bass, his married sister, claimed his medals.

The fiasco engendered a political crisis back in Britain when General Sir John French complained of the insufficient quantity and quality of the artillery shells. The Asquith government fell to be replaced by a coalition which included, for the first time, a minister of munitions, a post that would be occupied by David Lloyd George.

Percy Broad –
Gravesend Cemetery [above left and above] and Tom Britten –
Le Touret Memorial [below]

Arthur Percy Broad
Royal West Kent, 5th Battalion
Service No. 20079 - Private

Percy was born in September, 1876, the eldest child of Arthur and Sarah Broad. Arthur was born in 1849 and was a plumber and decorator. Sarah was four years his junior. There were four other children in the family – Bernard, born in 1880, Harold, born in 1882, Edith born in 1884 and Nellie born in 1886. The family lived at 2 South Street. There would be a double bereavement in the family as Harold, serving with the RWK 8th Battalion, would be killed in action some seven months later.

Percy was a house painter and plumber by profession.

He enlisted on September 21st, 1914 at Gravesend. The 5th Battalion was formed on April 1st, 1908 from the old 2nd Volunteer Battalion, The Queen's Own. On August 4th, 1914 it was mobilised with Head Quarters at Bromley. That September it divided into an "Overseas" and a "Home Service" battalion. The 1/5th formed at Bromley for those who volunteered for Overseas Service in 1914. In October it moved to India, remaining there throughout the war. The 2/5th formed at Eastry at the end of October from men of 5/RWK who did not volunteer for Overseas Service in 1914. In November it moved to Ascot and was attached to 2nd Kent Brigade in 2nd Home Counties Division (later re-styled 202nd Brigade, 67th Division) and became a Reserve Battalion. It remained in Kent, moving at various stages to Canterbury and Ashford.

BROAD.—On Feb. 5th, at the Military V.A.D. Hospital, Dartford, Arthur Percy Broad, Gravesend Co. N.R. Guards, aged 38 years.

GR 18/2/15 [Andrew Marshall]

However, Percy never made it to the 'front' - he died in Dartford Hospital of pneumonia contracted on February 5th, 1915. He is buried in Gravesend Cemetery.

Harold Broad
Royal West Kent, 8th Battalion
Service No. G/3422 - Private

Harold was the younger brother of Percy Broad and was a coach painter. Harold enlisted with the 8th Battalion. The 8th (Service) Battalion was raised at Maidstone on September 12th, 1914 as part of Kitchener's Third New Army and joined 72nd Brigade, 24th Division. They trained at Shoreham and moved to billets in Worthing for the winter in December, returning to Shoreham in April 1915. They moved to Blackdown in July for final training and proceeded to France on the 30th of August 1915, landing at Boulogne. The Division concentrated in the area between Etaples and St Pol on September 4th and a few days later marched across France into the reserve for the British assault at Loos, going into action on the 26th of September and suffering heavy losses. The Battalion was annihilated in this, its first action. The losses were the highest in a single action of any battalion of the Regiment in The Great War - 175 are known to have been killed; 286 other ranks were listed as wounded, 62 as wounded and "missing" and 182 "missing – of the missing 95 were later confirmed as prisoners of war. This from the compliment of 24 Officers and 800 ORs who went into battle.

Harold was one of the 87 "missing" who remained so; he has no known grave and is commemorated on the Loos Memorial.

Arthur Frank Brooman

Royal West Kent, 1st Battalion
Service No. G/968 - Private

Frank was born on October 15th, 1886 in Tonbridge. He was the son of Stephen Thomas and Rose, born in Aylesford, 1858, [Gammon] Brooman. Stephen was born in Tunbridge Wells in 1858 and was a cutler.

There were six children in the family – Eleanor, born in 1882, Arthur, Ethel, born in 1898, Albert, born in 1890, Dorothy, born in 1892 and Elsie, born in 1895. The family moved to Perry Street, Northfleet at the turn of the century from Tunbridge Wells.

Frank married Ada Elizabeth Jay on July 24th, 1912 in Stepney. The couple lived at 22 New Street. He was a baker by profession.

He enlisted at Gravesend on September 1st, 1914 being posted to the 6th Battalion. He was 5 foot 3½ inches tall and weighed 118lbs. He had a sallow complexion, had fair hair and brown eyes.

Army time keeping and keeping to a time schedule generally was not Frank's forte as between October 1914 and November 1915 he was on a charge six times; mostly for being late back when on a pass but also due to inattention when on the rifle range.

The sentences started with admonishment and finally stretched to nine days loss of pay.

He was posted to the 3rd Battalion on March 31st, 1915. On May 13th he joined the 1st Battalion, A Company.

On July 14th the Battle of Bazentin Ridge began with High Wood coming into the battlefield that evening. Despite the initial success over the following week the wood was re-occupied by the Germans. On the night of the 22nd/23rd the 4th Gordon Highlanders attacked the eastern corner of the wood as the 1st Royal West Kent attacked the south eastern part. There had been a preliminary bombardment but the defenders were mostly unaffected and the attackers made little ground with much losses, the Royal West Kents losing some 420 men including Frank who was killed in action on the 2nd in the initial attack.. He is buried at Caterpillar Valley Cemetery, Longueval.

His wife was granted a pension amounting to 12s. 6d. initially and subsequently of 10s.

MISSING.

BROOMAN.—Private A. Brooman, of 22, New-street, Gravesend, has been missing since July 22th, 1916. No. 968, R.K.A., "A" Company.

GR 16/9/16

Sidney Frederick Brown

Royal Garrison Artillery,
239th Siege Battery - 2nd Lieuten.

Sidney was born in Wimbledon in 1889. His parents were James and Ellen Brown 55 Norman Road, West Wimbledon. James was born in 1857 in Swanscombe and Ellen in Birling in 1860. He worked as an assistant in a grocery shop. There were just the two children in the family – Arthur, born in 1886 and Sidney. The family subsequently moved to Gravesend and lived at 32 Grange Road.

Sidney was a commercial clerk prior to enlisting.

Sidney was killed in action on May 15th, 1918. He is buried at Faubourg D'Amiens Cemetery, Arras.

GR 25/5/18

Killed In Action.

BROWN.—On May 15th, "Somewhere in France," Second-Lieut. Sidney Frederick Brown, Essex and Suffolk R.G.A., aged 29 years, dearly-loved younger son of Mrs. E. Brown, "Harford," Grange-road, Gravesend, and of the late Mr. James Brown, of Wimbledon.

Sidney Brown –
Faubourg D'Amiens Cemetery, Arras

Harold Broad – Loos memorial

FOR THE SALUTE
A WARRIOR'S HOME
GONE TO HEAR
THE GREAT "WELL DONE"

Arthur Brooman –
Caterpillar Valley Cemetery, Longueval.

174

William Edwin John Buck

Royal Naval Volunteer Reserve
Service No. Z/2280 – A/Seaman

William was born on August 9th, 1884 in Battersea. His father John from Shoreham was born in 1851 and his mother, Elizabeth Ann from Blackheath was two years his elder. John found employment on the dock as a labourer. The couple had eight children of whom only two survived. Prior to the Great War the family lived at 10 Crooked Lane. On John's death, Elizabeth and William moved to 3 Terrace Court.

William was an electrical labourer with the Borough. He was with the Royal Naval Volunteer Service on the outbreak of war and was posted to *HMS Russell*.

HMS Russell was laid down by Palmers at Jarrow in March 1899 and launched in February 1902. She arrived at Sheerness later the same month and went to Chatham Dock-yard for steam and gun-mounting trials.

When World War I began in August 1914, plans originally called for *Russell* to go in the 6th Battle Squadron and serve in the Channel Fleet, where the squadron was to patrol the English Channel and cover the movement of the British Expeditionary Force to France.

However, plans also existed for the 6th Battle Squadron to be assigned to the Grand Fleet, and, when the war began, the Commander-in-Chief, Grand Fleet, Admiral Sir John Jellicoe, requested that *Russell* and her four surviving sister ships of the *Duncan* class be assigned to the 3rd Battle Squadron in the Grand Fleet for patrol duties to make up for the Grand Fleet's shortage of cruisers.

Russell and her four *Duncan*-class sisters, as well as the battleships of the *King Edward VII* class, temporarily were transferred to the Channel Fleet in November 1914.

On November 6th, 1915, a division of the 3rd Battle Squadron consisting of battleships *Hibernia* (the flagship) and *Russell* was sent to reinforce the British Dardanelles Squadron in the Dardanelles Campaign.

Russell took up her duties at the Dardanelles in December 1915, based at Mudros with *Hibernia* and held back in support. Her only action in the campaign was her participation in the evacuation of Cape Helles from January 7th to the 9th, 1916, and she was the last battleship of the British Dardanelles Squadron to leave the area. She relieved *Hibernia* as Divisional Flagship, Rear Admiral, in January 1916.

After the conclusion of the Dardanelles campaign, *Russell* stayed on in the eastern Mediterranean.

Russell was steaming off Malta early on the morning of April 27th, 1916 when she struck two sea mines that had been laid by the German submarine *U-73*. A fire broke out in the aft part of the ship and the order to abandon ship was passed. After an explosion near the after 12-inch turret, she took on a dangerous list. However, she sank slowly, allowing most of her crew to escape. A total of 27 officers and 98 ratings were lost. John Cunningham served aboard her at the time and survived her sinking; he would one day become First Sea Lord. William was killed in action on April 27th, 1916. He has no known grave and is commemorated on the Chatham Naval Memorial.

Mined in the Mediterranean.

The above is a photograph of Able Seaman William Edwin John Buck, R.N.V.R., who was on H.M.S. Russell when she was mined in the Mediterranean on the 27th April. The only son of Mrs. Buck, 3, Terrace-place, he joined the R.N.V.R. in June last year. Previous to that he was for 11 years with the Corporation of Gravesend, and would have been 32 years of age on August 9th next. Great sympathy is felt for his widowed mother, who has thus given her only son for King and country.

GR 1/7/16 [Andrew Marshall]

Ernest John Buckmaster
Royal West Kent, 11th Battalion
Service No. G/7499 - Private

Ernest was born in Poplar in 1893. His father, Thomas, a blacksmith, died when Ernest was still in his teens. His mother Martha, born in 1866 married George Sheppard, born in 1869 in 1900. He was a ship's plumber. There were two surviving children from her second marriage – Florrie, born in 1908 and Leonard, born in 1909. There were four children from her first marriage – Veronica, born in 1887,

Thomas, born in 1889, Eveline, born in 1891 and Ernest. The family lived at 4 Park Avenue.

Ernest followed in his step father's footsteps as a ship's plumber before enlisting.

He was with the 11th (Lewisham) (Service) Battalion ("*Corfe's Irregulars*") which was raised in early May 1915 by the Mayor and a local committee. The battalion trained at Catford and in July 1915 was assigned to 118th Brigade in 39th Division; in October it was transferred to 122nd Brigade in 41st Division. The battalion moved to Aldershot in January 1916. On May 3rd, 1916 it landed in France.

The battalion suffered heavy casualties in its first action – of 610 in action 343 became casualties – at Flers on September 15th. It was then moved to the Ypres salient where it was in action on the first day of Third Ypres on June 7th, 1917.

At Messines the objectives gained but with losses of 7 Officers and 124 other ranks. Ernest was killed in action on July 31st.

He has no known grave and is commemorated on the Menin Gate.

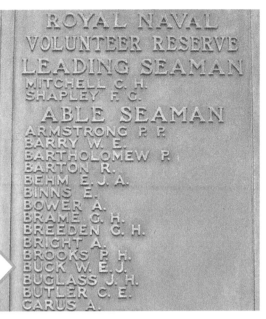

Chatham Naval Memorial,
Panel 20 – William Buck

Ernest Buckmaster – Menin Gate

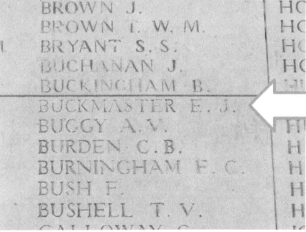

BUCKMASTER. — Machine-Gunner E. J. Buckmaster, R.W.K. Regt., aged 24 years, beloved son of Mrs. Sheppard and late Mr. Buckmaster; missing since July 31st, 1917; now officially reported killed.

GR 31/8/18 [Andrew Marshall]

Machine-Gunner E. J. Buckmaster (whose portrait appears above) is now presumed to be dead by the War Office. He was a son of the late Mr. T. Buckmaster and Mrs. Sheppard, 4, Park - avenue, Gravesend. Machine-Gunner Buckmaster, of the R.W.K. Regt., had been reported missing since July 31st, 1917, and information has just been received from the War Office to the effect that he must be presumed killed on or about that date in France. The place where he is presumed to have fallen is Hollibeke. Before the war he was employed by a shipping line at Tilbury Dock as a plumber. Joining up in February, 1916, he was sent to France in November of the same year. He returned home in February, 1917, owing to a severe illness, but having recovered was sent out again in June. Deceased, a single young man well-known and respected, was 24 years of age.

George Bull

Northumberland Fusiliers, 1st Bn
Service No. 9911 - Private

George was born in 1886 in Gravesend to Frederick and Elizabeth Bull of 54 Peppercroft Street. Frederick was born in 1851 in Gravesend. He was a bricklayer by profession. Elizabeth was born in 1849 and was also born in Gravesend.

George was a labourer on the docks prior to enlisting with the Northumberland Fusiliers in early 1915.

He died on September 27th, 1915 and is buried in St Andrew's and Jesmond Cemetery, Newcastle-upon-Tyne.

Thomas John Burles

R.G.A., 21st Siege Battery
2nd Lieutenant

Thomas was born in Gravesend in 1884. His father Thomas John was born in 1853 in Gravesend. He was a labourer on the docks. His mother Lydia was born 1858 and came from Chalk. They had eight children in all – Thomas, Arthur, born in 1885, Lydia, born in 1887, Annie, born in 1889, William, born in 1891, John, born in 1893, George, born in 1895 and Lily, born in 1899. The family lived at 28 Augustine Road.

Thomas was a grocer's assistant by profession. He subsequently moved to Plymouth by 1901. He and his wife Beatrice lived at 26 Adelaide Street, Stonehouse.

Thomas enlisted with the Royal Garrison Artillery; by 1911 he was an acting bombardier with RGA at Stamford Fort, Plymouth and was subsequently posted to 21st Siege Battery. The Battery proceeded to France in May 1915.

The Siege Batteries were deployed behind the front line, tasked with destroying enemy artillery, supply routes, railways and stores. The batteries were equipped with heavy Howitzer guns firing large calibre 4, 6, 8 or 9.2 inch shells in a high trajectory.

2nd Lieutenant Thomas Burles was killed in action on June 24th, 1917. He is buried in Ferme-Olivier Cemetery, some 7 km north west of Ypres.

We regret to announce the death of Lieut. T. J. Burles, who was killed in action on 24th June. One of the old Army, his career has been one of unchecked promotion, he being advanced to the rank of corporal (from that of bombardier) in August, 1914. After his recovery from wounds received in October he returned to France in 1915, and was promoted to sergeant in September. The June following he was sent to England to instruct a battery, was promoted to battery quartermaster-sergeant, and later (July) to battery sergeant-major (W.O., Class II.). Returning to France in November, 1916, he was brought into prominent notice by his services on the field of battle, for which services he received his lieutenancy. Mr. and Mrs. Burles, Augustine-road, Gravesend, have every reason to be proud of this their eldest son who, after fighting with the old Army and helping to train the new, has now laid down his life in the cause of righteousness and liberty.

GR 21/7/17 [Andrew Marshall]

Killed in Action.

BURLES.—Killed in action on June 24th, Lieut. T. J. Burles, the dearly beloved son of Mr. and Mrs. T. J. Burles, 28, Augustine-road, Gravesend.

Tom Burles – Ferme-Olivier Cemetery;

MAY HIS REWARD BE
AS GREAT AS HIS SACRIFICE
FROM HIS LOVING
BEAT

Menin Gate –
William Burles

The cemetery was used continuously between June 9th, 1915 and August 5th, 1917, with the 62nd, 16th, 9th, 11th, 129th and 130th Field Ambulances successively having dressing stations close by. Throughout this period, the village was just within range of the German artillery and a collective grave in Plot 2, Row E, contains the remains of 37 men of the 3rd Battalion, Monmouthshire Regiment killed on parade on December 29th, 1915 by a single shell fired from a naval gun in Houthulst Forest.

The cemetery contains 408 Commonwealth burials.

William Burles
Royal Sussex Regiment, 11th Bn.
Service No. TF/241467 - Private

William was born in Gravesend in 1898. His father Thomas was born in Essex in 1877. He was a general labourer. His mother Emma was born in 1878 and was from Gravesend. They married in 1897 and had seven children in all – Willie, Percy, born in 1900, Lizzie, born in 1903, Arthur, born in 1905, Nellie, born in 1906, Gracey, born in 1908 and Sidney, born in 1910. The family lived at 71 Clarence Street.

William joined the 11th Battalion and training took place at Cooden Camp, near Bexhill, from September 1914 until July 1915. At this stage the War Office took over direct control of the battalion and it moved to Detling Camp, near Maidstone in Kent. On 29th September 1915 the battalion moved to North Camp, Aldershot. In October it became part of 116th Brigade, 39th Division. This division had been formed at Winchester in August 1915, but concentrated at Witley via Aldershot in October/November 1915. From this

date until March 1916, the battalion stayed at Witley Camp.

It crossed to France via Southampton on March 5th/6th, 1916, landing at Le Havre. It served on the Western Front with 116th Brigade, 39th Division until the Spring of 1918.

William was killed in action on September 27th, 1917. He has no known grave and is commemorated on the Thiepval Monument.

After only serving a month in France, Private William Burles, Sussex Royal Regiment, son of Mr. and Mrs. Burles, 71, Clarence-street, was killed in action on September 27th, a year after his joining the Colours. Prior to then he had been in the employ of Messrs. W. T. Henley and Co. for four years. Deceased was 19 years of age. The official information of his death, with the letter of condolence from the King, were received on October 19th.

GR 3/11/17 [Andrew Marshall]

Killed in Action.

BURLES.—On Sept. 27th, 1917, William eldest son of Mr. and Mrs. Burles, of 71 Clarence-street, killed in action, aged 19 years.

Alexander Charles Burrill
Royal Naval Reserve –

Leading Deck Hand

Service No. 4339SD

Alexander was born on February 25th, 1895 in Chatham. His parents were Charles and Sarah Burrill of 32 Havelock Road. Charles was born in 1867 in Lambeth. He enlisted with the Royal Marines in 1884 but by 1910 he had left the service and was in receipt of an Army pension. By this time he was with H.M. Customs. He would re-enlist for service in the Great War, being a Lieutenant in the Service Corps. Sarah was born in 1882 and came from Sittingbourne. They married in 1882 and had something of a nomadic life together.

They had six children in all including Alexander, born in Chatham, Bessie, born in 1899 in Darlington, Glencoe, born in 1900 in Leeds, Charles, born in 1905 in Carlyle and Eleanor, born in 1906 in Rochester.

Alexander served on *H.M.S. Supernal*. Alexander accidently drowned on July 27th, 1917. He has no known grave and is commemorated on the Chatham Naval Memorial.

> **On Active Service.**
> BURRILL. — Alex Burrill, Gunner, R.N. Reserve, Trawler Section; who fell overboard and was drowned from H.M. Drifter "———" at sea, July 27th, aged 22 years, eldest son of Sergt. C. W. Burrill, R.M.L.I., of 32, Havelock-rd., Gravesend.

GR 4/8/17 [Andrew Marshall]

John Thomas Burville
The King's Liverpool Regiment

Service No. 6779

John was born in 1885 in Steyning, Sussex. He was the youngest son of John and Amelia Burville of 13 Eustace Street, Brighton. John was a general labourer. There were three children in the family – Kate, born in 1881, Charles, born in 1884 and John. John enlisted in the Liverpool Regiment on March 12th, 1900 in London. His attestation papers gives his address as unknown and his age - 13 year 6 months. He was 4 foot 7¼ inches tall and weighed a mere 69 pounds but was considered 'fit' for the army. He had brown hair, blue eyes and was of fresh complexion.

Two days later on the 14th, he joined the regiment in Dublin. He engaged for twelve years which he duly completed and was discharged in March, 1912.

However he found the re-adjustment to civilian life difficult as having found employment as an attendant at the London County Asylum in Bexley he re-enlisted with the Regiment in September, 1912 for a further four years. By now he was 5 foot 7 inches tall with brown hair and fresh complexion. Army life had affected him in several ways to include a colour change of his eyes – now brown. He had acquired a tattoo of Queen Victoria on his chest and a tattoo of a serpent on a tree on his left forearm.

He married Edith Banks on April 24th, 1915 and the couple lived at 18 Coombe Road. They had two children – Sidney, born in June 1916 and Vera born in September the following year.

On November 22nd, 1914 he was wounded and lost the hearing in his right ear being taken to 6th Field Ambulance initially before transferring to Rouen and back to England. He was back to the Front in 1917 and was killed in action on January 30th, 1918.

He is buried in Metz-en-Couture Communal Extension Cemetery. Metz-en-Couture is a village situated in the extreme south-eastern corner of the Department of the Pas-de-Calais.

The British Extension is next to the Communal Cemetery. The village was

Chatham Naval Memorial, Panel 26 –
Alexander Burrill

Metz-en-Couture Communal Extension
Cemetery –
John Burville

The Military Cemetery is adjacent to the [modern]
Communal Cemetery. Behind both is the pre Great War
Communal Cemetery. Not in use since 1914 it reflects the
ravages of war – the original Community being killed or
dispersed, never to return. [Courtesy of Jean Horent.]

captured by the 10th and 11th King's Royal Rifle Corps in April 1917, evacuated in late March 1918, and retaken by the 1st Otago Regiment the following September.

Felix George Bush
Mercantile Marine, Storekeeper

Felix was born on May 30th, 1887. His father John George Lewin Bush died before the turn of the century leaving his wife Mary Elizabeth nee Finch to bring up their five children. Felix was the eldest followed by Arthur, born in 1889, Harold, born in 1891, Elizabeth, born in 1893 and Ernest, born in 1895. All but Harold who was born in Dartford were born in Milton.

Mary was a dressmaker. She and her five children lived with her mother Harriet at 13 Christ Church Road, Milton. Harriet was a caretaker in the local church. They were boarders in the property with the landlady Mary Grubb and her daughter Gertrude also residing there. Mary was born in 1841 and came from Suffolk; Gertrude was born in Wadhurst, Sussex in 1884 and was employed as a shop assistant.

Felix was a store keeper on *H.M.S. Ulysses.* He died from pneumonia on December 11th, 1916 off Sierra Leone and was buried at sea.

> **DEATHS.**
> BUSH.—On Dec. 11th, 1916, on H.M.S. "Ulysses," of pneumonia, Felix George Bush, aged 29 years; buried at Sierra Leone:—[Australian papers copy.]

GR 21/1/17 [Andrew Marshall]

Daniel George Butcher
Royal Fusiliers, City of London
Service No. G/61527 - Private

Daniel was born in 1886 in Reigate. His father was born in 1855 in Charlwood, Surrey. He was a baker by profession in addition to running his own grocery shop. His mother Mary was born in 1846 in Benhall, Suffolk. Daniel was married to Minnie Heaver in Gravesend in 1911. They had two daughters and a son – Dorothy, born in 1915, Irene, born in 1918 and Daniel George, born in 1913.

Daniel was a career soldier having joined the Royal West Kent Regiment, Service No. G/16608

Daniel was with the 4th Battalion when he was killed in action on August 31st, 1918. He is buried at H.A.C. CWGC Cemetery at Ecoust-St. Mein.

Ecoust-St.Mein is a village between Arras, Cambrai and Bapaume. The German positions from Doignies to Henin-sur-Cojeul, including the village of Ecoust, were captured on April 2nd, 1917, by the 4th Australian and 7th Divisions. The cemetery was begun by the 7th Division after the battle, when 27 of the 2nd H.A.C., who fell (with one exception) on March 31st or April 1st, were buried. The 120 graves were the original H.A.C. Cemetery; but after the Armistice graves were added from the battlefields of Bullecourt and Ecoust and from a number of smaller burial grounds.

Henry Robert Byrne
Royal West Kent - 8th Battalion
Service No. S/752 - Col. Sgt.

Henry was born in 1867 in Windsor. He and wife Catherine, born in 1878, lived at Ivy Villa, Parrock Avenue. They had two children, Margaret who was born in 1901 and Henry who was two years younger. Henry was a self-employed carpenter and builder at the outbreak of war; prior to that he had been a career soldier, serving in both the Royal Marines and the Royal West Kent Regiment, 4th and 13th Battalions.

Dan Butcher –
Ecoust-St. Mein Cemetery.
He lies in a row of Royal Fusiliers,
all bearing the same date –
August 31st, 1918 – a stark
reminder of the wholescale
decimation of units.

HMAT Ulysses / A38 was built by Workman Clark, Belfast for the China Mutual SN Company, London, a subsidiary of the Blue Funnel Line, in 1913. Requisitioned in late 1914 as a transport ship it made seven voyages from Australia during the war; five carrying Medical Officers and twice carrying troops. The third voyage left Port Melbourne on October 25th, 1916 with Medical Officers. It was on this voyage that Felix Bush died.
Having survived one war *HMS Ulyssses* did not survive a second; on April 11th, 1942 *HMS Ulysses* was sunk by U-160 en-route from Liverpool to Sydney.

The Royal Navy did not fight any other ships after 1850 (until 1914) and became interested in landings by Naval Brigades. In these Naval Brigades, the function of the Royal Marines was to land first and act as skirmishers ahead of the sailor Infantry and Artillery. This skirmishing was the traditional function of Light Infantry. For most of their history, Marines had been organised as fusiliers. It was not until 1923 that the separate Artillery and Light Infantry forces were formally amalgamated into the *Corps of Royal Marines.*

The Royal Marines played a prominent role in the Boxer Rebellion in China (1900). For the first part of the 20th Century, the Royal Marines' role was the traditional one of providing shipboard Infantry for security, boarding parties and small-scale landings. The Marines' other traditional position on a Royal Navy ship was manning 'X' and 'Y' (the aftermost) gun turrets.

Henry was already 46 years old when he re-enlisted at Maidstone on September 14th, 1914. He was promoted Sergeant on enlisting and subsequently on January 6th the following year Colour Sergeant. He was 5 feet 10½ inches tall and weighed 149lbs. he had hazel coloured eyes and dark brown hair and was deemed physically fit for service.

The 8th (Service) Battalion, The Royal West Kent Regiment was raised at Maidstone on September 12th, 1914 as part of Kitchener's Third New Army and joined 72nd Brigade, 24th Division. They trained at Shoreham and moved to billets in Worthing for the winter in December, returning to Shoreham in April 1915. They moved to Blackdown in July for final training and proceeded to France on August 30th, 1915, landing at Boulogne. But Henry never made it to France as he died of brain cancer on January 10th, 1915

He is buried in Gravesend.

In Loving
MemoryOf
My Dear Husband
HENRY ROBERT BYRNE
(Late Col-Sergt. R.W.Kent Regt)
Died 10th Jan 1915
Age 46 Years.

Also In Beloved Memory of
CATHERINE FLORENCE BYRNE
Wife of the Above, Who Passed Away
12th Dec. 1949, Age 69 Years

Military Funeral.

THE LATE SERGEANT-MAJOR H. R. BYRNE.

IMPRESSIVE SERVICE AT GRAVESEND.

To every soldier that dies in this war against the Teuton the honour is not extended to meet this end in, perhaps, that more picturesque and romantic setting of action on the battlefield. But, nevertheless, there have been—and there will be still more —many that have donned the khaki who, though not in the trenches, have answered the last call in no less a glorious manner and for no less a glorious purpose than those who have died in action. Many there are—indeed, far too many have been those who have worn the uniform before—who have been unable to stand, like their younger and more strongly constituted comrades, and have broken down under the rigour and hardships that have attended the improvised camps for training that necessarily had to suffice for the first few months of hostilities.

In that number of patriotic men who had answered yet again the call of the trumpet, but who, in doing their duty in training those younger men quickly for the fighting forces, have succumbed to the intense hardships of the conditions prevailing, was a respected and popular resident of the town, Sergeant-Major Henry Robert Byrne, whose home was at Ivy Villa, Parrock-avenue.

MANY YEARS IN THE ARMY.

The deceased gentleman, who was only 46 years of age, had served practically the whole of his life in His Majesty's Forces. He was in the Royal Marines for 23 years, and after that he was transferred to the Volunteers. It was then, about twelve years ago, that he took up residence in the borough. His duties were primarily as drill instructor at the Cliffe and Chatham Stations, and in this connection he attained the rank of Colour-Sergeant Instructor. About five years ago, however, he retired, and took up business on the Kiosk, on the Promenade and in Harmer-street. In this capacity he became even better known and more popular, and he established a wide circle of friends.

At the outbreak of war, sacrificing all business considerations, he re-enlisted, and was promoted to the rank of Company Sergeant-Major in the 8th Battalion of the Royal West Kent Regiment, stationed at Shoreham. For quite a long period, Sergeant-Major Byrne stood the rigour of the almost unprecedented bad climatic conditions under soaked canvas tents and with bare covering at night-time. Day after day did he carry on his duties on the rain-sodden parade grounds and never did he complain. Never did the men complain; it was accepted as one of the inevitabilities of the war. But there came a time when "Sergeant-Major," as he was popularly known amongst the troops, did not take his place, and to the regret of all, he was taken to Brighton Hospital. For a month he laid there, and then he came home on sick leave. To all appearances he progressed favourably and grew stronger. On Sunday morning, the 10th inst., he went for quite a long walk. When he returned home in the early part of the afternoon he merely remarked to his wife that he had "overdone it." Dr. Dismorr was sent for, but by five o'clock the Sergeant-Major had passed away.

MILITARY HONOURS.

With full military honours, the deceased gentleman was laid to rest in Gravesend Cemetery on Saturday afternoon. The coffin, covered by the Union Jack, was conveyed upon a gun-carriage, and a firing party of the Middlesex Regiment followed immediately behind. A short but impressive service was conducted at the graveside by the Rev. G. W. Mennie, M.A., military chaplain; three volleys rang out, and as the coffin was lowered into the grave the "Last Post" was sounded, a fitting conclusion to the career of one who had devoted his life to the service of his country.

The chief mourners were: Mrs. Byrne (widow), Mr. and Mrs. Byrne (father and mother-in-law of the deceased), Miss Byrne (sister-in-law), Mr. John Byrne (brother-in-law), Colour-Sergeant Nicholson and Colour-Sergeant Ackland (fellow N.C.O.'s of the deceased).

By request there were only a few floral tributes sent. Among them were a wreath "from his loving wife. 'In the midst of life we are in death'"; from Mr. and Mrs. Byrne; a wreath "to our dear daddy, from his loving son and daughter"; from Mr. and Mrs. Norris; and from the Sergeants of the 8th Battalion Royal West Kents.

Mr. Allen carried out the funeral arrangements.

The Gravesend Town Band, in the absence

A B C D E

Left panel:

CABLE
CABLE W. (M.C.)

CARLAN J.
BAXTER G.T.
CHAMBERS R.
CHAPMAN G.W.
MARSHALL J.
CHILDS C.E.
CHILDS T.
CHRISTIAN A.R. (H.M.)
CHURCH T.
CLARKE E.W.P.
CLARKE H.V.
CLARKE S.J.
CLARKE W.R.
CLIFFORD S.
COLEQUENE J.W.
COLE A.
COLE G.
COLLEDGE H.C.
COLVILLE S.
COLVER-HENDERSON T.R. (H.M.)
CONNELLY J.V.R.

Right panel:

CONNOLLY T.
CONSTANT G.P.
COPPIN A.R.
COPPINS E.J.
CORDEN T.
COFFINS W.J.
CORRY
CORR
COSGROVE F.
COSGROVE L.G.
CRACKNELL W.R.
CALVERT J.V.
CREAMER A.H.
CREED A.V.
CREED C.R.
CRITTENDEN H.G.
CROCKETT A.J.
CRUTHALL G.
CROWHURST W.J.

ONLY THOSE WHO HAVE LOST
ARE ABLE TO TELL
HOW GREAT IS OUR LOSS
FOR HIM WE LOVED SO WELL

Albert Creed
Bethune Communal Cemeter

Bernard Francis Cadic
Royal Garrison Artillery
Service No. 4430 - Captain

Bernard was born in 1894, the eldest son of Lieutenant Colonel Ludvic 'Louis' Stephen and Ellen Cadic of Manor House, Chalk. Ludovic was born in Guernsey in 1868. He served with the Royal Engineers and after an army career settled to civilian life, no doubt using the expertise gained in the army, as a manager in road contracting. Ellen hailed from Boston, Lincolnshire and was a year older than her husband. The couple married in 1894 and had four children – Bernard, Lawrence, born in 1897, Agnes, born in 1905 and Oswald, born in 1910. Oswald, born on April 7th, would become an early aviation flyer – being awarded his Royal Aeronautical Club aviators' certificate on June 24th, 1934. He took his test in a Gipsy 1 at the Gravesend School of Flying.

He would be tragically killed on May 1st, 1936. He is buried in the family grave in Gravesend Cemetery.

Bernard was educated at St Lawrence College, Ampleforth and University College, London. In 1911 he enlisted in the Kent (Gravesend) Territorial Royal Garrison Artillery being promoted Captain in 1915.

After being wounded he returned to England for treatment. He died in hospital on August 20th, 1916 and is buried in Gravesend Cemetery. His death was as a result of a fall; at the time he was suffering from depression the consequence of his wounds, time at the front and influenza.

Terrible Fall at Fort Pitt.
YOUNG OFFICER'S SAD DEATH.
DEPRESSION AFTER INFLUENZA, TRENCH FEVER, AND WOUNDS.

GR 26/8/16 [Andrew Marsall]

The Late Captain B. F. Cadic.

TRAGIC DEATH AT CHATHAM.

The sympathy of a very wide circle of friends will be extended to Captain and Mrs. L. C. M. Cadic, of Manor House, Chalk, near Gravesend, in the great blow they have sustained by the death of their eldest son, Captain Bernard Francis Cadic, under tragic circumstances.

The deceased officer, who had served with the Royal Garrison Artillery in France for several months, was wounded and recently sent to Chatham Military Hospital. As a result of his injuries, his mind was a little deranged, and while taking exercise on Sunday evening he fell over a parapet from a height of 45ft. When picked up he was found to be terribly injured.

Educated at St. Lawrence College, Ampleforth, Captain Cadic showed great ability as a member of the O.T.C. Leaving College in 1912 he was gazetted to the Kent Royal Garrison Artillery. On the outbreak of hostilities he was placed on the Thames Defences, where he remained until October, 1915. He was then posted as Captain to the 62nd Siege Battery of the R.G.A., with which he fought in Flanders.

His father, Captain L. C. M. Cadic, R.E., late consular agent for the Republic of France at Gravesend, is commanding a company of Royal Engineers in France. Only a short time ago the other son, Lieut. William L. Cadic, was badly wounded.

When the last rites were performed at the Gravesend Cemetery yesterday (Thursday), crowds of people gathered to pay their final tribute, and full military honours were accorded. The first part of the service was performed at St. John's Roman Catholic Church, the Rev. Father Kilmartin officiating, assisted by Father Bourdelot. The coffin was borne in and out of the Church and to the graveside by Major Passby, Major Buckle, Captain Porter, Lieut. Ellison, Lieut. Rigden and Lieut. Fooks. The coffin was covered with the Union Jack and bore deceased's cap and sword. Immediately behind it came the bereaved father. Other mourners were Mrs. Cadic, Lieut. Wm. L. Cadic, Master and Miss Cadic, Col. Passby and Colonel Gadd were also present. The service at the grave-

Lieut. L. W. L. Cadic (Gravesend),
2nd Battalion Essex Regiment,
WHO HAS WON MILITARY CROSS

For conspicuous bravery in action, Lieut. Lawrence William L. Cadic has won the Military Cross. When his Commanding Officer was wounded, he continued to organise the men in the second line of the enemy's trench under heavy shell and machine gun fire. His fine example, the official report states, did much to steady the men under trying circumstances.

Lieut. Cadic is the eldest surviving son of Captain L. S. Cadic, R.E., and of Mrs. L. Cadic, Manor House, Chalk, Gravesend. He is only 19 years of age. He was educated at King's School, Rochester, where he was a member of the O.T.C. When 17 he entered Sandhurst and on December 23rd, 1914, was gazetted to the Essex Regiment. Early in March, 1915, he joined the 2nd Battalion Essex Regiment at the Front and soon afterwards took part in the second battle of Ypres. He was seriously wounded in three places on July 1st in the first fighting of the Battle of the Somme. During the last six months, he was Acting Adjutant to his Battalion, truly a wonderful record for a young Britisher. "Youth will be served."

KM 30/9/16 [Andrew Marshall]

KM 26/8/16 [Andrew Marshall]

Lawrence William Cadic, M.C.
Essex Regiment, 2nd Battalion
Captain

Lawrence was the younger brother of Bernard, being born on December 20th, 1896. He was educated at the King's School, Rochester and at Sandhurst, passing out in 1914. He was commissioned into the Essex Regiment in December, 1914. He joined the 2nd Battalion at the Front in March, 1915. He fought through 2nd Ypres.

He was wounded three times and won the Military Cross for conspicuous gallantry in action on the opening day, July 1st, of the Battle of the Somme. The M.C. was gazetted on September 23rd that year; when his C.O. was wounded, he continued to reorganise his men in the second line of the enemy trench under heavy shell and machine gun fire. His fine example did much to steady his men under trying circumstances. In this action he

received three wounds himself. [London Gazette, September 22nd, 1916.

> **CAPT. L. W. CADIC, M.C.**
>
> With much regret we last week reported that Capt. Laurence W. Cadic, Essex Regt., eldest son of Capt. L. S. Cadic, R.N., had fallen mortally wounded during an engagement with the enemy at Poelcappel. At the same time we reviewed his military experience, and now reproduce his photograph, which we were unable to obtain in time for our last issue. Meanwhile, we may add that the bereaved parents have received many expressions of sympathy.

GR 27/10/17 [Andrew Marsall]

He died of wounds on October 9th, 1917 and is buried in Cement House Cemetery.

> **CAPT. L. W. CADIC, M.C.**
>
> It is with much regret we learn that Capt. Laurence William Cadic, Essex Regiment, eldest son of Capt. L. S. Cadic, R.N., fell mortally wounded on the 9th October, while gallantly leading his company into action at Poelcappel. Much sympathy is felt for the bereaved parents, who are well-known in Gravesend and district. The deceased young officer was born in December, 1895. Educated at King's School, Rochester, he passed into the Military Academy, Sandhurst in September, 1914, from where he was gazetted on his eighteenth birthday to the Essex Regt., proceeding to France early in March, 1915, and soon afterwards took part in the second Battle of Ypres. He was seriously wounded in three places on July 1st in the first fighting of the Battle of the Somme, being mentioned in despatches for conspicuous gallantry in action and awarded the Military Cross, the official report stating: — "When his Commanding Officer was wounded he continued to re-organise the men in the second line of the enemy trenches under heavy shell and machine-gun fire, his fine example doing much to steady the men under trying circumstances." Capt. Cadic was a universal favourite with his brother officers and men, for those that came in contact with him were inspired by his splendid work and keenness. He was buried in the battlefield close to where he fell and the spot is now within our lines. The gallant officer was only 20 years of age. R.I.P.

> CADIC.—On October 9th, while gallantly leading his Company into action, Capt. Laurence William Cadic, M.C., Essex Regiment, second son of Mr. and Mrs. L. Cadic, Manor House, Chalk, Gravesend, aged 20.

GR 20/10/17 [Andrew Marsall]

GR 20/10/17 [Andrew Marsall]

Lawrence Cadic –
Cement House Cemetery, Ypres

Gravesend Cemetery – the Cadic family grave and headstone; the military tradition continued with Lieutenant-Colonel Edward Cadic, R.A., M.B.E., T.D., who died in December, 1995.

Lawrences Auctioneers of Crewkerne
Two Day Sale of Militaria, Coins, Medals, Collectors and Sporting, May 10 & 11th, 2012.

FAMILY MEDALS/DEATH PLAQUES/SCROLLS etc A 1914/15 Trio to Lt-Capt (later Lt Col) L S Cadic Royal Engineers with Oak Leaf also his MID certificates.(2) Lt Colonel Cadic lived at the Manor House , Chalk, Gravesend in Kent. Both dated 16th March 1919. The British War Medal, Death Plaque and Scroll awarded to Lt Bernard Francis Cadic of the Kent Royal Garrison Artillery. After being wounded in 1916 he returned to England from F&F for treatment but died in hospital soon thereafter. He is buried at Chalke, the eldest son of the family he was educated at St Lawrence College, Ampleforth, University College London. Original plaque and scroll/Kings Letter envelopes are included addressed to L S Cadic Esq, also his Commission Scroll dated 1911 Kent RGA. Died 20/8/1916. The Death Plaque, Scroll and Kings letter to Captain Lawrence William Ludovic Cadic Military Cross of the Essex Regt. Commissioned into the Essex Regt in December 1914 he was just 19 years old when he was awarded the Military Cross for the 1st July 1916 Battle of the Somme action. Educated at Kings School , Rochester he was the second son of Lt Colonel and Mrs L Cadic, joining the 2nd Battalion Essex Regt at the front in March 1915. His MC was gazetted 23 Sept 1916. For Conspicuous Gallantry in Action. When his CO was wounded, he continued to reorganise the men in the second line of the enemies trench under heavy shell and machine-gun fire. His fine example did much to steady the men under trying circumstances. In this action he received three wounds himself, he had already fought through the second Battle of Ypres. He succumbed to further wounds in F & F on the 10/10/1917. His birth certificate slip for 20/12/1896, original copy of the Daily Telegraph dated 23/09/1916 MC awards section etc. Original photographs of his father and himself also his older brother Bernard , newspaper cuttings etc are with this lot. Various R Artillery badges and buttons etc.

Estimation:

£500 - £700

James Callan
R.N. Vol. Res. - Able Seaman
Service No. London Z/2423

James was born on October 19th, 1898 the son of William and Eliza Callan of 4 Constitution Hill, Milton. William was born in 1863 in Liverpool. He was a stoker with the Waterworks before becoming a fireman. Eliza was born in 1876 in Hastings. The couple married in 1896. They had two sons – William, born in 1896 and James.

James was a nursery man and enlisted on June 15th, 1915 with the Royal Naval Reserve. He held the rank of able seaman. He was drafted for the M.E.F. on December 5th, 1915 and joined the Hawke Battalion at Mudros on February 7th, 1916.

The Naval Division was formed in August 1914. The Admiralty realized that with the mobilization they would have between 20-80,000 men of the Reserve, for whom there would not be room on any ship of war. This surplus would be sufficient to form two naval Brigades and a Brigade of Marines available for Home Defence or for any special purpose. From this they formed the "Naval" Division.

Having landed in Gallipoli in April, 1915 the Division was evacuated in early January, 1916 to Mudros and split up. The Division did not reform until arriving back in France in May, 1916. During this time the Naval Division were transferred from the Admiralty to the War Office (Army).

The Battalions landed in France at Marseille with Hawke being the last to arrive on May 23rd, 1916. In France the Naval Division were numbered the 63rd (Royal Naval) Division and the Brigades were numbered the 188th, 189th and 190th.

In 189th Brigade were the Hood, Nelson, Hawke and Drake Battalions. On October 7th the 190th Brigade took over a sector of the line from Serre to Beaumont Hamel, the 188th and 189th Brigades holding the trenches in the sector in front of the village of Hamel down to the Ancre River. The weather was execrable and trenches had been destroyed by the enemy, there were virtually no dugouts and the communication trenches ran across a conspicuous ridge under constant aimed fire. 63rd Division's sector was about 1,200 yards in width, was immediately north of the Ancre River, the front running at right angles to the river valley which ran almost due east to Beaucourt, the Division's objective.

The preliminary British bombardment began on November 6th concentrating on those areas around Beaumont Hamel and St. Pierre Divion. Zero hour was at 5.45am on November 13th, but troops of the 63rd Division had reached the assembly area at 9pm the previous evening and had to lie out in the open and in the rain only 200 yards from the German line. At 5.45am the British barrage opened on the German lines and the troops moved forward keeping well up to the shrapnel barrage which moved on about 100 yards in 5 minutes. It was abnormally dark and with a thick mist. The two Naval Brigades led the attack with the 188th Brigade on the left next to the 153rd Brigade of the 51st Highland Division. The 189th Brigade was on the right of its line being the valley of the Ancre. 190th Brigade was in support.

On the right, the Hood Battalion followed by the Drake encountered strong opposition, sweeping machine-gunfire from the left causing considerable loss. Still the German front line system was captured with 300 prisoners. On the left of the advance the Hawke and Nelson Battalions had attacked in the mist at 5.45am. but as the first wave approached the German trenches and with the barrage still on the German first line, a devastating German machine-gun fire broke out from a Redoubt between the first and second enemy lines and opposite the Hawke Battalion front. Nearly 400 of the officers and men became casualties mainly falling round the Redoubt.

Understandably on the night of November 13th/14th there was considerable confusion with trenches obliterated and distances impossible to calculate. The attack on Beaucourt village at 7.45am was the task of 190th Brigade which had managed to collect near Beaucourt Station. At this critical point Colonel Freyberg, although wounded again, led the assault himself with a mixed detachment from the Hood, Drake, Hawke and Nelson battalions.

The capture of Beaucourt was reported at 10.30am That afternoon the hold on Beaucourt was consoledated. At midnight the 37th Division began the entire relief of the 63rd Division, the 63rd Brigade of the 37th Division taking over the whole front, with the 111th Brigade remaining in support and in the old enemy front line the remains of the 188th and 189th Brigades. In the afternoon of the 15th November the 188th and 189th Brigades were finally relieved to march back to Engelbelmer, the 190th Brigade remaining temporarily to clear up the battlefield.

The losses of the 63rd Division were approximately 100 officers and more than 1600 men killed, 160 officers and 2,377 men wounded almost the whole in the twelve infantry battalions and machine-gun companies and more

than three-quarters of these in the two Naval Brigades, 188th and 189th, whose allotted task in the Battle of the Ancre had inevitably exacted higher casualties than those suffered by the four Army battalions in 190th Brigade.

James was among those killed in action on November 13th. He was originally buried where he fell in a shell hole near the German 3rd line. He is buried in Ancre Cemetery, Beaumont-Hamel.

Ancre British Cemetery is about 2 km south of the village of Beaumont-Hamel. The village was attacked on July 1st, 1916 by the 29th Division, with the 4th on its left and the 36th (Ulster) on its right, but without success. On November 13th and 14th, the 51st (Highland), 63rd (Royal Naval), 39th and 19th (Western) Divisions finally succeeded in capturing Beaumont-Hamel. The majority of those buried in the cemetery died on July 1st, September 3rd or November 13th, 1916.

There are now 2,540 casualties buried or commemorated in the cemetery. 1,335 of the graves are unidentified, but special memorials commemorate 43 casualties known or believed to be buried among them. There are also special memorials to 16 casualties know to have been buried in other cemeteries, whose graves were destroyed by shell fire.

CALLAN:—On November 13th, killed in action: James Callan, the dearly loved youngest son of W. and E. Callan, The Waterworks, Nurstead, aged 18 years, "Peace, perfect peace."

GR 16/12/16 [Andrew Marsall]

Mr. and Mrs. W. Callan, of the Waterworks Cottages, Nurstead, have received intimation that their youngest son, James Callan (A.B., R.N.D.), was killed in action in the taking of Beaumont Hamel. He was only 18 years of age. He joined up in June, 1915, and after four months' training at the Crystal Palace was on active service for 14 months. His only brother, William was wounded in the same engagement.

James Callan – Ancre Military Cemetery.

Lijssenthoek CWGC Cemetery – George Carter

George Tristam Carter
Royal Fusiliers, 1st Battalion
Service No. 50917 - Private

George was the son of George and Caroline Carter of Tatton, Cheshire. He was born in 1876. His father was a land agent and died in 1879 leaving Caroline to bring up her three sons, Cuthbert, born in 1873, George and William who was two years younger. The family subsequently moved to Hendon and then to Deptford.

George married Florence Helen Roberts in August, 1906 in Deptford. Florence was born in Bermondsey. The couple moved to 89 Pelham Road with George being employed as a broker's clerk. They had two sons – Tristam, born in 1907 and Lionel born in 1909. They moved to 28 King Street and then 19 Lennox Avenue.

He initially was posted to the 24th Battalion, Royal Fusiliers. The 24th (2nd Sportsman's) Battalion, The Royal Fusiliers (City of London Regiment) was raised at the Hotel Cecil in the Strand, London, on the 25th of September 1914 by E. Cunliffe-Owen. In June 1915 they joined 99th Brigade, 33rd Division at Clipstone camp near Mansfield in Nottinghamshire in July 1915. In August they moved to Salisbury Plain for final training and firing practice. In November they received orders to prepare to proceed to France and the Divisional Artillery and Train were replaced by the units raised for the 54th (East Anglian) Division.

George was now posted to the 1st Battalion.

1st Battalion, The Royal Fusiliers (City of London Regiment) were in Kinsale when war broke out, serving with 17th Brigade, 6th Division. They returned to England and proceeded to France on the 10th of September 1914, landing at St Nazaire. They marched to the Aisne to reinforce the hard-pressed BEF.

They moved north to Flanders and were in action at Hooge in 1915. On the 14th of October 1915 17th Brigade transferred to 24th Division. In 1916 they suffered in the German gas attack at Wulverghem and then moved to The Somme seeing action in The Battle of Delville Wood and The Battle of Guillemont. In 1917 they were in action at The Battle of Vimy Ridge in the Spring, The Battle of Messines in June and Third Battle of Ypres in October. George was killed in action on August 4th, 1917 and is buried at Lijssenthoek CWGC Cemetery .

George Challenor
Australian Pioneers
Service No. 3819A - Private

Over the first half of 1919 much correspondence was made over the fate of George Challenor; the Australian Army authorities and the Red Cross made every effort to ascertain what in fact happened to George who died as a Prisoner of War a week after the Armistice. It was not until September that it was confirmed that George had died of dysentery almost a year earlier. His sister, Eleanor Everist was keen to ascertain the circumstances of his death on behalf of herself and their elderly mother, Ellen, their father being already deceased.

George was born on March 18th, 1866, the son of Edwin and Ellen Challenor of 55 Knights Alms Houses, Perry Street, the fifth of ten children. Edwin was born in Bermondsey in 1832 and was a cooper. Ellen was born in 1834 in Ulcomb.

George was a Thames Waterman before migrating to Australia where his sister, Eleanor lived. She maintained the Gravesend connection, living at Rosherville, Henry Street, Sydney. George sought employment as a labourer and at the time of his enlistment was staying at the Young Australian Hotel, Bundaberg, Queensland.

He enlisted on January 26th, 1917 at Maryborough, Queensland and was initially posted to the 14th Depot Battalion. He was 5 feet 5½ inches tall, weighed 138lbs, had light brown hair, blue eyes and was of dark complexion. He was transferred to the 4th Pioneers on February 22nd.

Each Division in the A.I.F. was allocated a Pioneer Battalion. The 4th Pioneers were the Pioneer Battalion of the 4th Division. Pioneer Battalions were essentially light military combat engineers organised like the infantry and located at the very forward edge of the battle area.

They were used to develop defensive positions, construct command posts and dugouts, prepare barbed wire defences and to facilitate the mobility of friendly forces while taking whatever action they could to deny it to the enemy.

Their skills and capability were broad from building, construction and maintenance to road and track preparation and maintenance. They could also, and did quite often, fight as infantry.

During the war there was a much heavier reliance on field work and roads and railways needed to be maintained. Engineers alone could not meet the heavy demand, while rifle men were always needed at the front. Therefore, pioneer battalions were raised to meet the needs of both and trained to support engineers and infantry.

The 4th Pioneers were engaged in every action undertaken by the 4th Division, starting at Pozieres and Mouquet Farm in mid-1916 through Bullecourt, Messines and Third Ypres in 1917, culminating in the final stages of the Hundred Days campaign in late 1918.

He sailed for Europe on the *Hororata* on June 14th, arriving in Liverpool on August 27th.

He was sent to the Front on January 26th. George was taken prisoner on April 7th, 1918. He was at Forbach Prisoner of War Camp where conditions gradually worsened over the following months.

In a letter sent in response to enquiries by the Red Cross by another prisoner at the St. Gobian Bois Camp, Arthur Cook wrote of the conditions, describing them as being very difficult – *we were doing very heavy work cutting down trees etc., being very badly clothed and fed and also very*

Australian War Memorial, Canberra

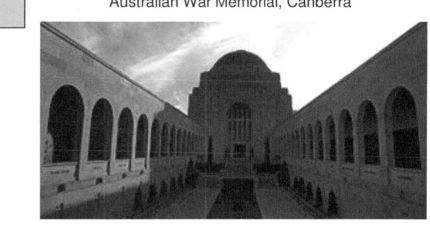

unsanitary. 10 or 12 men per day or two days went away sick out of 130 men, then the Camp would be reinforced. Arthur himself was among those *taken to a convalescent camp leaving this man behind, although he was looking very thin and ill.*

He died of dysentery on November 20th, 1918 at Forbach Reserve Hospital. He is buried in Perreuse Chateau Franco British Cemetery. He left his effects to his mother; the instructions being that these were to be forwarded to his sister, Eleanor, for her to send on to Northfleet. These were duly forwarded to his mother on October 31st, 1919. But the records indicate that the effects to include the medals awarded were finally returned to Base as undeliverable.

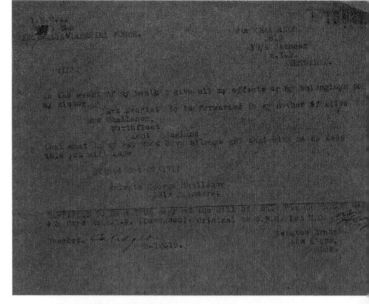

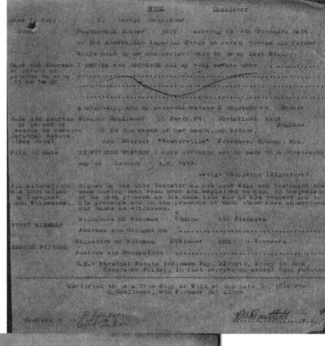

George's last will and testament October 1917, above right and January 1918, right and inventory of personal effects, below.

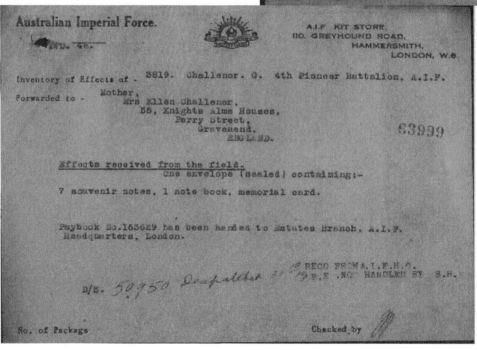

The request for
information on George.
July 1919.

The formal response, August and September, 1919.

COPY.

A.I.F. 4th Pioneers. Bttn.   CHALLENOR.
                                             George 3819a.
                                        22, Upper Grosvenor Street.
                                             Park Lane W.L.
                                             6th Sept 1919.

Dear Sir,
        In reply to your note of enquiry for George
Challenor 3819a., the description certainly answers to one of
the Australians in the same working camp in the St. Gobian Bois.
There we were doing very heavy work cutting down trees etc.,
being very badly clothed and fed and also bery unsanitary.
10 or 12 men per day or two days went away sick out of 130
roughly. Then the camp would be reinforced. Eventually I was
sent with a party of men to a convalescent camp, leaving this
man behind, although he was looking very thin and ill the last
time I saw him. Another party followed my party to the Convalescent camp a few days after who said this man was ill. Then I
heard again after that he had died. This I should say happened
about this time last year or perhaps a few days sooner, Two
other Australians named "Connel and "Stack" were in the St.
Gobian Bois camp with me could probably tell you more as they
knew him better than I.
        I do hope this will help you in some way am sorry
I cannot tell you more for the sake of his poor people who
would like to know his fate for certain.
        I am yours very sincerely.
                        (Sgd) Arthur Cook.
(Copy of letter rec. from Officer i/c Records A.I.F. Hdqrs 16.9.19.
in reply to enquiries from A. Red Cross 9.9.19.
London.   B.
19.9.19.

COPY.

A.I.F. 4th Pioneers. Bttn.

CHALLENOR.
George 3819a.
22,Upper Grosvenor Street.
park Lane W.L.
6th Sept 1919.

Dear Sir,

In reply to your note of enquiry for George Challenor 3819a ., the description certainly answers to one of the Australians in the same working camp in the St.Gobian Bois. There we were doing very heavy work cutting down trees etc., being very badly clothed and fed and also very unsanitary. 10 or 12 men per day or two days went away sick out of 130 roughly. Then the camp would be reinforced. Eventually I was sent with a party of men to a convalesment camp, leaving this man behind, although he was looking very thin and ill the last time I saw him. Another party followed my party to the Convalesent camp a few days after who said this man was ill. Then I heard again after that he had died. This I should say happened about this time last year or perhaps a few days sooner. Two other Australians named "Connel and "Stack" were in the St. Gobian Bois camp with me could probably tell you more as they knew him better than I.

I do hope this will help you in some way am sorry I cannot tell you more for the sake of his poor people who would like to know his fate for certain.

I am yours very sincerely.

(Sgd)Arthur Cook.
(Copy of letter rec.from Officer i/c Records A.I.F.Hdqrs 16.9.19. in reply to enquiries from A.Red Cross 9.9.19. London.
19.9.19.

B.

Replies from former soldiers regarding George's fate.

A.I.F. 4th Pioneers Bttn.

CHALLENOR.
George. 3819a.

<u>P. of W.</u>

In reply to your letter inquiring about information concerning
3819a Pte George Challenor of the 4th Pioneers Battalion A.I.F
The last as I seen of him was when we were working at a Saw
Mills, in Alsace Lorraine. We never did get to Friedrichsfeld
at all. That was in August last 1918 but just before we were
repatriated we were all gathered together ready to be handed
over to the French, but the Germans did not hand us exactly
over to the French soldiers, they took us to the Border, and
then told us to find our own way there. But very few arrived
there, they died on the way and that is all the information
I can give you. Probably Pte David Watson of Stewart Street,
Edinburgh, Scotland,late of the Royal Scots, can give you a
bit more information concerning Pte G.Challenor.
     (Letter from Pte F.Cook, 122052, 3rd Sherwood
       Foresters, Military Guard, White Lund, R.F.F.
        near Morecambe, dated Sept.16th 1919.)

London.
18.9.19.

B.

Replies concering
George.

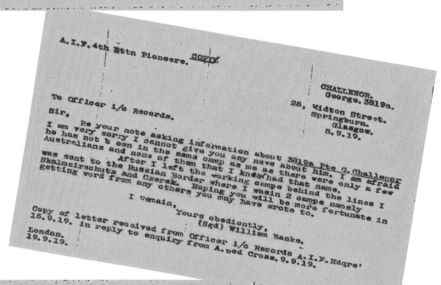

A.I.F. 4th Bttn Pioneers. <u>COPY</u>

CHALLENOR.
George. 3819a.
28, Widton Street.
Springburn.
Glasgow.
8.9.19.

To Officer i/c Records.
Sir,
    Re your note asking information about 3819a Pte G. Challenor
I am very sorry I cannot give you any news about him. I am afraid
he has not been in the same camp as me as there were only a few
Australians and none of them that I knew had that name.
    After I left the working camps behind the lines I
was sent to the Russian Border where I was in 2 camps namely
Skalmeirschutz and Czersk. Hoping you will be more fortunate in
getting word from any others you may have wrote to.
    I remain,
        Yours obediently,
        (Sgd) William Banks.
Copy of letter received from Officer i/c Records A.I.F. Hdqrs'
16.9.19. in reply to enquiry from A.Red Cross. 9.9.19.
London.
19.9.19.

B.

A.I.F.4th Pioneers.

CHALLENOR.
G. 3819a.

<u>"Prisoner of War"</u>

"In answer to your letter I regret to say while working in a forest
in a place named Crippe in Germany, 2 Australians were killed
with falling trees. I do not know their names as they had no books
on them or anything by which they could be identified.
    There were only 4 Australians in our company,
and I regret to say that L/Cpl J.Stewart died of dysentary
in a French Hospital as I happened to be a patient in the same ward,
and I believe he was buried at Narmr. Hoping you have some better
news from other enquirers to send to their relatives.

       Letter from T.Gorsor.
       Sou Pinas Road.

       17.4.19.

London.
8.9.19.

B.

204

Robert Samuel Chambers
Machine Gun Corps [motor]
Service No. 296 - Gunner

Robert was born in 1891 in West Ham. Prior to the war he lived with his step father William Osborne and his mother Minnie at 60 Lynton Road South. William was born in 1876 in Brixton and was a shop manager. Minnie was born in in 1872 in Dovercourt, Essex. His father, Joseph was born in 1860 in Bishopsgate and was a QMS with the Royal Engineers. He died in 1907 in Gravesend.

Robert was a chauffeur prior to enlisting in 1914.

Robert held the rank of gunner in the 5th Battery, Machine Gun Corps. He arrived in France on March 3rd, 1915.

Robert was killed in action on April 18th, 1915. He has no known grave and is commemorated on the Le Touret Memorial.

We regret to announce that Gunner Robert Chambers, of No. 5 Battery, Motor Machine Gun Service, was killed in action at Neuve Chapelle on the 18th April. His mother, who is a widow, resides at 60, Lynton-road South, Gravesend, and the sad news was received by her on Sunday. The deceased was the son of the late Q.M.S. Chambers, R.E., for many years at Tilbury Fort. He received his education at the Gravesend Modern School under Mr. Waldegrave, and no doubt will be remembered by many of his old school chums. Robert, for three years, was chauffeur to Dr. C. Golding-Bird, at Meopham, and whilst occupying that position made many friends owing to his genial disposition. At the beginning of the war he joined the West Kents, but was afterwards transferred to the Motor Machine Gun Battery, in which he was serving when killed. He had only been in France about two months, and his early death is much to be regretted, for he had proved himself a very capable soldier. Our sympathy goes out to his mother, who has lost her only son and child.

Mrs. Chambers received the following letters from the Lieutenant of the section, and the Quarter-Master-Sergeant, while there was also forwarded an extract from the Battery Orders paying a high tribute to the worth of the deceased:—

"Dear Madam,—As officer commanding your son's section, I feel it my duty to drop you a line expressing my very deepest sympathy in the loss of your son. I don't think any of his pals felt the loss more than I do, as he was such a plucky and thoroughly good lad, one I could rely upon at any time.. He very fortunately did not suffer at all, as he was hit through the head. Allow me, dear madam, to express my deepest regret, and condole with you from the bottom of my heart.—Yours sincerely, H. G. MEERTINO."

"Dear Mrs. Chambers,—I am sending you something which belongs to your dear boy. I hardly know how to write these few lines, for Bob and I came out of the same Regiment (West Kents), and he has been in my section ever since he came to this Battery. From the bottom of my heart I offer you my sincere sympathy. You have lost a brave son and our Battery a noble comrade. I have had a nice cross made with his name and Battery on it, and will take it up to-morrow. He is buried a few yards behind the trenches where he fell—a brave British soldier. God bless you and help you to bear up in this hour of trouble. I have sent you an extract from Battery Orders, for I know it will cheer you up to know your dear boy was loved by both officers and men.—Yours very sincerely, W. THOMPSON, Q.M.S."

Extract from Battery Orders.—20-4-15. "The O.C. regrets to state that Gunner R. Chambers was killed in action at Neuve Chapelle at 8.30 p.m. on 18th April. Gunner Chambers was a good and popular soldier. His loss will be deeply felt both by the officers and men of No. 5 Battery."

George William Chapman
Royal West Kent, 6th Battalion
Service No. G/979 - Private

George was the son of John and Charlotte Chapman of 65 Peacock Street. He was born in Higham in 1896. Both John, born in 1867 and Charlotte, born in 1871 were from Shorne. They married in 1890 and had six children – Edith, born in 1890, John, born in 1893, George, Harry, born in 1898, Edward, born in 1901, Doris, born in 1905 and Vera, born in 1910. John was an engine driver with the Borough. George was an errand boy initially on leaving school but subsequently became an engine attendant.

George enlisted on September 1st, 1914 at Gravesend. He was 5 foot 3¾ inches tall, weighed 114lbs, had blue eyes, brown hair and had a fresh complexion. He was with 4th Company, 6th Battalion.

The 6th (Service) Battalion, The Royal West Kent Regiment was raised at Maidstone on the 14th of August 1914 as part of Kitchener's First New Army and joined 37th Brigade in 12th (Eastern) Division. They trained at Colchester and moved to Purfleet in September 1914 they spent the winter in billets in Hythe from December. They moved to Aldershot for final training in February 1915 and proceeded to France on the 1st of June 1915 landing at Boulogne, they concentrated near St Omer and by 6th of June were in the Meteren-Steenwerck area with Divisional HQ being established at Nieppe. They underwent instruction from the more experienced 48th (South Midland) Division and took over a section of the front line at Ploegsteert Wood on the 23rd of June 1915. They were in action in The Battle of Loos from the 30th of

September, taking over the sector from Gun Trench to Hulluch Quarries consolidating the position, under heavy artillery fire. On the 8th they repelled a heavy German attack and on the 13th took part in the Action of the Hohenzollern Redoubt, capturing Gun Trench and the south western face of the Hulluch Quarries. By the 21st they

Private George William Chapman, who was serving in D. Company, 6th Battalion, Royal West Kent Regiment, was killed at Loos on 8th October, 1915. From a letter received by his father, we learn that he had fought hard in the Battle of Loos, and in the advance around that part volunteering to fetch water for his comrades under shell fire, and while engaged in doing so he jumped into a dug-out for temporary shelter, but no sooner had he done so than a shell burst overhead and killed him instantly. Private Chapman was employed at the Imperial Paper Mills until August, 1914, when he enlisted, his home being 64, Peacock-street. Mr. Chapman has now two sons serving the country, one in the R.F.A. (France) and the other with the R.N.D.

GR 6/11/15 [Andrew Marsall]

moved to Fouquieres-les-Bethune for a short rest, returning to the front at the Hohenzollern Redoubt until the 15th of November, when they went into reserve at Lillers.

George did not survive the Battle of Loos being among those killed in action on the 8th. His body was not recovered and he has no known grave. He is commemorated on the Loos Memorial.

Marine Barracks, Chatham.

John Chibnall
Royal Marine L't Inf – Lance Corp.
Service No. CH/16588

John was born on January 2nd, 1892 in Shorne to John and Alice Chibnall of 38 Raphael Road, Gravesend.

He was with the Chatham Battalion, Royal Naval Division having enlisted in 1909.

The Royal Marines are not part of the British Army but are an integral part of the Royal Navy. In WW1 there were Royal Marine Light Infantry (RMLI) & Royal Marine Artillery (RMA). They were organised into three Grand Divisions Based at Chatham, Portsmouth and Plymouth. these divisions did not have an operational role as such but acted in the same way as an Army Regiments depot, they supplied drafts and reinforcements to man the RN ships and the RM Battalions in the 63rd (Royal Naval) Division. Every RN Ship had an home

The Main Entrance, RM Barracks.

port of Chatham, Plymouth or Portsmouth and normally they were manned by sailors and Marines from that Depot. Both RMLI & RMA together manned at least one main turret on Capital Ships and Cruisers so a ships RM detachment could have both RMLI & RMA men. The RMLI men being trained as naval gunners as well as infantry soldiers.

The Royal Marine Brigade was moved to Ostend on August 27th, 1914, although it returned four days later. On September 20th it arrived at Dunkirk with orders to assist in the defence of Antwerp. The two other Brigades moved to Dunkirk for the same purpose on 5 October 1914. In the haste to organise and move the units to Belgium, 80% went to war without even basic equipment such as packs, mess tins or water bottles. No khaki uniform was issued. The two Naval Brigades were armed with ancient charger-loading rifles, just three days before embarking. The Division was originally titled the Royal Naval Division, and was formed in England in September 1914. At this stage, it had no artillery, Field Ambulances or other ancillary units.

RND units that managed to successfully withdraw from Antwerp returned to England, arriving in mid-October. John was promoted Corporal on January 7th.

After a lengthy period of refit and training (scattered in various locations, and still short of many of the units that ordinarily made up the establishment of a Division), the Division moved to Egypt preparatory to the Gallipoli campaign. On February 6th, 1915 Plymouth and Chatham Battalions entrained at Shillingstone near Blandford and moved to Devonport. They are temporarily known as the "Royal Marine Special Service Force". The Chatham Battalion sailed on the Cawdor Castle. After a five day stay in Malta in mid-February, the Battalion sailed for Lemnos arriving on February 24th. There followed delays due to bad weather and rerouting before on April 28th the "Gloucester Castle" and "Cawdor Castle" ordered to move and anchor off Gaba Tepe. The Chatham and Portsmouth Battalions ordered to disembark and come under orders of 1st Australian Division on arrival. On completion of disembarkation the Brigade was ordered to take over No 2 Section of defences held by Australian and New Zealand forces. This was the western edge of Lone Pine plateau.

George Chapman – Panel 96, Loos Memorial

Charles Edward Childs
East Surrey Rgt, 9th Battalion
Service No. 30771 - Private

Charles was born in 1897 the son of Frederick and Margaret Childs of 61 Parrock Street. Frederick, born in 1867 and Margaret, born a year later, were both from Farnham. There were six children in the family – Eva, born in 1883, Margaret, born in 1889, Frederick, born in 1891, Charles, Hilda, born in 1895 and Gracie, born in 1902. Frederick's job as a Chief Chef with Royal Mail took him around the country but eventually to Gravesend.

John was mortally wounded in early June and died of wounds on the 16th at the 11th Casualty Clearing Station and is buried in Lancashire Landing Cemetery.

The 9th Battalion, The East Surrey Regiment was raised at Kingston-upon-Thames in September 1914 as part of Kitchener's Third New Army. They trained at Worthing, moving to Shoreham by April 1915 the moving to Blackdown, Aldershot in June for final training. They proceeded to France, landing at Boulogne on September 1st, 1915. The Division concentrated in the area between Etaples and St Pol and marched across France into the reserve for the assault at Loos, going into action on the 26th and suffering heavy losses. In 1916 they suffered in the German gas attack at Wulverghem and then moved to The Somme seeing action in The Battles of Delville Wood and Guillemont. In 1917 they were in action at The Battle of Vimy Ridge in

Charles, left with his father, Frederick and his brother, Frederick.

the Spring, The Battle of Messines in June and Third Battle of Ypres in October before moving south where they were in action during The Cambrai Operations. In 1918 they were in action on the Somme and at Cambrai and the Final Advance in Picardy.

He was killed in action on September 23rd, 1918 and is buried in Aix-Noulette Communal Cemetery Extension. Aix-Noulette is 13km south of Bethune on the main road to Arras. The Cemetery Extension was begun by French troops early in 1915, and the two French plots are next to the Communal Cemetery. It was taken over by the 1st and 2nd Divisions in February, 1916, and used by fighting units and Field Ambulances until October, 1918.

Frederick Childs
Royal Horse Artillery, Q Battery
Service No. 33137 – Lance Bomb.

Frederick was born in Haningfield, Essex in 1888. His father, William was born in 1853 and was a brick maker; his mother Mary was born in 1857. They had seven children – William,

born in 1877, Walter, born in 1880, Eliza, born in 1882, James, born in 1884,Frederick, Mary Ann, born in 1890, Arthur, born in 1893 and Alfred, born in 1896.

Frederick was a labourer at the Ammunition Stores in Cliffe. He lived with his wife, May at 42 Kempthorne Street. The couple married in 1910 and had a daughter Pearl, born in 1913.

He enlisted with the Yorks and Lancs Regiment, service number 7453. He subsequently moved to the Royal Horse Artillery with the rank of Lance Bombardier. The RHA was responsible for light, mobile guns that provided firepower in support of the cavalry. It was the senior arm of the artillery, but the one that developed and grew least during the Great War. In 1914 the establishment of the RHA was one battery to each brigade of cavalry.

Abattery had six 13-pounder field guns and included 5 officers and 200 men.

He was killed in action through an air raid on May 26th, 1918.

On Active Service.

CHILDS.—On active service, " Somewhere in France," Frederick Childs, R.H.A. (just rejoined his battery from hospital), killed by shrapnel from aeroplane bomb, aged 30 years, the loving husband of May Childs (née Gamage), late of Northfleet, leaving one little girl to mourn her loss.

I can take my child upon my knee, and look upon his picture which is on, so dear to me, and think and say, with pride your Dad, my dear, did his duty for King; Country, You and I.

GR 22/6/18 [Andrew Marsall]

Frederick is buried at Daours Communal Cemetery Extension.

The preparations for the Somme Offensive in 1916 brought a group of casualty clearing stations to Daours.

The Allied advance in the spring of 1917 took the hospitals with it and no further burials were made there until April, 1918, when the Germans advanced. From April until mid-August the cemetery was on the Front line. In August and September the casualty clearing stations went forward and in September the cemetery was closed.

There are 1,231 Commonwealth servicemen of the Great War buried or commemorated in Daours Communal Cemetery Extension. The adjoining communal cemetery contains two Great War burials one being that of Frederick.

Arthur Robert Christian, M.M
Royal West Kent, 7th Battalion
Service No. G/18364 - Private

Arthur was born in 1880. He and his wife Isabella, who was three years younger, were married in 1904. Both came from Gravesend. They had three daughter and a son - Phillis who was born in July, 1908, Doris, born in June 1911, Elsie, born in June 1913 and Arthur William born in December, 1914. The family home was at 152 Wellington Street.

He enlisted at Gravesend on November 29th, 1915 – service number 3014, Royal Sussex Regiment. He was 6 foot tall and weighed 172lbs. He was posted to the reserves due to being diagnosed with mitral stenosis [narrowing of the heart valve]. His teeth were also in a bad state of decay although this was secondary to his heart condition. He was mobilised to the 3rd Battalion on June 9th, 1916 – the shortage of man power in the army superceding any physical ailments. On September 13th he was posted to the 7th. It was with the 7th Battalion, service number 12614, that he was awarded the Military Medal on September 21st, 1916.

He was transferred to the 7th Battalion, RWK in October, 1916. The 7th (Service) Battalion was raised at Maidstone on September 5th, 1914 as part of Kitchener's 2nd New Army. After initial training near home, they moved to Colchester in April 1915 and then to Salisbury Plain in May for final training.

THE MILITARY MEDAL.

"I have read with great pleasure the report of your Regimental Commander and Brigade Commander regarding your gallant conduct and devotion to duty in the field on 18th November, 1916." Such are the words on the parchment, signed by the Major-General of his Division, handed to Private A. Christian, of the Royal West Kent Regiment, and his officer, Capt. R. Anstruther, wrote to him: "My heartiest congratulations on the Military Medal. Jolly good work." Private Christian is the husband of Mrs. Christian, 152, Wellington-street, Gravesend, and he was formerly employed by Mr. Cooper and at Tilbury Docks. He had been at the Front four months when he earned his distinction. Writing to his mother, he says: "I am pleased to tell you that I have made quite a name for myself this time in what we call a bombing stunt. We had to take a section of trench on Friday evening, and I had the section and took the trench in a very short time with no casualties on our side, and the General sent a runner to congratulate us on our performance and requested the name of the leader to be sent to him. I was congratulated by the Captain of my own Company in front of the rest of the Company, and my name has been forwarded with three others for the Military Medal or Cross, I don't know which. They are all proud of 'A' Company, as the trench was a strong German point, but we frightened the life out of Fritz. I can tell you that I feel quite proud, and have received congratulations all round because I was the first volunteer to go up to the trench." That was the true Gravesend spirit, and Gravesend is proud of it.

GR 27/1/17 [Andrew Marsall]

They proceeded to France on the July 27th landing at Le Havre. In 1916 they were in action on The Somme in The Battle of Albert capturing their objectives near Montauban, The Battle of Bazentin Ridge including the capture of Trones Wood, The Battle of Delville Wood, The Battle of Thiepval Ridge, The Battle of the Ancre Heights playing a part in the capture of the Schwaben Redoubt and Regina Trench and The Battle of the Ancre. In 1917 they took part in the Operations on the Ancre including Miraumont and the capture of Irles, they fought during the German retreat to the Hindenburg

Line and in The Third Battle of the Scarpe before moving to Flanders. Arthur was killed in action on May 6th, 1917. He has no known grave and is commemorated on the Arras Memorial.

Another of the gallant West Kents has given his life in this great war in the person of Private A. Christian, husband of Mrs. Christian, of 152, Wellington-street, and son of Mrs. E. Christian, of 46, Kempthorne-street. Second-Lieut. Knight, writing to Mrs. Christian a letter of condolence on the loss of her husband, says: "If ever there was a brave man it was your husband. He was admired and respected by all, and I am sure there is not a man in our company who is not grieved and pained at having lost him. I was quite close to him when he was killed; he was right up in the front of the fight, and game and cheerful to the last. It will, I am sure, be some comfort to you to know that he did not suffer much. After being hit he passed peacefully away in two or three minutes. He was buried by his own comrades with all due reverence. You have, I can assure you, the deepest sympathy of every officer and man in our company. Your husband was in my platoon, and I cannot speak too highly of him. He was a man to be proud of. We have most of us lost dear ones in this horrible war, and the only consolation we have is that they died a hero's death and fighting for their King and country." In our issue of January 27th we recorded the fact that Private Christian received the Military Medal, having been at the Front four months when he received his distinction. He was decorated by the General commanding his division, and Capt. Anstruther wrote of the deed which gained the medal, "Jolly good work," while Private Christian himself said that the point on which he led a bombing attack was taken and that they "frightened the life out of Fritz."

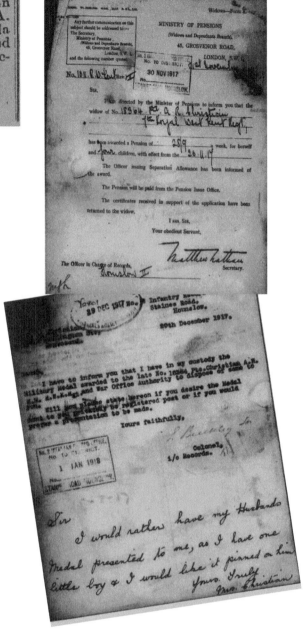

CHRISTIAN.—On May 3rd, 1917, killed in action, "Somewhere in France," Pte. A. Christian, beloved husband of Isabella Christian, of 152, Wellington-street, and son of Mrs. E. Christian, 46, Kempthorne-street.

He died for his King and his Country,
With the bravest of the brave,
All there is left is his photo,
Since he has found a soldier's grave.

GR 19/5/17 [Andrew Marsall]

When the Ministry wrote to Isabella asking whether she wanted Albert's Military Medal sent or presented to her, she wrote back stating that she wished it pinned on their only son's chest; Arthur William was just four years old!

Frederick Victor Church
Royal West Kent, 6th Battalion
Service No. G/12897 - Private

Frederick was born in 1890, to Francis and Elizabeth Church of Fern Villa, 42 Havelock Road. Both were born in 1853 with Francis hailing from Milton and Elizabeth from Sussex. He worked as a coal porter on the docks. The couple married in 1879 and had eight children – Elizabeth, born in 1879, Francis, born in 1881, Lewis, born in 1883, Daisy, born in 1885, Benjamin, born in 1887, Frederick, Harold, born in 1893 and Leonard, born in 1895. Benjamin was a wire winder at the Cable Works and Frederick was a stores man at the Brewery.

He married Florence Clark on December 26th, 1912 and the couple lived at 7 Union Street. They had three

Charles Childs –
Aix-Noulette Communal Cemetery Extension

Frederick Childs – Daours
Communal Cemetery Extension

Arras Memorial – Arthur Christian, M.M.

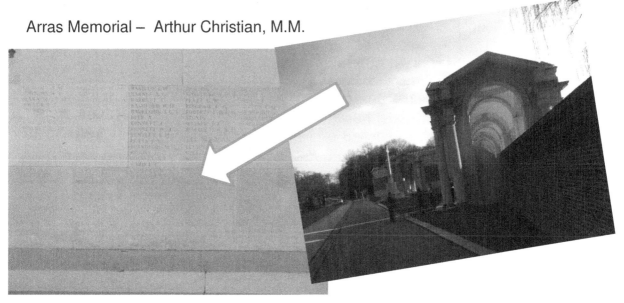

children – Frederick Francis, born August 1913, Katherine, born February 1915 and Leonard, born March 1916.

Frederick enlisted in December, 1915. He was 5 feet 4 inches tall and described as being of good physical development. He suffered from chronic arthritis and so initially was posted to the Reserve from which he was mobilised on March 31st, 1916. He was posted to the 3rd Battalion on September 1st, 1916. The 6th (Service) Battalion, The Royal West Kent Regiment was raised at Maidstone on the 14th of August 1914 as part of Kitchener's First New Army and joined 37th Brigade in 12th (Eastern) Division.

They trained at Colchester and moved to Purfleet in September 1914 they spent the winter in billets in Hythe from December. They moved to Aldershot for final training in February 1915 and proceeded to France on the 1st of June 1915 landing at Boulogne, they concentrated near St Omer and by 6th of June were in the Meteren-Steenwerck area with Divisional HQ being established at Nieppe. They underwent instruction from the more experienced 48th (South Midland) Division and took over a section of the front line at Ploegsteert Wood on the 23rd of June 1915. They were in action in The Battle of Loos from the 30th of September, taking over the sector from Gun Trench to Hulluch Quarries consolidating the position, under heavy artillery fire. On the 8th they repelled a heavy German infantry attack and on the 13th took part in the Action of the Hohenzollern Redoubt, capturing Gun Trench and the south western face of the Hulluch Quarries. By the 21st they moved to Fouquieres-les-Bethune for a short rest then returned to the front line at the Hohenzollern Redoubt until

the 15th of November, when they went into reserve at Lillers. On the 9th of December, 9th Royal Fusiliers assisted in a round-up of spies and other suspicious characters in the streets of Bethune. On the 10th the Division took over the front line north of La Bassee canal at Givenchy. On the 19th of January they began a period of training in Open Warfare at Busnes, then moved back into the front line at Loos on the 12th of February 1916. In June they moved to Flesselles and carried out a training exercise. They moved to Baizieux on the 30th June and went into the reserve at Hencourt and Millencourt by mid morning on the 1st of July. They relieved the 8th Division at Ovillers-la-Boisselle that night and attacked at 3.15 the following morning with mixed success. On the 7th they attacked again and despite suffering heavy casualties in the area of Mash Valley, they succeeded in capturing and holding the first and second lines close to Ovillers. They were withdrawn to Contay on the 9th July. They were in action in The Battle of Pozieres on the 3rd of August with a successful attack capturing 4th Avenue Trench and were engaged in heavy fighting until they were withdrawn on the 9th.

CHURCH. — Officially reported missing October 7th, 1916, now officially reported killed on or since that date, Private Frederick Victor Church, Royal West Kent Regiment, fourth and dearly loved son of Mr. and Mrs. F. R. Church, Fern Villa, Havelock-road, Gravesend.

Sleep on, dear son, in your soldier's grave.
Our tears shall not awake you,
We only wait till death doth take,
Then those you loved sha'l meet you.

—From Mother, Father, Sisters and Brothers.

GR 18/8/17 [Andrew Marsall]

The above is a photograph of Private Frederick Victor Church, of the Royal West Kents, and husband of Mrs. Church, of 7, Union street, Gravesend, who, having been reported missing since October 7th, 1916, was on the 9th August officially reported killed. Before the war the deceased worked for many years at Russell's Brewery, and, joining up on the 30th March, 1916, was sent to France in September, being killed a fortnight later. A comrade, who saw him killed instantly by a shell, wrote at the time informing Mrs. Church, and his commanding officer also wrote stating that he could not say whether he had been killed or taken prisoner. He was only 26 years of age, and leaves a widow and three children.

GR 25/8/17 [Andrew Marsall]

Frederick was listed as missing, being killed in action on October 7th, 1916. He has no known grave and is commemorated on the Thiepval Monument. Florence was awarded a pension of 26/3 a week for herself and the three children

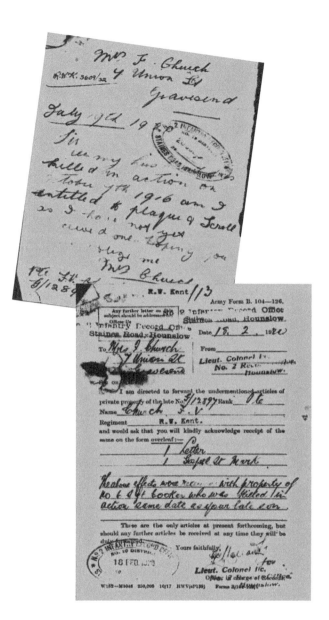

Frederick Cooker, D.C.M.
Royal West Kent, 6th Battalion
Frederick was born in 1893, the son of Walter and Mary Cooker of 69 Melville Road, Maidstone. Frederick enlisted at Maidstone.

Lance Corporal Cooker was awarded the Distinguished Conduct Medal *for conspicuous gallantry during operations. When our bombers had* *been driven back, he immediately reorganised the party under heavy bomb fire and erected a new barricade. Later he climbed over the barricade and brought in a wounded man from close to the enemy.* [The London Gazette, September 26th, 1916].

Fredrick was killed in action on October 7th, 1916. He has no known grave and is commemorated on the Thiepval Monument.

Army records of Frederick Church note that a letter and Gospel of St Mark had been held by Frederick Cooker and returned with his personal effects. They were killed on the same day but indicated that Frederick Cooker had taken them to return to the family of Frederick Church.

In Loving Memory
FREDERICK
VICTOR CHURCH
WHO WAS KILLED ON THE SOMME

Frederick Church –
Gravesend Cemetery, above
and Thiepval Monument, right.

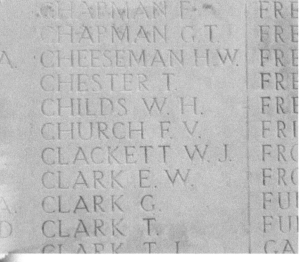

Thiepval Memorial –
Frederick Cooker, D.C.M.

Alfred Charles Clarke
Royal Sussex Rgt., 3rd Battalion
Service No. G/10129 - Private

Alfred was born in Gravesend in 1894. His father, Frederick was born in 1861 and came from Gravesend. He was a carpenter and joiner by profession. His mother, Elizabeth died in 1910

Elizabeth was born in 1861 in Poplar, London. There were six boys and two girls in the family – William, born in 1881, Harriet, born in 1885, Thomas, born in 1890, Frederick, born in 1893, Alfred, Robert, born in 1897, James, born in 1899 and Nelly born in 1900.

All the sons joined their father in the building trade.

Alfred enlisted with the 3rd Battalion, The Royal Sussex Regiment.

Wounded at the Front he was sent back to England to recuperate. He died of his wounds on July 1st, 1918 and is buried in Gravesend Cemetery.

Charles W. F. Clarke
Army Pay Corps [Hounslow]
Service No. 17635 - Private

Charles was born in 1878 in Bury St. Edmunds, the son of Charles Henry and Elizabeth Clarke of 13 Dashwood Road. Charles was born in 1846 and was an Insurance Agent. Elizabeth was born in 1854 and like her husband was from Bury St Edmunds. They had three children in all – Charles, William, born in 1881 and Phillip, born in 1887. Prior to enlisting Charles was a clerk with a granite merchant.

He enlisted with the Royal West Kents, service number G/28595. He subsequently was with the Army Pay Corps, based in Hounslow. He died on June 25th 1918 at the Royal Herbert Hospital, Woolwich and is buried in Gravesend Cemetery.

John James Gordon Clarke
Essex Rgt, 13th Battalion – Capt.

Captain John Clarke was born in 1893 in Gravesend. He was the son of John and Elizabeth Clarke of 'Lyndhurst', St James' Road. John [father] was born in 1859 in Sydenham and was a foreman, engine fitter with a steamship company. Elizabeth was a year younger and came from London. The couple married in 1887 and had seven children – Donald, born in 1891, John, Dorothy, born in 1895, Elsie, born in 1896, Arthur, born in 1898, Philip, born in 1900 and Kathleen, born the following year. The family lived in Grays before moving to Northfleet in 1898.

He married Muriel Mary Simmonds in September 1916 and the couple lived at Briscoe Lodge, Lennox Road, later moving to 'Maryville', Cobham Street. John worked as a clerk with a shipping company.

GR 15/7/16 [Andrew Marsall]

He enlisted with the Essex Regiment, 13th Battalion. He was subsequently attached to the 1st Battalion, Oxford and Bucks Light Infantry. He was promoted 2nd Lieutenant on December 24th, 1915 and made temporary captain the following year. He was killed in action on April 28th, 1917.

The diary of the 13th Battalion faithfully records the action resulting in his death –

27th April – Battalion moved to Roclincourt, leaving Maroeuil at 11am and practising the attack route, arriving at Roclincourt at 2pm, where dinner was served after which men rested until dusk. Battalion then moved up to the assembly trenches beyond Bailleul [Oppy Sector] and formed ready for attack. All ranks appeared confident of success and cheerful.

Each man carried chocolate and two cheese sandwiches and were given a rum issue before moving off.

Disposition of the 6th Brigade; 13th Essex on right, 17th Middlesex on left.

Disposition of the Battalion, right to left; 'B', 'C'. 'D' and 'A'.

Each company – a footage of 120 yards.

The artillery barrage is the guiding factor as to the pace of the infantry advancing. It must be impressed on all ranks taking part in the attack that it is absolutely essential to advance close up to the barrage and they must assault any portion of the enemy trench or portion opposite them immediately the barrage lifts.

A contact aeroplane, from No. 5 Squadron, will fly over our line at 7am. Flares will be lit and mirrors flashed. This will be done when the contact aeroplane sounds his klaxon horn or fires a Very Light.

A contact patrol was essentially an aeroplane, or flight of aeroplanes, flying low over the battlefield to determine the relative positions of the opposing front lines during an attack. In theory the aeroplane would fly along the front, sometimes sounding a klaxon to alert the troops below to its presence. When the aeroplane was overhead, the attacking force would fire a flare to indicate their position. Not surprisingly, many infantrymen

Gravesend Cemetery

Charles Clarke –

IN LOVING MEMORY

CHARLES WATTS FREELOVE CLARKE

UNTIL THE DAWN BREAKS AND SHADOWS FLEE AWAY

John James Gordon Clarke –

CAPTAIN 13TH ESSEX REGIMENT

WHO MADE THE SUPREME SACRIFICE

ON 28TH APRIL 1917 AGED 24

opted not to fire flares that would also disclose their position to the enemy artillery, so the airmen would have to rely on noticing if the muddy uniforms below were khaki or field grey.

Dress; Fighting Order. One days ration and iron rations to be carried and water bottles filled. The following will also be carried; 2 bombs per man [No. 5 Mills], bombers will carry 10 bombs. 2 sandbags per man. Every man to carry one flare and 120 rounds SAA.

Every man to have a round in the chamber when advancing.

28th April – the heavy fighting continued and at 9am the troops were ordered to fall back, hold and consolidate the German Front Line. All the officers of the Battalion had become casualties and the majority of the non-commissioned officers and what was left of the Battalion was quite disorganised and exhausted.

The officer commanding 'D' Coy, 2nd Lt [Temporary Captain] E C Lowings was severely wounded. Three ORs were killed outright. 4 officers and 79 OR's were wounded, 8 officers and 240 OR's were missing.

T/Captain John James Gordon Clarke [OC 'C' Coy] and T/Captain C W Ritson OC 'B' Coy] were killed.

John has no known grave and is commemorated on the Thiepval Monument.

> We deeply regret to have to announce that Captain J. J. G. Clarke, Essex Regt., second son of Mr. and Mrs. John Clarke, of Lyndhurst, St. James's-road, Gravesend, fell in action on the 28th April. Mr. Clarke joined the Territorials on September 7th, 1914, soon after the outbreak of the war, and after about a year's service in the ranks he received his commission in the Essex Regt. He proceeded to France on active service at the beginning of September last. Major A. D. Derniche Jones, commanding the battalion, writes of the captain that he had penetrated some way into positions, leading his men most gallantly, when he fell to an enemy sniper. In adding his expression of sympathy, the chaplain of the regiment concludes with these words: "For him it is better, although it is difficult to realise, for all who knew him know what his religion was to him." Capt. Clarke was married to Miss M. M. Simmonds, daughter of Mr. and Mrs. Sidney Simmonds, of Cobham-street, in July last.

GR 19/5/17 [Andrew Marsall]

> CLARKE.—Killed in action, in France, on April 28th, Captain J. J. G. Clarke, Essex Regt., greatly loved husband of Muriel Mary Clarke (née Simmonds), of Malville, Cobham-street, and dearly loved and second son of Mr. and Mrs. John Clarke, of Lyndhurst, St. James's-

Valentine Herbert Clarke
On the Memorial as *H V Clarke*
Mercantile Marine Reserve

Valentine was born near Aylesford in 1878. His father Charles was born in 1836 and was from Gravesend. He worked in a nursery and subsequently as a bill distributor. His mother Mary was born in 1844 and from Gravesend. The couple had five children – Agnes, born in 1867, Gertrude, born in 1869, Edith, born a year later, Frances, born in 1874 and Valentine. The family home was at 16 Alma Cottage, Northfleet before moving to 1 Marion Villas, Dover Road.

Valentine was a carpenter by profession and found employment in Enfield by the turn of the century. He was living at 70 Gordon Hill, Enfield with his widowed mother prior to the war. On being called to the colours his mother returned to Gravesend being resident at 134 Parrock Street.

Valentine was in the Mercantile Marine Reserve and served on board *H.M.S. Isonzo*. The *Isonzo* was a passenger liner under the flag of the P & O Line from 1898 through to requisitioning.

She was built by Caird & Co. of Greenock.

She was just over 90m long and a breadth in excess of 11m and had a maximum speed of 20 knots.

BLAND LINE R.M.S. "GIBEL-SARSAR"

Isonzo's passenger capacity was 74 first class. She had a crew of 155 on the outbreak of War - 20 British, 95 Italian.

Valentine was killed when *H.M.S. Isonzo* was sunk on May 7th, 1918. His body was lost at sea and he is commemorated on the Plymouth Naval Memorial.

18518

CLARKE.—Drowned at sea, on the 7th inst., Valentine Herbert Clarke, only son of Mrs. M. A. Clarke, of 134, Parrock-street, and the late Charles Joseph Clarke.

GR 18/5/18 [Andrew Marsall]

Gravesend Cemetery –

And In Loving Memory Of
VALENTINE H. CLARKE
Drowned In The Great War 1917

221

Wilfrid Randall Clarke
R.F.A. / R.F.C. - Lieutenant

Wilfrid was born in Gravesend in 1891, the son of Richard Feaver Clarke of 'Henbury', New Milton [Hampshire]. Richard was born in Wincanton, Somerset and was a pharmaceutical chemist. He became a J.P. on retirement. His mother Rebecca was born in Brompton in 1852. There were five children in the family – Dorothy, born in 1885, Edith, born in 1887, Annie, born in 1888, Winifred, born in 1890 and Wilfrid. The family lived, prior to moving, at 'Daneholme', Pelham Road.

Wilfrid was educated at St Lawrence College in Ramsgate and enlisted in the Territorials in October, 1908 with the 4th H.C. [Howitzer] Brigade, Royal Artillery which was based at Erith. At the time he was an apprentice with Vickers and Maxim, Queen's Road, Erith. He was 5 feet 10½ inches tall and of good physical development. Over the following four years he undertook his fortnightly training at Lydd or Dover [1911]. He secured his Instructor's Certificate for Instruction of Signalling in his training.

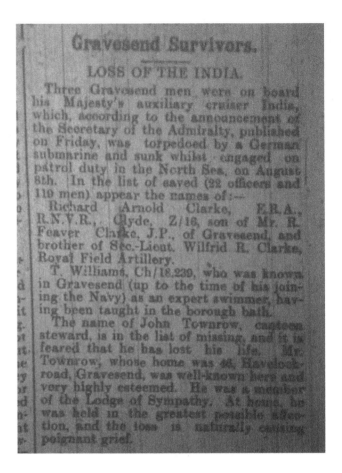

Gravesend Survivors.

LOSS OF THE INDIA.

Three Gravesend men were on board his Majesty's auxiliary cruiser India, which, according to the announcement of the Secretary of the Admiralty, published on Friday, was torpedoed by a German submarine and sunk whilst engaged on patrol duty in the North Sea, on August 8th. In the list of saved (22 officers and 119 men) appear the names of:—

Richard Arnold Clarke, E.R.A., R.N.V.R., Clyde, Z/16, son of Mr. R. Feaver Clarke, J.P., of Gravesend, and brother of Sec.-Lieut. Wilfrid R. Clarke, Royal Field Artillery.

T. Williams, Ch/18.239, who was known in Gravesend (up to the time of his joining the Navy) as an expert swimmer, having been taught in the borough bath.

The name of John Townrow, canteen steward, is in the list of missing, and it is feared that he has lost his life. Mr. Townrow, whose home was 44 Havelock-road, Gravesend, was well-known here and very highly esteemed. He was a member of the Lodge of Sympathy. At home, he was held in the greatest possible affection, and the loss is naturally causing poignant grief.

He died on February 4th, 1918 and is buried in Grantham Cemetery.

A SUPPLEMENT to the "London Gazette," published Monday, November 23rd, contains the announcement that Wilfrid Randall Clarke is gazetted second lieutenant in the R.F.A., from the 3rd Batt. of the University and Public Schools' Brigade, Royal Fusiliers, Epsom, Surrey. Lieut. W. R. Clarke, A.M.Inst.C.E., is the elder son of Mr. R. Feaver Clarke, J.P., 9, The Avenue, Gravesend. Mr. Feaver Clarke's younger son, Richard Arnold Clarke, also a student-member of the Institute of Civil Engineers, is serving in the Royal Naval Volunteer Reserve (Clyde Division), now stationed at the Royal Naval Barracks, Chatham.

GR 5/12/14 [Andrew Marshall]

He joined the Royal Flying Corps on October 14th, 1915. He was promoted Lieutenant and became a flying officer.

On Active Service.

CLARKE.— On February 4th, accidentally killed whilst flying at Grantham, Lieut. Wilfrid Randall Clarke, R.F.A., attached to Royal Flying Corps, aged 26 years, elder son of R. Feaver Clarke, J.P., Gravesend.

GR 9/2/18 [Andrew Marshall]

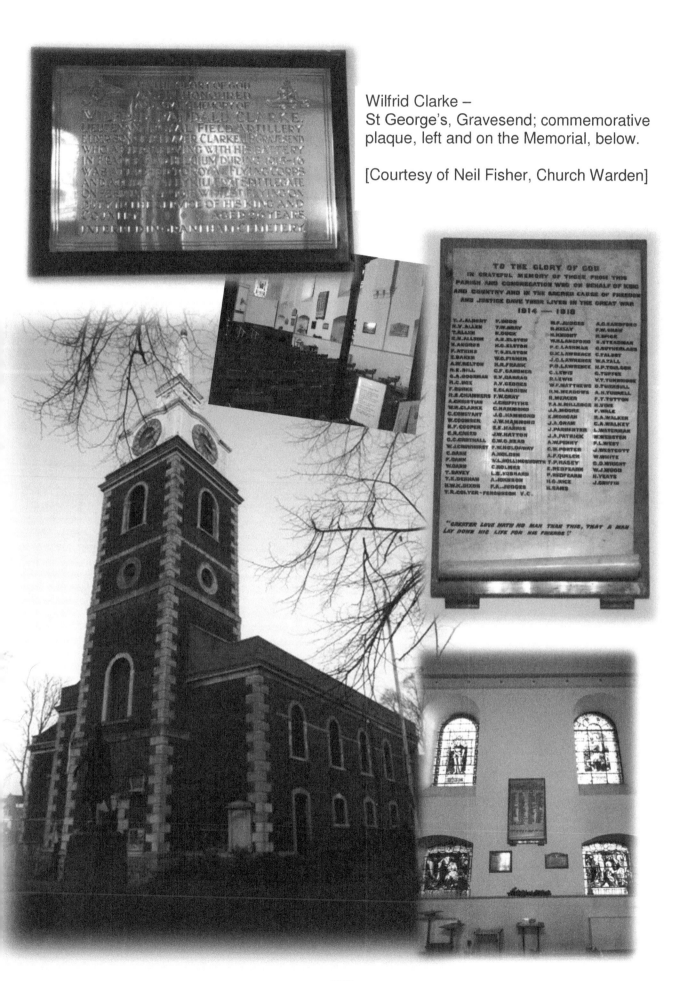

Wilfrid Clarke –
St George's, Gravesend; commemorative plaque, left and on the Memorial, below.

[Courtesy of Neil Fisher, Church Warden]

223

Lieutenant Wilfrid Randall Clarke, R.F.A. (attached to Royal Flying Corps), whose death we briefly announced in our last issue, was born on the 15th June, 1891, at Gravesend, and entered upon his school life at St. Lawrence College, Ramsgate, September, 1904, where he remained four years. On leaving the College he was apprenticed at Messrs. Vickers, Ltd., Erith, to learn engineering. Upon the completion of the term of his apprenticeship, this firm retained his services, and while so working he passed his examination, upon which he became an Associate Member of the Inst. C.E. During his residence at Erith he joined the 4th Home Counties Howitzer Brigade as a private, and at St. Lawrence College he was also a private in the Cadet Corps. Upon the outbreak of war in August, 1914, Lieut. Clarke resigned his appointment at Messrs. Vickers to join the colours, selecting the Public Schools Battalion training at Epsom. He was given a commission and gazetted Second-Lieut., Royal Field Artillery, on November 20th, 1914. Further training followed at Salisbury and Berkhamsted until October, 1915, when he went with his Battery to the front, and during the winter of 1915 was at Ypres and Arras. After being six months at the front he was transferred to the Inspection Department (Carriages), Royal Arsenal, Woolwich, where he remained until September, 1917, when he volunteered for the Royal Flying Corps, and being accepted went into training. He was enthusiastically devoted to this work and made good progress, passing his examinations successfully. He went home on February 1st for two days' leave in the fullest vigour of young healthy manhood, stimulated with the anticipation of taking his final examination at the end of the month to secure qualification for the granting of his "wings." He returned from Gravesend early on the morning of February 4th, and in the evening of the same day his father received the sad intelligence that he had met with a fatal accident whilst flying in the afternoon. He received his promotion to First Lieutenant in the R.F.A. on July 1st, 1917. Lieut. Clarke was buried in Grantham Cemetery on Thursday afternoon of last week with full military honours. His father and two of his sisters, Miss Edith R. Clarke and Miss Winifred S. Clarke, being present.

Mr. Feryer Clarke's younger son is a prisoner of war, interned in Norway. He was one of the survivors of H.M.S. "India," sunk by German submarine in the Arctic Circle on August 8th, 1915. Fortunately he obtained leave for a month on parole in England last November, and arriving had three days with his brother. A singular coincidence occurred in the fact that the two boys joined the colours the same day, one in Kent, the other in Glasgow, without previous communication either to each other or to their father.

Squadron Commander, R.F.C., writes:—"If sincere sympathy can take any weight off such a blow, then the sympathy that the whole of my squadron has for you may help, for we all loved him. He was my own pupil, and I have often remarked that if all pupils were as keen and hard-working as your son was, our work would be much easier. Always cheerful, always ready for any work, he set a fine example, and his death was a great shock to us all." The Chaplain, R.F.C., writes:—"It is with the greatest regret that I have heard of your son's death to-day, and I should like to send you and his family my deep sympathy. I hear on all sides what a good fellow he was, keen and plucky. . . . It is a heavy price we have to pay for the training of the men who serve their country in the air." The Bishop of Chelmsford sends the following tribute:—"I know how poor human words must be at such a time as this, but you have his memory, which must be of great value to you now. I well remember his visit to me at Bethnal Green and how he delighted us all by his clean and wholesome life. You must thank God for what he was, and what he is, for surely he is in the Service above. . . . . ." A Friend writes:—"Poor Will! So splendid in physique, so courteous, so tender, so genuine, so clean. The world is a loser when such as he are taken, for to know him was to love and respect him."

———

Preaching at St. George's Church, Gravesend, on Sunday morning, from the words, "I do set my bow in the cloud" (Genesis ix., 13), the Rev. Canon Gedge alluded to the death of Lieut. Clarke. "Man's extremity is God's opportunity," he observed, and continued: "You must be thinking of one whose sudden death, in a sense, marked the passing of the last week. Only last Sunday morning, in the bloom of life and in the flush of youth he was with us. He would come to his early Communion, saying that he must always remember that with him and those with him it was one moment in the air and the next in eternity. The words were of singular significance. It was even so with him in a few hours. He left us the next morning to go back to Grantham, to ascend 1,500 feet and then to fall like a stone. A sudden faintness must have prevented his releasing the controls which would automatically have righted the machine, and thus he went to his death, probably unconscious. Very early in the war we lost one of our best, well known to us here, by a fatal and insidious disease then little understood. Since then again and again we have had to face this tragic effect of this war, costing us our young, and brave and bright. That is the peculiar effect of this war. It takes the young. We feel it to-day and are repeatedly conscious of it. And yet, who would have it otherwise than it is? If the cause is sacred, if it is the cause of God, then by an instinct, which has prompted men in all ages to make the sacrifice of the best, we are giving to God our best and strongest, our youngest and our bravest. As the Bishop of Chelmsford says, writing about our young friend, who was also his friend, and who has worked with him — 'He is serving still.' He is in the service of God above. In the service! That is what

significance. It was even so ...
few hours. He left us the next morning, to
go back to Grantham, to ascend 1,500 feet
and then to fall like a stone. A sudden
faintness must have prevented his releasing
the controls which would automatically have
righted the machine, and thus he went to his
death, probably unconscious. Very early in
the war we lost one of our best, well known
to us here, by a fatal and insidious disease
then little understood. Since then again and
again we have had to face this tragic effect
of this war, costing us our young, and brave
and bright. That is the peculiar effect of
this war. It takes the young. We feel it
to-day and are repeatedly conscious of it.
And yet, who would have it otherwise than
it is. If the cause is sacred, if it is the
cause of God, then by an instinct, which has
prompted men in all ages to make the
sacrifice of the best, we are giving to God
our best and strongest, our youngest and our
bravest. As the Bishop of Chelmsford says,
writing about our young friend, who was
also his friend, and who has worked with him
—'He is serving still.' He is in the service
of God above. In the service! That is what
these young souls are, living and dying. It
is the proud title which indicates their relation to their sovereign and their country.
Their motto is the motto of the Heir
Apparent—'I serve.' They serve, alike in
life and in death. It is the supreme test of
service unto death. So we must not grudge
it. Like another young spirit which fled only
a week or two ago, he would have had his
wings. And he has had them. The
heathen said 'Whom the gods love die
young.' We can but realise that it may be
in great mercy and tenderness they are taken
away from the evil to come. Our young
friend was suddenly dashed to the ground,
broken like the potter's vessel. It might
well be he would almost cry in those great
words which the Russian novelist puts into
the mouth of his escaping prisoner when he
falls dying—'Fly on, my soul.' Yes, fly on
my soul! The body's work is done, the
service rendered, his part in the world,
apparently so short and so abruptly ended,
fulfilled. Soul, fly on. This lad, as you
know, has always been one of us. He used
to help us in our Band of Hope, he was a
regular communicant, a member, and a
fellow-worker. Who shall say what he does
for us still? Are they not ministering
spirits, those whom God sets free from the
trammels of earth? He breaks the clay but
sets the spirit free. Why, and for what?
Surely for some purpose, some service to be
rendered. And so, on the dark cloud of
widespread sorrow which now broods over our
nation, on the bosom of that dark cloud of
anxiety and apprehension which looms so
large in the face of the great assault which
must soon come and the tremendous sacrifice
it must involve, God paints for you and me
once more the rainbow of immortal hope.
The boy who took with us last Sunday
morning the bread of life, the food of
immortality gives this parting message to
all—'a moment in the air; another moment
in eternity!' So may we learn that to live
is Christ; to die is gain."

Edward Clifford
Royal West Surrey Rgt, 2nd Bn
Service No. L/12133 - Private
Edward was the son of Edward and Eliza Clifford of 3 Albion Parade. Edward [father] was born on 1869 and worked as a coal porter on the Thames. Eliza, born in 1871 was also from Milton. They were married in 1890 and had nine surviving children – Sarah, born in 1892, Eliza, born in 1895, Edward, born in 1897, Robert, born in 1899, Emma, born in 1901, Margaret, born in 1903, Lily, born in 1905, William, born in 1908 and Frederick, born in 1910.

He enlisted with the Royal West Kents, service number 10736 before joining the 2nd Battalion, The Queen's. He was killed in action on October 29th, 1918 and is buried at Tezze Commonwealth Cemetery.

Frederick William Colbourne
Royal Army Ordnance Corps
Service No.   Private
Frederick was born in 1887 in Paddington, the son of Henry, born in 1856 in Blakemere, Hereford and Annie, born in 1859 in Marylebone, [Stallion] Colbourne. They married on June 12th, 1882. Henry was a butler to James and Mary Frater of 2 Clifton Place. James was a rather successful solicitor as Henry was one of five servants in the house.

The Colbourne family lived at 23 Stanyforth Road, Paddington with three other families on the premises. There were four children in the Colbourne family – Albert, born in 1893, Emily, born in 1895, Frederick and Edwin.

Frederick was employed as a lawyer's clerk in Gravesend. He had a room with Alice Offen, a widow, who ran a boarding house at 136 Milton Road.

He married Margaret Walton on April 17th, 1911 at St Luke's Church, Paddington. She was born in 1886 and was also from Gravesend, the Walton family living at 145 Windmill Street. The couple lived at 157 Parrock Street. They had two children – Freda, born December 1912 and Kathleen, born December 1914.

He was promoted Lieutenant on April 14th, 1918. Frederick died of pneumonia on February 25th, 1919. He is buried in Tincourt Cemetery.

George Cole - Menin Gate

George Barclay Cole
Royal West Kent, 1st Battalion
Service No. S/8483 - Private

George was born in Gravesend in 1894. His father, George, was born in 1862 and was also from Gravesend. He had a sister Doris who was two years younger. The family lived at 8 Darnley Street.

George [father] was a cab proprieter and a widower since shortly after Doris' birth.

George enlisted with the 1st Battalion, Royal West Kent in Gravesend.

George was killed in action on April 18th, 1915 and has no known grave. He is commemorated on the Menin Gate.

Harry Charles Colleer
Royal West Kent, 7th Battalion
Service No. 240828 - Private

Harry was born in Brightlingsea in 1890. He was the son of Charles and Lottie Colleer of 68 Darnley Road. The couple were married in 1890 and they had three children – Harry, Wilfrid, born in 1894 and Dorothy, born in 1897. Charles, born in 1860 in Colchester, was a Preventive Officer

Pozieres Memorial – Harry Colleer

with H.M. Customs. Lottie was born in 1866 in Brightlingsea where the three children were also born. Harry worked as a clerk with the Port of London Authority and Wilfrid worked for the Tramway Company.

He was killed in action on March 28th, 1918. He has no known grave and is commemorated on the Pozieres Memorial.

Lce.-Cpl. H. C. Collier.
R.W.K. Regt.

GR 21/12/18 – note the mis-spelling!

Samuel Colville

Royal Navy - P/Officer, 1st Class
Service No. 169942

Sam was born on June 10th, 1876 in Swanscombe. He married Mary Ann in 1904 and they had no family. She was from Chatham and was two years his junior. Sam worked in the Coast Guard service and so the couple were constantly on the move. Prior to the Great War they had moved from South Shields to the Coast Guard Station at Leigh-on-Sea.

GR 16/1/15 [Andrew Marsall]

Sam enlisted in the Royal Navy at the outbreak of war. He was a Petty Officer, 1st Class when he was killed in action on board HMS Formidable on January 1st, 1915.

He has no known grave and is commemorated on the Naval Memorial in Chatham.

GR 4/1/19 [Andrew Marsall]

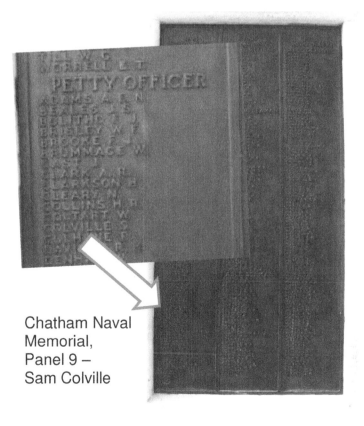

Chatham Naval Memorial, Panel 9 – Sam Colville

Thomas Riversdale Colyer-Fergusson, V.C.
Northamptonshire Regt, 2nd Batt.
Captain

Thomas Riversdale 'Riv' Colyer-Fergusson was born at 13 Lower Berkley Street, London, on the 18th February 1896, the third and youngest son of Thomas Colyer Fergusson, a former High Sheriff of Kent, and his wife Beatrice [Muller]. He inherited the name Riversdale, with its Irish connections, a maternal grandmother, a daughter of Riversdale Grenfell.

His father, Thomas Colyer-Fergusson, was a Kentish Squire with homes at Wombwell Hall, Gravesend, and Ightham Mote

He was descended from Sir William Ferguson, Queen Victoria's doctor, and Sir James Rankin Fergusson, a distinguished barrister.

The name Colyer came to the family through Sir James Fergusson's first wife, Mary Soames, elder daughter of Thomas Colyer of Wombwell Hall. It was added by Sir Thomas in 1890 on succeeding to his grandmother's house, Wombwell Hall near Gravesend.

The family also owned the Scottish seat of Spitalhaugh and rented a London house, 13 Lower Berkley Street, for the season.

Sir Thomas divided his time between these properties, but in his later years he stayed mainly at the Mote, and there he brought up his large family. He was a much respected man and a serious genealogist, working through the parish register to compile 24 manuscript volumes on the descent of local families. Following the tradition of the house, he was High Sheriff of Kent in 1906.

Sir Thomas Colyer-Fergusson married twice. All his six children were by his first wife, Beatrice, the daughter of Professor Friedrich Max Müller, a renowned philologist and Professor of Modern European Languages at Oxford, where he was Keeper of the Bodleian Library and a Fellow of All Souls. They lost two sons to the World Wars - In 1917 their third son, Riv died aged 21 in the Third Battle of Ypres, winning a posthumous Victoria Cross. Their elder son Max was killed at the age of 49 in a bombing raid on an army driving-school near Tidworth in 1940.

Sir James Ranken Fergusson [1835-1934] on left with Thomas Colyer-Fergusson [1865-1951] on right; Max [1890-940] is standing behind his son James [1917-2004].

Wombell Hall; the entrances, top left and top right, and a part of the original gardens are all that remains of the original Wombell Hall, above. Northfleet School for Girls now occupies much of the original site.

Robert Hiscock in his A HISTORY OF GRAVESEND describes Wombell Hall –
now part of the Technical School, the present building, erected in 1860 for Thomas Colyer, occupies the site of at least two earlier houses of this name. The first erected in 1471 by Thomas Wombwell, who came from a village of that name in Yorkshire, and the second by James Fortrey in 1663. The last family to live there were the Colyer-Fergussons, who were there until 1937.

In the years following the purchase of the house, 1890-1, Sir Thomas carried out much repair and restoration, and this perhaps is the greatest memorial, for without his dedication the house might scarcely have survived, having suffered from centuries of neglect. He made it more habitable, converting an old lumber room into a billiard room, inserting bathrooms and a primitive form of central heating. He was the first to undertake the work which the National Trust resumed, on a larger scale, a hundred years later.

Ightham Mote

One of the Colyer-Fergussons' three daughters, Mary, always known as Polly, married Walter Monckton, who as a lawyer and politician achieved great national distinction. He was married from there in 1914, became Edward VIII's closest confidant during the Abdication Crisis of 1936 and was promoted to the Cabinet in Minister of Labour in Churchill's second government. On retiring in 1957 he was created a Viscount, and at his death in 1965 he was succeeded by his son Gilbert, later a Major-General, who was born at the Mote and christened in its chapel.

On Sir Thomas's death at the age of 86 in 1951, the property and baronetcy passed to Max's son, James, who was and remained a bachelor. From childhood his main interest had been in railways, and he rose to responsible positions within British Rail.

Riv as he was known in the family, was taught at Summer Fields, Oxford, and then went on to Harrow in 1909. There he joined the Officer Training Corps, eventually attaining the rank of Sergeant.

As a youngster, he developed a passion for country sports. A keen follower of the hounds, he was also an accomplished shot. He kept a pet falcon in his younger days and was a keen supporter of the West Kent Hounds Hunt.

In the summer of 1914 he was due to take his place at Oriel College, Oxford,

but the war intervened. He enlisted in the Public Schools Battalion of the Middlesex Regiment in September. He was posted to T Company as 1021 Private T. R. Colyer-Fergusson. He was 5 foot 7 inches tall and weighed 134lbs.

The following February he was granted a temporary commission as a 2nd Lieutenant with the 3rd Battalion, the Northamptonshire Regiment. He was posted to the 2nd Battalion and went to France in November 1915, qualifying him for the 1914-1915 Star.

He applied for a regular commission which was granted. His commission took effect on July 4th, 1916 as a 2nd Lieutenant.

Riv was in action in the opening phases of the Battle of the Somme. He was wounded in the right arm, gunshot wound, at Contalmaison on July 7th. He was evacuated to Boulogne two days later and on to England the following day. On October 6th, he appeared before a Medical Board at Fort Pitt Military Hospital in Chatham. He was declared fit for active service. He returned to his unit in November and the following month was given a permanent commission.

In January 1916, age 20, he was promoted to acting captain and given command of B Company. The following month, as the Germans pulled back to the Hindenburg line, he led his men in a dashing attack on the ridge overlooking Bouchavesnes. Sweeping across two lines of enemy trenches, they burst into the third line, captured a machine gun and bombed a dug out before realising they had advance beyond their objective. Pulling back, they helped consolidate and newly won position and held it against five counter-attacks. The action cost the Northants almost 250 causalities, but Riv emerged unscathed with his reputation enhanced.

A contemporary account described the young officer as *a fine type of healthy English boyhood.* His high spirited behaviour and appearance however belied his mature leadership qualities. He was a general favourite and had a particularly frank and open manner which gained him the affection of all classes on whom he came in contact. One of his commanding officers spoke of his *adroitness in managing the men under him.* Leslie Wilkinton, the machine gun officer who came to know him shortly before the 3rd Ypres, describe him as *a keen young regular, obviously greatly liked by the men.*

The Battle of Pilckem Ridge began with an initial assault on July 31st, 1917. Riv was in command of B Company, 2nd Battalion. The Regiment's objective was to capture the Bellewaarde Ridge by advancing through the area to the east of Bellewaarde Lake and Chateau Wood, above right.

The night of the 30th/31st July 1917 was dark and cloudy with the threat of rain as the men of the 2nd Northamptonshire's shuffled towards their assembly positions in front of Bellewaarde Ridge.

B Company was last to arrive, led by Riv. Two of his platoons formed part of

the battalion's third wave in the coming attack, the remainder being employed as mopping up teams. The Northants had been allotted stretches of the Kingsway and Kingsway Support trenches, but shortly after midnight, Riv keen to avoid any retaliatory bombardment, moved his men, together with a supporting section of machine gunners, 100 yards forward.

By 2am they were in position. The night was quite with little shelling or rifle fire. *We lay there quite happily to wait for the off,* observed 2/Lt Leslie Wilkinton, the officer in command of the machine gunners of the 24th Machine Gun Company. One of the men handed round humbugs which he had just received from home.

That morning the men of 11 Corps, of which the 2nd Northants were part, faced the most important task to be undertaken by General Sir Hubert Gough's Fifth Army. Operating south of the Ypres Roulers Railway, three divisions, the 8th, 30th, and 24th, were to capture the entire Pilckem Ridge, the most heavily defended enemy sector along the Ypres front. Three main defence zones and no fewer than seven lines of fortifications ran across the high ground. Once freckled with woods, the plateau had become a *wilderness of fallen trees* masking a lethal network of pillboxes and machine gun nests that had survived intact the British bombardment. The Northants were the left hand Battalion of the 24th Brigade, and their task was to capture Bellewaarde Ridge, one of the enemy's key observations posts.

At 3.50 am the barrage came down with *tremendous roar* and the battalion advanced under its cover. Perfect order prevailed, the battalion keeping its formation just as if they were still in the practice trenches back at Bomy. 2/Lt Hubert Essame, the acting adjutant, recorded - *The blast was so deafening that we jammed our fingers in our ears; the ground shook. We could see the flashes of the barrage in the murk ahead. The swish of the 18 pdr shells tempted us to crouch down. In fact, although we could not see them, the two leading companies advancing on compass bearings were clinging to the barrage and moving forward each time it jumped a further 25yds.*

A and D Companies led the advance, followed by Riv's B Company ready to push on to the Battalion's main objective on the ridge. Little remained of the enemy wire or their forward trenches as they advanced into Chateau Wood. According to the Northants' war diary, the *defenders were too dazed to put up a fight.* As the leading waves occupied Ignis Trench and Ignorance Support, mopping up parties netted sixty prisoners from the craters around Hooge and scattered outposts along the Menin Road.

B and C Companies, meanwhile, skirted Bellewaarde Lake and a line of smouldering dugouts treated to a barrage of Thermite (incendiary mortar bombs). 2nd Lieutenant Essame, who had moved forward with Lieutenant-Colonel C.G. Buckle DSO, MC, the second Northants' 26 year old CO, saw them *ploughing through the mud* on their way towards the crest of Bellewaarde Ridge.

As they advanced, Riversdale realised there was an enemy stronghold in front

of them, with machine-gun crews positioned nearby. If they lost the cover of the barrage, the assault would almost certainly fail. He decided to push through the barrage in order to reach "Jacob" trench. Riv collected ten men, including Sergeant W.G. Boulding and his orderly Private B. Ellis, and dashed forward under cover of the shelling.

Forming up for the final approach, however, proved difficult. Riv realised his company was in danger of losing the barrage. Ahead lay Jacob Trench, covered by a machine gun in a wired strongpoint, missed by the bombardment. Knowing a delay could prove disastrous, he attacked.

Just as they gained a footing in the enemy position, a German company was spotted advancing en masse barely 100 yards away. The regimental history recorded that Riv and *his picked men knocked out 20 or 30 of them with rifle fire, and the remainder put up their hands. The men of his company were beginning to come up, when the German machine gun came into action. Leaving his company to hold the trench, and assisted by his orderly alone, [Private Basil Hannant Ellis] Captain Colyer-Fergusson attacked and captured the gun. He then turned it on to another group of the enemy, killing a large number of them and driving the remainder into* the hands of another British unit. Later, assisted only by Sgt Boulding and Pte Ellis (both later awarded DCMs), he attacked and captured a second machine gun.

This enabled the rest of B Company to arrive and ensure the capture of Jacob trench and complete.

At around 5.30 am, when the young company commander reported to his CO, consolidation was under way. Buckle, who had signalled the ridge's capture to a patrolling scout plane, ordered B and C Companies to push on 100 - 200 yards to establish a line of outposts, and it was while directing this operation, shortly afterwards that Riv was hit in the head by a snipers bullet, dying instantly. No one had done more to ensure the success of the operation. As the unit war diary recorded - he *had done magnificently. The capture of Jacob Trench was largely due to his courage and initiative.*

He was 21 years old when his heroism on the occasion resulted in he being awarded the Victoria Cross, the citation reading - *For most conspicuous bravery, skilful leading and determination in attack. The tactical situation having developed contrary to expectation, it was not possible for his company to adhere to the original plan of deployments, and owing to the difficulties of the ground*

and to enemy wire, Captain Colyer Fergusson found himself with a Sergeant and five men only. He carried out the attack nevertheless, and succeeded in capturing the enemy trench and disposing of the garrison. His party was then threatened by a heavy counter-attack from the left front, but this attack he successfully resisted. During this operation, assisted by his Orderly only, he attacked and captured an enemy machine gun and turned it on the assailants, many of whom were killed and a large number driven into the hands of an adjoining British unit. Later, assisted only by his Sergeant, he again attacked and captured a second enemy machine gun, by which time he had been joined by other portions of his company, and was enabled to consolidate his position. The conduct of this officer throughout forms an amazing record of dash, gallantry and skill, for which no reward

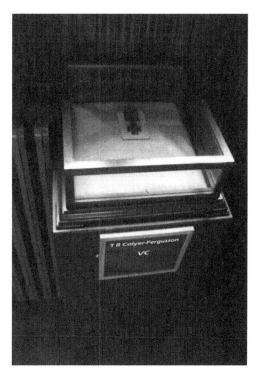

Thomas' Victoria Cross is displayed at the Museum of the Northamptonshire Regiment [48th and 58th Foot].

can be too great, having regard to the importance of the position won. This gallant officer was shortly afterwards killed by a sniper. - The London Gazette.

GR 5/9/17 [Andrew Marsall]

Riv was a most popular office in the field. A staff officer from divisional headquarters wrote to his parents as follows - *I cannot, however, tell you that he behaved with quite exceptional gallantry on July 31st, and set an example which everybody in the division is proud of.*
But not only did he display exceptional gallantry, but also sound military knowledge and tactical insight far beyond his years, and in so doing enabled us to secure all objectives which would have cost many lives but for his prompt and gallant actions.
A fellow Officer of his wrote - *There is, however a great comfort to me, and I know it will be to you, in the manner and circumstances of Riv's death.*
He died in the best of spirits in the very moment of success, and a success which was rendered possible by his own brave action.
No men could wish for a finer or more manly ending to this life. God grant, when my time comes, that I may meet it in a like manner.

In the letter from Lieutenant-Colonel Buckle, Riv's commanding officer, to the family - *In this last attack I selected his company for the most difficult portion of trench within the battalion objective. He carried out his task most brilliantly. For the capture of a certain line of German trenches, his company had to follow our barrage through a very broken wood, which proved to be full of wire. He soon saw that it would be impossible to keep his whole company up with the barrage for the final assault, and if he failed to keep up with it would probably fail to capture the trench, so he picked out ten or a dozen men and with them pushed on ahead, and without any further assistance captured his portion of the*

German trench. Almost as soon as he got in he perceived a company of Germans advancing against him in mass formation and a bare 100 yards away. He and his picked men knocked out 20 or 30 of them with rifle fire, and the remainder of them surrendered as the rest of his company came up.

He came and reported to me in the same trench about half an hour later, when I got up to him. Five minutes later he was shot through the forehead by a German machine gun bullet. I think his death was more deeply felt in the regiment than any other I have known. To my own mind he was the most promising officer under my command. I cannot hope ever to be able to replace him he, besides being a first rate officer, such a through

sportsman and the cheeriest of companions.

Riv is buried in the Menin Road South Commonwealth War Graves' Commission Cemetery. The inscription on his headstone reads. *My son, my son. No reward can be too great.* Thomas' brother, Max was killed in action in World War 2.

Died of Wounds.
COLYER-FERGUSSON.—On the 31st July, of wounds received same day, Thomas Riversdale Colyer-Fergusson, Second-Lieutenant (Acting Captain), Northamptonshire Regt., dearly-loved youngest son of Thomas Colyer-Fergusson, of Ightham Mote and Wombwell-Hall, Kent, in his twenty-second year.

GR 25/8/17 [Andrew Marsall]

Lieut. T. R. Colyer Fergusson, V.C.

Mayoral Chambers, Woodville Halls, Gravesend –
Portrait and citation. [courtesy John Càller]

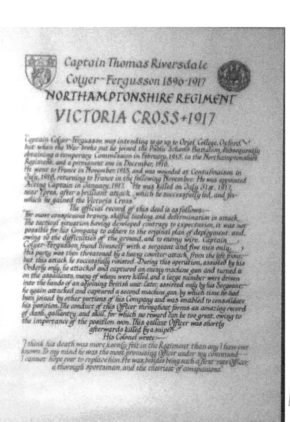

The original grave marker, above at
Ightham Mote and Riv's grave, below in
the Menin Road South Cemetery, Ypres –
MY SON, MY SON
NO REWARD CAN BE TOO GREAT

His name is also on the Ightham
War Memorial and there is a plaque
and window in St Peter's Church,
Ightham dedicated to Thomas.

NORTHFLEET'S V.O. WINNER.—The Northfleet Council have written to the Gravesend
Corporation politely calling attention to the
fact that the late Lieut. T. R. Collyer-Fer-
guson, V.O., whose name appears on the
memorial tablet outside the Town Hall, really
belongs to Northfleet parish.

GR 22/2/19 – whose hero?
[Andrew Marsall]

The Colyer Arms in Station Rd,
Betsham

A Service of Dedication of the Plaque
in Memory of

Thomas Riversdale Colyer-Fergusson
V.C.

8 May 2006

at

Northfleet School for Girls
and
Northfleet School for Boys

R.I.P. 31st July 1917

Northfleet School for Girls –
the memorial to Riv.

The service of dedication was on May 8th, 2006, left.

The memorial is at the back of the school – above and left.

The main entrance, below.

The school is sited on the grounds of Wombell Hall.

[courtesy Northfleet School for Girls]

John Victor Michael Connolly
Royal West Kent Rgt, 6th Bn
Service No. G/14958 - Private

John was born 1897. He was the eldest of three children born to Michael and Susan Connolly of 7 Lower Range Road, Denton.

Michael was born in 1875 and worked locally as a coal porter. Susan was born in 1880. The couple married in 1897. John had two sisters – Kathleen, born in 1907 and Rosaleen in 1910.

John enlisted with the 6th Battalion, Royal West Kents. The battalion moved to Boulogne on June 1st, 1915 and then proceeded to the Ypres sector.

On January 19th, 1916 they began a period of training in Open Warfare at Busnes, then moved back into the front line at Loos in mid-February 1916.

In June they moved to Flesselles and carried out a training exercise. They moved to Baizieux on the 30th June and went into the reserve at Hencourt and Millencourt by mid-morning on July 1st. They relieved the 8th Division at Ovillers-la-Boisselle that night and attacked the following morning with mixed success.

On the 7th they attacked again and despite suffering heavy casualties in the area of Mash Valley, they succeeded in capturing and holding the first and second lines close to Ovillers.

They were withdrawn to Contay on July 9th. They were in action in The Battle of Pozieres on August 3rd with a successful attack capturing 4th Avenue Trench and were engaged in heavy fighting until they were withdrawn on the 9th.

He was killed on October 7th, 1916. He has no known grave and is commemorated on the Thiepval Memorial.

GR 25/8/17 [Andrew Marsall]

Thomas Connolly
Royal Sussex Regiment, 5th Bn
Service No. TF/241330 - Private

Tom was born in 1876 in Chorlton, Lancashire. He worked as a printer's stereotyper. His wife, Annie was born in Dublin in 1879. They had five children – Alice, born in 1901, John, born in 1902, Thomas, born in 1904, Michael, born in 1907 and Albert, born in 1910. The family moved to Gravesend in 1901 and lived at 17 Enfield Terrace.

The family had moved to Huddersfield and Annie died before he enlisted on August 26th, 1914 with the West Riding Regiment. He was 5 feet 6 inches tall and weighed 115lbs and was deemed fit for service. However he was discharged on January 29th, 1915 – not likely to become an efficient soldier.

He re-enlisted with the Royal Sussex Regiment in Maidstone.

Tom was killed on September 30th, 1917 and is buried at Duhallow A.D.S. Cemetery. Duhallow Advanced Dressing Station, believed to have been named after a southern Irish hunt, was a medical post 1.6 kilometres north of Ypres. The cemetery was begun in July 1917 and in October and November 1918, it was used by the 11th, 36th and 44th Casualty Clearing Stations.

After the Armistice, the cemetery was enlarged when graves were brought into this cemetery from isolated sites and a number of small cemeteries on the battlefields around Ypres. Special memorials commemorate a number of casualties known to have been buried in two of these cemeteries, Malakoff Farm Cemetery, Brielen, and Fusilier Wood Cemetery, Hollebeke, whose graves were destroyed by shellfire.

There are now 1,544 Commonwealth casualties of the First World War buried or commemorated in the cemetery.

The records indicate that his son John had also enlisted in late 1914 being listed with the 1st Leinster Regiment, service number 1225.

> It is with deep regret that the death is announced of Pte. Connolly, of 27, Shrubbery-road, who was killed by a shell in France on Sept er 30th. He was 41 years of age, and leaves a wife and six children. Previous to joining the Royal Sussex Regt. on June 16th 1916, he was employed at the Amalgamated Press, where he had been since February 1901 Mr. Connolly will be remembered as one of the best and most popular members of the Harmsworth football and cricket team, and also as a member of the Gravesend Town Band. Mrs. Connolly has received a letter from his officer (Lieut. E. Bruce Gilson commenting on his sterling qualities and p ?arity with his comrades. He was always c rful, an excellent worker, and best of all a b e man. Much sympathy has been expresse to his wife and family by his late comrads, y whom he will be sadly missed.

GR 15/12/17 [Andrew Marsall]

Charles Edward Constant
Able Seaman

Charles was born in 1893, the youngest of eleven children and lived with his widowed mother, Sarah at 23 Thames Terrace. Sarah was born in 1851 and was self-employed as a shrimp merchant. Her husband, Amos died in the mid-1890s. Six of her surviving children, including Charles, lived at the address. Charles and his older brother, Robert, born in 1890, worked as shrimpers.

Charles later joined in the Mercantile Marine. He was on the *S.S. Marquette* out of West Hartlepool when it was sunk by a German submarine. He was killed in the engagement.

The *SS Bodicea* (as she was first called), was originally built for the Wilson & Furness-Leyland Line with accommodation for 120 1st class passengers. Launched on November 25th, 1897, she made her maiden voyage from Glasgow to London and New York on January 15th, 1898. Later that year she became one of 5 sister ships acquired for the Atlantic Transport Line.

She made only one trip across the Atlantic in service with her new owners before, on September 15th, 1898, she was renamed *SS Marquette*. She then began further regular sailings across the Atlantic. By September 1905, she had been transferred to the Red Star Line and, once fitted with radio, she commenced the Antwerp to Philadelphia service for that Company.

By the end of 1914, she had completed her final Atlantic crossing, as Antwerp and other Belgian ports had fallen into German hands. She was then requisitioned for use as a British war transport ship, for which she was re-painted grey.

The *H.M. Transport S.S. Marquette,* under command of Captain John Bell Findlay, left Alexandria Harbour,

Anvers
S. S. „Marquette" de la Red Star Line

Egypt in the late afternoon on October 19th, 1915 for Salonica, Greece. A rousing send off with cheers and songs by British and French sailors manning warships in port was interrupted by a fault in the steering gear which caused the *Marquette* to suddenly swing round. A fire in a case on the deck caused a further diversion until it was thrown overboard. At dusk the transport was joined by its escort and the portholes were blacked out. The passengers and crew carried out lifeboat drills, as there were rumours there was German U-boats in the area. On the evening of the fourth day the escort, the French destroyer *"Tirailleur"*, left the convey. At 0915 the next morning, October 23rd, Capt. Dave Isaacs NZMC (the Quarter-master) was out strolling on deck with several nurses and drew their attention to a *straight thin green line about 50 yards away streaking through the water towards the ship,* a periscope was seen cutting the water, and a terrific explosion on the forward starboard side signalled the ship had been struck by a torpedo. At once the steamer *Marquette* began to list to port, but righted herself and then began to sink by the bow.

Both in Cairo and Salonica the news that the *Marquette* had been struck was released some hours before the happening took place. She sank in thirteen minutes with a heavy loss of life - 128 troops including (17 NZMC staff), 10 nurses and 29 crewmen. She had 14 lifeboats and 35 rafts - combine carrying capacity 1,196. Rafts and lifebouys were thrown overboard.

She was a legitimate target carrying 22 officers and 588 other ranks of the 29th Division Ammunition Column, Royal Field Artillery with its vehicles and animals, and staff (8 officers, 9 NCO's, 77 other ranks of the NZMC), equipment and stores of the No. 1 New Zealand Stationary Hospital including the thirty-six nurses of the NZANS as well as the *Marquette* crew of 95. She was also loaded with ammunition and 541 animals including many horses and mules. She was torpedoed off Platanona Point, 30 to 36 miles (57.5 kilometres), south from the anti-submarine net at Salonica Bay, which would have meant safety, by the *U-35* under Lt-Cdr Waldemar Kophamel.

Some lifeboats were not lowered efficiently and overturned as they were launched. One of the lifeboats on the port side fell on another already in the water, and the nurses from that boat spilled out in the confusion. On the starboard side a boat filled with nurses was lowered at one end but not the other leaving it hanging vertically sending the occupants into the sea. This boat had to be abandoned as it had huge hole on one side. Other lifeboats were not seaworthy, as they had been damaged by the mules on board. Many of the deaths and injuries to the nurses were due to inexperienced men (soldiers helping out as some crew members had not turned up at their stations for various reasons) lowering the lifeboats and the angle of the sinking ship.

Only one lifeboat filled with nurses managed to get away and that was half filled with water. The survivors floated for hours in intense cold clinging to rafts and debris before being picked up utterly exhausted by rescue ships.

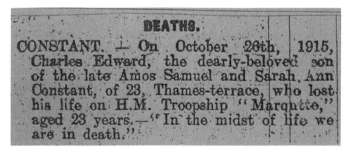

DEATHS.

CONSTANT. — On October 26th, 1915, Charles Edward, the dearly-beloved son of the late Amos Samuel and Sarah Ann Constant, of 23, Thames-terrace, who lost his life on H.M. Troopship "Marquette," aged 23 years.—"In the midst of life we are in death."

GR 13/11/17 [Andrew Marsall]

By the time the ship was almost on her side the second officer shouted *Every man over the side.* Some of the survivors were in the water until 1700 hours. Major Acland who later became a prominent surgeon in Christchurch was picked up after seven hours. Survivors were given dry clothes, hot drinks and brandy. It is said that one nurse was saved because her veil –

the regulation head-dress - was seen floating on the surface of the water.

The International Press circulated a story that the nurses had requested the rescuers to *take the fighting men first.* It had great public appeal.

Charles was among the 29 crewmen to have died. He has no known grave and is commemorated on the Tower Hill Memorial.

The Tower of London; The 'Poppy Memorial', August-November, 2014.

Thiepval Memorial – John Connolly.

Duhallow A.D.C. Cemetery, Ypres - Tom Connolly [right] and St Quentin Cabaret Cemetery, Messines – Charles Constant.

Charles Edward Constant –
Tower Hill Memorial, above and
Gravesend Cemetery, below.

Albert George Cooper

Royal West Kent Regiment, 6th Bn
Service No. G/3042 - Corporal

Albert was born in Shorne in 1894, the son of John and Eizabeth Cooper of 17 Providence Cottages, Upper Higham. John was born in 1843 in Chalk and was an agricultural labourer. Elizabeth was born in 1853 in Maidstone. There were five children in the family – Mary, born in 1878, Elizabeth, born in 1884, Emma, born in 1890, Albert and Mary, born in 1895.

Albert married Eleanor Emma Leadbetter in 1913 and the couple living at 16 Carters Road, Perry Street. They had two children – Eliza, born in 1913 and John, born in 1915.

He enlisted in September 1914 in Chatham.

He was killed in action on May 3rd, 1917. He has no known grave and is commemorated on the Arras Memorial.

Frederick and **William Coppins**, whose biographies now follow, were brothers.

Frederick John Coppins

Manchester Regiment, 1st/10th Bn
Service No. 54213

Frederick was born in Gravesend in 1895 to William and Annie Coppins. There were seven children in the family, he being the second youngest. On leaving school he became a milkman's assistant progressing to being a milkman. The family home was at 6 Mead Road.

Signaller Frederick Coppins, Manchester Regt., is home on leave after serving twelve months on active service in France. His brother, Pte. W. Coppins, Australian Forces, was killed on the Western Front a year ago.

Frederick enlisted with the East Surrey Regiment, service number 33552. He subsequently was with the Manchester Regiment.

Frederick died of wounds on November 15th, 1918 and is buried in St Sever Cemetery Extension, Rouen. During the First World War, Commonwealth camps and hospitals were stationed on the southern outskirts of Rouen.

Almost all of the hospitals at Rouen remained there for practically the whole of the war. They included eight general, five stationary, one British Red Cross, one labour hospital, and No. 2 Convalescent Depot. St. Sever Cemetery contains 3,082 Commonwealth burials of the First World War.

The second son of Mr. and Mrs. W. Coppins, 6, Mead-road, Gravesend, has been called upon to make the supreme sacrifice. Signaller Frederick John Coppins, of the Manchester Regt.—his photograph appears above—died November 15th from wounds received in action. Deceased, 23 years of age and of bright and cheerful disposition, joined the Army about two years ago, and had only just recently been married. In civil life he worked at Messrs. Henley's Cable Works. Mr. and Mrs. Coppins's elder son was killed twelve months ago; they have one other son.

GR 30/11/18 [Andrew Marsall]

GR 5/10/18 [Andrew Marsall]

William James Coppins
A.I.F., 41st Battalion
Service No. 3699

William was born in 1893, the son of William and Annie Coppins of 6 Mead Road. The couple were married in 1885 and there were seven surviving children in the family – Elizabeth, born in 1886, Rose, born in 1888, Phoebe, born in 1889, Catherine, born in 1891, William, Frederick, born in 1896 and Albert, born in 1899.

William attended Milton Road Council School. On leaving school he got a job as a deck boy on the Orient mail line steamer – the *Orotova*.

Orotava was built by Barrow Shipbuilding Co, and was launched in 1889 for the Liverpool-Valparaiso service of Pacific Steam Navigation Co. *Orotava* made two voyages in that service in 1889, and was then placed under Orient Line management for service from Liverpool to Australia via Suez. She made her first sailing in that service on June 6th, 1890.

Except for service as a troopship during the Boer War (1899-1903), *Orotava* remained in Orient Lines' Australia service until 1906. In 1906, however, Pacific Steam's Australian service was acquired by Royal Mail Steam Packet Co., which dissolved the alliance with Orient in 1909. *Orotava* was then placed in Royal Mail's West Indies service. After serving as an armed merchant cruiser during World War I, *Orotava* was broken up in 1919

In 1908 William settled in Brisbane and became a fireman. He was stationed at the St Ann's Fire Station.

William enlisted at Wolloongabba, Queensland and was posted to the 41st Battalion.

The 41st Battalion was raised at Bell's Paddock Camp in Brisbane in February 1916 with recruits from Brisbane, northern Queensland and the northern rivers district of New South Wales. It formed part of the 11th Brigade of the 3rd Australian Division.

After training in Australia and Britain, the 41st Battalion arrived in France on November 25th, 1916. It entered the front line for the first time on Christmas Eve and spent the bleak winter of 1916-17 alternating between service in the front line, and training and labouring in the rear areas.

Compared to some AIF battalions, the 41st experience of the battles in Belgium during 1917 was relatively straightforward. It had a supporting role at Messines in June, captured its objectives at Broodseinde on October 4th, and was spared the carnage of Passchendaele a week later. It was some of the battalion's more "routine" tasks that proved its most trying experiences. At the end of June 1917, the 11th Brigade was ordered to establish a new front line west of Warneton, in full view of the Germans. Work carried on night and day under

Albert Cooper –
Arras Memorial, above
and
Frederick Coppins –
Ste Sever CWGC
Cemetery, Rouen.

William Coppins –
Tyne Cot.

251

heavy shellfire and the period became known to the battalion as "the 18 days". The start of August found the 41st holding ground captured by two of its sister battalions in a feint attack on July 31st. Enduring continual rain, flooded trenches and heavy shelling many of the battalion's platoons dwindled from 35 men to less than ten. William was killed in action on October 5th, 1917 at Broodesende and is buried in Tyne Cot Cemetery.

GR 27/10/17 [Andrew Marsall]

There is an additional **W Coppins** listed on the Memorial. However there is no trace of ant soldier in the records with a Gravesend connection. It is assumed that this is an error.

William Jack Corby
East Kent Regiment, 6th Battalion
Service No. L/9084

Jack was born in 1891 the son of Henry and Janet Corby of 2 Terrace Street. Henry was born 1858 and was a native of Gravesend. He worked on the river as a waterman. Janet was born in 1861 and came from Northfleet.

There were six children in all in the family – Denise, born in 1878, Henry, born in 1881, Gordon, born in 1887, Minnie, born in 1889, Jack, Donald, born in 1893, Greta, born in 1895 and Violet, born in 1897.

On leaving school he worked as a labourer before joining the army for six years' service. He enlisted in Gravesend on October 20th, 1908. He was 5 feet 6 inches tall and weighed 125lbs. Jack had a chest measurement of 36 inches which he could expand another 2 inches. He had blue eyes and brown hair. Not surprisingly he was considered fit for service when attending his medical examination on October 22nd in Maidstone

He was posted with the 2nd Buffs in January, 1909. With the Buffs he was in Aldershot from January, 1909 until October 1910 and thereafter he travelled with the 2nd Buffs to Singapore, October, 1910 to January, 1913 and onto India where the Battalion remained until November, 1914.

Arriving 'home' on November 16th, 1914, the Battalion departed to France on January 16th the following year.

The 6th were in action in the opening phase of the Somme Offensive on July 3rd in the vicinity of Ovillers. They attacked at 3.15am. Some 11 officers and 263 other ranks were lost in the attack and despite being readied for another assault five hours later that attack was cancelled. The 6th were back at the Front in the Ovillers sector on July 27th having been hastily refitted and brought up to strength.

Jack meanwhile had been among the wounded and was brought back to Rouen and then onto Etaples. On recovery he was transferred to and joined the 6th Battalion on July 27th, 1916.

The 6th were based in the neighbourhood of Beaumetz and Betrencourt, some seven or so miles south east of Arras for six weeks or so from mid-August through September. This sector was generally quiet at this time with the exception of trench-mortar activity. The ground was so bad that transport proved difficult and troops had to rely exclusively on pack animals for the supply of necessary food and supplies.

On October 6th, the 6th were in the front line when operation orders came through that the general advance would be resumed. The Buffs were on the right of their Brigade with the Royal West Kent on the left.

The attack was ordered to be carried out in four waves at fifty yards interval – each platoon extended to two yards interval, bayonets fixed and magazines charged. The zero hour was 1.45pm on the 7th. The artillery was to lift every minute and fifty yards at a time. However, at 12.45pm the positions of the 6th were heavily shelled and at 1.30pm the Germans opened a tremendous machine-gun fire and shrapnel barrage on the front line trenches. At 1.45pm the attack started to be met with an excessively heavy machine-gun and rifle fire. The first objectives were secured and held

CORBY.—On October 7th, killed in action, Private Jack Corby, The Buffs, third son of the late Capt. W. H. Corby, H.M. Customs, and Mrs. Corby, aged 25 years. "Requiescat in pace."

GR 21/10/16 [Andrew Marsall]

despite severe losses. Jack was among those killed in action on October 7th. He has no known grave and is commemorated on the Thiepval Monument.

John Cork
Mercantile Marine - Fireman

John was born in Bermondsey in 1883. He married Eliza Johnson in 1904 and the couple lived at 1 Duke of York Court, Milton and subsequently at 9 Robert Street. They had two children – Clara, born in 1906 and John, born in 1908.

John was a sailor with the Mercantile Marine. He was on board the *S.S. Minnehaha* when it was sunk by U48, a German submarine on July 7th, 1917. He was among the 43 fatalities. His body was not recovered and he is commemorated on the Tower Hill Memorial.

Fred and **Louis Cosgrove**, whose biographies now follow, were brothers.

Fred Cosgrove
Mercantile Marine
Service No. 39804

Fred was born in 1885 in Chatham. His father, Matthew, was born in London in 1852 and his mother, Caroline was born in Dover in 1859. Matthew was corporal with the Royal Engineers and on retiring from the Army became a carpenter at the Royal Engineers' Works, Chatham. The couple were married in 1887 in Dover and they had seven surviving children. Their birth places reflect the itinerant nature of their father's employment – Catherine was born in Cork in 1883, Fred and Jesse, 1893 were born in Chatham with Dorothy, 1896, Louis and Bernard, 1899 born in Gravesend.

The family by 1914 lived at 30 Wellington Street.

Fred on leaving school and became a plumber. He and his wife, Theresa lived at 2 Cambrian Grove.

He joined the Mercantile Marine and died when the ship he was serving on, the Clan McNaughton disappeared on February 3rd, 1915.

HMS Clan McNaughton was a 4985 ton passenger cargo vessel, built in 1911 and requisitioned November 1914 from the Clan Line Steamers Ltd, Glasgow, when she returned to her home port of Tilbury. She was then hastily converted into a fighting ship, which would have included mounting guns up on deck - well above her normal centre of gravity. A crew was then cobbled together for her – career RN officers, although her engineer officers had all been Merchant Navy with some RN but many of the rest of the crew were reservists including some men from Newfoundland, plus no less than 50 boys straight

out of the training shore base at Shotley, *H.M.S. Ganges.*

She sailed for patrol duties in the North Atlantic a few days before Christmas 1914, but had to put into Liverpool on the way. She was in radio contact at about 6 a.m. on the morning of February 3rd, 1915 and reported terrible weather conditions. Nothing further was ever heard of her. Some floating wreckage was found about a fortnight later in the approximate area of her last known position but it could not be identified as having come from her. The mine theory was put forward as a possible cause of the loss.

There is some speculation that as she had a new crew who were generally unfamiliar with the vessel, and that the armaments added to the deck destabilised her making the McNaughton vulnerable to such severe weather as was found on the day she lost contact.

COSGROVE.—In Feb., drowned on the H.M.S. Clan McNaughton, Fred, third beloved son of Mr. and Mrs. Matthew Cosgrove, 30, Wellington-street.—Rest in peace.

COSGROVE.—Fred Cosgrove, the dearly-beloved husband of Teresa E. Cosgrove, who was drowned on H.M.S. Clan McNaughton, in February, aged 30 years.—R.I.P.

GR 27/2/15 [Andrew Marsall]

wreck, who solicit your orders and recommendation.—Advt.

LOST ON THE CLAN McNAUGHTON.—Mr. Fred Cosgrove, plumber, late of the H.M.S. Clan McNaughton, the armed merchant cruiser, was among those drowned off the Irish coast last month during the bad weather which prevailed at that time. For several years he was employed by the late Messrs. Stone, of High-street, and of late years by Mr. W. L. Allan, of Queen-street. He was thirty years of age and leaves a widow and two young children, and was the third son of Mr. and Mrs. Matthew Cosgrove, of Wellington-street. He joined the ship at Tilbury as a volunteer only last December, and both his bereaved wife and parents are bearing their sad loss in a true and patriotic spirit.

WHAT THE PRIVATE SAW.—Pte. E. Fountain, of the 1st Northampton Regiment

Thiepval Memorial – William Corby.

Tower Hill
Memorial –
John Cork.

Gravesend Cemetery

ALSO OUR TWO SONS KILLED IN ACTION

[Photograph – Andy White]

St. Martin Calvaire Cemetery –
Louis Cosgrove

Pte. L. G. Cosgrove (Gravesend).
Durham Light Infantry.
KILLED IN ACTION.

We regret to announce the death in his 20th year of Private Louis Geo. Cosgrove, seventh son of Mr. and Mrs. M. Cosgrove, of 30, Wellington Street, Gravesend, who has been killed whilst serving his country in France. Pte. Cosgrove, who had been in France since February, was a member of a Lewis gun team and the circumstances, attending his death are related in a sympathetic letter received from Co. Sergt. Major T. W. Robinson, who writes:—"'Toby,' of my Company, was killed to-day at 4.30 p.m. He was holding a trench with some pals of his gun team when a shell dropped right at their feet, killing poor Toby and seriously wounding two others. He never spoke after he was hit. We did all we could for him, but it was no good. Myself and all his chums wish to express our deepest sympathy, and sincerely trust that the knowledge of a brave steadfast and staunch soldier will be your stay in this time of great trouble. We have not buried him yet, but he will receive the last rite from our hands with all reverence. Again accept my deepest sympathy."

Prior to joining the Army, Pte. Cosgrove was employed by the P.L.A. at Tilbury. One of his brothers perished by the sinking of the Clan MacNoughton, and two others are serving in the Army. One of the latter has been wounded three times. The Cosgroves are indeed a fighting family. The father Mr. M. Cosgrove, has himself retired from the Army, and fought from 1884 to 1886 in the Egyptian campaign as a corporal in the Royal Engineers.

KM 6/10/17 [Andrew Marshall]

256

Louis George Cosgrove
Durham Light Infantry, 1/6th Bn
Service No. 273083 - Private

Louis was born in 1897 in Gravesend. He was the younger brother of Fred Cosgrove.

Louis was killed in action on September 15th, 1917. He is buried in St Martin Calvaire Commonwealth Cemetery, St Martin-sur-Cojeul. The village of St. Martin-sur-Cojeul, south east of Arras, was taken by the 30th Division on April 9th, 1917. It was lost in March 1918 but retaken in the following August.
St. Martin Calvaire British Cemetery was named from a Calvary which was destroyed during the war. It was begun by units of the 30th Division in April 1917 and used until March 1918. The cemetery contains 228 Commonwealth burials of the First World War, five of them unidentified.

William Henry Cracknell
Royal Dublin Fusiliers, 2nd Battalion
Service No. 28984 - Private

William was born in Gravesend in 1897. He was the son of Joseph and Emily Cracknell of 14 East Terrace.
Joseph was born in Brentwood in 1864 and worked on the docks as a labourer. Emily [Hills] was from Single-

The death of Pte. Louis George Cosgrove is announced this week. He is the seventh son of Mr. and Mrs. M. Cosgrove, of 30, Wellington-street, Gravesend, and brother of Mr. M. A. Cosgrove, of 1 and 2, Perry Street, Northfleet. Previous to joining up, the deceased was employed by the P.L.A. He had been serving in France since February on a Lewis gun team, and the circumstances attending his death are told in the following letter from Colour-Sergt.-Major T. W. Robinson: — "'Toby,' of my company, was killed to-day at 4.30 p.m. He was holding a trench with some pals of his gun team, when a shell dropped right at their feet, killing poor 'Toby,' and seriously wounding two others. He never spoke after he was hit, and we did all we could for him, but it was no good. Myself and all his chums wish to express our deepest sympathy, and sincerely trust that the knowledge of a brave, staunch, and stedfast soldier will be your stay in this time of great trouble. We have not buried him yet, but he will receive the last rites from our hands with all reverence."—One of the deceased's brothers perished by the sinking of the "Clan McNaughton," whilst two others are serving in the Army, one of the latter having three times been wounded. The father of the deceased retired from the Army, having fought from 1884-6 in the Egyptian Campaign as a Corporal in the R.E.'s.

GR 13/10/17 [Andrew Marsall]
GR 6/10/17 [Andrew Marsall]

Killed in Action.

COSGRAVE.—Killed in action on September 15th, 1917, Private Louis George, seventh son of Mr. and Mrs. Matthew Cosgrave, of 30, Wellington-street, aged 20 years.

GR 2/2/18 [Andrew Marsall]

IN MEMORIAM.

COSGROVE.—In loving memory of my dear husband, Fred Cosgrove, who was lost at sea on H.M.S. "Clan McNaughton," February 3rd, 1915, aged 30 years.—R.I.P.

Three years to-day has passed away,
Since this great sorrow fell,
But in my heart I mourn the loss,
Of one I loved so well.

—Teresa.

COSGROVE.—In loving memory of our dear dada, Fred Cosgrove, who was lost at sea February 3rd, 1915.—Dearly loved and sadly missed by his loving little daughters (Nina and Kathleen).

well and was born in 1867. The couple were married in 1885 and had eleven children. Prior to the war, Emily's father Thomas, born in 1839 and from Ash, lived with the family. He was a farm labourer. He enlisted with the Royal West Surrey Regiment, service number 4870 before being posted to the 2nd R.D.F. They were in action in October 1918 in the Battles of the Hindenburg Line, The pursuit to the Selle and the Final Advance in Picardy.

The Battle of the Selle began on October 17th. Fourth Army troops attacked at 5.20am on that Thursday; infantry and tanks, preceded by a creeping barrage, moved forward on a ten mile wide front south of Le Cateau. The centre and left of the Fourth Army forced crossings of the river despite unexpectedly strong German resistance and much uncut barbed wire. Fighting was particularly fierce along the line of the Le Cateau – Wassigny railway. The right of the attack, across the upland watershed of the Selle, made most progress and by nightfall enemy defences had been broken and Le Cateau captured. Severe fighting continued on October 18th and 19th, by which time Fourth Army, much assisted by the French First Army on its right, advanced over five miles, harrying the Germans back towards the Sambre-Oise Canal.

The British Third and First Armies, immediately to the north of Fourth Army, maintained the offensive pressure the following day. In a surprise joint night attack in the early morning of October 20th, Third Army formations secured the high ground east of the Selle. Following a two day pause, to bring up heavy artillery, the attack was renewed on October 23rd, with a major combined assault by Fourth, Third and First Armies; the fighting, which continued into the next day, resulted in further advances. At

this stage, the German Army was retreating at a forced but controlled pace. On October 24th, the German Army counterattacked at the Canal de la Dérivation, but were repulsed and pushed back by the Belgian Army.

William was killed in action on the opening day of the Battle, on October 17th. He is buried in Highland Cemetery, Le Cateau. After the Battle of Le Cateau (August 26th, 1914), the town remained in German hands until the middle of October 1918. The original cemetery was made by the 50th (Northumbrian) Division after the fighting of October 17th; the name of Highland Cemetery is suggestive at once of the comparatively high ground on which it stands and of the 32 graves of the 13th (Scottish Horse) Battalion, Black Watch, buried here. The cemetery was greatly enlarged after the Armistice when graves of October and November 1918 were brought in from isolated positions on all sides of Le Cateau.

Highland Cemetery now contains 624 First World War burials.

John Henry Craven
Royal Dublin Fusiliers, 2nd Bn
Service No. 10575 – Lance Corp.

John was born in Birmingham in the Summer of 1892. He was the only son of John, born in 1870 and Ellen, born in 1873, Craven. He had a younger sister Maggie, born in 1894. John [father] worked in the iron foundry. The family lived at 4 Highgate Street, Aston.

John was married to Kate Lydia [Jackson] and the couple lived at 7 Clifton Grove. They had one son, John, who was born in June, 1916. He enlisted with the 2nd Battalion, Royal Dublin Fusiliers.

The 2nd Battalion were in Gravesend when war broke out in August 1914.

Part of 4th Division they were held back from the original British Expeditionary Force by a last minute decision to defend England against a possible German landing. The fate of the BEF in France and the lack of any move by the Enemy to cross the channel, reversed this decision and they moved to Harrow to prepare to join them. The 2nd proceeded to Boulogne on August 22nd, 1914 arriving in time to provide infantry reinforcements at the Battle of Le Cateau, the Artillery, Engineers, Field Ambulances and mounted troops being still en-route at this time. They were in action at the The Battle of the Marne, The Battle of the Aisne and at The Battle of Messines in 1914.

In 1915 they fought in The Second Battle of Ypres and in 1916 moved south to The Somme taking part in the Battles there.

GR 7/7/17

In 1917 they fought at the The Battle of Messines and The Battle of Langemark, during the 3rd Battle of Ypres.

However Lance-Corporal Craven did not participate in either as he was killed in action on June 2nd, 1917. He is buried in La Laiterie Military Cemetery. The cemetery, 7km south of Ypres, named from a dairy farm, was begun in November 1914 and used until October 1918 by units holding this sector of the front. The different plots were, to a great extent, treated as regimental burial grounds. After the Armistice, graves were brought into the cemetery from the battlefields north and north-east of Kemmel.

GONE BUT NOT FORGOTTEN

Killed in Action.

CRAVEN. — In loving memory of my dear husband, Lance-Corpl. John Henry Craven, Royal Dublin Fusiliers, killed in action, in France, June 2nd, 1917, aged 25 years.

He bravely answered his Country's call,
He gave his life for one and all,
but the far away grave is the bitter blow,
None but aching hearts can know.

Little I thought when I bade him good-bye,
He'd left me for ever, he'd left me to die,
Not even his last farewell look did I see,
But always his memory will cling to me.

—From his loving wife and child.

259

Alfred William Creamer
Royal Dublin Fusiliers – 2nd Bn
Service No. 7218 – Lance Corp.

Alfred was born in Lambeth in 1888. He had a brother, Fred who lived in Chislehurst.

He enlisted on his 14th birthday on August 18th, 1900 in the Royal Dublin Fusiliers for 12 years as a Bandsman. He was 4 feet 7 inches tall and weighed a mere 71lbs at the time. He had a fresh complexion and blue eyes. He and his wife, Elizabeth Maud Gamble had their home at Victory House, St. Osyth Road, Clacton-on-Sea. They were married in the local parish church on September 7th, 1912. The couple had the one child – Alfred Robert, born on June 29th, 1913.

He was promoted Lance Corporal on September 9th, 1909 and re-engaged on June 11th, 1912, for a total of 21 years' service.

2nd Battalion, The Royal Dublin Fusiliers were in Gravesend, as part of 10th Brigade, 4th Division when war broke out in August 1914. 4th Division was held back from the original British Expeditionary Force by a last minute decision to defend England against a possible German landing. The fate of the BEF in France and the lack of any move by the enemy to cross the channel, reversed this decision and they moved to Harrow to prepare to join them. The 2nd Dublin Fusiliers proceeded to France landing at Boulogne on August 22nd, 1914 arriving in time to provide infantry reinforcements at the Battle of Le Cateau, the Artillery, Engineers, Field Ambulances and mounted troops being still en-route at this time. They were in action at the The Battle of the Marne, The Battle of the Aisne and at The Battle of Messines in 1914.

Lance Corporal Creamer was killed in action on August 27th, 1914. He has no known grave and is commemorated on the La Ferte-sous-Jouarre Memorial. La Ferte-sous-Jouarre is a small town 66 kilometres to the east of Paris. The monument is constructed of white Massangis stone and surmounted by a sarcophagus onto which military trophies are laid. At the four corners of the pavement on which the monument stands are stone columns supporting urns which bear the coats of arms of the four constituent nations of the United Kingdom. The memorial was designed by George H. Goldsmith, a decorated veteran of the Western Front, and unveiled by Sir William Pulteney, who had commanded the III Corps of the BEF in 1914.

His wife Elizabeth was awarded a pension of 15/- a week.

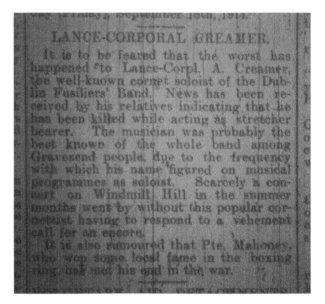

Albert Victor Creed
Norfolk Regiment, 9th Battalion
Service No. 29814 – Private

Albert was born in Dartford in 1883. He was the son of Joseph and Alice Creed of 5 Clifton Terrace, Whitehill Road. Joseph was born in 1844 in Gravesend and was a customs' officer. Alice was born in 1849 and was also from Gravesend. They had 3 sons and a daughter – William, born in 1879, was a cab driver, Alfred, born in 1882, was a gardener and Albert was a

Albert Victor Creed –
Bethune Town Cemetery

ONLY THOSE WHO HAVE LOST
ARE ABLE TO FEEL
HOW GREAT IS OUR LOSS
FOR HIM WE LOVED SO WELL

house painter. Florence was the youngest of the children being born in 1890.

He enlisted in December, 1915 in Gravesend and was initially posted to the 3/5 Leicester Regiment. He was 5 feet 10 inches tall and weighed 140lbs. he was mobilized in March 1916 and posted to the Norfolk Regiment on August 25th, 1916.

In 1916 the 9th Battalion was in action at Battle of Flers-Courcelette on The Somme, and again in The Battle of Morval and The Battle of Le Transloy, in 1917 they were in action at Hill 70 and Cambrai.

He died of wounds on March 26th, 1917 and is buried in Bethune Town Cemetery.

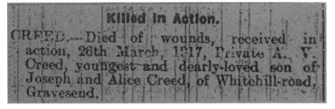

Killed In Action.

CREED.—Died of wounds, received in action, 26th March, 1917, Private A. V. Creed, youngest and dearly-loved son of Joseph and Alice Creed, of Whitehill-road, Gravesend.

GR 7/4/17 [Andrew Marsall]

For much of the First World War, Bethune was comparatively free from bombardment and remained an important railway and hospital centre, as well as a corps and divisional headquarters. The 33rd Casualty Clearing Station was in the town until December 1917. Early in 1918, Bethune began to suffer from constant shell fire and in April 1918, German forces reached Locon, five kilometres to the north. The bombardment of May 21st did great damage to the town and it was not until October that pressure from the Germans was relaxed.

Charles Richard Creed
Border Regiment, 1st Battalion
Service No.22647 - Private

Charles was born in 1895 in Gravesend. He was the second eldest child of James and Winnie Creed of 16 Mount Pleasant. James, born in Gravesend in 1870 was a labourer. Winnie was also from Gravesend and was born in 1873. The couple were married in 1893 and they had nine children – James, born in 1894, Charles, George, born in 1898, Emma, born in 1900, Alexandra, born in 1902, William, born in 1904, Thomas, born in 1907, Doris, born in 1908 and Lilian, born in 1911.

He enlisted with the Royal West Kents, service number 10772, on May 13th, 1915 in Gravesend. he was 5 feet 6 inches tall and weighed 132lbs. He had blue eyes, brown hair and was of fresh complexion. He was transferred to the 3rd Border Regiment on November 9th. He was posted with the 1st to join the M.E.F. and left Devonport on November 24th, arriving in Cairo on January 20th, 1916. Shortly after arriving in Egypt he was hospitalised with scabies, February 4th. He was eventually discharged to duty on April 19th. He sailed for France from Alexandria on the City of Edinburgh on May 8th and arrived in Marseilles on the 18th. The Battalion arrives in the Somme sector on the 31st.

He went into the line on June 23rd and was killed in action on July 1st, 1916. He has no known grave and is commemorated on the Thiepval Monument.

Howard George Crittenden
Royal Navy - Stoker, 2nd Class
Service No. K/39087

Howard was born in Lambeth on September 27th, 1891. He was the youngest of three children to Alfred and Alice Crittenden. Alfred, born in 1857 in Higham, was a labourer on the docks. His wife, Alice was a year older and came from Wellington in

Shropshire. They had three children in all – Ernest, born in 1884, Hilda, born in 1889 and Howard. The family lived at 8 Sheppey Place.

Howard worked in a print shop. He married Mable Butcher and the couple lived at 18 Roseriggs Road, Clapham.

He served in the Royal Navy as a Stoker 1st Class. He was on HMS Foyle when she struck a mine on March 15th, 1907.

HMS Foyle was a Laird Type River Class Destroyer ordered by the Royal Navy under the 1902 – 1903 Naval Estimates. Named after the River Foyle in County Limerick, she was the first ship to carry this name in the Royal Navy.

Laid down at Cammel Lairds shipyard in August 1902, the Foyle was launched in February of the following year and entered service thirteen months later in 1904. 225 feet long with a top speed of twenty five and a half knots, the Foyle was armed with four twelve pounder guns and two torpedo tubes. At first her slower speed caused concern, but it was soon realised that the sturdiness of her design allowed her to maintain her top speed in all but the worst conditions, and soon her critics were silenced.

When War broke out the Foyle found herself performing patrol and escort duties in the killing ground of the Dover Straights. On the night of March 15th, 1917 she hit a mine, and the force of the explosion blew away the whole of her bows forward of the bridge, killing twenty-seven of her crew of seventy. Unbelievably the stern half stayed afloat, and it was decided to tow this to Plymouth, presumably to graft on another bow. What the thoughts were of the tug crews who had to place the tow on a helpless drifting hulk in the middle of a potential minefield we can only guess, but eventually the tow was established and the Foyle was led away towards Plymouth. But, after surviving the minefield and slipping through a screen of marauding E boats, the salvage crew on the Foyle could not keep up with the water pouring through her ruptured plates, and only a few miles from Plymouth HMS Foyle sank in fifty meters of water miles off the Mewstone.

Howard was among the 27 killed in the explosion; his body was lost at sea and he has no known grave. He is commemorated on the Chatham Naval Memorial.

Alfred James Crockett
R.E., 1st/3rd Kent Field Company
Service No. 2564 - Sapper

Alfred was born in 1898 in Gravesend to James and Eliza Crockett, being the eldest son. James was born in 1858 in Tring, Herts, being a seaman working on steamships. Eliza was born in 1871 in Gravesend. There were six children in the family – Alfred, James, born in 1899, Annie, born in 1902, Hilda, born in 1904, William, born in 1905 and Inez, born in 1909.

Alfred enlisted in Gillingham – Brompton Barracks – with the 1/3rd Kent. In May 1914 the 1/3rd Kent Fortress Royal Engineers came into being because the existing No 3 Company in the Medway Area had difficulty recruiting and a decision to disband it was made. Thus was created the 1/3rd Kent (Fortress) Royal Engineers. They were initially

Thiepval Memorial – Charles Creed.
The name above has been erased
signifying identification of found
remains since the name was
inscribed on the Memorial.

Gravesend Cemetery - Alfred Crockett

**ALSO THEIR SON ALFRED JAMES
DROWNED OFF GALLIPOLI
OCT. 28th 1917. AGED 17 YEARS**
His brother James was also lost at sea.

[Photograph – Andy White]

Chatham Naval Memorial, Panel 24 –
Stoker 2nd Class Howard Crittenden and
Stoker 2nd Class George Crothall.

responsible for the protection of the coastline, for searchlights and defence. They were mobilised on August 4th, 1914.

During the initial stage of the First World War the company remained at home and continued to train. They were converted to a Field Company from a Works Unit. In July 1915 they were at least 185 strong.

Royal Engineers were required in the Dardanelles to fill vacancies no doubt caused by the appalling loss there.

The company had a farewell dinner on October 11th, 1915 and they went onto Devonport and boarded *H.M.T. Scotian*. They sailed to Malta before heading for Lemos Island, Mudros Bay. Orders were received that they were to proceed to Sulva Bay but this was then changed to Cape Helles. Number 1 company was also travelling with them. There were two ships available - *HMS Redbreast* and the *HMS Hythe*.

The 1/3rd were allocated HMS Hythe. Because the Hythe had no passenger accommodation a fabric awning was rigged on her deck to help protect the crowded deck from spray and the weather. The Hythe left Mudros and had 50 miles to go to Cape Helles. It was travelling in a darkened state to avoid enemy bombardment. They were due to land and some forty minutes remained of their journey when there was a warning that *HMS Sarnia* was bearing down on them. She had landed her cargo and troops and was leaving the Peninsula.

Several attempts at a change of course by both ships, failed to avoid a collision. The *Sarnia* struck the *Hythe* on her port side. *Hythe* stopped dead in the water with the foremast falling onto the fabric awning. Some 129 members of 1/3rd Company were lost as were 15 other Army personnel and 11 crew from the *Hythe*. The disaster was compounded by the lack of life jackets and poor organisation and could have been avoided by shipping following a set route inward and outward bound from Cape Helles.

Alfred was among the casualties on the *Hythe* which sank on October 28th, 1915. He has no known grave and is commemorated on the Helles Memorial.

George John Crothall
Royal Navy – Stoker 2nd Class
Service No. K/39194

George was born on August 30th, 1883 in Wapping, , the son of John and Caroline Crothall. John was born in 1860 in Gravesend and was a coal porter. Caroline was born in 1861. There were eight children in the family – John, born in 1886, Charles, born in 1887, Florence, born in 1891, Alice, born in 1894, William, born in 1897, Caroline, born in 1900 and Alfred, born in 1904. The family home was in Burch Road, Rosherville.

He married Agnes Lear, born in 1890 in Gravesend in 1910. The couple had four children – Agnes, born in 1911, Alice, born in 1913, Eleanor, born in 1914 and Hilda, born just after George's death in 1917. The family home was 25 Church Street. George was a steam crane driver by profession before enlisting with the Royal Navy. He was a Stoker 2nd Class initially serving on *H.M.S. Hannibal*.

Hannibal was a majestic class pre-dreadnought battleship. In 1906 she underwent a refit, which included a conversion from a coal burner to using oil. She was in reserve from 1907 being mobilised in July 1914.

From August 1914 to February 1915 *Hannibal* was a guard ship at Scapa Flow. Later that year, her main armament was removed and she was converted to a troopship, serving in this capacity in the Dardenelles.

George subsequently served on *H.M.S. Arcadian* and was killed in action on April 15th, 1917 when *Arcadian* was sunk by a submarine.

His body was not recovered and he is commemorated on the Chatham Naval Memorial.

GR 19/5/17 [Andrew Marshall]

GR 13/7/18 [Andrew Marshall]

Walter James Crowhurst
Royal West Kent, 10th Battalion
Service No. G/15327 - L/Corp

Walter was born in Gravesend in 1887 to Samuel and Elizabeth Crowhurst of 35 Railway Terrace, Rugby. Samuel was born in 1863 in Gravesend and was a carpenter's machinist. Elizabeth was born in 1863 in Deal. There were six children in the family – Florence, born in 1886. Walter, George, born in 1890, Frances, born in 1892, Alfred, born in 1896 and William, born in 1900.

He married Minnie Ethel George at St James', Milton on October 30th, 1910. The couple lived at 15 Mead Road and had two children – Freda, born on July 2nd, 1913 and Kathleen Doris, born July 13th, 1915.

He enlisted in Gravesend in May, 1915 with the 10th Battalion. He was 5 feet 3½ inches tall and weighed 130lbs.

The 10th (Kent County) Battalion, The Royal West Kent Regiment was raised at Maidstone on May 3rd, 1915 . After initial training close to home they joined 118th Brigade, 39th Division in July. In October they transferred to 123rd Brigade, 41st Division. They moved to Aldershot for final training in January 1916 and proceeded to France in early May, concentrating between Hazebrouck and Bailleul. In 1916 they were in action at The Battle of Flers-Courcelette and The Battle of the Transloy Ridges on the Somme. In 1917 they fought during The Battle of Messines, The Battle of Pilkem Ridge and The Battle of the Menin Road.

The 10th went back into the trenches near Hollebeke on July 31st, 1917 after a three day rest behind the Front line. The trenches were in an appalling condition and the enemy plied the positions with constant shelling. The main incident of this four day stay in the Front line was a raid by a 15 strong party which cleared several machine gun placements resulting in the taking of 40 prisoners. There was only the one casualty in this raid.

Lance Corporal Crowhurst was killed in action on this raid on August 8th. He has no known grave and is commemorated on the Menin Gate.

Minnie was awarded a pension of 22/11 a week to maintain herself and her two children.

KM 7/9/17 [Andrew Marshall

Lce.-Corpl. W. J. Crowhurst (Gravesend),
Royal West Kent Regiment.
KILLED IN ACTION.

The Captain has written to Mrs. Crowhurst, of 35, All Saints' Road (late of Mead Road), Gravesend, informing her of the sad news that her husband Lance-Corpl. Walter James Crowhurst, Royal West Kent, was killed during very heavy fighting in France on August 8th. Lance-Corpl. Crowhurst, who was 29 years of age, had been in France since November, 1916, having joined the Army the previous May. In the Gravesend district he was well known. For about five years he acted as a bell ringer at St. George's Parish Church. He was employed at Messrs. Allen and Sons, Harmer Street and afterwards at the Amalgamated Press Works. Two of his brothers and five brothers-in-law are serving in the Army. The lance-corporal leaves a young widow and two children, with whom much sympathy is expressed.

KR 25/12/18 [Andrew Marsall]

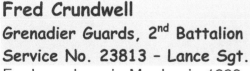

CROWHURST.—On Aug. 17th, "Somewhere in France," Lance-Corpl. Walter James Crowhurst, of 35, All Saints-road, late of Mead-road, aged 29 years.

Fred Crundwell
Grenadier Guards, 2nd Battalion
Service No. 23813 – Lance Sgt.

Fred was born in Marden in 1893, the son of Frederick and Ada Crundwell of Collier Street, Maidstone. Frederick was born in 1871 in Yalding and was a farm labourer. Ada was born locally in 1873. The couple were married in 1890 and had seven children – Fred, George, born in 1896, William, born in 1898, Florence, born in 1899, May, born in 1903, Ernest, born in 1906 and Harry, born in 1909.

Fred, George and William all were farm labourers in the pre Great War years. Fred enlisted with the 2nd Battalion, The Grenadier Guards.

The 2nd Battalion, Grenadier Guards was based in Chelsea with 4th (Guards) Brigade, 2nd Division when war broke out in August 1914. On August 15th, 1914 they proceeded to France, landing at Le Havre. They were in action in The Battle of Mons and the subsequent retreat, The Battle of the Marne, The Battle of the Aisne, the First Battle of Ypres and the Winter Operations of 1914-15. In 1915 they were in action during The Battle of Aubers and then on August 20th, 1915 they transferred to the newly formed 1st Guards Brigade, Guards Division. They saw action in The Battle of Loos. In 1916 they fought on The Somme in The Battle of Flers-Courcelette and The Battle of Morval, capturing Lesboeufs. In 1917 they were in action in The German retreat to the Hindenburg Line, the Third Battle of Ypres and The Battle of Cambrai. In 1918 they fought on The Somme, during the Battles of the Hindenburg Line, The pursuit to the Selle, The Battle of the Selle and The Battle of the Sambre.

The German strategy for the 1918 Offensive or *Kaiserschlacht*, a series of attacks that achieved the deepest advances along the Western Front by either side since 1914. The four German attacks had the code names Michael, Georgette, Gneisenau and Blücher-Yorck.

On day 7, March 27th, of the Offensive the town of Albert was relinquished during the night of March 26th/27th. With the choice of holding the old position on the heights east of Albert, on the left bank of the Ancre, or the high ground west of the devastated town, it had been decided to adopt the latter course. The ruins of Albert were therefore abandoned to the enemy.

March 27th saw a series of continuous complex actions and movements during the defensive battle of XIX Corps against incessant German attacks from the north, east and north-west around Rosières, less than 20 miles east of Amiens.

The focus of the German attack changed again on the 28th. This time, in an attempt to get the direction of the offensive back on track, it was the Third Army, around Arras, that would be the target of Operation Mars.

Lance Sergeant Crundwell was killed in action on March 27th, 1918. He has no known grave and is commemorated on the Arras Memorial.

His brother George also fell.

268

A B C D E

DADSON W J
DALY P
DANN E J
DANN W
DARBY T N
DAVIS I F
DAY G J
DEADMAN C
DEADMAN E J
DEAKIN A R
DEARING A
DENHAM T
DENNIS F R
DICKS J
DIX G
DIX W J
DIXON H H
DODD F
DODD P E
DRAKE H R
DRAY T W

DRENNAN R H
DRIVER A J
DRYDEN A
DUCK E
DULEY F J
DUMBRUL P A
DUNLOP J E

DUNLOP G R

Frederick Dennis - Maurois Cemetery

Oliver Stanley Dack
Royal Horse Guards
Attached to Machine Gun Corps
Service No. 1564 - Lance Corporal

Oliver was born in Snodland in 1896 to Samuel and Eliza Dack. Samuel was born in Maidstone in 1852. He worked as a general labourer on the railway. Eliza was born in 1857 and came from East Peckham. The family lived at 1 Cottage Place, Milton. They were married in 1876 and had eight children, Oliver being the youngest.

Oliver worked as an errand boy on leaving school before enlisting with the Kent Fortress Regiment Special Reserve, Royal Engineers at Sheerness on August 7th, 1912, service number 763. After thirty three months working for the shop owner he was let go due to insufficient business. He was now an assistant caretaker.

He joined the 3rd Battalion Royal West Kents, on November 28th, 1912 at Gravesend, service number 8631. He was 5 feet 11½ inches tall and weighed 149lbs. he was described as being very obliging and trustworthy in every way by the Secretary to the Education Committee who gave his reference. With three months training completed he applied to enlist with The Royal Horse Guards. Described as a tall good looking upstanding youth he was referred to Hyde Park Barracks by the 50th R.A.M. Corps, Maidstone on March 10th, 1913. Army life suited him as he was now 6 feet and ¾ inch tall and weighed 158lbs! He had brown eyes, brown hair and was of pale complexion.

On April 30th he arrived at Windsor where he would spend the year. In July he was injured when his horse threw him during drill and when in the process of jumping, Oliver was kicked in the back. He subsequently suffered twice from boils no doubt through his acquaintance with the art of riding a

horse! On April 29th, 1914 he was back in London on duty.

He left Southampton with his unit on April 7th, 1915. By now he had acquired the necessary qualifications in the use of the machine gun. On March 3rd, 1916 he was attached to the 8th Machine Gun Company.

The 8th Machine Gun Company was formed from the Machine Gun Sections of the 8th Brigade, 3rd Division on January 22nd, 1916 they took part in The Actions of the Bluff and St Eloi Craters then moved to The Somme for The Battle of Albert, The Battle of Bazentin helping to capture Longueval, The Battle of Delville Wood and The Battle of the Ancre.

On July 14th Oliver was appointed Lance Corporal. He was killed in action on August 17th, 1916 in operations in Delville Wood. He is buried in Authuile (now Authuille), 5 km north of Albert. The village was held by British troops

The Machine Gun Corps Memorial,
Hyde Park Corner.

from the summer of 1915 to March, 1918, when it was captured in the German Offensive on the Somme; it was ruined by shell fire even before that date.

The Military Cemetery was used by Field Ambulances and fighting units from August, 1915 to December, 1916. There are now over 450, 1914-18 war casualties commemorated in this site. Of these, nearly 40 are unidentified and special memorials are erected to 18 soldiers known or believed to be buried among them.

Killed in Action.

DACK. — Killed in action, on or about August 20th, Lance-Corpl. Oliver Stanley Dack, Royal Horse Guards, aged 20 years, the dearly-loved youngest son of Samuel and the late Eliza Dack, 71, Parrock-street, Gravesend. — Deeply mourned by his brothers and sisters.

Gravesend has to mourn the death of another gallant son in the person of Lance-Corpl. O. Stanley Dack, Royal Horse Guards. Born in Snodland twenty years ago he was brought to Gravesend when a child and received practically the whole of his education at the Milton-road Board School. Being a lad of fine physique he determined to make the Army his profession and with that end in view became one of the initial members of the Kent Fortress Engineers. When approaching army age he joined the Royal West Kent Training Schools and from there transferred straight to the Royal Horse Guards. Sixteen months ago, he then having become a machine gunner, he proceeded with a draft of his regiment to France and with the exception of a week, a few months ago, when he was granted special leave to attend, what proved to be, the deathbed of his mother and sister, has been through all the engagements his regiment has taken part in.

He was killed instantaneously on or about the 20th inst., and was buried the following day. Appended is a letter received from his platoon officer : —

8th Machine Gun Squadron, B.E.F., France.

August 22nd, 1916.

Dear Mr. Dack, — Although a complete stranger, I write to offer you my most sincere sympathy on the very sad loss which has come to you. Your son was one of my best men and a very first-class machine-gunner, and he had been under me for nearly a year. I therefore miss him not a little myself. It may perhaps be some slight consolation to you to know that his death was instantaneous and that he suffered nothing. I attended his burial myself — just the usual simple service that all men who die for their country here are given — and we have placed a simple wooden cross with his name and date of death written on it over his grave. If sympathy is of any help to you in your sorrow, you have mine in full measure. — Yours truly,

DENYS R. TREFUSIS, Lieut.

GR 2/9/16 [Andrew Marshall]

GR 2/9/16 [Andrew Marshall]

William Dadson

Royal West Surrey Rgt, 2nd Bn
Service No. L/9329 - Sergeant

William was born in Northfleet in 1890, the son of Henry and Sarah Dadson of 82 West Street. Henry was born in 1857 in Northfleet with Sarah born in 1866 and also from Northfleet. They were married in 1892 and had five surviving children. They ran a lodging house and in 1911 had 16 lodgers! William found employment as a farm labourer until enlisting on May 1st, 1908 in Maidstone. He was 5 feet 4 inches tall and weighed 115lbs. he had grey eyes and brown hair and was of ruddy complexion. He was sent to Guildford and on to Colchester on June 23rd remaining here until October when he and the Battalion sailed for Gibraltar. William found army life

difficult as he was on a series of charges including being on parade with a dirty rifle, dirty equipment, a dirty rifle [again] and rusty bayonet and not complying with instructions. There were other incidents including having shaving gear in the cook house and malicious damage to public property. Whereas all carried 3 to 4 days punishment, confined to barracks, the latter incurred a custodial sentence.

He was now an assistant cook and impressed some of his superiors, being described as a sober and hardworking individual. However the misdemeanours continued unabated and ranged from a dirty rifle, insolence, insubordination, creating a disturbance [in the barrack room at 11.30pm], inappropriate language and being absent while on duty. The sentences ranged from 3 to 8 days confinement to barracks. From Gibraltar he was posted to Bermuda and in January, 1914, South Africa where his conduct remained poor.

However, worse followed. William was found guilty of maliciously breaking a glass case containing bottles and glasses, the damages being £6. He was found guilty with two fellow privates in the civil courts of a criminal act by the Civil Powers on June 16th. All three were given three months hard labour and were to be dishonourably discharged from the Army. But on August 11th the Office of the Adjutant-General of South Africa waived any discharge due to the onset of War.

He was wounded in September 1914 and was back in Gravesend convalescing from the 20th until October 3rd. He was promoted Corporal the following Summer but life at the Front affected him. He was twice treated for impetigo and once for eczema later that year.

Worse followed in the Spring and Summer, 1916. He was wounded on February 7th and in the right shoulder on July 15th, having been promoted Sergeant on the 4th. He was given leave and returned to Gravesend in December suffering from a synovitis knee, the effects of trench life.

Sergeant Dadson was killed in action on May 11th, 1917 and is buried in H.A.C. Cemetery, Ecoust-St Mein.

Doignies to Henin-sur-Cojeul, including the village of Ecoust, were captured on April 2nd, 1917, by the 4th Australian and 7th Divisions. After the Armistice graves were added from the battlefields of Bullecourt and Ecoust and from a number of smaller burial grounds.

> Mrs. Fry, 10, Lansdowne-place, Perry Street, has received the intimation that her brother, Sergt. W. J. Dadson, of the Queen's (Surrey) Regt. has been killed in action. Sergt. Dadson was for a long time employed on Mr. Redsell's farm at Singlewell, and, joining the Army in 1908, had nearly completed nine years' service. He went to France soon after war broke out, and was killed on the 11th of May. His platoon officer, Second Lieut. F. P. Movdit, writing to Mrs. Fry, says: — "I am writing with regret to let you know of your brother's death. He was killed in action on the 11th May, doing his duty for his King and country. We all feel very proud of him, and the whole company join in expressing our deepest sympathy for you in this bereavement. He gave his life willingly, always cheerful and an example to his men. Everything possible is being done to mark the spot where he is resting, so that any time you may be able to see it for yourself."

GR 9/6/17 [Andrew Marshall]

Oliver Dack –
Authuile Military Cemetery

Bill Dadson –
H.A.C. Cemetery, Ecoust-St Mein

GR 18/5/18

A **_P Daly_** is listed on the Memorial; on the original Memorial boards he is listed as **_P Dailey_** – his birth name. The family changed the surname from **_Dailey_** [1901 Census] to **_Daly_** [1911 Census] thus ensuring the confusion!

Patrick Dailey
Royal West Kent Rgt, Private
Service No. 8421

Patrick was born in 1894 in Deptford. His father William was born in 1864 in Deptford. He was a labourer on the docks. Hs mother Johanna was born in 1866. The couple had four children – Patrick, William, born in 1898 in Gravesend, Sophia, born in 1900 in Rochester and Mary, born in 1903 in Gravesend. The family home was at originally The Terrace but subsequently 14 Crooked Lane, Gravesend. William, Patrick's father, died prior to the Great War, leaving Johanna to bring up the younger children on her own.Patrick was a ship's cook when he enlisted in the Army Reserve, Royal West Kent, for six years' duration on November 8th, 1911 in Gravesend. He was 5 feet 2½ inches tall and weighed 118lbs. He had blue eyes and brown hair.

His army records indicate that Patrick was in poor health as he was declared temporarily unfit for service in April, 1912. However, he was appointed Lance Corporal on July 31st, 1914. Patrick was mobilised on August 5th with the 3rd Royal West Kent Regiment but was demoted to Private on September 7th.

Patrick attended a Medical Examination in late November at Fort Pitt, Chatham. The Board found that he was not fit for Army service, suffering from Pulmonary Tuberculosis. He was discharged as being no longer physically fit for war service on December 11th.

Patrick died in December, 1916.

Fort Pitt and the Military Hospital

Fort Pitt's construction was completed in 1812. The Royal Marine Artillery occupied the fort from 1814 to 1815. Then wounded troops returning from the battle of Waterloo were looked after at the fort, which was to be the start of the fort's long life as a Military Hospital which was to last until 1919.

In 1828 the fort became a depot for Invalid Soldiers. New Hospital building construction began in 1832 and an Asylum was added in 1847. The central tower was demolished at this time to make way for the new buildings.

Florence Nightingale established the first Army Medical School at the fort, this came to an end in 1863 when it was moved to Netley in Hampshire.

The Great War was a very busy period for the fort when it had a large number of out-stations. Many soldiers who died there were buried at the nearby Military Cemetery.

The Hospital finally closed in 1919 when it had become run down and was shut as a post-war economy measure.

Part of the fort's ditch was filled in to provide work for the local unemployed after WWI.

Crimea Block, part of the former Hospital. [www.MedwayLines.com, 1914]

Francis Joseph Dann
Royal Marine Light Infantry
Service No. CH/11623 - Private

Francis was born in Plumstead, London on June 15th, 1883.

He married Nellie Lloyd in 1905 and the couple lived at 71 Havelock Road. Nellie was born in 1883 and was from Cliffe. He was a milk carrier. They had one child – Sidney who was born in 1911.

He served on board *HMS Hogue*. HMS *Hogue* was a *Cressy*-class armoured cruiser built for the Royal Navy in 1900. Upon completion she was assigned to the Channel Fleet and the China Station. In 1906 she became a training ship for the North America and West Indies Station before being placed in reserve in 1908. Re-commissioned at the start of World War I, she played a minor role in the Battle of Heligoland Bight a few weeks after the beginning of the war.

On the morning of September 22nd, 1914 *Hogue* and her sisters, *Aboukir* and *Cressy*, were on patrol without any escorting destroyers as they had been forced to seek shelter from bad weather. The three sisters were in line abreast, about 2,000 yards apart, at a speed of 10 knots. They were not expecting submarine attack, but they had lookouts posted and had one gun manned on each side to attack any submarines sighted. The weather had moderated earlier that morning from the storm that had been raging and Tyrwhitt was en route to reinforce the cruisers with eight destroyers.

U-9, commanded by Otto Weddigen, had been ordered to attack British transports at Ostend, but had been forced to dive and take shelter from the storm. On surfacing, she spotted the ships and moved to attack. She fired one torpedo at 06:20 at *Aboukir* that struck her on the starboard side; the ship's captain thought he had struck a mine and ordered the other two ships to close to transfer his wounded men.

Aboukir quickly began listing and capsized around 06:55. As *Hogue* approached her sinking sister, Captain Wilmot Nicholson realized that it had been a submarine attack and signalled *Cressy* to look for a periscope.

Having stopped and lowered all her boats, *Hogue* was struck by two torpedoes around 06:55. The sudden weight loss of the two torpedoes caused *U-9* to broach the surface and *Hogue*'s gunners opened fire without effect before the submarine could submerge again. The cruiser capsized about ten minutes after being torpedoed as all of her watertight doors had been open and sank at 07:15.

Cressy attempted to ram the submarine, but did not hit anything and resumed her rescue efforts until she too was torpedoed at 07:20. She too took on a heavy list and then capsized before sinking at 07:55. Several Dutch ships began rescuing survivors at 08:30 and were joined by British fishing trawlers before Tyrwhitt and his ships arrived at 10:45. The combined total from all three ships was 837 men rescued and 62 officers and 1,397 enlisted men lost. Of these, *Hogue* lost a total of 48 men.

Francis was among the 375 casualties on *Hogue*. He has no known grave and is commemorated on the Chatham Naval Memorial.

In 1954 the British government sold the salvage rights to all three ships to a German company and they were subsequently sold again to a Dutch salvage company which began salvaging the wrecks' metal in 2011.

Francis Dann,
Panel 7, Chatham Naval Memorial

Francis Dann – mentioned in the report in the *GRAVESEND REPORTER* of September 26th, 1914 and the entry in De Ruvigny, below.

GR 30/9/16 [Andrew Marshall]

Frank Dann's biography follows; he is not listed on the Memorial but was a brother of **Wilfred Dann** whose biography follows and who is listed on the Memorial.

Frank Dann
A.I.F. 15th Battalion
Service No. 126 - Private

Frank was born in Dartford in 1887, the son of Henry and Elizabeth Dann of 36 Pelham Road. Henry was born in 1852 in Bexley, Elizabeth was three years younger. The couple married in 1874 and had five children – Kate, born in 1880, Thomas, born in 1881, May, born in 1884, Frank and Wilfred, born in 1887.

Henry was an auctioneer and land agent. The family employed four servants and a governess to attend to the children.

Frank attended the King's College, Canterbury and served with the London Rifle Brigade before emigrating to Australia. He arrived in Sydney on January 13th, 1913. He settled in Peeramon, Cairns and was a selector.

He enlisted on September 16th, 1914 in Townsville, Queensland. He was 5 feet 10 inches tall and weighed 159 lbs. He had brown eyes, light brown hair and of fair complexion.

He left for Gallipoli on April 12th, 1915.

He served with 'A' Company. On May 3rd his medical report noted that *he was behind the trenches when hit by a bullet in left side of chest. Bullet penetrated lung. Empyema developed subsequently.*

The SS Nevassa, on which Frank was taken back to England after being wounded in Gallipoli, was launched on December 12th, 1912. She was built by Barclay, Curle & Co, of Glasgow at their Clydeholm Yard.

She made her maiden voyage – London to Calcutta in March, 1913. The Nevassa survived both wars and was broken up in March 1948 in Glasgow.

Owned initially by British India Steam Navigation Co. Ltd., Glasgow, the *Nervassa* was 1914 Requisitioned as troopship in 1914. The following year she was used as an Hospital ship in the Gallipoli Campaign. From 1916 she had various Trooping/Hospital duties until converted to Troopship Duties full time from

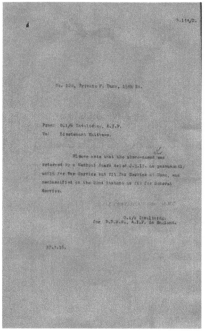

Communications regarding status of Frank Dann and his wounds, above left and above right, and the reply regarding his grave dated April 27th, 1922.

280

Gravesend Cemetery –

IN LOVING MEMORY

ALSO TWO SONS
FRANK & WILFRED
KILLED IN ACTION 1916-1917

[Photograph – Andy White]

Frank and Wilfred Dann

Wilfred Dann - Lijssenthoek CWGC Cemetery

281

Frank was severely wounded and was taken initially on the Gascon to the General Hospital, Alexandria, arriving on the 7th. On the 12th he was taken on the Nevassa to England and admitted to the 2nd Western Hospital, Manchester on May 28th. On May 30th he was operated on – empyema.

On August 30th he was transferred to the Middlesex Hospital in Harewood. On September 2nd Frank was re-commended by a Health Board to be sent back to Australia for home service being deemed unfit for active service. However he was reclassified on the 22nd as fit for General Service. In mid-December he was sent to Weymouth.

He recovered sufficiently to be discharged to Perham Downs, Salisbury on July 7th, 1916. Frank embarked on July 16th to the 4th Training Battalion at Etaples and on the 26th was in the 2nd Draft re-joining the 15th Battalion.

Frank was killed in action on August 13th, 1916. It appears his body was recovered and he was buried in a field grave at Pozieres. However his grave was lost and Frank is commemorated on the Villers-Bretonneux Memorial.

Wilfred Dann
Gloucestershire Rgt, 12th Bn
2nd Lieutenant

Wilfred was born in Dartford in 1887 and the younger brother of Frank. Like his brother he attended the King's College, Canterbury.

Wilfred was an architect before enlisting. He joined the 12th Battalion on October 25th. There is no mention of him in the Battalion War Diary, perhaps due to his recent arrival. On the 27th the Battalion was in reserve at Ridgewood. The following day the Battalion paraded at 11am and then moved forward relieving the 16th Warwickshire Regiment. They moved via Bedford House to Sanctuary Wood. They left the Wood at 5.30pm with one company in the front line and another in support with the other two companies supporting the 1st Devons and the 1st D.C.L.I. Casualties included 2nd Lieutenant E.G. Fowler being killed at Battalion Head Quarters but otherwise casualties were light and nothing of importance was reported.

The Battalion was still in the front line on the 30th. German artillery was active in the morning. There were casualties at Clapham Junction but casualties were light. On the 31st the Battalion was still in the front line with the situation again reported as being normal and the weather fine and, surprisingly, no mention of Second Lieutenant Dann.

Wilfred was wounded on October 29th, 1917 and died of his wounds the following day. He is buried in Lijssenthoek Military Cemetery.

During the War, Lijssenthoek was situated on the main communication line between the Allied military bases in the rear and the Ypres battlefields. Close to the Front, but out of range of most German field artillery, it became a natural place to establish casualty clearing stations. The cemetery was first used by the French 15th Hopital D'Evacuation and in June 1915, it began to be used by casualty clearing stations of the Commonwealth forces. From April to August 1918, the casualty clearing stations fell back before the German advance and field ambulances (including a French ambulance) took their places. The cemetery contains 9,901 Commonwealth burials of the First World War. There are 883 war graves of other nationalities, mostly French and German.

The cemetery, designed by Sir Reginald Blomfield, is the second largest Commonwealth cemetery in Belgium.

	25	...ys at disposal of Company Commanders during the morning. Battalion paraded at 2 pm and moved forward to RIDGEWOOD. Transport and Administrative branch proceeded to same area as when Battalion was last in the line (N.W. central). Draft of 56 O.R. joined Bn as reinforcements and the following Officers: 2 Lts A.H.HAY, R.W.HARRIS, W.DANN M.CALVERT, G.H.ROGERS and T.R.BRIDGFORD.
	26 27	Battalion in Divisional Reserve at Ridgewood
Do	28	Bn paraded at 11 am. and moved forward to relieve the 16th Bn. R.WARWICKSHIRE REGT in the front line. Battalion proceeded via BEDFORD HOUSE & SANCTUARY WOOD, leaving Sanctuary Wood at 6.30 pm. One Company was in the front line. One Company in close support. Two Coys in support to 7 Devons & 10 C.L.I. B. H.Q. SERR HOUSE. I.15. H. 9.b. 2/Lt E.G. FOWLER was killed at B. H.Q. Casualties were very light.
	29	Battalion holding front line, Casualties ... ... nothing of importance to report
Do	30	Battalion holding front line. Enemy's artillery was very active during the morning and ration party had great difficulty in getting forward with rations. I O.R. of Transport was killed at CLAPHAM Junction otherwise situation normal. Casualties light
Do	31	Battalion in front line. Situation normal. Weather fine

J.H.Haywood ...

12th Battalion Gloucestershire Regiment; War Diary.

Thomas Neville Darby
3/1st West Kent Yeomanry, Private Service No. 2531

Thomas was born in Gravesend in 1884 the son of Thomas and Eliza Derby of 46 The Grove, Milton. Thomas senior was born in 1856 in Grays. He had his own drapery business. Eliza was born in Gravesend in 1855.

There were three children in the family – Thomas, Charles, born in 1886 and Nellie, born in 1887. Also living at their home was Ada Sullivan who was born in 1878 in Bristol and was employed as a servant.

Thomas married his wife Emily in 1909. The couple lived at 36 Brandon Street, Gravesend. Thomas inherited his father's drapery business with Emily assisting Thomas in the shop. They were well enough off to employ a servant, Beth Whiting who was born in Northfleet. Prior to the Great War the couple moved to Florence Villa in Wrotham Road, Gravesend.

Thomas enlisted with the Queen's Own West Kent Hussars, a battalion of the Household Cavalry Regiment. The Queen's Own West Kent Yeomanry can trace its origins to 1794 when local volunteer troops were raised to assist the civil powers. Each troop was about 50 strong with three officers.

In 1827 the government disbanded the Yeomanry Regiments in those districts where they had not been mobilised in the previous 10 years. The Kent Regiment was stood down. But for this gap in service, the Kent Yeomanry formations would have been the most senior Yeomanry Regiments in the country in terms of the date of acceptance of its senior troop - the Cinque Ports Cavalry. In 1830 the West Kent Yeomanry was reformed and in 1864 the West Kent Yeomanry was awarded the title Queen's Own and became known as the Queen's Own West Kent Yeomanry.

In accordance with the Territorial and Reserve Forces Act 1907 the TF was intended to be a home defence force for service during wartime and members could not be compelled to serve outside the country. However, on the outbreak of war on August 4th, 1914, many members volunteered for Imperial Service. Therefore, TF units were split in August and September 1914 into 1st Line (liable for overseas service) and 2nd Line (home service for those unable or unwilling to serve overseas) units. Later, a 3rd Line was formed to act as a reserve, providing trained replacements for the 1st and 2nd Line regiments

The 3rd Line regiment was formed at the end of 1914 at Canterbury. In June 1915 it was affiliated to 3rd Reserve Cavalry Regiment at Canterbury. In the summer of 1916 it was dismounted and attached to the 3rd Line Groups of the Home Counties Division at Crowborough as its 1st Line was serving as infantry.

In November 1916 it was at Tunbridge Wells. The regiment was disbanded in February 1917 with personnel transferring to the 2nd Line regiment or to the 4th (Reserve) Battalion of the Royal West Kent Regiment at Crowborough.

Thomas was attached to the 13th Middlesex Regiment. The 13th (Service) Battalion, Middlesex Regiment (Duke of Cambridge's Own) was raised at Mill Hill in September 1914 as part of Kitchener's Third New Army. They trained on the South Downs, spending the winter billets in Hove. They moved to Shoreham in May then to Pirbright in June for final training.

They proceeded to France on the September 2nd, 1915, landing at Boulogne. The Division concentrated in the area between Etaples and St Pol on September 4th and a few days later

Killed in Action.

TROOPER T. N. DARBY.

Trooper Thomas Neville Darby (elder son of Mr. T. G. Darby), who carried on the business of a draper in Parrock-street, was very popular in Gravesend, where his amiable manner and upright character were fully appreciated by an exceptionally large number of friends and acquaintances. His death at the front, the news of which was received on Wednesday, will be universally regretted, while the utmost sympathy will be felt for the bereaved widow and parents. From the outbreak of the war he was fired with a desire to do "his bit" for the country, and many times he expressed the hope that he would have his share in, defeating the frightful Huns. He was a trooper in the West Kent (Queen's Own) Yeomanry, and on joining up he was attached to the 13th Middlesex. He went into training at Crowborough camp, and about a month ago he was sent to France, where he was killed in action, dying, as the sergeant of his company stated in a letter to his parents, like a brave Britisher, with his face to the foe. The sad news was conveyed in the Sergeant's letter already referred to, in which the deceased was spoken of as a splendid personality and an excellent soldier. A short time ago, the deceased sent home three letters—one to his parents, one to his wife, and one for a solicitor—to be opened "after his death" should that occur, and, needless to say, the contents revealed him as a most affectionate and devoted husband and son, and showed his conviction that he was only doing a Britisher's duty by giving his services to his country. The deceased was given as good a burial as the circumstances would permit. The widow, who has one son about three years old, is naturally broken-hearted at the sad occurrence, as also are the parents, and the deceased's many friends will share in this great sorrow. Mr. and Mrs. T. G. Darby have a second son who has enlisted, and also a son-in-law (Mr. Parkes, dairyman, Southend), who is joining up, necessitating, we understand, the closing of his business.

marched across France into the reserve for the British assault at Loos, going into action on the 26th of September and suffering heavy losses. In 1916 they suffered in the German gas attack at Wulverghem and then moved to The Somme seeing action in The Battle of Delville Wood and The Battle of Guillemont.

Thomas was killed in action on August 31st, 1916; the Battalion war diary for the 30th and 31st details his final moments -

August 30th - Left E13 & 14 at 1 p.m. in pouring rain. Marched via DERNANCOURT - MEAULT to MEMETZ where teas were served and guides of 4th SUFFOLKS met platoons who marched independently to GREEN DUMP and eventually completed relief of TEA TRENCH, WORCESTER TRENCH-PONT STREET & ORCHARD TRENCH – at 7.30 A.M.

August 31st - Trenches knee deep in mud & blocked by troops. At 8.30 a.m. enemy bombardment commenced on all trenches – increasing up to 2 p.m. when attack was launched – driving 'B' Coy out of TEA TRENCH and 'A' Coy back up WORCESTER TRENCH to MACDOUGAL C.T. and PONT ST.Enemy advanced to ORCHARD TRENCH where they were stopped by 2/LT GREEN with about 12 men of 'D' Coy and a L.G. This party forced to retire did so in good order, holding up enemy until support could be brought up.
'A' Coy withdrawn from PONT ST. to CARLTON TRENCH also remnants of B & 1 platoon 'D' & 'C' Coy. Gas shells at night.

Thomas has no known grave and is commemorated on the Thiepval Monument.

His probate came to the good sum of just under £3,934.

Joseph Frederick Davis, M.C.
Royal Engineers – Lieutenant
Service Number – 954 & 504208

Joseph was born in 1893 in Gravesend, the son of Joseph and

Minnie Davis of 10 Park Place. Joseph was born in 1854 in Ashton-under-Lyme. Minnie was born in 1867 in Bath. The couple were married in 1891 and they had three children – Doris, born in 1892, Joseph and William, born in 1902. All three were born in Gravesend.

Joseph [father] was a civil engineer and the manager of the Gravesend Gas Company. His son Joseph was articled to his father prior to enlisting.

Joseph was in the Territorials before the war, serving with The Royal Engineers, service number 954. He was called up on the declaration of war. He arrived in France on December 21st, 1914.

He served with distinction through the war rising to the rank of 2nd Lieutenant. He was awarded the Military Cross in July, 1918 – the award being made *for conspicuous gallantry and devotion to duty. He constructed forward gun* positions in full view of the enemy and under continual shell fire. He displayed great determination and skill.

Joseph died on March 19th, 1919. It is somewhat ironic that having survived four long years of warfare he would succumb to the 'Spanish 'Flu'. He is buried in Aldershot Military Cemetery.

George Jesse Day
Merchant Marine, Master

George was born in Hoo in 1873. His father George was born in 1840 in Hoo. He was a labourer at the Cement Works. Hs mother Amelia was also from Hoo, being born in 1843. The couple had five children, May, born in 1867, George, Harry, born in 1875, Frank, born in 1878 and Amy, born in 1880. The family home was at 8 Hill Row, Lower Upnor.

George married Florence Ellen Rose in Strood in December, 1904. The couple had two children – Olive Florence, born in Gravesend in June, 1906 and Jessie, born in Gravesend in September, 1914. The family home was 6 Raphael Road, Gravesend.

George worked on boats that plied their trade on the river to include the *Isabell Little*. The Thames was a major route for traffic making their way up river to London and beyond or sailing down river towards the North Sea with various ports, great and small being used to load or deliver goods and passengers.

In the final year of the war, and now 46 years old, George was Master of the ketch, The *Lord Roseberry*, ship number 99922. The *Lord Roseberry* was built in 1893 in Upnor by James Little of Strood. She was a ketch-rigged barge of 72 tons.

George was killed on September 14th, 1918 when he drowned some 5 miles north east of Le Treport in the Channel.

George and *Thomas Deadman* whose biographies now follow, were cousins.

George Deadman
Royal Marine Light Infantry
Service No. CH/16154 – Private

George was born in 1889 in Northfleet to Absolom and Mary Deadman of 85 Nelson Road, Perry Street. Absolom was born in 1859 in Ifield; he was a labourer at the cement works. Mary was from Chatham, being born in 1864. The couple had nine children – Arthur, born in 1885, Absolom, born in 1886, May, born in 1888, George, Emily, born in 1891, Amy, born in 1893, Ellen, born in 1896, Thomas, born in 1899 and Walter, born in 1900.

Lieut. Joseph Frederick Davis, M.C., R.E.

FULL MILITARY HONOURS AT FUNERAL.

Last week we briefly recorded the sad death of Lieut. Joseph Frederick Davis, M.C., R.E., at Cambridge Hospital, Aldershot, following a severe double operation for gastric ulcer in the stomach and appendicitis. As then stated he was the son of Mr. Joseph Davis, general manager and engineer of the Gravesend and Milton Gas-Light Company. He was educated at the Dartford Grammar School, and upon leaving was articled to his father, after which he entered the service of the above Company as assistant engineer, and remained with them until he joined up in September, 1914. He held 1st class certificates at the City and Guilds of London Institute for gas engineering and gas distribution. He was a member of the Eastern Counties Gas Managers' Association, in which he took strong interest and gave great assistance to his father during the time the latter was honorary secretary. He was in his 26th year, and died on Wednesday, the 10th inst.

year, and died on Wednesday, the 10th inst.

MILITARY CAREER.

The deceased officer enlisted as a sapper in the Royal Engineers as early as September, 1914, proceeding overseas in December of that year. He remained on the Western Front throughout these early and difficult days of the campaign until the latter part of 1915, when he returned to England to take up a commission in the Engineers. After being gazetted he again proceeded to France and was all through the severe fighting and the momentous days of the Huns' great attack in the early part of last year. During those operations he was awarded the Military Cross for services thus described in the "London Gazette" Supplement: — "He constructed forward gun positions in full view of the enemy and under continual shell-fire. He displayed great determination and skill." Whilst home on a brief, but well-earned, leave in October last he was unfortunately taken ill, which necessitated his removal to a London Hospital. After a somewhat lengthy period of sickness there he was sent to re-join his company at Aldershot. It is to be regretted, however, that he had not made a complete recovery, and he was, therefore, sent into Hospital again. Shortly after admission it was found necessary to perform a serious operation, from the effects of which he unfortunately succumbed.

THE FUNERAL.

His remains were interred in the Military Cemetery, Aldershot, on Monday last, full military honours being accorded, the whole of the arrangements being carried out by the Authorities. The body, enclosed in a polished oak coffin, was conveyed on a gun-carriage drawn by six horses. The Colonel of the Royal Engineers wrote a very sympathetic letter to the parents, and deeply regretted his inability to be at the funeral owing to an important official engagement. The Officer Commanding the Royal Engineers, however, was present, as also were all the Officers of the Mess, and the full band of the Regiment. The committal of the body was followed by a volley fired by a party of 30 men, after which the "Last Post" was sounded by the buglers.

A number of beautiful wreaths were sent, these being from the bereaved Widow; Father and Mother (Mr. and Mrs. Jos. Davis, "Oaklands," St. James's-road, Gravesend); Doris (sister); Grandma and relatives at Bath; Officers of the Royal Engineers' Mess; N.C.O.s Officers' Mess; Fellow Officers in Ward 19, Cambridge Hospital, Aldershot; the R.E. Office Staff; the officers of the Gravesend and Milton Gas Works; also foreman and workmen of the Gas Co.; Mr. and Mrs. Lines; Larry and Dorothy (London); Uncle Will and Auntie Bertie (Gravesend); Mrs. Beaver (London); Mrs. Sanderson (London); Miss Turner (London); Mr. O. V. Starkey; Mr., Mrs. and Miss Dean (Gravesend); Lizzie Dagner (London); Doris and Brownie Kerr (Bristol); Nellie Lacy and Minnie Hoffall (London); "From all friends" (London).

Aldershot CWGC Cemetery – CWGC

GR 29/3/19 [Andrew Marshall]

George enlisted with the Royal Marine Light Infantry when old enough. George married Daisy Eileen Search in March 1913. They had one son, George, born in December. The couple lived at 15 Stone Street.

George was stationed on the *Endymion* in 1911 before joining *HMS Vanguard*. HMS *Endymion* was a first class cruiser of the *Edgar* class. Built in 1901 she served in China during the Boxer Rebellion and later in the First World War. She served in the First World War in the Gallipoli Campaign, and was sold for breaking up at Cardiff in March 1920.

The ninth HMS *Vanguard* was a *St. Vincent*-class battleship, an enhancement of the "dreadnought" design built by Vickers at Barrow-in-Furness. She was designed and built during the Anglo-German naval race and spent her life in the Home Fleet.

At the outbreak of World War I, *Vanguard* joined the First Battle Squadron at Scapa Flow, and fought in the Battle of Jutland as part of the Fourth Battle Squadron. As one of twenty-four dreadnoughts in Jellicoe's Battle Fleet, she did not suffer any damage or casualties.

On the afternoon of July 9th, 1917, the ship's crew had been exercising, practising the routine for abandoning ship. She anchored in the northern part of Scapa Flow at about 18.30. There is no record of anyone detecting anything amiss until the moment of the explosion at 23:20.

A court of inquiry heard accounts from many witnesses on nearby ships. They accepted the consensus that there had been a small explosion with a white glare between the foremast and "A" turret, followed after a brief interval by two much larger explosions. The Court decided, on the balance of the available evidence, that the main detonations were in either "P" magazine, "Q" magazine, or both.

Although the explosion was an explosion of the cordite charges in a main magazine, the reason was much less obvious. The inquiry found that some of the cordite on board, which had been temporarily offloaded in December 1916 and catalogued at that time, was past its stated safe life. It was also noted that a number of ship's boilers were still in use, and some watertight doors which should have been closed in war-time, were open as the ship was in port. It was suggested that this might have contributed to a dangerously high temperature in the magazines. The final conclusion of the board was that a fire started in a 4-inch magazine, perhaps when a raised temperature caused spontaneous ignition of cordite, spreading to one or the other main magazines and exploding.

George was among the 804 casualties, there being just the two survivors. He has no known grave and is commemorated on the Chatham Naval Memorial.

GR 21/7/17 [Andrew Marshall]

DEADMAN.—On July 9th, on H.M.S.
"Vanguard," Private George Deadman,
R.M.L.I., dearly beloved husband of
Daisy Deadman, of 15, Stone-street.
Gravesend, aged 29 years.

George Deadman – Chatham Naval Memorial

Gravesend Cemetery –

GEORGE DEADMAN
Who Lost His Life on HMS
Vanguard
July 9th 1917, Aged 29 Years
HIS DUTY NOBLY DONE

Pte. G. Deadman (Gravesend),
Royal Marine Light Infantry.
LOST ON H.M.S. VANGUARD.

Among those who perished on H.M.S. Vanguard was Pte. George Deadman, of 15, Stone
Street, Gravesend, whose loss is deeply
mourned by his relatives and a wide circle
of friends. He was a particularly bright,
upright and intelligent young man. A son
of Mr. and Mrs. A. Deadman, of Perry Street,
he was educated at the Dover Road School,
and after serving six years' apprenticeship
with Mr. Drake, Perry Street, joined the
Royal Marines ten years ago. He had served
on many famous war vessels—the Endymion,
the Africa (when Prince Louis of Battenburg,
to whom he was orderly, was admiral), the
Falmouth (lost since the war began), the London, and, finally, the Vanguard, which he
joined some time before war broke out. He
was a great favourite on ship as well as on
shore. He was popularly known on board as
"Taffy," whilst his ship mate and friend,
Harry Styles, of Snodland, who, alas, also
also perished, was known as "Patsy"—the
names being characters they represented in
an entertainment. Pte. G. Deadman, who
was 29 years of age, was exceedingly indus-
trious, and had a penchant for making mats
and other nick-nacks for the home, at which he
was very clever. He leaves a widow and
a charming little son to mourn their loss. It
was a pathetic fact that after being away
many months at sea, deceased was expected
home this week on leave. Two of his
brothers are at the Front, one with the West
Surreys and the other with the Buffs.

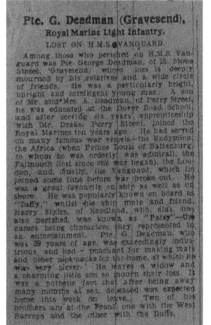

GM 21/7/17 [Andrew Marshall]

Pte. T. L. Deadman (Meopham).
Royal Fusiliers.
KILLED IN ACTION.

His mother has received an intimation that Pte. Thomas Leonard Deadman, Royal Fusiliers (youngest son of Mrs. Deadman, late of Camer Street, Camer, near Meopham), was killed in action on June 7th. Before joining he was employed as an under gardener on the estate of Mr. Foa, Hollywell Park, Wrotham. He went to France in May, 1916. He had been there only a few days, when his father was struck by lightning, with fatal results. Later Pte. Deadman was twice in hospital in France through wounds. With reference to his death, a chaplain, writing to his mother, states that he found her son, together with several more of his boys, had been killed through the bursting of a shell, and that he was buried beside his comrades and his young officer, who had also fallen in the great battle. A cross had been erected at the grave, bearing his name, regimental number, and corps. Two letters belonging to Pte. Deadman picked up on the day following the battle, by one of the sergeants of the Middlesex Regiment, were thoughtfully returned to his relatives.

Thomas Deadman –
Voormezeele Enclosure No. 3.

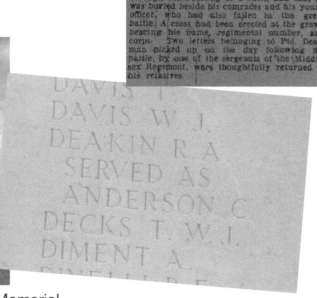

Robert Arthur Deakin – Thiepval Memorial

Thomas Leonard Deadman
Royal Fusiliers, 32nd Battalion
Service No. 24411 - Private

Thomas was born in Perry Street, Northfleet in 1893. He was one of six children born to William and Mary Deadman of 117 Sun Lane. William was born in 1852 in Ifield. He was a foreman on a farm. Mary was born in 1854 and was born in Bapchild; she also worked on a farm. They married in 1874. By the eve of the Great War the family lived in Camer Street, Meopham.

Thomas was a domestic gardener before enlisting with the 32nd Battalion. The 32nd (East Ham) Battalion, The Royal Fusiliers (City of London Regiment) was raised in London on October 18th, 1915 by the Mayor and Borough of East Ham. After initial training close to home they joined 124th Brigade, 41st Division at Aldershot in November 1915. They proceeded to France on May 5th, 1916, the division concentrating between Hazebrouck and Bailleul. In 1916 they were in action at The Battle of Flers-Courcelette and The Battle of the Transloy Ridges on the Somme. In 1917 they fought during The Battle of Messines and it was here that Thomas was killed in action on June 7th, 1917. He is buried in Voormezeele Enclosure Number 3 Cemetery.

Robert Arthur Deakin –
Served under the name;
Robert Arthur Anderson
Royal West Surrey Rgt, 8th Bn
Service No. L/10908 - Private

Robert was born in Northfleet in 1898. He was the son of Robert and Emma Deakin of Hope Villa, Park Avenue, Northfleet. Robert [father] was born in Northfleet in 1868 and was a foreman baker. Emma was born the same year

in Gravesend. They married in 1893 and had seven children – Gertrude, born in 1893, Lilian, born in 1895, Elsie, born in 1896, Robert, Edgar, born in 1901, Harold, born in 1904 and Ethel, born in 1906.

He enlisted at Chelsea under the name Robert Arthur Anderson, presumably to conceal his true age.

The 8th Battalion, The Queen's Royal Regiment (West Surrey) was raised at Guildford in September 1914 as part of Kitchener's Third New Army and joined 72nd Brigade, 24th Division. The Division was established in September 1914 as part of Kitchener's Third New Army and began to assemble in the area of Shoreham. The division suffered from a lack of equipment and a lack of trained officers and NCOs to command the volunteers. In late June 1915 they moved to Aldershot for final training and they proceeded to France at the end of August. The Division concentrated in the area between Etaples and St Pol in September and then marched across northern France into the reserve for the British assault at Loos, going into action on September 26th, with heavy losses. In 1916 they suffered in the German gas attack at Wulverghem and then moved to the Somme seeing action at Delville Wood and Guillemont.

One of the most famous incidents to occur on the first day of the battle of the Somme was the 8th Battalion's famous 'football' charge towards the German trenches at Montauban. Captain W. P. Nevill provided four footballs for his platoons to kick across No Man's Land as they advanced and the image had soon captured the imagination of the British public.

Robert was killed in action on September 2nd, 1916 during the closing stages of the Battle of Delville Wood. He has no known grave and is commemorated on the Thiepval Monument.

"The Surrey's Play the Game" by R. Caton Woodville, published in the *Illustrated London News*, July 27th, 1916 (Incorrectly captioned as occurring at Contalmaison)

Pte. R. A. Deakin, son of Mr. and Mrs. Deakin, 38, Victoria-road, Gravesend, was killed in action by shrapnel in the Battle of the Somme on the 2nd September. Announcing the death, Lieut. M. H. Lansdown, of the 8th Queen's Regt., has written:—"He was an excellent soldier, and his loss is deeply felt in the company. His friends have asked me to convey their sympathy. It will probably be a comfort for you to know that he was killed instantaneously whilst doing his duty in the trenches." Sergt. Park writes: "I can only say he was a good lad since I joined the platoon in December, 1915. I have just lost a brother myself on this front, so can sympathise more fully." Pte. Deakin was a cadet in the Territorials, and would liked to have joined up when war broke out. However, in February, 1915, though only 16 and 8 months, he felt the call, and enlisted in the Queen's Own Royal West Surrey Regt. He went to France on the 13th October, and has been to and from the trenches ever since. He was a member of Wycliffe Chapel, and well-known in the district. His chums will miss him very much. He was a loyal friend and a devoted son. One of the kindly acts by which he will be remembered was to fetch and take home Mr. G. Turner, who has lost his eyesight. He was a good correspondent, and took a kindly interest in his fellow-members at Wycliffe. He also read with interest the "Reporter," and sent a letter, which we published, signed "A Perry Street Boy."

GR 30/9/16 [Andrew Marshall]

Alfred Henry Dearing
Royal Navy Reserve
Service No. 17820DA – Deck Hand

Alfred was born in Cliffe in 1888. His father William was born in 1860 in Snodland. He was a labourer at the Cement Works. Alfred's mother, Alice, was born in 1862 in Higham. They were married in 1882 and had three children – Alice, born in 1885, James, born in 1887 and Alfred. The family lived at 16 Church Street, Gravesend.

Prior to being on active service Alfred worked as a labourer at the Cement Works, like his father.

Alfred was a deck hand on board *H.M. Drifter Hastfen.* Hastfen was a 77 ton steam powered drifter.

She was built in Killybegs, County Donegal in 1911. On September 24th, 1917, Hastfen was sunk by a mine laid by UC-11 under the command of Karl Dobberstein south of the Shipwash Sands.

Alfred was among the crew of four killed. He has no known grave and is commemorated on the Chatham Naval Memorial.

Thomas Edwin Denham
London Rifle Brigade, 5th Battalion
Service No. 318375 - Rifleman

Thomas was born in 1899 in Gravesend. His father Thomas was born in 1868 and came from Portsmouth. He was a stone mason's labourer. His mother Harriet was born in 1878 and was from Surbiton. The couple were married in 1899 and they had three children – Thomas, Doris, born in 1904 and Leonard, born in 1906. The family lived at 221 Old Road West.

Thomas enlisted in the 15th London Regiment, service number 537392. He was subsequently with the 5th [City of London] Battalion [London Rifle Brigade]. The London Rifle Brigade (LRB) were affiliated to the Rifle Brigade, and wore black buttons and shoulder titles. Their headquarters was at Bunhill Road, and in August 1914 they were at their annual camp at Crowborough, in Sussex. They crossed to France in November 1914, joining the 11th Brigade, 4th Division, serving with them in the trenches at Ploegsteert. Men from the battalion took part in the Christmas Truce in December 1914.

They took part in Second Ypres and in

It is with great regret we have to record the death of Alfred Henry Dearing, which took place on September 24th, at the early age of 29 years. He adds one more to the daily list that are heroically giving their lives to save others, to uphold the cause of right against might, and our humanitarian principles against the cursed militarism of the Hun. The deceased lad was the son of Mr. William Dearing, the well-known and respected proprietor of the Waterman's Arms, Church-street. The circumstances of the lad's death are particularly sad, as he had only joined the Colours a month ago in the R.N.R. Trawling Section. He was engaged on a mine-sweeper, which had a crew of 10. Whilst engaged in the act of picking up floating mines one touched the vessel and exploded, and four of the crew were launched into eternity instantaneously, the ship sinking at once. Previous to his joining the Colours he was in later years employed in turn on the pontoon bridge as a donkeyman, mate of a barge in Jurvis's firm, Transport Service, P.L.A., and cement worker for many years at the late I. C. Johnson's factory. By his happy and jovial disposition, fondness of sport, and kindness of heart, Alf. was immensely and deservedly popular, and claimed a large circle of friends. Always the first to help in any charitable cause, with heart and pocket too, and beloved by all who knew him, this young life will be sadly missed, not only by his sorrowing parents and relatives, but by the numerous friends who enjoyed the pleasure of his acquaintance. God rest his soul. As the remains have not been discovered, a memorial service was held at St. George's Church on Sunday, Canon Gedge impressively officiating.—Communicated.

GR 6/10/17 [Andrew Marshall]

April-May 1915 they lost 16 officers and 392 men. Due to the losses they formed a composite battalion with other London units until August 1915 when they became part of the 3rd Division. They served with them until the formation of the 56th (London) Division in March 1916 when they joined the 169th Brigade. They lost heavily at Gommecourt on July 1st, 1916, and fought again at Leuze Wood and Combles. In 1917 they were in the Battle of Arras and Third Ypres, and also took part in the Battle of Cambrai. They were heavily involved in the

Chatham Naval Memorial, Panel 26 - Arthur Dearing

Gravesend Cemetery – Thomas Denham

[Photograph – Andy White]

March 1918 German Offensive at Arras, and took part in the fighting on the Hindenburg Line.

Thomas was killed in action on November 6th, 1918. He is buried in Angreau Communal Cemetery. The village of Angreau is located south-west of Mons.

The two plots in the communal cemetery contain the bodies of soldiers of the 56th (London) Division, who fell on November 4th to the 7th, 1918. The cemetery contains 39 Commonwealth burials of the First World War.

Above is a photograph of the late Pte. Thomas Edwin Denham, London Rifle Brigade, who was killed in action just previous to the signing of the armistice. He was educated at St. James's school under Mr. L. Rusbridge, and from there he went to Messrs. B. and F. Tolhurst, solicitors, New-road, to commence a promising career. He was held in very high esteem by all the staff, and all with whom he came into contact. From the outbreak of war he was a member of the Kent V.A.D. 37 and served at the Yacht Club Hospital under the Commandant of the Men's Detachment (Mr. H. L. Tatham). Under the supervision of this gentleman deceased arranged and carried out much transport work, and was always in demand as a stretcher bearer at operation cases, and well worthy of the distinction for which he was recommended in 1916. On attaining the age of 18, he joined the Civil Service Rifles, and after four months' training was drafted to France. He was then transferred to the London Rifle Brigade, serving with this regiment until called upon to make the supreme sacrifice. Extremely popular and having a wide circle of friends, his death will be regretted by all who knew him.

GR 18/11/18 [Andrew Marshall]

Frederick Richard Dennis
Essex Regiment, 10th Battalion
Service No. 42991 - Private

Frederick was born in 1899 in Gravesend the son of William and Sarah Dennis of 61 Peppercroft Street. Both were born in 1863; William in Balham Hill and Sarah from Gravesend. They married in 1886. William worked for the dairy as a milkman. There were five children in the family – William, born in 1887, Edith, born in 1890, Beatrice, born in 1892, Dorothy, born in 1897 and Frederick.

10th (Service) Battalion, The Essex Regiment was raised at Warley in September 1914 as part of Kitchener's Second New Army and joined 53rd

Brigade, 18th (Eastern) Division. They moved to Shorncliffe and then to Colchester and to Codford St Mary in May 1915 for final training. They proceeded to France on July 26th, 1915, landing at Boulogne, the Division concentrating near Flesselles. In 1916 they were in action on The Somme in The Battle of Albert capturing their objectives near Montauban, The Battle of Bazentin Ridge including the capture of Trones Wood, The Battle of Delville Wood, Thiepval Ridge, the Ancre Heights playing a part in the capture of the Schwaben Redoubt and Regina Trench and The Battle of the Ancre. In 1917 they took part in the Operations on the Ancre including Miraumont and the capture of Irles. They fought during The German retreat to the Hindenburg Line and in the Third Battle of the

Scarpe before moving to Flanders. They were in action in The Battle of Pilkem Ridge, Langemarck and The First and Second Battle of Passchendaele. In 1918 they saw action during The Battles of St Quentin and of the Avre, The actions of Villers-Brettoneux, The Battles of Amiens and of Albert where the Division captured the Tara and Usna hills and Trones Wood. They fought in The Second Battle of Bapaume, The Battles of Epehy, the St Quentin Canal, the Selle and the Sambre.

At the front, German resistance was falling away. Unprecedented numbers of prisoners were taken in the Battle of the Selle, and a new attack was quickly prepared. The French First Army and the British First, Third, and Fourth Armies were tasked with advancing from south of the Condé Canal along a 30-mile front toward Maubeuge-Mons, threatening Namur. Together with the American forces breaking out of the forests of Argonne, this would, if successful, disrupt the German efforts to reform a shortened defensive line along the Meuse.

At dawn on November 4th, 17 British and 11 French divisions headed the attack. The Tank Corps, its resources badly stretched, could provide only 37 tanks for support.

The first barrier to the northern attack was the 60–70 foot wide Sambre Canal and the flooded ground around it. German guns quickly ranged on the attackers, and bodies piled up before the temporary bridges were properly emplaced under heavy fire. Even after the crossing the German forces defended in depth, and it was not until midday that a 2 mile deep by 15 mile wide breach was secured.

Further north, IV and V Corps attacked into Forêt de Mormal. At Le Quesnoy, the Germans defence was haphazard. The advance continued and the battle objectives were reached. This resulted in bridgehead almost 50 miles long, to a depth of 2–3 miles.

From this point, the northern Allies advanced relentlessly until the Armistice line of November 11th.

Frederick was killed in action on October 31st, on the eve of the Battle.

He is buried in Maurois Communal Cemetery, 5km south-west of Le Cateau.

Frederick Richard Dennis, private in the 10th Essex Regt, 19 years of age and second son of Mr. and Mrs. W. Dennis, 61 Peppercroft-street, Gravesend, has succumbed to wounds received in action in France on Oct 31st, 1918. Deceased, whose portrait will be recognised above and who was in civil life employed by the Gravesend Gas Company had served in the Army for about thirteen months, eight being spent in France Describing the circumstances of the lad's death in a letter to the father, Lieut.-Col. Forbes (commanding the regiment) states:— " Your son, Pte. F. Dennis, was moving up the line near Bousies on the evening of O 31st, when a shell landed in the middle of party, killing several and wounding a go many more. Your son was very bad wounded, but he was removed at once to b pital. I know your son very well and had great regard for him; he was so cheer under adverse conditions and so cool a courageous in action. He was also ve popular with his comrades, who mourn th loss. Please accept my very since sympathy."

GR 15/11/18 [Andrew Marshall]

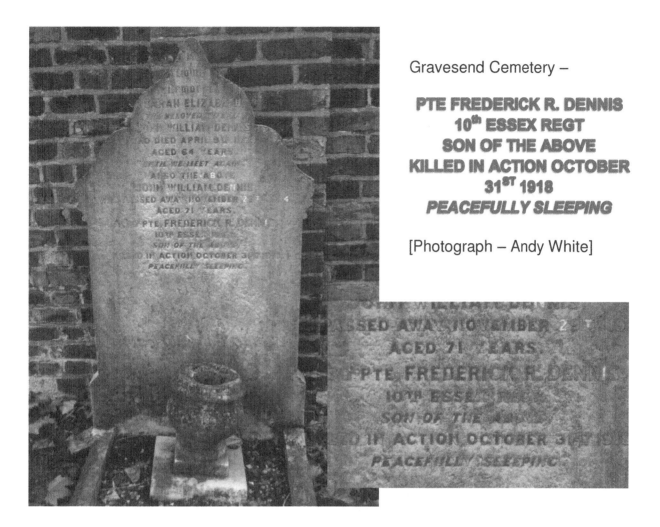

Gravesend Cemetery –

**PTE FREDERICK R. DENNIS
10th ESSEX REGT
SON OF THE ABOVE
KILLED IN ACTION OCTOBER
31ST 1918
PEACEFULLY SLEEPING**

[Photograph – Andy White]

Frederick Dennis

Maurois Communal Cemetery.

John Dicks

A.I.F., 9th Battalion
Service No. 2810 – Private

John was born in 1874 to William and Joyce Dicks. William was born in 1830 in Strood. He was a general labourer before joining the navy. Joyce was born in 1844 and was from Gravesend. The couple married in 1861 and had five children – Caroline, born in 1870, Thomas, born in 1872, John, Martin, born in 1876 and Edward, born in 1880. The family originally lived in Rotherhithe before moving to 44 Southill Road, Gravesend.

John was a potman at the Neptune Pubic House, Rotherhithe on leaving school and subsequently enlisted with the Royal Marine Light Infantry. He served on *H.M.S. Hotspur*, a 2nd Rate Port Guard ship. He served a total of twelve years and two months before leaving.

It had been recognised that a ship, while it might carry weaponry, was itself a potent weapon if used as a missile against other ships. In the era of sail-powered warships with their intrinsic limitations of speed and manoeuvrability the practice of ramming opponents fell by default into disuse, although the concept remained alive. With the advent of steam-powered vessels, with their enhanced speed and lack of dependence for direction on the wind, the ram as a potent weapon of attack gained credibility in Naval circles and in Ship Constructors' departments. This first became apparent in the American Civil War, when many attempts were made by ships on both sides to ram their opponents, with almost uniform lack of success.

The battle which influenced the faith in the ram as a weapon was the battle of Lissa between Austria-Hungary and Italy in 1866. The Austrian *Ferdinand Max* rammed the (stationary) Italian *Re d'Italia*, which immediately keeled over and sank. This resulted in all ironclad battleships designed for the next forty years being built to carry a ram; a weapon which, while causing the loss of a number of ships accidentally, never sank another major enemy warship of any nationality.

Hotspur was designed to work with the Fleet, to bring into action her main weapon, her ram. This projected some ten feet (3 m) ahead of her bow perpendicular, and was reinforced by an extension of the armoured belt.

It was assumed that the bearings upon which a usual turret turned would not survive the shock of the impact consequent upon the use of the ram against an enemy ship. Her single 12-inch (305 mm) gun was therefore positioned in a fixed cupola perforated by four firing-ports through which the gun could be discharged. None of these ports allowed the gun to be fired straight ahead, where a potential ramming target would be situated. It was therefore only possible to engage these targets with the gun if the ramming attack missed.

As the maximum speed of *Hotspur* was less than virtually all of her potential targets, it quickly became apparent that ramming attacks on ships under way were almost guaranteed to miss, and she quickly descended from being a ship held to be of great military value to be the most useless member of the battle-fleet.

Hotspur was commissioned at Devonport in 1871, and remained in reserve until 1876. She served with *HMS Rupert* in the Sea of Marmara during the Russo-Turkish war of 1878. She then returned to Devonport, where she remained until her major reconstruction, undertaken by Laird & Sons Co. between 1881 and 1883. Her only active service thereafter was with the Particular Ser-

[top left] The Neptune Public House, Rotherhithe. [top right] 9th Battalion Lines - Mena Camp, Egypt, December, 1914. [above] Rue-de-Bacquerot Cemetery and [left] John Dicks' headstone in the Cemetery.

H.M.S. Hotspur

vice Squadron of 1885. She was guard ship at Holyhead until 1893, was again in reserve until 1897, and was posted thereafter to serve as guard ship at Bermuda, where she stayed until sold.

John emigrated to Australia and found employment as a groom in Sydney.

John enlisted with the 9th Battalion on August 18th, 1915. He was 5 feet 7 inches tall and weighed 167lbs. he had grey eyes, dark hair and was of fresh complexion.

The 9th Battalion was among the first infantry units raised for the AIF during the First World War. It was the first battalion recruited in Queensland, and with the 10th, 11th and 12th Battalions it formed the 3rd Brigade.

The battalion was raised within weeks of the declaration of war in August 1914 and embarked just two months later. After preliminary training, the battalion sailed to Egypt, arriving in early December. The 3rd Brigade was the covering force for the ANZAC landing on April 25th, 1915, and so was the first ashore at around 4.30 am.

The battalion was heavily involved in establishing and defending the front line of the Anzac beachhead. It served at Anzac until the evacuation in December 1915.

After the withdrawal from Gallipoli, the battalion returned to Egypt. It was split to help form the 49th Battalion and

bought up to strength with reinforcements. In March 1916 the battalion sailed for France and the Western Front. From then until 1918 the battalion took part in operations on the Western Front.

The battalion's first major action in France was at Pozières in the Somme valley. The 9th Battalion attacked on the extreme right of the line. But by then John was dead.

John was killed in action on April 20th, 1916. He is buried in Rue-du-Bacquerot [13th London] Cemetery, Laventie.

Laventie is a village some 6 km south-west of Armentieres and 11 km north of La Bassee. The 13th London Graveyard was begun by the 1st Royal Irish Rifles in November 1914, and during and after the following December graves of the 13th London Regiment (The Kensingtons) were added.

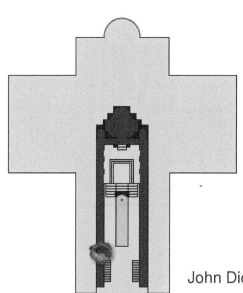

John Dicks – Australian War Memorial, Canberra

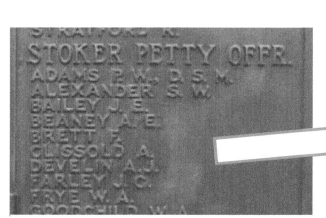

Chatham Naval Memorial, Panel 29 –
Arthur Develin

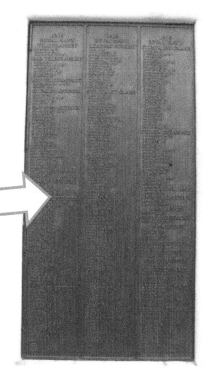

George Dix – Thiepval Memorial

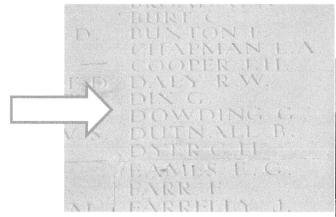

George and *Walter Dix*, whose biographies now follow, were brothers.

George Dix
Royal West Kent Regiment, 6th Bn
Service No. G/845 - Lance Corp.

George was born on August 11th, 1890. His parents were Charles and Harriet Dix of 19 Norfolk Road. There were eight children in the family – Harriet, born in 1869, Florence, born in 1871, Alice, born in 1875, April, born in 1881, Walter, born in 1882, Ernest, born in 1888, George and Jessie, born in 1894.

George was a sailor; he worked as a deck hand on board the steam tug, *The Warrior*. The tug under the command of William Cowes operated in Falmouth. It had a crew of nine, seven of whom were born in Gravesend with William Addy, the fireman, from Faversham and William Cowes from Eton.

He enlisted with the Royal West Kent Regiment at Gravesend on August 31st, 1914 and was posted to the 6th Battalion on September 4th. He was 5 feet 5½ inches tall and weighed 123lbs. He was appointed a Lance-Corporal on March 4th, 1916.

The 6th (Service) Battalion, The Royal West Kent Regiment was raised at Maidstone on August 14th, 1914 as part of Kitchener's First New Army and joined 37th Brigade in 12th (Eastern) Division. They trained at Colchester and moved to Purfleet in September 1914 they spent the winter in billets in Hythe from December. They moved to Aldershot for final training in February 1915 and proceeded to France on the June 1st landing at Boulogne. They concentrated near St Omer and by June 6th were in the Meteren-Steenwerc. They underwent instruction from the more experienced 48th (South Midland) Division and took over a section of the front line at Ploegsteert

Wood on the June 23rd, 1915. They were in action in The Battle of Loos from September 30th, taking over the sector from Gun Trench to Hulluch Quarries consolidating the position. On the 8th they repelled a heavy German infantry attack and on the 13th took part in the Action of the Hohenzollern Redoubt, capturing Gun Trench and the south western face of the Hulluch Quarries. During this period at Loos, 117 officers and 3237 men of the Division were killed or wounded. By the 21st they moved to Fouquieres-les-Bethune for a short rest then returned to the front line at the Hohenzollern Redoubt until mid-November, when they went into reserve at Lillers.

On December 9th, 9th Royal Fusiliers assisted in a round-up of spies and other suspicious characters in Bethune. On the 10th the Division took over the front line north of La Bassee canal at Givenchy. On January 19th they began a period of training in Open Warfare at Busnes, then moved back into the front line at Loos on February 12th, 1916. In June they moved to Flesselles and on the 30th went into the reserve at Hencourt and Millencourt on July 1st. They relieved the 8th Division at Ovillers-la-Boisselle that night and attacked at 3.15am the following morning with mixed success. On the 7th they attacked again and succeeded in capturing the first and second lines close to Ovillers. They were withdrawn to Contay on July 9th.

Lance-Corporal Dix was killed in action on July 3rd. He has no known grave and is commemorated on the Thiepval Monument.

DIX.—Lance-Corpl. George Dix, Royal W. Kent Regt, missing since July 3rd, 1916, officially reported killed, aged 26 years; son of Mr. and Mrs. Dix, 19, Norfolk-road, Gravesend.

GR 8/6/18 [Andrew Marshall]

Gravesend Cemetery

IN
LOVING MEMORY OF
Lieut ROBERT
BROWN ANDERSON, 5th Batt.
R.S.F.
Who Died Feby 15th 1918
Also Corpl. WALTER JAMES DIX
Killed in Action April 14th 1918,
Also his brother GEORGE
Killed in Action July 3rd 1916.

Also mentioned on the memorial is Alice,
elder sister of George and Walter –

Beloved Wife of
ROBERT BROWN ANDERSON
Died January 15th 1933 Aged 53 Years
SWEET REST

[Photograph – Andy White]

And listed on the
Ploegsteert Memorial

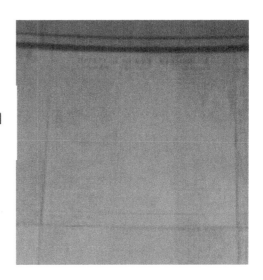

GR 8/6/18 [Andrew Marshall]

Walter Dix
Sherwood Foresters, 2nd/6th Bn
Service No. 102982 - Corporal

Walter was born in Gravesend in 1882, the son of Charles and Harriet Dix. He was the older brother of George.

He was a postman and was married to Isabella Murdoch. They lived at 15 Prospect Road. They had two children – Walter, born December 8th, 1912 and Margaret, born September 9th, 1915.

He enlisted at Gravesend with the East Surrey Regiment on December 7th, 1915. He was 5 feet 5 inches tall and weighed 128lbs.

The 2nd/6th was formed at Chesterfield on September 14th, 1914 as a second line unit. It moved on November 2nd to Buxton, with Battalion HQ occupying the Empire Hotel.

The Battalion moved to Luton in January 1915 and placed under command of 2nd Notts & Derby Brigade. In August 1915 the formation became the 176th Brigade, 59th Division. It moved to Watford after a few weeks at Dunstable. In April 1916 the Battalion was sent to Dublin to quell the rebellion there.

On January 12th, 1917 it was sent to Fovant and landed at Boulogne February 25th from here the Battalion was sent to the Ypres salient and it was here that Walter was killed in action on April 16th, 1918. He has no known grave and is commemorated on the Ploegsteert Memorial.

Henry William Dixon
RGA, 319th Siege Battery
Service No. 128557 - Gunner

Henry was born in 1896 in Brentford, the son of Henry and Emily Dixon of 15 Salisbury Road, Gravesend. The couple were married in 1889. Henry was born in Kennington in 1865. He was an engineer's labourer. Emily was born in 1867 in Marylebone.

The family moved to Gravesend before the turn of the century from Acton.

They had four children – Albert, born in 1891, Cecily Maud, born in 1894, Henry and Ellen, born in 1902. Henry was a shop assistant before enlisting in Gravesend with the Royal Garrison Artillery.

Henry was killed in action on October 6th, 1917. He is buried in Klein Vierstraat Cemetery.

Klein-Vierstraat British Cemetery is located 6 km south-west of Ypres. The village of Kemmel and the adjoining hill, Mont Kemmel, were the scene of fierce fighting in late April 1918, in which Commonwealth and French forces were engaged.

The cemetery was begun in January 1917 by field ambulances and fighting units before the middle of January 1918. More burials were added in April 1918. After the Armistice, graves were brought in from the surrounding area. Klein-Vierstraat British Cemetery now contains 805 First World War burials, 109 of them unidentified.

The above is a photograph of Gunner H. W. Dixon, R.G.A., youngest son of Mr. and Mrs. Dixon, 15, Salisbury-road, Gravesend, who was killed in action in France on October 6th, at the age of 21 years. Before joining the Colours, which was at the outbreak of war, he was employed at the Imperial Paper Mills for nearly four years. He had only been in France four months before he was killed, the circumstances attending his death being told in the following letter from Second-Lieut. Anthony Bristow: —"It is with greatest regret I have to inform you of the lamentable death of your dear son, which occurred at 7.20 p.m. last night. Whilst remembering that he died for his country, I just mention that he made the proudest sacrifice a gunner can make, inasmuch as his detachment were answering an infantry 'S.O.S.' distress signal, and he thus truly laid down his life for his countrymen. He was killed almost instantaneously, being alive, though uncon-

scious, only a few moments. We buried him in a cemetery especially consecrated and set apart for British soldiers, where the private lies next to the colonel—officer and men mutually bound together in the defence of the Motherland. The Padre administered the burial service while we surrounded his grave. We sang 'Jesu, Lover of my Soul,' as the priest (C.E. Chaplain) committed his soul to God's keeping. Your son was a good soldier and liked by us all. We mourn his loss, and you may be sure that a substantial and permanent cross shall mark his grave, a token of respect and affection from all of us." Mr. and Mrs. Dixon have one other son serving, and he is at present in France with the anti-aircraft guns.

GR 27/10/15 [Andrew Marshall]

Frank Dodd
Middlesex Regiment, 4th Battalion
Service No. G/42480 - Private

Frank was born in 1884 in Gravesend. He was the son of William and Lois Dodd. William was born in Cobham in 1850. He was a gardener. Lois was born in Ifield in 1859. The couple were married in 1877 and had six children – Frank, Edith, born in 1886, William, born in 1889, Percy [Percy's biography follows], born in 1893, Elsie, born in 1896 and Stanley, born in 1902. The family lived at 24 Clarence Place.

Frank was a grocer's assistant before enlisting in Maidstone with the Royal West Kent Regiment, service number 23423. He subsequently served with the 4th Battalion [B Company] of the Duke of Cambridge's Own [the Middlesex Regiment].

4th Battalion, The Middlesex Regiment (Duke of Cambridge's Own) was based in Devonport with 8th Brigade, 3rd Division when war broke out in August 1914. They proceeded to France on August 14th, 1914 landing at Boulogne. They saw action in The Battle of Mons and the rear guard action at Solesmes, The Battle of Le Cateau, The Battle of the Marne, The Battle of the Aisne, at La Bassee,

Klein-Vier-Straat CWGC Cemetery

Henry Dixon

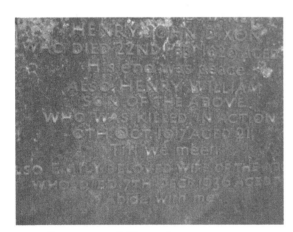

Gravesend Cemetery –

ALSO HENRY WILLIAM
SON OF THE ABOVE
WHO WAS KILLED IN ACTION
6th OCT. 1917 AGED 21

Abide with me.

[Photograph – Andy White]

306

Attack on Bellewaarde and the Actions at Hooge.

On November 14th, 1915 they transferred to 63rd Brigade in 21st Division In 1916 they were in action in Battle of The Somme, on July 8th, 1916 they moved with the Brigade to 37th Division. They went into action in The Battle of the Ancre. In 1917 they fought in The Second Battle of the Scarpe and The Battle of Arleux.

Frank died of wounds received during the Battle of the Scarpe on May 18th, 1917. He is buried in Etaples Cemetery. Etaples is 27 km south of Boulogne.

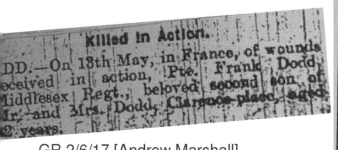

Killed in Action.

DD:—On 18th May, in France, of wounds received in action, Pte. Frank Dodd, Middlesex Regt., beloved second son of Mr. and Mrs. Dodd, Clarence-place, aged 22 years.

GR 2/6/17 [Andrew Marshall]

During the First World War, the area around Etaples was the scene of immense concentrations of Commonwealth reinforcement camps and hospitals. It was remote from attack, except from aircraft, and accessible by railway from both the northern and the southern battlefields. In 1917, 100,000 troops were camped among the sand dunes and the hospitals, which included eleven general, one stationary, four Red Cross hospitals and a convalescent depot, could deal with 22,000 wounded or sick. In September 1919, ten months after the Armistice, three hospitals and the Q.M.A.A.C. convalescent depot remained.

The cemetery contains 10,771 Commonwealth burials of the First World War, the earliest dating from May 1915. 35 of these burials are unidentified.

As will be remembered, in our issue of three weeks ago, we reported that Mrs. Dodd, of 24, Clarence-place, was anxiously awaiting further news of her son, Pte. Frank Dodd, of the Middlesex Regt. (transferred from the West Kents), who was reported dangerously wounded in the head. Although receiving every attention at the 26th General Hospital, France, and for a time he appeared to rally, news has been received of his passing away on the 18th inst. Seeking to alleviate somewhat the terribly sad news, the lady who has kept Mrs. Dodd informed as to the progress of her son since he was wounded, on the 23rd of April, writes that the wound was on the occipital bone, and therefore had he lived there was hardly any grounds for hope that his reason would have been unimpaired. The kind writer goes on to say that Pte. Dodd would be buried in the cemetery attached to the chapel, where each grave is marked with a cross bearing the name of the fallen one. For 1 years Frank Dodd worked for Mr. Malloney, Princes-street, who was as a second father to him, and who keenly feels his loss. He was a great favourite, too, with the customers, who had known him from a boy. At Princes-street he was a valued teacher in the Sunday-school. He was in his ... year when he laid down his life for his King and country. As well as losing this (their second) son, Mr. and Mrs. Dodd have been also bereaved of their fourth son, Percy Edward, who was in the London Scottish, confirmation of his death being received by them just after Easter only, though he had been reported wounded and missing since the previous July.

GR 2/6/17 [above] & 18/5/18 [below] [Andrew Marshall]

DODD.—In affectionate remembrance of our dear son, Pte. Frank Dodd, Middlesex Regt., who died of wounds in France, May 18th, 1917. From his loving Mum, Dad, Sisters and Brothers

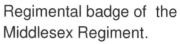

Regimental badge of the Middlesex Regiment.

24 Clarence Place, home of the Dodd family prior to the Great War. Coincidentally, number 24 is directly opposite the Windmill Hill Memorial.

Frank Dodd –
Etaples CWGC Cemetery

Percy Dodd
London Regiment, 14th Battalion
Service No. S/1897 – Lance Corp.

Percy was born in 1893.

He enlisted in London with the 14th [County of London] Battalion [London Scottish]. 14th (1st London Scottish) Battalion, The London Regiment, a Territorial unit had their headquarters at 59 Buckingham Gate when war broke out in August 1914. They were attached to 4th London Brigade, 2nd London Division and were quickly mobilised and moved to Abbotts Langley.

They proceeded to France, landing at Le Harve on September 16th, 1914. They saw their first action at Messines on October 31st, 1914 under the command of the Cavalry Corps. On November 7th, 1914 the battalion joined 1st Brigade, 1st Division and were in action during the Winter Operations of 1914-15. In 1915 they were in action during The Battle of Aubers and The Battle of Loos. On February 8th, 1916 they transferred to the newly arrived 168th Brigade, 56th (London) Division who were assembling in the Hallencourt area. In 1916 they were in action on The Somme taking part in the diversionary attack at Gommecourt on the 1st of July and it was there that Percy was killed. He has no known grave and is commemorated on the Thiepval Memorial.

Killed in Action.

DODD.—Killed in action, on July 1st, 1916, "somewhere in France," Pte. Percy Edward Dodd, of the London Scottish, fourth son of Mr. and Mrs. W. Dodd, 24, Clarence-place, Gravesend.

GR 21/4/17 [above] & 6/7/18 [below]
[Andrew Marshall]

IN MEMORIAM.

DODD.—In ever-loving memory of our dear son, Private Percy Edward Dodd, London Scottish Regiment, who was killed in action July 1st, 1916.—From his loving Mum, Dad, Sisters and Brothers.—"Ever in our thoughts."

Hugh Rivers Drake
Royal West Kent Regiment, 1st Bn
Service No. G/7668 - Private

Hugh was born in 1897 in Gravesend, the son of Abraham and Laura Drake of 36 Darnley Road. Abraham was born in 1857 in Earshaw, Norfolk. He was a draper and milliner and had his own business. Laura was born in 1861 in Bury St Edmund. They had two children – Gladys, born in 1896 and Hugh.

Hugh enlisted in Maidstone with the 1st Battalion. 1st Battalion, The Royal West Kent Regiment was based in Dublin when war was declared in August 1914. They proceeded to France landing at Le Havre on the August 15th. They were in action in The Battle of Mons and the subsequent retreat and subsequently to Ypres where they saw action at Messines and The First Battle of Ypres.

In 1915 they were in action at The Second Battle of Ypres and the Capture of Hill 60. In autumn 1915, many units were exchanged with units from the newly arrived volunteer 32nd Division, to stiffen the inexperienced Division with regular army troops, but the 1st West Kents remained with 5th Division. In March 1916 5th Division took over a section of front line between St Laurent Blangy and the southern edge of Vimy Ridge, near Arras. They moved south in July to reinforce The Somme and were in action at High Wood, The Battle of Guillemont, The Battle of Flers-Courcelette, The Battle of Morval and The Battle of Le Transloy. In October they moved to Festubert and remained there until March 1917 when they moved in preparation for the Battles of Arras. On September 7th, 1917 the 5th Division moved out of the line for a period of rest before, being sent to

Gravesend Cemetery

In Memory of
PERCY DODD

[Photograph – Andy White]

Thiepval Memorial, below.

Pte. P. E. Dodd (Gravesend),
London Scottish.
KILLED IN ACTION.

Mr. and Mrs. W. Dodd, of 24, Clarence Place, Gravesend, have just learnt officially that, after having been reported missing since July 1st, 1916, their fourth son, Pte. Percy Edward Dodd, of the London Scottish, was killed in action. Pte. Dodd was 24 years of age and enlisted in September, 1915. He was a brother of Pte. Frank Dodd, of the Middlesex Regiment (now serving in France), and of Mr. William Dodd, of Windmill Street, Gravesend.

GM 21/4/17 [Andrew Marshall]

Gravesend Cemetery

also HUGH RIVER DRAKE
Killed in Action in France
Octr 4th 1917 in His 21st Year
"Sleep on Beloved, Sleep and Take Thy Rest"

Tyne Cot – Panel 107

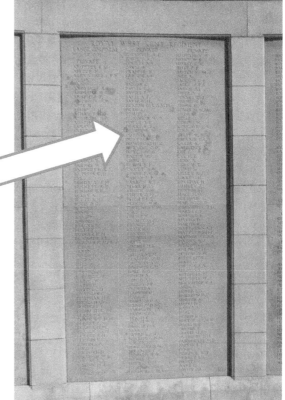

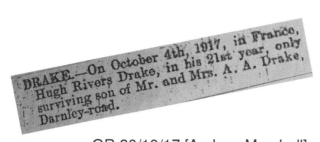

GR 20/10/17 [Andrew Marshall]

Flanders where they were in action during the Third Battle of Ypres.

Hugh was killed in action on October 4th. He has no known grave and is commemorated on the Tyne Cot Memorial.

Local Casualties.

Another Gravesender has been added to the list of townsmen who have sacrificed themselves for King and country. Mr. and Mrs. A. A. Drake, Darnley-road, received information on Monday morning that their only son, Hugh Rivers Drake, of the Royal West Kents, had been killed in action in France. Deceased was at one time a pupil with Messrs. Carnell and Son, Swanley and Eynsford, the noted rose and fruit growers. On his 18th birthday, February, 1915, he joined the West Kent Yeomanry, but was subsequently transferred to the Royal West Kents, and soon embarked for France. He had recently been in hospital for two months and had only gone back to the front for a fortnight when the end came.

Thomas William Dray
A.I.F., 14th Battalion
Service No. 1462 - Private

Thomas was born in 1890 in Gravesend. His father Thomas was born in 1863 and was a store man; his mother Kate was born in 1861 in High Wycombe. The family lived at 14 Wakefield Street.

His father died shortly after Thomas was born. Kate remarried in 1898 to one James Frist who was seven years older and from Brighton. He was a brick maker. He had a son Albert, born in 1896, from his previous marriage. The couple settled into James' home, a few houses away, at 44 Wakefield Street and had two children from the marriage - Kate, born in 1899 and Christian, born in 1901.

Thomas was a labourer before becoming a sailor, being a trimmer on the *Otway*. He settled in Sydney after the *Otway* arrived there in December 1911, having sailed from London on October 26th.

SS Otway was a British ocean liner owned by the Orient Line, built by Fairfield Shipbuilding and Engineering Company of Glasgow, Scotland and launched in 1909.

S.S. "Otway."

She had five sister ships; *Orsova*, *Osterley*, *Otranto*, *Orvieto*, and the *Orama*. These ships allowed the Orient Line a prized attraction to the travelling public: fixed sailings every other week to Australia and New Zealand. Requisitioned by the Royal Navy and deployed as an armed merchant cruiser, *Otway* was torpedoed and sunk by *UC-49* off the Hebrides on July 23rd, 1917 with the loss of 10 lives.

Thomas enlisted with the 14th Battalion when first raised in Melbourne in September 1914 as part of the Australian Imperial Force (AIF), which was an all-volunteer force raised for overseas service during World War I. Forming part of the 4th Brigade which was commanded by Colonel John

Monash, the battalion was assigned to the New Zealand and Australian Division. After undertaking initial training at Broadmeadows, the battalion embarked for Egypt in December 1914, arriving there the following month.

GR 20/5/16 [Andrew Marshall]

In Egypt further training was undertaken and then on April 25th, 1915 the battalion took part in the landing and subsequent campaign at Gallipoli. For defensive operations as the beachhead was established before being committed to the August Offensive during which they were involved in attacks upon Hill 971 and Hill 60. The offensive failed to achieve the breakout that was designed and a period of stalemate followed before the decision was made to evacuate the peninsula in December 1915.

Thomas was killed in action on August 8th, 1915. He has no known grave and is commemorated on the Lone Pine Memorial.

The Memorial stands on the site of the fiercest fighting at Lone Pine and overlooks the whole front line of May 1915. It commemorates more than 4,900 Australian and New Zealand servicemen who died in the Anzac area - the New Zealanders prior to the fighting in August 1915 - whose graves are not known. Others named on the memorial died at sea and were buried in Gallipoli waters.

The memorial stands in Lone Pine Cemetery. The original small battle cemetery was enlarged after the Armistice when scattered graves were brought in from the neighbourhood, and from Brown's Dip North and South Cemeteries, which were behind the Australian trenches of April-August 1915.

There are now 1,167 Commonwealth servicemen of the First World War buried or commemorated in this cemetery. 504 of the burials are unidentified. Special memorials commemorate 183 soldiers (all but one of them Australian, most of whom died in August), who were known or believed to have been buried in Lone Pine Cemetery, or in the cemeteries at Brown's Dip.

Robert Hugh Drennan, MB
Royal Army Medical Corps
Service No. 5159 - Captain

Annebank House, Annbank, Ayrshire, Scotland
(home to James & Catherine Drennan prior to Carse Hall)

Robert was born in 1865 in Newtown Limavady, the youngest son. His parents were James William Drennan and Catherine Stewart Wilson. James was born in 1810 and was a 'coal miner'. His brother Hugh was a chaplain to the Forces being based at Shoeburyness for many years. Catherine was some twelve years younger than her husband being born in 1823. They originally lived at Annebank House, Tarbolton, Ayrshire before moving to Limavady.

James and Catherine would live to be 84; James dying in 1894 and Catherine in 1908.

James came to Carse Hall in 1855 and created a farm of some repute in the subsequent years. There were six sons and two daughters in the family – John Wallace, born in 1840, Matthew, born in 1843, William, born in 1846, James Wilson, born in 1849, Alexand-er, born in 1854, Isabella Cowan, born in 1855, Robert Hugh, born in 1866 and Cassie, born in 1860.

Isabella married William Dickie in the summer of 1895 in Limavady. The couple lived in Eastwood, Renfrewshire. Her mother, Catherine, would visit her there regularly in the years after her husband's death in 1894. Isabella died in Glasgow on September 14th, 1930.

Cassie – Catherine Agnes – died in her teens in 1877 at Carse Hall.

The Drennan family - back row, from left; Matthew, Isabella, Alexander and John; front row, from left; William, Catherine, Robert [the future Doctor R.H. Drennan, M.B.], James, Cassie and James. [Hugh Mackrell]

Carse Hall,
Limavady.
The house.
[Hugh Mackrell]

Carse Hall, Limavady.
General view.
[Hugh Mackrell]

The Drennan Family at
Carse Hall, 1894 –
[Hugh Mackrell]

Back row, from left – William, John, Isabelle, Robert, James and Alexander.
Middle row, from left – Jeanie [Gault, Alexander's wife], Catherine [Cherry, wife of John], James, Catherine, Agnes [Lawson, wife of James] and Alexander [eldest son of Alexander].
Front row, from left – James [the future Lieutenant], Anna [James' daughter], James [son of Alexander], Catherine [James' daughter], Mary [William's daughter] and Isabella [James' daughter].   [Hugh Mackrell]

John Wallace Drennan, C.B.E., inherited Carse Hall on the death of his father in 1894. He would carry on the work of his father and develop the farm further becoming a prominent and noted Clydesdale breeder.

He married Catherine, his wife, in 1891 and the couple had seven children, the eldest being James, born in 1893. The other children were Kathleen, Mary, John, Margaret, Alice [Aileen], William Wallace and Matthew.

Kathleen and James Wilson [HM]

Ireland in the immediate pre-war era was in turmoil. The Drennan family were among many caught up in the politic problems that were sweeping through Ireland in these turbulent years.

Prime Minister H.H. Asquith introduced the Third Home Rule Bill to the House of Commons on 11 April 1912. It provided for a parliament in Dublin with limited powers, and it met with strong oppositions from Ulster Unionists who saw it as the first step to Irish independence. On 'Ulster Day', 28 September 1912, the Ulster Covenant was signed by 237,368 men and 234,046 women who pledged themselves to use 'all means which may be found necessary to defeat the present conspiracy to set up a Home Rule Parliament in Ireland'.

There were a number of places within Limavady Borough Council area where people could sign the Ulster Covenant and Declaration. The main location was Limavady Market Place where over 2000 people signed. Other places included the Bellarena Rectory,

Ballykelly Parochial Hall and Banagher Lecture Hall.

Aaron Callan writes of the events -
In 1912, Limavady, like any many other towns across Ulster, celebrated 'Ulster Day' with great energy and enthusiasm. Throughout the local area, 4,385 men and women signed the Covenant and Declaration with signings in Dungiven, Ballykelly, Bellarena and Boveva in various locations including Orange Halls, Church and Civic Buildings. With around 3,000 attending a united humiliation and prayer service in the Market Yard in the centre of town led by Rev. Canon R.G.S. King, Rev. William Browne and Rev. Samuel Houston. Local Businesses closed for the day from 1pm to 4pm to accommodate the signing of the Covenant and the Services. The Bishop of Derry and Raphoe George Chadwick subsequently wrote in the Londonderry Sentinel the following – *I never in my life saw anything like*

Ulster Day. The churches were filled; and when emptied the multitude did not even cheer: there was only one grim and fixed determination on a thousand faces, to live as freemen or to die. They simply signed.

Catherine signed the Declaration at the Ballykelly Presbyterian Hall, Drumcaw with John and his son, James signing the Covenant at the North Ballykelly Parochial Hall.

On Thursday, April 16th, 1914 Sir Edward Carson visited Limavady. Aaron Callan relates that work for the visit of Carson commenced in earnest in the months leading up to April. A committee was formed of the leading Unionists in the town who were key in the 'Ulster Day' organisation and the forming of the local U.V.F. (Ulster Volunteer Force). Many of the names are well known and some not so well known. They included the Deputy Lieutenant of

SIGNING THE COVENANT, LIMAVADY

County Londonderry Rt. Hon. Maurice Marcus McCausland, Edward M.F.-G. Boyle, F.S.N. Macrory, James W. Drennan, Dr James Claude B. Proctor, William Alexander Ingram and Fredrick CB Trench to name a few.

Commentary about the day from the contemporary press state that - *The streets of Limavady were ablaze with colour and those in charge of the decorations are to be complemented upon the thoroughness with which they carried out their work. Every street had one or more arches containing either a greeting to the great Ulster Leader or an expression of their feelings on the subject which transcends all others in the political arena at the present moment. In some of the streets it seemed as if there was not a house, be it big or small, from which a loyal emblem was not displayed.*

Sir Edward travelled from Garvagh where he had reviewed the South Derry U.V.F. Regiment in a morning inspection to Limavady. He was escorted by thirty two dispatch riders drawn from Coleraine, Limavady, Londonderry and Ballymoney. Along the route groups of people gathered to cheer him and special trains were laid on to bring thousands of volunteers and spectators to the town.

The purpose of the visit was to review the North Derry U.V.F. Regiment which took place at Drenagh the family home of the McCausland family just on the outskirts of Limavady. In addition to this, a new U.V.F. Drill Hall, which was situated on the present day site of Limavady Baptist Church, was to be opened. The men of Limavady and surrounding Roe Valley area were eager to show their loyalty and by 1914 the Second Battalion of the North Derry Regiment, from the Roe Valley, had 900 volunteers under the command of thirty officers.

In total, the county strength was 5,360 men, headed up by M.M. McCausland and included a number of notable people including J.W. Drennan. *The Northern Constitution* reported that in June 1913 guns were smuggled into the town, estimated to be 3,183.

Dr H.S. Morrison, a prominent South Derry Unionist, in his book Modern Ulster gives us a first-hand account of the 16th April 1914 as he accompanied Carson to Limavady –

At the field for the review in Limavady, we, that is the party of Sir Edward Carson, were received by Sir James Craig MP, H.T. Barrie MP, and John Gordon MP, and the inspection was carried out in customary fashion. Quite 4,000 Volunteers from Derry City and North Derry were on parade, and Major Cunningham, at this time commander of the South Derry Regiment, said to me - I would not ask to lead a finer body of men on any battlefield.

Officers of the U.V.F. on the steps of Drenagh House, Limavady before the war. The motorcyclist is Major Macrory; Lt. Drennan is standing next to him. [courtesy Willie Wilson]

A young James Wilson [HM]

John died on July 29th, 1916. His effects came to £2,593 and 9 pence, 2nd Lieutenant James Wilson Drennan, the eldest son, being the beneficiary.

John's eldest son, James enlisted with the 10th Royal Iniskilling Fusiliers. The 10th was formed at Finner Camp on August 15th, 1914.

DEATH OF MR. J. W. DRENNAN.

We regret to record the death of Mr. John W. Drennan, Carse Hall, Limavady. Not only in the North-West but in other parts of Ireland and in Scotland and England, where he was known and esteemed, particularly among agriculturists, the news of the death of Mr. Drennan will convey a sense of great loss. He had been in failing health for the past six months, but was able to be out and about till within a week of his death, which took place on Saturday night. The news was received in the Limavady district and in Derry with feelings of deep regret. By many connected with agriculture the news was received as being in the nature of a personal bereavement, so highly was his friendship and counsel esteemed and so heartily was his genial presence welcomed in the market and on the farm. As an agriculturist Mr. Drennan's record of practical work and progress stands almost unequalled in Ireland. Under his management land reclaimed from the sea was transformed, and where once was forbidding, dreary slob there is now an expanse of countryside which is the admiration of all who visit the North. His farming methods were up-to-date, and "thorough" seemed to be a guiding principle. In buildings, stock, machinery, and arrangement the Carse Hall holding of hundreds of acres is a model to all who wish to achieve success. These and other aspects of Mr. Drennan's success as an agriculturist have been dealt with appreciatively already by some of the highest authorities on farming and breeding in the agricultural magazines, and a year or two ago we had the pleasure of reproducing one such article in which a visit to Carse Hall was enthusiastically and fully described, and due attention paid to the owner's progressive spirit in all that tends to the advancement of Ireland's most important industry.

As would be expected, full and frequent use was made by the agricultural communities of the North of Mr. Drennan's sound knowledge and counsel, and for several years he occupied, with the utmost acceptance the position of vice-chairman of the North-West of Ireland Agricultural Society. Both as an officer of the society and as an exhibitor of prize stock he took a prominent and valued part in raising the show to its present high position.

A native of Ayr, Mr. Drennan was quite a young man when he came over from Scotland to the Limavady district. He took up farming in Ireland some fifty years ago, and was 76 years of age. He was a member of Second Limavady Presbyterian Church, on the session and committee of which he acted with devoted and thoroughly sympathetic interest. He was one of the members of the Limavady Technical Instruction Committee appointed by the county council, and a member of North Derry Unionist Association. With the widow, a daughter of the late Mr. James Cherry, Thornhill, Ballykelly, and her four sons and four daughters there will be the deepest sympathy in their great bereavement. One of the sons is Lieutenant Drennan, at present serving in France with the 10th Battalion (Derry U.V.F.) Royal Inniskilling Fusiliers.

The 'Derrys' crossing Bann Bridge, Coleraine, May, 1915 and marching into Limavaday on the way to Randalstown.

The drum, left, and flag, right, carried into battle by the 10th. Both are in the United Services' Club, Limavady. [Courtesy of Limavady Storyfinders]

Officers, 10th Battalion – James Drennan is on back row, first left.

The Battalion was made up of four companies which comprised men from the following areas –

'A' Company –
Londonderry/Derry City
Company Commander –
Major Macrory

'B' Company
Londonderry/Derry
Company Commander –
Major Waring Smyth

'C' Company
Coleraine/Limavady & district
Company Commander –
Major Trench

'D' Company
Rural Districts & villages of the County
Company Commander –
Captain Miller

At 3.50am on July 31st, 1917 nine Divisions attacked in what has become known as the Battle of Passhendaele / 3rd Ypres. The bombardment prior had ensured a landscape covered in craters and with the drainage system in the area destroyed by the bombardment, these quickly began to fill with water. In the late afternoon the German counter attack coincided with heavy rain.

The attack was suspended on the 2nd but it continued to rain until the 4th. On the 7th the 10th Inniskillings moved up to the front line. Trenches as such did not exist and conditions were dreadful. At 1am as the 10th were relieving the 15th Rifles the artillery was active. However the Germans started using a new shell type – 'mustard' gas'. This was in liquid form and was dispersed as a splattered spray as the shells impacted on the ground.

The situation continued through the following days. August 11th was the date set for the attack. As the 10th were readying for the assault between 4am and 5am the Germans, anticipating such an event, unleashed a torrid bombardment. 15 were killed including 2nd Lieutenant Alfie Bogle, the noted boxer.

On August 11th the positions were again under heavy bombardment.

Two noteworthy events occurred –
a private from the Liverpool Irish staggered into the positions held by the 10th – he had been part of the attack on the 2nd and had been in 'no man's land' surviving as best he could until he got back to the safety of the 10th and

2nd Lieutenant Drennan was mortally wounded. He died the same day, the day before the 10th were relieved and sent back to Vlamertinge.

He is buried in Brandhoek New Military Cemetery.

BRANDHOEK
NEW MILITARY
CEMETERY

JAMES WILSON DRENNAN

INNISKILLING
27

HE DIED THAT WE MIGHT LIVE

LIEUTENANT J. W. DRENNAN FATALLY WOUNDED.

Official intimation has been received of the death from wounds received in action on the 12th inst. of Lieutenant James W. Drennan, Royal Inniskilling Fusiliers (Ulster Division). Deceased, who was aged twenty-three years, was the eldest son of the late Mr. John W. Drennan, Carse Hall, Limavady Junction. Prominently identified with the U.V.F. movement from its inception, the deceased officer was a company commander in the North Derry Regiment, and at the outbreak of war he immediately volunteered for active service with the Ulstermen, and went out to France with the original Division. Mr. Drennan had been recently home on leave in connection with the management of very extensive agricultural interests which had devolved on him since the death of his father about a year ago, the Carse Hall farm being widely known as a model holding, and one of the largest in the North of Ireland. He returned to the front only a few weeks ago. The news of his death has evoked very general feelings of regret, and sincere sympathy is felt for his mother and other members of the family in their sorrow.

James' younger sister, Margaret married the Reverend Colin Montgomery, T.D., the son of the Rt. Reverend Henry Hutchinson Montgomery, K.C.M.G. of New Par, Donegal. 1927 was an auspicious year for the Montgomery family as the then Lieutenant-Colonel [and later Field Marshall] Bernard Law Montgomery married Elizabeth Carver on July 27th. Elizabeth Carver, née Hobart, was the widow of Oswald Carver, Olympic rowing medallist who was killed in the First World War. Their son, David, was born in August 1928. Elizabeth Carver was the sister of the Second World War commander Percy Hobart. The service was conducted by his father and Colin who had just been ordained Minister. Colin's first parish was in Northfleet!

Province. It was here that he died on August 28th, 1958.

The Reverend James Wilson Drennan was the fourth son being born in 1856. He moved to Glasgow in his 'teens to study at Glasgow University. He was awarded an M.A. from Edinburgh University in 1871 and became a teacher. He subsequently married and he and his wife Agnes had four daughters – Anna, born in 1888, Catherine, born in 1890, Isabella, born in 1894 and Agnes, born in 1897. They lived in Markinch, Fife.

From 1882 he was a minister with the United Presbyterian Church [Scotland] at Innerleven

It was formed in 1847 by the union of the United Secession Church and the Relief Church, and in 1900 merged with the Free Church of Scotland to form the United Free Church of Scotland, which in turn united with the Church of Scotland in 1929. For much of its existence the United Presbyterian Church was the third largest Presbyterian Church in Scotland, and stood on the liberal wing of Presbyterianism in the country.

James died on May 27th, 1901.

Colin, who was born in 1901, had been teaching in Foyle College before going to Durham University from where he was ordained in early 1927.

Later that year Colin married Margaret. The couple moved to Wallasey in 1932 becoming Vicar at St John's. Subsequently in February, 1935 he was appointed a Chaplain to the Forces. After the war the couple travelled the Commonwealth with appointments in South Africa, Natal Province, then Aklavik, Canada and back to South Africa, to Cape

Robert Hugh, the youngest of the brothers, moved to Scotland to study medicine at Edinburgh University, staying with his brother James and sister-in-law Agnes. He duly qualified in 1892.

Four years later, in 1896, Robert took over the medical practice of Alfred Parker, M.R.C.S., moving into his practice at 56 Parrock Street. Robert settled quickly in Gravesend, the

Hugh on graduation,
Edinburgh University. [HM]

From FRANCIS M. CAIRD, M.B., C.M., F.R.C.S., &c.,
Edinburgh; *Extra-mural Lecturer in Surgery; Assistant
Surgeon, Royal Infirmary, Edinburgh.*

21 RUTLAND STREET,
EDINBURGH, 8th *November*, 1892.

IT gives me great pleasure to state
that Mr. R. H. DRENNAN was a most diligent Student
of Surgery, and, that from personal observation, I
have formed a high opinion of his capabilities.

I believe that he will prove a conscientious, hard
working, and trustworthy practitioner.

FRANCIS M. CAIRD,
F.R.C.S., Edin.

From Professor ALEXANDER RUSSELL SIMPSON, M.D., *Professor of Midwifery and Diseases of Women and Children,
and of Clinical Medicine, in University of Edinburgh;
President, Royal College of Physicians, Edinburgh;
Obstetric Physician, Royal Maternity Hospital, Edinburgh;
Physician to Royal Infirmary, Edinburgh.*

52 QUEEN STREET,
EDINBURGH, 28th *December*, 1892.

I HAVE much pleasure in testifying to
the intelligence and industry displayed by Mr. ROBERT
HUGH DRENNAN, M.B, and C.M., as a Student of
Medicine in the University of Edinburgh.

In the department of Midwifery and the Diseases
of Women and Children, he worked with zeal and
success, and passed his examination with credit.

He will be found well qualified for the duties of
his profession.

A. R. SIMPSON.

From S. D. HENDERSON, M.D., &c., Brighouse, Yorkshire.

BRIGHOUSE,
YORKS, 24th *April*, 1893.

IT gives me very much pleasure to
bear testimony to the admirable manner in which
Dr. ROBERT H. DRENNAN has filled the office of
"*Locum Tenens*," during my absence.

It is gratifying to hear from my numerous patients
the indefatigable and painstaking way in which he
performed his duties, even during so short a period of
time, he seems to have gained their complete confidence.

Besides having an opportunity of knowing his
professional skill, he is a gentleman of the highest
character, and I cannot speak too highly of him pro-
fessionally, morally, or socially.

I therefore can strongly recommend him to any
medical gentleman who may require his services.

S. D. HENDERSON, M.D., &c.

From Professor T. GRAINGER STEWART, M.D., &c., *Professor
of Practice of Physic and of Clinical Medicine in the
University of Edinburgh; Physician in Ordinary to Her
Majesty the Queen for Scotland, Physician to the Royal
Infirmary, Edinburgh.*

UNIVERSITY OF EDINBURGH,
November 11, 1892.

I HAVE much pleasure in certifying
that Mr. R. H. DRENNAN, M.B. and C.M., of this
University, was a diligent and successful student, and
clinical clerk, and that I consider him, in all respects,
well prepared to enter upon the duties of practice.

T. GRAINGER STEWART.

Robert and Daisy. [HM]

practice developing keeping him busy as both a General Practitioner and as a surgeon.

Next door, at Number 57, lived Henry and Emily Buckle. Henry was a shipping clerk. He was born in 1855 and was born in Birkenhead. Emily came from Bow, London and was also born in 1855. There were five children in the family, 2 boys and three girls, the eldest of whom, Daisy, was born in 1880. In 1901 Robert and Daisy married and she moved next door!

Robert with Emily and Henry Buckle at the back and Daisy, right. [HM]

They had the one child, a daughter – Sylvia Catherine who was born in 1902. Sylvia was better known by the name 'Girlie' given her as a 'pet name' by her parents. They had one domestic servant, Edith Bettis, born in 1884 in Essex.

Hugh's reputation ensured his practice developed and he opened a second surgery at 19 Dover Road, Northfleet. His unassuming and charitable disposition ensured his ever increasing popularity in the community.

With the onset of war in the summer of 1914 Robert volunteered. He was declined on account of his age – now being 48 years old. He remained determined to have an active role in the conflict. He organised a VAD

Hospital at the Yacht Club, lectured on nursing to those volunteering in such hospitals and organised the training of men as stretcher bearers. Such was his success he was presented with a silver cigarette case on the conclusion of duties at the Club.

The ever increasing number of casualties being returned to England for further treatment ensured a greater need for qualified medical staff. The following year, 1915, Robert again volunteered and on this occasion he was accepted, being appointed a Captain in the Royal Army Medical Corps. His commission came on May 25th, 1915.

Robert now tended to wounded servicemen in hospitals being stationed in several various locations including Alexandra Palace, Newmarket, Bedford, Hemel Hempstead and Brightlingsea.

Robert, Daisy and Sylvia. [HM]

Letter [courtesy of Hugh Mackrell] sent from Sylvia in August 1915 to her Aunt, Dorothy, [right] Daisy's sister and sister-n-law to Robert Drennan. Dorothy had a rather romantic relationship with an officer in the American Navy.

There is much mention of her father in Sylvia's letter with Captain Drennan on leave and the family obviously enjoying the presence of the father back home in Gravesend. There is also much reference to events and places in Gravesend and the war.

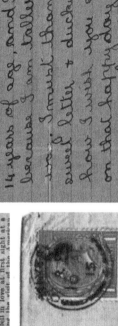

U.S. FLEET FLAGSHIP ROMANCE.

Miss Dorothy Buckle, with whom an officer on the United States flagship Minnetta fell in love at first sight at a reception on board during the visit of the American...

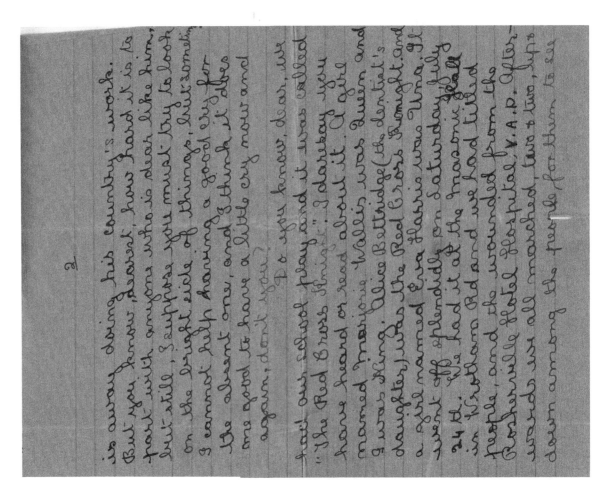

2

is away doing his country's work. But you know, dear, how hard it is to part with anyone who is dear like him, but still, I suppose you must try to look on the bright side of things, this somehow I cannot help having a good cry for the absent one, and I think it does me good to have a little cry now and again, don't you?

Do you know, dear, we had our school play and it was called "The Red Cross Knight." I daresay you have heard or read about it. A girl named Marjorie Wallis was Queen and I was King. Alice Betteridge (the dentist's daughter) was the Red Cross Knight and a girl named Eva Harris was Una. It went off splendidly on Saturday July 24th. We had it at the Masonic Hall in Kirkham Rd and we had titled people, and the wounded from the Amberville Hotel Hospital, V.A.D. After we all marched, two & two, up the ___ down among the people for them to see

[left] Robert with Daisy [Buckle] and Sylvia and, below, the cast of the school play mentioned in the letter; Sylvia is seated centre left beside the 'Queen'.

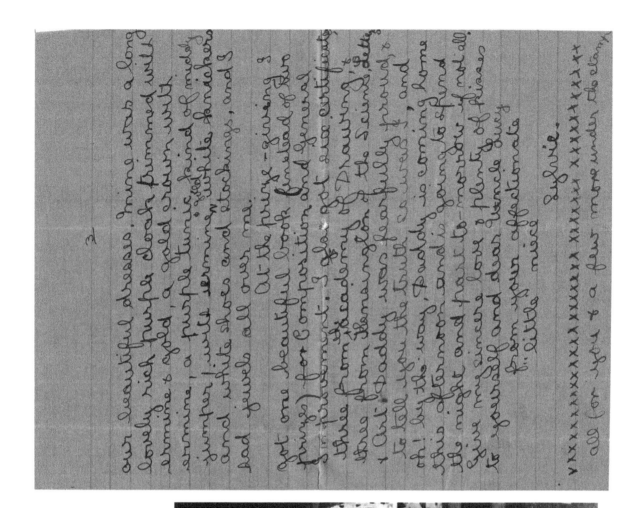

3

our beautiful dresses. Mine was a long lovely rich purple cloak trimmed with ermine & gold, a gold crown with ermine, a purple tunic & a kind of muslin jumper with ermine, white & mauve and white shoes and stockings, and I had jewels all over me.

At the hinge-giving I got one beautiful book finished of and a [hinge?] for Composition and General Improvement. I also got six certificate[s], three from Bermington of Drawing, two one from Bermington of the Scands, letters. Daddy was fearfully proud & to tell you the truth so was I, and oh! by the way, Daddy is coming home this afternoon and is going to spend the night and has to morrow if not all. Give my sincere love & plenty of kisses to yourself and dear Uncle Guy from your affectionate little one

Sylvie.

xxxxxxxxxxxxxxxxxxxxxxxxxx xxxxxxxxxxxxx
all for you & a few more under the elastic

Sylvia; portrait, bottom left and as the 'King' in the school play mentioned in the letter.

329

Robert, probably in Brightlingsea

Daisy and Sylvia [HM]

It was while he was in command of a Prisoner of War Camp that winter of 1916/1917 that he contracted T.B. Robert was taken to Colchester Military Hospital to be treated and for rest in March, 1917. The following month he was discharged from the Army and returned to Gravesend.

But his health further deteriorated and he died on July 26th, 1917.

Robert was buried with full military honours; the fife and drum band of the 1st [Reserve] Battalion of the Suffolk Regiment preceded the funeral cortege on the way to Gravesend Cemetery. The coffin, draped with the Union Flag, was borne on a gun carriage. To the accompaniment of three volleys from the firing party and a bugler sounding the 'Last Post' Robert was buried.

Hugh's effects came to £480, 16 shillings and 5 pence

I do however have very strong memories of his wife, Daisy my Great Grand Mother , who came out to South Africa (where I was born and raised) to help out her and Robert Hugh's daughter Sylvia, who was raising two young children (one of which was my Mom) as she separated and then divorced from her husband. Daisy was the most wonderful Great Grand Mother in the world and she lived in a small flat on her own in Durban South Africa where she died when I was about 5 - but she was very loving and doting and called me "Duckie" which I think was something from her Gravesend background. My Gran Sylvia was also the loveliest of people and I always felt so sad for her being an only child and losing he father who she absolutely adored when she was only 16. – Hugh Makrell, Hugh's great grandson.

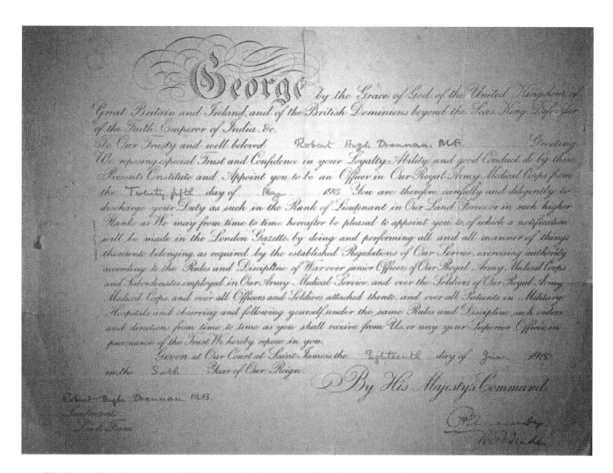

National, above, and Borough, below, Certificates of Honour.
[courtesy of Hugh Mackrell]

DEATH OF DR. DRENNAN.

We regret to record the death of Dr. Robert Hugh Drennan, M.B.U.M., R.A.M.C., which took place on Wednesday evening at the age of 51. The late Dr. Drennan was of Scotch descent, his family originally coming from Ayr, but his father, Mr. James Drennan, J.P., lived at Carse Hall, Limavady Junction, Ireland. He came to Gravesend about 20 years ago, and carried on a practice at 56, Parrock-street, and also at Northfleet, and married Miss Daisie Emily Buckle, eldest daughter of Mr. and Mrs. H. R. Buckle, of Cross-lane East, Gravesend, who is left, with a daughter of 15, to mourn her loss. Dr. Drennan was a prominent Freemason, having passed the chair of the Lodge of Freedom. On the outbreak of war he tried to join the Army, but did not succeed. Two years ago, when there was such a demand for doctors, his services were accepted, and he was successively located at the Alexandra Palace, at Newmarket, Colchester, and Brightlingsea. At the latter place he was taken seriously ill and was removed to Colchester, from whence he was brought home about eight weeks ago. Despite the assiduous attention of Dr. Pinching, jun., and unremitting care in nursing, he passed away as stated. During the time he had been on service his practice had been carried on by Dr. Knight and other brothers in his profession, and for this he was always deeply grateful. Many in Gravesend will mourn the decease of this kind-hearted and popular doctor, and friend, for it is well known that, apart from undertaking charitable work in the town, the poorer classes benefited by his skill in many instances without question of monetary return.

GR 28/7/17 [Andrew Marshall]

GR 28/7/17 [Andrew Marshall]

On Active Service.

DRENNAN.— On the 26th inst., at 56 Parrock-street, Gravesend, Captain R. H. Drennan, M.B.C.M., R.A.M.C., the dearly-loved husband of Daisie Drennan and youngest son of the late James Drennan, Esq., J.P., of Carse Hall, Limavady Junction, Ireland.

GR 28/7/17 [Andrew Marshall]

Gravesend Cemetery –
before, above, and now, right.

In Ever Loving Memory
Capt, Robert Hugh Drennan
M.B. C.M. R.A. M.C.
Who Died in Active Service
July 26th 1917, Aged 51
"FOR EVER WITH THE LORD"

A J Driver is listed on the memorial. There is no *A J Driver* with Gravesham connections listed in any records.

Arthur Johnson [1879-1918] may be the soldier mis-transcribed on the memorial; he served with the 200th Field Company, Royal Engineers with the rank of driver.

Arthur Dryden

Served under the name;

Arthur Goulding

Mercantile Marine - Trimmer

Arthur was born in 1897 in Leicester to John and Emma [Goulding] Dryden. John was from Scotland, being born in 1833. He was a school teacher. Emma was born in 1865 in Hounslow. They had ten surviving children in all. This was John's second marriage, there being six children from his first. The family settled in Cliff at the turn of the century before coming to Gravesend in 1906. The family lived at 17 Terrace Street. John died in 1900 and Emma remarried.

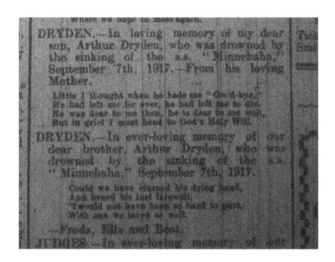

We regret to report the death, at the age of 22, of Arthur Dryden, who sailed under the name of Arthur Goulding, of 17, Terrace-street, Gravesend, his ship having been sunk by enemy submarine on the 7th September, and unfortunately was drowned off the coast of Ireland. This was his sixteenth trip on the vessel that was sunk. He was educated at Church-street School and was well-known and greatly respected in Gravesend. For some time he was employed at H.M. Customs. Deceased was the youngest son of Mrs. Williams, who was the late Mrs. Dryden; he has a brother serving in France, Royal Fusiliers, and one in the Royal Flying Corps, whilst another brother is a seaman.

GR 27/10/17 [Andrew Marshall]

Arthur was a trimmer on board the *SS Minnehaha*.

He was among the 43 casualties when the Minnehaha sunk after being torpedoed by U-48 on September 7th, 1917.

He has no known grave and is commemorated on the Tower Hill Monument.

DRYDEN.—In loving memory of my dear son, Arthur Dryden, who was drowned by the sinking of the s.s. "Minnehaha," September 7th, 1917.—From his loving Mother.

Little I thought when he bade me "Good-bye,"
He had left me for ever, he had left me to die.
He was dear to me then, he is dear to me still,
But in grief I must bend to God's Holy Will.

DRYDEN.—In ever-loving memory of our dear brother, Arthur Dryden, who was drowned by the sinking of the s.s. "Minnehaha," September 7th, 1917.

Could we have clasped his dying head,
And heard his last farewell,
T'would not have been so hard to part,
With one we loved so well.

—Freda, Ella and Beat.

GR 7/9/18 [Andrew Marshall]

Arthur Dryden –
Tower Hill Memorial

Gravesend Cemetery –

**ALSO OF OUR DEAR BROTHER ARTHUR DRYDEN
KILLED BY ENEMY ACTION IN THE S.S. MINNEHAHA, ON SEPT. 7TH 1917. AGED 20 YEARS**

Photograph – Andy White]

Edward Duck

Royal Navy – Ordinary Seaman
Service No. J/16642

Edward was born in Gravesend on August 4th, 1896. His father Henry was born in 1872 in Faversham. He worked as a general labourer in the Paper Mills. His mother Mary was born in 1870 in All Hallows. The couple had four children – Edward, Henry, born in 1897, Edith, born in 1901 and Victor, born in 1906. The family lived at 39 Cecil Road.

Henry followed his father and secured employment in the Paper Mills although in Edward's case, as a blacksmith striker.

He served as an ordinary seaman on *HMS Pathfinder*. HMS *Pathfinder* was the lead ship of the *Pathfinder* class scout cruisers, and was the first ship ever to be sunk by a locomotive torpedo fired by submarine She was built by Cammell Laird, Birkenhead, launched in July 1904, and commissioned on July 1905. She was originally to have been named HMS *Fastnet*, but was renamed prior to construction.

At the beginning of September 1914 Otto Hersing of *U-21* ventured to the Firth of Forth, home to the major British naval base at Rosyth. Hersing is known to have penetrated the Firth of Forth as far as the Carlingnose Battery beneath the Forth Bridge. At one point the periscope was spotted and the battery opened fire but without success. Overnight Hersing withdrew from the Forth, patrolling the coast from the Isle of May southwards. From distance, on the morning of September 5th he observed the SSE course of HMS *Pathfinder* followed by elements of the 8th Destroyer Flotilla. The destroyers altered course back towards the Isle of May at midday while HMS *Pathfinder* continued her patrol. Hersing spotted *Pathfinder* on her return journey from periscope depth at 1530. This time he resolved to make an attack. At 1543 Otto Hersing fired a single 50 cm (20 in) Type G torpedo.

It was a sunny afternoon. At 1545 lookouts spotted a torpedo wake heading towards the starboard bow at a range of 2,000 yards. The officer of the watch, Lieutenant-Commander Favell gave orders for the starboard engine to be put astern and the port engine to be set at full ahead while the wheel was fully turned in an attempt to take avoiding action. At 1550 the torpedo detonated beneath the bridge. The cordite charges may have then been ignited, leading to a flash causing a second, massive explosion within the fore section of the ship as the magazine blew up. The fore mast and No 1 funnel collapsed and then toppled over the side. The forensic evidence of the wreck is that everything before the first funnel disintegrated. The majority of the crew below decks in the forward section had neither the time nor the opportunity to escape. Although the explosion was well within sight of land, Captain Martin-Peake knew it was essential to attract attention. He ordered the stern gun to be fired. The king-pin must have been fatally damaged by the explosion because after firing a single round, the gun toppled off its mounting, rolled around the quarter deck, struck the after screen then careered over the stern, taking the gun crew with it. There was no list but there was insufficient time to lower boats. Indeed the remains of a lifeboat davit and rope can still be seen on the

Esplanade, looking S., Largs.

Postcard sent the year before hostilities opened, 1913 – censorship not in force; *we are at Harwich … we keep going out to sea for firing; a torpedo boat smacked into us*! [Courtesy of Andrew Marshall]

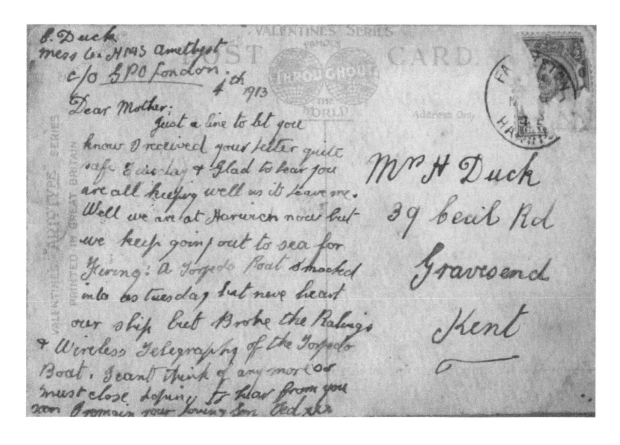

GR 7/9/18
[Andrew Marshall]

wreck. The propeller belonging to the ship's boat lies on the deck nearby.

The bow section sheared off under the strain as the stern heaved up to a sixty degree angle. Then it quietly slipped below the surface.

Eyemouth fishing boats were first on the scene and encountered a field of debris, fuel oil, clothing and body parts. Destroyers HMS *Stag* and *Express* had spotted the smoke and headed for the pall of smoke.

There is significant confusion regarding the numbers of survivors. *The Times* declared that 58 men had been rescued but that four had died of injuries. The fact that it is impossible to determine how many were on board that day, adds to difficulties but research indicates that 268 personnel were on board plus two civilian

canteen assistants. There were just eighteen known survivors.

The explosion was seen by Aldous Huxley (while staying at Northfield House, St. Abbs) who recorded the following in a letter to his father sent on September 14th, 1914 –

I dare say Julian told you that we actually saw the Pathfinder explosion — a great white cloud with its foot in sea.

The St. Abbs' lifeboat came in with the most appalling accounts of the scene. There was not a piece of wood, they said, big enough to float a man—and over acres the sea was covered with fragments—human and otherwise. The explosion must have been frightful. It is thought to be a German submarine that did it, or, possibly, a torpedo fired from one of the refitted German trawlers, which cruise all round painted with British port letters and flying the British flag.

Despite the events having been easily visible from shore, the authorities attempted to cover up the sinking and *Pathfinder* was reported to have been mined. Admiralty came to an agreement with the Press Bureau which allowed for the censoring of all reports. *The Scotsman* however published an eye-witness account by

an Eyemouth fisherman who had assisted in the rescue. The account confirmed rumours that a submarine had been responsible, rather than a mine. However *The Scotsman* also reported that *Pathfinder* had been attacked by two U-boats and had accounted for the second one in her death throes. Admiralty intelligence later claimed that cruisers had cornered the U-boat responsible and shelled it to oblivion. The sinking of *Pathfinder* by a submarine made both sides aware of the potential vulnerability of large ships to attack by submarines.

Edward was killed in the action. He has no known grave and he is commemorated on the Chatham Naval Memorial.

GR 12/9/14 [Andrew Marshall]

a day or two before the ship went under Mrs. Duck received a brief but happy letter, from 'Ted, which, he said, left him 'A1. at present.' Only last month he finished his boy's service and at the age of eighteen became an ordinary seaman after nearly three years in the Navy. He and Leonard Waterman were at Shotwell Barracks together, joining the Navy practically at the same time. It will be seen that in the lists their official numbers differ only by six.

Edward Duck –

Gravesend Cemetery

**ALSO OF EDWARD DUCK
SON OF THE ABOVE
WHO LOST HIS LIFE ON H.M.S. PATHFINDER
1914.
AGED 18 YEARS.**

[Photograph – Andy White]

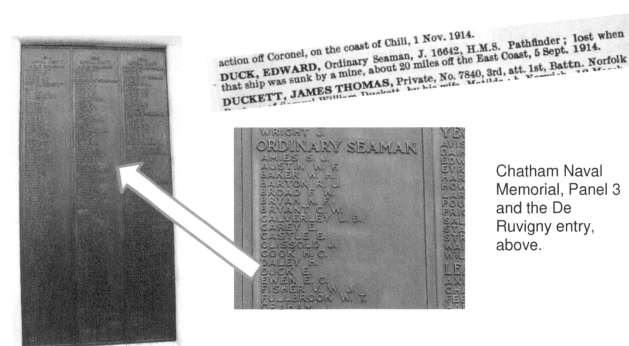

action off Coronel, on the coast of Chili, 1 Nov. 1914.
DUCK, EDWARD, Ordinary Seaman, J. 16642, H.M.S. Pathfinder; lost when that ship was sunk by a mine, about 20 miles off the East Coast, 5 Sept. 1914.
DUCKETT, JAMES THOMAS, Private, No. 7840, 3rd, att. 1st, Battn. Norfolk

Chatham Naval Memorial, Panel 3 and the De Ruvigny entry, above.

Edwin Duley –

**BELIEVED TO BE BURIED
IN THIS CEMETERY**

A.I.F. Burial Ground, Flers

Percy Dumbrill -
St. Sever Cemetery, Rouen

Edwin Joseph Duley
Border Regiment, 7th Battalion
2nd Lieutenant

Edwin was born in 1887 in Great Yarmouth to Edward and May Duley. Edward was born in 1848 in Northampton and was a fish merchant; May was a year younger. The couple had nine children – Emilia, born in 1870, Eliza, born in 1874, Ada, born in 1876, Maud, born in 1878, Frederick, born in 1883, Amy, born in 1885, Agnes, born in 1886, Edwin and Arthur, born in 1892. The family lived in Great Yarmouth before moving to 11 Suffield Road, Gorleston-on-Sea.

Edwin was a solicitor's clerk before enlisting with the 7th Battalion in Gravesend. The 7th (Service) Battalion, The Border Regiment was raised in Carlisle on September 7th, 1914. They trained at Andover. moving to Bovington in January 1915 and on to Winchester in June. They proceeded to France on July 15th, landing at Boulogne. The Division concentrated near St Omer undergoing trench familiarisation moving to the front in the Southern part of the Ypres Salient.

In the Spring of 1916 they were in action near the Bluff on the Commines Canal, south east of Ypres. They then moved to the Somme and saw action in the Battle of Albert where the Division captured Fricourt, and the Battle of Deville Wood.

2nd Lieutenant Duley was killed in action on November 2nd, 1916. He has no known grave and is commemorated in the A.I.F. Burial Ground, Flers.

Percy James Dumbrill
Royal Garrison Artillery,
13th Heavy Trench Mortar Battery
Service No. 130892 - Gunner

Percy was born in 1885 in Gravesend. His parents were William and Emily Dumbrill of 39 Bath Street. The couple were married in 1870 and had five surviving children - Emily, born in 1873, Edith, born in 1876, Albert, born in 1879, Leonard, born in 1881 and Percy who was the youngest. William was born in 1852 in Gravesend. He was a builder. Emily was born in 1846 and came from Essex.

Percy married shortly before the war. He and his wife Lilian [Gray] lived at 35 Cobham Street. They were married in St Albans on May 10th, 1913. They had one child, Emily who was born on May 8th, 1914. Percy was a mechanical engineer before enlisting in the Royal Garrison Artillery on November 25th, 1916 in Gravesend. He was 5 feet 6½ inches tall and weighed 130lbs.

13th Heavy Battery was raised for 13th (Western) Division as part of Kitchener's First New Army. The division began to assemble on Salisbury Plain in August 1914. Near the end of February 1915 the Division concentrated at Blackdown in Hampshire for final training.

13th Heavy Battery left the Division and were sent to France May 30th, 1915 as part of XVII Heavy Brigade. On October 23rd they joined 28th Division who were preparing to sail and five days later the first units left Marseilles for Alexandria in Egypt arriving in late November and they went on to Salonika on January 4th, 1916. Later in the year they were in action during the occupation of Mazirko and the capture of Barakli Jum'a. In 1917 they were involved in the capture of Ferdie and Essex Trenches (near Barakli Jum'a) and then the capture of Barakli and Kumli. In mid-1918 a number of units returned to France. The remainder of the Division were later in action at the Battle of Doiran and the pursuit to the Strumica Valley. When hostilities with Bulgaria ceased at the end of September the 28th Division was in the area of Trnovo. They moved in early

November to Gallipoli and occupied the Dardanelles Forts.

Percy died on December 8th, 1918 at 25 Sty Hospital, Rouen. The cause of death was described as measles and broncho-pneumonia.

GR 14/12/18 [Andrew Marshall]

The Base Hospital was part of the casualty evacuation chain, further back from the front line than the Casualty Clearing Stations. They were manned by troops of the Royal Army Medical Corps, with attached Royal Engineers and men of the Army Service Corps. In the theatre of war in France and Flanders, the British hospitals were generally located near the coast. They needed to be close to a railway line, in order for casualties to arrive (although some also came by canal barge); they also needed to be near a port where men could be evacuated for longer-term treatment in Britain.

There were two types of Base Hospital, known as Stationary and General Hospitals. They were large facilities, often centred on some pre-war buildings such as seaside hotels. The hospitals grew hugely in number and scale throughout the war. Most of the hospitals moved very rarely until the larger movements of the armies in 1918. Some hospitals moved into the Rhine bridgehead in Germany and many were operating in France well into 1919. Most hospitals were assisted by voluntary organisations, most notably the British Red Cross.

Number 25 at Rouen was opened in March 1915, closing in May 1919.

Percy is buried in St Sever Cemetery Extension, Rouen. During the First World War, Commonwealth camps and hospitals were stationed on the southern outskirts of Rouen. A base supply depot and the 3rd Echelon of General Headquarters were also established in the city.

The hospitals included eight general, five stationary, one British Red Cross, one labour hospital, and No. 2 Convalescent Depot. A number of the dead from these hospitals were buried in other cemeteries, but the great majority were taken to the city cemetery of St. Sever. In September 1916, it was found necessary to begin an extension. St. Sever Cemetery contains 3,082 Commonwealth burials of the First World War.

Lilian was granted a pension of 20s. 5d. for herself and her child.

George and *John Dunlop*, whose biographies now follow, were brothers. On May 2nd, 1915 *George* died of wounds, *John* was killed in action — both serving with the A.I.F. in Gallipoli.

George Alfred Dunlop
A.I.F., 10th Battalion
Service No. 312

George was born in Gravesend in 1883. His father was Charles Dunlop, born in 1852 and his mother was Elizabeth, born in 1855. Charles worked on the docks as a labourer. The couple had four children – Annie, born in 1876, Charles, born in 1879, George and John, born in 1886. The family lived at 20 Upper Kempthorne Street and subsequently at 10 Parrock Street.

HMAT Ascanius – pre Naval career and with the 10th boarding.

George was a seaman. He arrived in Australia in 1911 and settled in Portpirie. He married Annie Mary Skinner in 1906. They had three children – Alfred, Nellie and George. On George's death Annie would return to England and remarry. She and her new husband would live at 4 Wakefield Street.

He enlisted on August 28th, 1914 at Morphetville, South Australia. He was 5 feet 8 inches tall and weighed 154lbs. He had brown eyes and brown hair and was of dark complexion. He was posted to B Company, 10th Battalion.

The 10th Battalion was raised shortly after the outbreak of World War I as part of the Australian Imperial Force (AIF), which was an all-volunteer force raised by Australia for overseas service. Drawing personnel from South Australia, it came into being on August 17th, 1914 at the Morphettville Racecourse in Adelaide. Under the command of Lieutenant Colonel Stanley Price Weir, it was attached to the 3rd Infantry Brigade, 1st Division, along with the 9th, 11th and 12th Battalions, and was among the first units of the AIF raised for the war. With an establishment of 31 officers and 974 other ranks spread across eight companies, the battalion conducted a short period of individual training throughout September, culminating the presentation of the regimental colours on September 17th and a march past the state Parliament House on September 21st. The following month collective training was undertaken at Belair National Park and at Glenelg, South Australia.

On October 20th the battalion embarked on the ex-passenger liner, HMAT *Ascanius*; they were the first South Australian infantry unit during the war to deploy overseas. George was now in C Company.

After briefly stopping in Albany, where their convoy was delayed due to concerns over the presence of German warships en route, the battalion departed Australian waters in November and proceeded towards Egypt. Initially the plan had been for the battalion to proceed through to the United Kingdom; however, poor conditions and overcrowding in the training camps that they had been destined, resulted in the decision to disembark the Australians in Alexandria instead. Arriving there on December 4th, 1914, the

344

battalion was sent into camp at Mena, near Cairo.

George was in trouble on three occasions – being absent from a 6.45am parade on December 28th [one day confined to barracks], absent without leave on January 6th [forfeited six days' pay] and disobeying an order on January 9th [14 days confinement to barracks].

A period of desert training followed in January and February 1915 during which the battalion was reorganised around a four company structure. Designated 'A' to 'D', each company consisted of 228 men that were spread across four platoons. In late February, the 3rd Infantry Brigade received orders that it was being committed to an operation in the Dardanelles and, after moving by rail to Alexandria, they boarded *Ionian*, a Greek steamer on March 1st. On reaching Lemnos, a shortage of fresh water on the island meant that the battalion was housed on the ship for the next seven weeks, although this was spent ashore conducting exercises and mounting guard duty. In early April, planning for a landing on the Gallipoli Penin-sula began and as this went ahead, on April 15th the battalion was issued its distinctive blue and purple Unit Colour Patch.

On April 24th, the 10th Battalion embarked for Gallipoli. Two companies and the battalion headquarters were allocated to the battleship HMS *Prince of Wales*, while the other two companies proceeded on board two destroyers, *Scourge* and *Foxhound*. At around 4:30 am on April 25th, 1915, the 10th Battalion was one of the first units to come ashore at Anzac Cove as part of the covering force – drawn from Colonel Ewen Sinclair-Maclagan's 3rd Brigade – for the main Anzac landing. Troops from the battalion landed near the centre of the cove and, ascending the Ariburnu Ridge, attempted to push inland towards the Sari Bair Range. They are believed to have penetrated further inland than any other Australian unit.

Following this, the battalion remained at Gallipoli until the evacuation in December, taking part in defending the beachhead before being withdrawn from the peninsula along with the rest of the Allied forces and returning to Egypt. They remained in Egypt until early 1916 as the AIF was expanded and re-organised in preparation for its deployment to the European battlefield.

George died of wounds received in action on May 2nd, 1915 on board *HMT Devanha*.

He has no known grave; the army records note that his body was taken away probably for burial at sea. He is commemorated on the Lone Pine Memorial.

The photograph is of Pte. G. A. Dunlop, of the 10th Battalion Australian Imperial Forces, who has died of wounds received in action at the Dardanelles. Pte. Dunlop was the son of Mr. and Mrs. Chas. Dunlop, of 100, Peacock-street, Gravesend. He left the town for Australia some four years ago, and had not seen his parents since. Soon after the outbreak of war he volunteered to serve with the Australian forces. His brother, John Edgar, is also serving with the Australian troops at the Dardanelles, and another brother, James, is in France with the A.S.C.

GR 5/6/15 [Andrew Marshall]

The HMAT *Devanha* lifeboat, which carried soldiers of the 12th Battalion and 3rd Field Ambulance into Anzac Cove on April 25th, 1915, arrived at the Shrine of Remembrance, Melbourne on Sunday, May 4th, 2014 at 9.30am.

The *Devanha,* on loan from the Australian War Memorial, arrived for installation in the First World War (1914-18) Gallery. The Galleries opened to the public in November 2014. The image above depicts the *Devanha* landing boat in the First World War (1914-18) Gallery.

John Edgar Dunlop
A.I.F., 16th Battalion
Service No. 1153

John was born in 1886 in Gravesend, the brother of George.

He joined the Royal Naval Reserve in 1907.He was a seaman.

John enlisted at Morphetville, South Australia on September 16th, 1914 with the 16th Battalion. He was 5 feet 6 inches tall and weighed 146lbs. he had brown hair and brown eyes and was described as being of healthy complexion.

The 16th Battalion AIF (Australian Imperial Force) was composed of South Australians and Western Australians under the command of Lieutenant Colonel Harold Pope. The unit was a cross-section of the 1914 rural and urban environments of both states.

The battalion trained first at Blackboy Hill near Perth, and on November 21st, 1914 left Freemantle for Melbourne. There they joined the other three battalions of the 4th Australian Infantry

The 16th Battalion marching through Melbourne in 1914.

Brigade AIF under Colonel John Monash at Broadmeadows Camp to complete their organisation and training.

On December 22nd, 1914, the 16th Battalion embarked 32 officers and 979 other ranks on the transport *A40 Ceramic* at Port Melbourne. The men had left Broadmeadows after two days of continuous rain, and they and their equipment were saturated and muddy - *All ranks embarked thoroughly wet and with symptoms of a great*

prevalence of influenza!

They sailed for Egypt at 2.30 pm that afternoon.

The ship reached Albany, Western Australia, on December 27th, and Aden in the Persian Gulf on January 20th, 1915. On February 3rd, 1915, the battalion disembarked at Alexandria, Egypt. They travelled by train to camp at Heliopolis and remained there, undergoing training, until early April. The 16th left by train for Alexandria on April 11th where they boarded the troopship *Hyda Pasha* and on the afternoon of April 25th off the Gallipoli peninsula the battalion assembled in the ship's hold - *There, for the last time in this world, many of us stood shoulder to shoulder. As I looked down the ranks of my comrades, I wondered much which of us were marked for the Land Beyond. We were transferred from the transport to the destroyer, which took us close into the shore, and then we were transferred into the ship's boats and rowed to the shore, amidst a hail of shells.*

[Ellis Silas, 'The Last Assembly']

At about 6 pm, the 16th went ashore at Anzac Cove and made their way into the hills. The column occupied a sharp edge of spur that afterwards bore their commanding officer's name, Pope's Hill. They spent the night digging in along the edge under intense rifle fire. For the next five days they stayed there, holding the hill, with Turkish troops to their front and rear.

During the darkness of their first night on Gallipoli, there was confusion about Indian troops who were supposedly in the same area, when in fact they were Turkish soldiers. A small party led by Colonel Pope went forward to speak to their commanding officer. Pope, discovering the mistake, jumped over a ridge and escaped but three other men with him were captured and became prisoners of war. Now that they knew that they were surrounded by Turks, not Indians, defences were improved and fighting was fierce. Snipers, who had penetrated the nearby ridge at Russell's Top and were at the rear of the battalion's trenches, caused many casualties.

At dawn on April 26th, the warships shelled Russell's Top, breaking up the Turkish ranks, but there were still many accurate snipers. All that day, the battalion's two machine-guns sniped back at the Turks on Russell's Top and many of the original gun crew were killed or wounded. During the next two days, there were attempts to reinforce the battalion, and on April 27th the 2nd Battalion took Russell's Top and, together with a reinforcement of New Zealanders, manned it strongly. At about 2.30 that afternoon, the Turks organised a six-line attack, advancing on Walker's Ridge, Russell's Top and Pope's Hill. Shells from the navy ships stopped the attack but they continued to snipe. Later that night, there was another determined attack, but the Turks were practically annihilated by machine-gun and rifle fire.

On the evening of Friday April 30th, after being in action for five days, the 16th was relieved by the 15th Battalion. They moved down one of the gullies to a spot called 'rest camp' where they rested until May 2nd. However, during those 2 days they lost 50 more men from enemy sniper fire.

At nightfall on May 2nd, the 16th went into attack again up the Bloody Angle towards Quinn's Post. After the bombardment of the Turkish positions ceased, the 16th made their way up the steep side of the valley, towards the Bloody Angle. The Turks held their fire until the battalion reached the top of the ridge, then directed heavy fire opened on it, mostly from their positions at The Nek and the Chessboard. The battalion fought and dug in throughout the night, extending the trench line from Quinn's Post. Some of their men found an abandoned Turkish trench on the crest of the Bloody Angle and occupied it. During the attack the Otago Battalion failed to reach their objective at Baby 700 and were forced to dig in near The Nek. The 13th positioned themselves on the other side of the gully, to the left of the 16th, but each battalion was uncertain of each other's location and could not join up.

The battalion's exposure to continual firing made it very dangerous to carry ammunition to them - *Again and again volunteers were shot as they scrambled up with heavy cases; others took their places only to fall dead across the boxes they were dragging, or to roll down the steep side of the hill.*

[Captain C Longmore, *The Old Sixteenth: being a record of the 16th Battalion, AIF, during the Great War 1914-1918*, Perth, 1929]

At dawn on May 3rd, the New Zealanders withdrew under heavy fire and the Turks occupied their line. The Turks in front of the 16th attacked, but were driven back. The 16th then attempted to attack a Turkish position, from which heavy rifle fire was coming, but the Turks were alerted to the attack and their machine gun fire from Baby 700 raked the line. In addition, nearby Turks threw bombs and expended heavy fire on the men of the 16th. The dead lay thickly between their respective positions.

As the sky lightened, the Turks crept through the scrub towards the 16th and inflicted further heavy casualties. Although attempts were made to reinforce the 16th, the Turkish fire made it impossible to reach them. The battalion gradually withdrew through the day, and the Turks took over their trench line. Having lost support from both their left and right flanks, the 13th then withdrew during the night.

The 16th suffered very high casualties at the Bloody Angle. Entering the action with 17 officers and 620 men, they lost eight officers and 330 men. The battalion's dead remained unburied until after the war, when their remains were recovered by the Graves Registration Unit and buried in the newly established Quinn's Post cemetery nearby.

John was killed in action on May 2nd. A note on his casualty form records that *paybook received at Australian Records Section, Alexandria, with apparent bullet mark through book. 22/9/15.*

John has no known grave and is commemorated on the Lone Pine Memorial.

PRIVATE J. E. DUNLOP.

have already announced the death of Private G. A. Dunlop. He died of wound on Sunday, May 2nd, and remarkable to relate on the same day his brother was killed in action. The parents have received a letter from the captain of the battalion, stating with regard to the death of Private J. E. Dunlop: " I am sorry to inform you that he was killed on Sunday, May 2nd, during an assault of the enemy's position. When last seen by his company sergeant-major he was in the front line, and he thus died fighting gamely."

Fred Leist, *THE TAKING OF LONE PINE*

In January 1919 tattered pieces of uniform were found lying among the bones of the men of the 16th Battalion, who were killed trying to advance at the Bloody Angle on May 2nd, 1915. These items were recovered by Lieutenant William Hopkin James, who headed a small party to Gallipoli for the Australian War Records Section (the precursor to the Australian War Memorial). They arrived at Gallipoli in mid-December 1918, and remained there until late March 1919. With the assistance of members of the 7th Light Horse Regiment, who were stationed in the area at the time, they collected items, and photographed the area. In February 1919 they were joined by the Australian Historical Mission, led by Official Historian C E W Bean.

Remains of a 16 Bn shoulder strap

The fragile pieces of collars and shoulder straps were found in a gully between Dead Man's Ridge and Quinn's Post, leading up to the Bloody Angle. The photograph shows the area to the left of Quinn's Post, with the gully where the bodies of the 16th Battalion men were found leading up to the Bloody Angle.

The change from metal unit shoulder titles to cloth unit colour patches was ordered while the battalions were training in Egypt in March 1915. However these members of 16 Battalion, were still wearing their shoulder titles in early May. It is possible they had not received their patches before the battalion left Egypt in April; or they had been allocated their patches, but retained their metal numerals out of affection for them

The remains of the 16th Battalion men killed at the Bloody Angle in May 1915, remained there until they were buried at Quinn's Post Cemetery after the war. Most of the remains could not be identified and have no known graves, so their names are commemorated on the Lone Pine Memorial. Only a small number of the men recovered from the Bloody Angle have marked graves. They were identified from details recorded on identity discs, equipment or personal possessions that were found when their bodies were recovered.

EADES W. J.
EASTWOOD F. A.
EASTWOOD W. F.
EDGELEY
EDWARDS
EDWARDS
ELFORD
ELKIN A.
ELLEY A.
ELLINGHAM
ELLINGHAM
ELLIOTT
ELSTON A. E.

ELSTON
ELSTON
ELLIOTT
EVANS

A B C D E

HE LOVED DUTY
MORE THAN HE FEARED DEATH

Joseph Edgley -
Duisans Cemetery, Etru

Ernest James Eades
London Regiment, 24th Battalion
Service No. 4084 - Private

Ernest was born in 1895 in Wandsworth. Hs father, after whom he was named, was born in 1872 in Wandsworth. He was a boot maker by profession. His mother Ada was born in 1873 in Pimlico. They married in 1892 and had eight surviving children – Winifred, born in 1894, Ernest, Margaret, born in 1900, George, born in 1903, Ada, born in 1904, Alexander, born in 1906, Colin, born in 1908 and Ivy, born in 1911. The family moved to Gravesend from Wandsworth in 1905 and lived at 56 Milton Road.

Ernest followed his father as a boot maker.

He enlisted with the 24th County of London Battalion, 'The Queens'. 24th (The Queen's) Battalion, The London Regiment, were a Territorial unit with their headquarters at 71 New Street, Kennington Park Road, serving as part of 6th London Brigade, 2nd London Division in 1914. The Division had just arrived for their annual summer camp on Salisbury Plain when war was declared in August 1914, they were at once recalled to their home base and mobilised for war service. The Division concentrated in the St Albans area for training. They proceeded to France on the 16th of March 1915, landing at Le Havre, being only the second TF Division to arrive in theatre. The 5th London Brigade was ordered to Cassel, and the remainder of the Division concentrated near Bethune and were joined by 5th London Brigade near the end of the month. On the 11th of May 1915 the formation was renamed 142nd Brigade, 47th (2nd London) Division. They saw action in The Battle of Aubers Ridge, The Battle of Festubert, The Battle of Loos and the subsequent actions of the Hohenzollern Redoubt, In 1916 they fought during The German attack at Vimy Ridge, and on The Somme in The Battle of Flers-Courcelette capturing High Wood, The Battle of the Transloy Ridges in which they captured Eaucourt l'Abbaye and The attacks on the Butte de Warlencourt.

Ernest died on September 17th, 1916 and is buried in Abbeville Communal Extension Cemetery. For much of the First World War, Abbeville was headquarters of the Commonwealth lines of communication and No.3 BRCS, No.5 and No.2 Stationary Hospitals were stationed there variously from October 1914 to January 1920. The communal cemetery was used for burials from November 1914 to September 1916, the earliest being made among the French military graves. The extension was begun in September 1916.

Edward Edwin Hugh Eastwood
East Kent Regiment, 2nd Battalion
Service No. L/8986 - Private

Edward was born in 1899 in Gillingham. His father Edwin Lewin Eastwood was born in 1858 and was a private with the Royal Marines. His mother Sarah Elizabeth was born in Shoreham in 1867. They lived at 95 Medway Road when Edward was born. On leaving the Marines Edwin moved to Gravesend and the family lived at 15 Clifton Grove.

Edward was a labourer before enlisting with The Buffs, 3rd Battalion, on July 21st, 1908 in Chatham. He was 5 feet 5½ inches tall and weighed 112lbs. he had brown hair and hazel eyes.

He served with the 2nd Battalion, C Company. 2nd Battalion, The Royal East Kent Regiment (The Buffs) were in Madras when war broke out in August 1914. As soon as a territorial unit arrived to take over the garrison,

**SACRED TO THE MEMORY
OF ERNEST JAMES EADES
GRENADIER PLATOON
LONDON REGT
AND 1/24TH LONDON
WHO FELL ON THE SOMME
INTERRED AT ABBEVILLE
R.I.P.**
"HAPPY WARRIOR"

Ernest Eades – Gravesend Cemetery, above, and
Abbeville Communal Cemetery, below.
"HAPPY WARRIOR"

the 2nd Buffs returned to England, arriving on the 23rd of December. They joined 85th Brigade, 28th Division who were assembling near Winchester. They proceeded to France from Southampton, landing at Le Havre between the 16th and 19th of January, they concentrated in the area between Bailleul and Hazebrouck, being joined by additional Territorial units. In 1915 they were in action in The Second Battle of Ypres and The Battle of Loos. He was killed in action on May 24th, 1915. He has no known grave and is commemorated on the Menin Gate, Ypres.

DEATHS.
Killed in Action.
EASTWOOD.—On the 24th May, killed in action in France, Edwin Hugh, the beloved eldest son of Mr. Edwin and Mrs. Eastwood, of 15, Clifton-grove, Gravesend, age 25.

GR 19/6/15 [Andrew Marshall]

William Frederick Eastwood
Duke of Wellington's, 1st/7th Bn
Service No. 25479 - Private
William lived with his mother Sarah Jane and younger sister Marion, born in 1893, at 9 Brunswick Retreat. He was born in 1890. His father died before the turn of the century. Sarah worked as a laundry hand and on leaving school William worked as a delivery hand for a Draper's Shop.

William subsequently worked as a railway porter at Gravesend Railway Station, being employed by the Midland Railway.

William enlisted at Gravesend on December 12th, 1915. He was 5 feet 3½ inches tall and weighed 120lbs. his attestation papers note under the heading *slight defects but not sufficient to cause rejection - complete absence of scalp hair*!

He was called to the colours in June 1917 and served with the Duke of Wellington's [West Riding Regiment]. The 1/7th Battalion was a territorial unit based in Milnsbridge, serving with 2nd West Riding Brigade, West Riding Division. When war broke out in August 1914, the units of the Division had just departed for their annual summer camp, they were at once recalled to their home base and mobilised for war service, taking up position on the coastal defences near Hull and Grimsby. On the 5th of November they moved to billets in Doncaster for the winter. They trained in South Yorkshire and Lincolnshire in preparation for service overseas. They proceeded to France on the 17th of April 1915, sailing from Folkestone to Boulogne. The Division concentrated in the area around Estaires. On the 15th of May the formation was renamed 147th Brigade, 49th (West Riding) Division. Their first action was in The Battle of Aubers Ridge in May 1915. In 1916 they were in action in the Battles of the Somme. In 1917 they were involved in the Operations on the Flanders Coast and the The Battle of Poelcapelle during the Third Battle of Ypres. In 1918 they were in action during the Battles of the Lys, The pursuit to the Selle and the Final Advance in Picardy

William was killed on April 13th, 1918. He is buried in Trois Arbres Cemetery, Steenwerck. Steenwerck village remained untouched for much of the First World War, but on April 10th, 1918 it was captured by the Germans and remained in their possession until the beginning of October. Trois Arbres passed into German hands a day later than Steenwerck, after a rearguard defence by the 34th Division. The site for Trois Arbres Cemetery was chosen for the 2nd Australian Casualty Clearing Station in July 1916, and Plot 1 and the earlier rows of Plot

II, were made and used by that hospital until April 1918. A few further burials were made in the cemetery after the German withdrawal at the end of 1918 and after the Armistice, over 700 graves were brought into it from the battlefields of Steenwerck, Nieppe, Bailleul and Neuve-Eglise.

Joseph William Edgley
Royal Engineers - Sapper
Service No. 67894

Joseph was born in 1886 in Sunderland to Joseph and Margaret Edgley. Joseph [father] was born in 1860 in Sunderland and was a sailor. Margaret as born in 1856 and was also from Sunderland. There were three children in the family – Joseph, Edith, born in 1888, Margaret, born in 1891 and Samuel, born in 1893. The family home was at 30 Percy Terrace.

Joseph's uncle George – his father's brother – lived at 130 Darnley Road, Gravesend. He was born in 1861 and was married to Frances also born in 1861. Both were from Sunderland. George was a Trinity House Pilot.

Joseph was employed as a joiner before enlisting with the Royal Engineers on February 19th, 1915. He was 5 feet 6 inches tall, weighed 140lbs with a chest measurement of

35 inches, expanding two inches extra. His expertise as a carpenter proved invaluable in his new role with the Engineers.

He was absent without leave on August 30th when stationed in Boston and forfeited 10 days' pay as a consequence. It seems that proximity to home and family ensured his one misdemeanour in army life!

Joseph arrived in France on October 7th, 1915 with 135th Company. He was

A request regarding pension and pay.

wounded in mid-November 1916 and sent back down the line to Etaples. He was discharged on the 24th and the following day joined 146th Company. In early March 1917 he was transferred to the 93rd Field Company.

Joseph was badly wounded on April 20th and died of wounds the following day, on April 21st. He is buried in Duisans Cemetery, Etrun.

Killed In Action.
EDGELY.—Killed in France, on April 21st, Sapper J. Edgely, aged 31 years, eldest son of Mr and Mrs. J. Edgely, Sunderland, and nephew of Mr. and Mrs. G. Edgely, 130, Darnley-road, Gravesend.

GR 25/5/17 [Andrew Marshall]

Menin Gate, Ypres –
Edward Eastwood

William Eastwood –
Trois Arbres Cemetery

Joseph Edgley –
Duisans Cemetery, Etrun

Charles Alfred Edwards
Royal Army Medical Corps
Service No. 45575 - Private

Charles was born in 1878 in Gravesend to James and Sarah [East] Edwards. James was born in 1862 in Gravesend. He was a photographer. Sarah was born in Northfleet. On leaving school she was a domestic servant to John Willis in Gravesend who coincidentally was also a photographer.

By the early 1880s Sarah lived at 18 Union Street and was now earning a living as a dressmaker. Working as a dressmaker with her at the same premises was Sarah Hayes, who was born in 1857. Boarders in the house were Charlotte Edwards, a needle-woman. She was born in 1838 and was a widower. She had her three children with her – James, Jane, born in 1866 and Alfred, born in 1871.

James would marry Sarah in 1888. He is already listed as a photographer in the 1881 census.

By 1891 James and Sarah are living at 3 Windmill Street. The couple were married in 1878. There were six children in the family – Charles, William Willis, born in 1882, John, born in 1885, Caractacus James, born in 1887, Florence, born in 1889 and Blanche, born in 1890. James died in the early years of the century and the family subsequently moved to 23 Dover Road, Northfleet. Prior to the Great War Sarah still had five of the children still living at home – Florence being the only one of the children to have left home! William married Lillian Ethel in 1905 and both lived with his mother and his brothers and sister Blanche in the six bedroomed house in Dover Road.

Charles was a stevedore at Tilbury Docks before enlisting with the Royal Medical Corps in 1914 on the outbreak of war. He arrived in France on February 1st, 1915 and served at the Front until taken prisoner of war.

Private Edwards died on February 12th, 1918. He is buried in Hamburg. Hamburg Ohlsdorf Cemetery is the biggest non-military cemetery in the world. There are 3 Commonwealth War Graves plots - 1914-1918, 1939-1945 and Post War.

Charles Alfred Edwards, aged 43 years, son of Mrs. Edwards, a widow, residing at 43, Dover-road East, Northfleet, died on Feb. 12th, 1918, at Parchim, Germany, from dysentery. He had served in the Navy for 20 years, at the expiration of which time he was invalided out. Joining the New Army in 1914, he served with the R.A.M.C. in France, and on November 30th he was taken prisoner at Cambrai by the Germans. A second son of Mrs. Edwards, C. J. Edwards, was killed in France in 1915. Both were members of the R.A.O.B., and well-known in Gravesend and Northfleet.

GR

During the First World War, Hamburg Cemetery was used for the burial of over 300 Allied servicemen who died as prisoners of war. In 1923, it was decided that the graves of Commonwealth servicemen who had died all over Germany should be brought together into four permanent cemeteries. Hamburg was one of those chosen, and burials were brought into the cemetery from 120 burial grounds. The majority died as prisoners, but a few were sailors whose bodies were washed ashore on the Frisian Islands.

There are now 708 First World War servicemen buried or commemorated at Hamburg. This total includes special memorials to three casualties buried in Parchim Prisoners of War Cemetery whose graves could not be found, and 25 unidentified sailors whose remains were recovered from *HM Submarine E24*, which was sunk by a mine off Heligoland in March 1916, when the vessel was raised in July 1974.

The Commonwealth section of the cemetery also contains 1,466 Second World War burials, servicemen who died with the occupying forces, or airmen lost in bombing raids over Germany. There are also 378 post Second World War graves.

Charles was baptised ***Caractacus James***; on the 1891 census, aged 4, as on the 1901 census, aged 15, he is entered as ***James***. On the 1911 census, now aged 25, he is listed as ***Cractacus James***. The Commonwealth War Records list him as ***Charles J.***

As it was his elder brother William who returned the 1911 census the assumption is that Caractacus was using his birth name in everyday use and the name he would want to be known by.

Charles James Edwards
London Regiment, 16th Battalion
Service No. 8790 – Rifleman

Caractacus on leaving school was employed by the Post Office as an 'errand boy'. He subsequently secured employment as a carman, working in a laundry. Prior to the war he was unmarried and living at home at 23 Dover Road, Northfleet. His father James had died over two decades earlier leaving his mother Sarah as head of the family. She, now in her mid-50s, had retired from being a 'char woman' to, no doubt, look after the household.

Hamburg Ohlsdorf Cemetery, Hamburg
Charles Edwards

Living in the same home was his elder brother Charles, a stevedore at Tilbury, William, a fitter's labourer at the Cement Works, and his wife Lillian Ethel, John, a labourer at the Cement Works and his younger sister Blanche who helped her mother run the household.

It was as Charles J. that he enlisted with the 2nd London Regiment, service number 3278. The 2nd was formed in London in September 1914. By December 1914, it had moved to Kent. In February 1915 the 2nd was in Malta and on August 27th moved to Egypt, before landing on September 25th at Suvla Bay, Gallipoli, joining the 88th Brigade in 29th Division. The arrival in Egypt is noted on his 'medal card', making him eligible for the '1914/1915 Star' [medal].

In January 1916 the 2nd was evacuated from Gallipoli and moved to Egypt, joining the 53rd (Welsh) Division. In April 1916 it moved independently to France and in June was disbanded at Rouen.

Caractacus was transferred to the 16th (County of London) Battalion (Queens' Westminster Rifles), service number 554512. With the formation of the Territorials in 1908 the Westminsters became the 16th QWR. It was in the 2nd London Division at the outbreak of war, but left the division and landed in France in November 1914. For the first six months the battalion was in the Armentieres sector before moving to Ypres in May 1915. The next eight months were spent in the Salient where they occupied practically every portion of the northern half from the Ypres-Roulers railway to Wieltje. Then it was down to the Somme front where, with 48th, their division took part in the disastrous diversionary attack on Gommecourt on July 1st which cost them 600 casualties out of the 750 who went into action. Subsequently they were in action in The Battle of Ginchy on September 9th. The capture of Ginchy and the success of the French 6th Army in mid-September, enabled both armies to make much bigger attacks, which captured much more ground and inflicted c. 130,000 casualties on the German defenders during the month. Caractacus was killed in action on September 10th at Ginchy. He has no known grave and is commemorated on the Thiepval Monument.

BOMBARDIER C. J. EDWARDS.
Official notice was received on July 17th by Mrs. Edwards, 28, Dover-road East, of the death of Bombardier C. J. Edwards, who has been missing since 10th September, 1916. A valued employee of the New Falcon Laundry Co. for 10 years, Bombardier Edwards joined the Royal London Fusiliers in November, 1914, and was afterwards transferred into the 1st Queen's Westminster Rifles, his fields of service being Malta, Egypt, Gallipoli and France. Bombardier Edwards was Primo in the R.O.A.B., and was well-known in Gravesend and surrounding districts for his versatile talents as a comedian and dancer.

EDWARDS.—Bombardier C. I. Edwards, of the 1st Queen's Westminster Rifles, killed in action, September 10th, 1916.

GR 21/7/17 [Andrew Marshall]

GR 21/7/17 [Andrew Marshall]

William Thomas Cyril Edwards
Lancashire Fusiliers, 2nd Battalion
Service No. 56609 - Private

William was born in 1899 in Gravesend. His father Thomas Standish was born in 1874 in Gravesend. He was a pianoforte tuner. His wife Lavinia May was born in 1872 in Norwich. The couple were married in 1895 and had two children – William and Dorothy Winifred, born in 1906. The family lived at 2 Warwick Terrace, Singlewell Road.

William enlisted with the 2nd Battalion, Lancashire Regiment. He was in D Company. In August, 1914 the Battalion was stationed at Dover as part of the 12th Brigade of the 4th Division.

On August 20th, 1914 it mobilised for war and landed at Boulogne. The Division engaged in various actions on the Western Front in 1914 including The Battle of Le Cateau, The Battle of the Marne, The Battle of the Aisne, The Battle of Messines. In December the Battalion took part in the Christmas Truce and the following year in The Second Battle of Ypres.

In 1916 the Battalion was involved in The Battle of Albert and The Battle of Le Transloy. During 1917 there was involvement in The First Battle of the Scarpe, The Third Battle of the Scarpe, The Battle of Polygon Wood, The Battle of Broodseinde, The Battle of Poelcapelle and The First Battle of Passchendaele. The following year the Battalion saw action in The First Battle of Arras, The Battle of Hazebrouck, The Battle of Bethune, The Advance in Flanders, The Battle of the Scarpe, The Battle of Drocourt-Queant, The Battle of the Canal du Nord, The Battle of the Selle, The Battle of Valenciennes.

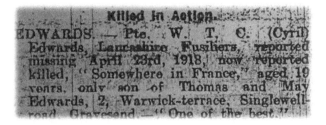

Pte. W. T. Cyril Edwards, Lancashire Fusiliers, only son of Mr. and Mrs. T. S. Edwards, 2, Warwick-terrace, Singlewell-road, Gravesend, is reported missing, after an engagement in France, since April 23rd. He was 19 years of age. Before joining up he was employed at the Technical Institute, and was a member of Northfleet Church Choir. Any further information respecting him would be gratefully received.

GR

He was killed in action on April 23rd, 1918. He has no known grave and is commemorated on the Loos Memorial.

Killed in Action.
EDWARDS. — Pte. W. T. C. (Cyril) Edwards, Lancashire Fusiliers, reported missing April 23rd, 1918, now reported killed, "Somewhere in France," aged 19 years, only son of Thomas and May Edwards, 2, Warwick-terrace, Singlewell-road, Gravesend.—"One of the best."

GR 5/10/18 [Andrew Marshall]

Charles Edwards –
Thiepval Memorial.

William Edwards –
Panel 46, Loos Memorial.

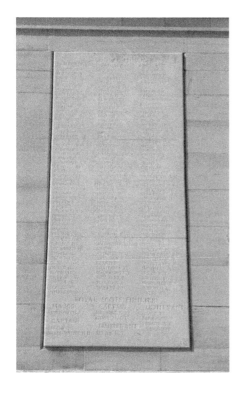

Charles William Elford
Royal Garrison Artillery
Service No. 772 - Gunner

Charles was born in Milton in 1888. He was the son of Charles and Emily Elford of 59 Peppercroft Street. He was a carman by profession. He and his wife Mary lived at 5 Melborne Pier, West Street. They married in 1913 and had one child, Ada, born in 1914.

Charles enlisted with the Royal Garrison Artillery, Kent Heavy Battery on March 26th, 1913 in Gravesend. Charles was 6 foot 1 inches tall and of good physical development with good eyesight. He was a labourer.

Home Counties (Kent) Heavy Battery was part of the 44th (Home Counties) Division at the outbreak of war in August 1914 the division was mobilised and the brigade artillery took up position at the defensive forts on the south coast. On September 22nd, 1914 the Indian Government agreed to exchange 52 regular British and Indian army battalions for 43 Territorial Battalions and the infantry battalions of Home Counties (Kent) Heavy Battery TF was selected to be sent to India. The Artillery, Medical Corps and Royal Engineers remained in Europe. The Home Counties (Kent) Heavy Battery proceeded to France in December 1915.

He died as a result of a fall on March 20th, 1915 at Cliffe Fort. It appears that he died of injuries – fractured skull - sustained in a fall when on sentry duty. The Commanding Officer of the Fort, Captain Edward Goldsmith, No. 2 [H.S.] Co., Kent R.G.A. reported that Charles *was found about 5.45 am on Saturday March 20th lying dead on the roof of a store below the parapet of the S.E. corner of this fort, where he had been on duty as a Maxim sentry.*
In my opinion the man had been leaning or sitting on the railing at this spot and had overbalanced, the

ELFORD.—On March 20th, 1915, Gunner C W. Elford, K.R.G.A., aged 27, who wa killed by a fall at Cliffe Fort while o sentry duty,—Deeply regretted by hi Mother, his comrades, and all that kne him. "In the midst of life we are i death."

GR 17/4/15

ground being somewhat slippery owing to frost.
He is buried in Gravesend.

ELFORD.—In loving memory of Charl loved brother of F. and M. Sedge, who di at Cliff Fort, March 20th, 1915.—"Un the day breaks."

GR 10/4/15 [Andrew Marshall]

Arthur Walter Elkin
Army Service Corps - Private
Service No. M2/200842

Arthur was born in Grays, Essex in 1883. His parents moved to Gravesend shortly after Arthur was born. He and his wife Elizabeth, born in 1886 in Northfleet, had no children. The couple lived at 16 Cutmore Street. Arthur was a carman.

Arthur enlisted with the Army Service Corps but was attached to the 152nd Siege Battery, Royal Garrison Artillery. Siege Batteries RGA were equipped with heavy howitzers, sending large calibre high explosive shells in high trajectory, plunging fire. The usual armaments were 6 inch, 8 inch and 9.2 inch howitzers, although some had huge railway - or road - mounted 12 inch howitzers.

As British artillery tactics developed, the Siege Batteries were most often employed in destroying or neutralising the enemy artillery, as well as putting destructive fire down on strongpoints, dumps, stores, roads and railways behind enemy lines.

DOUBLE BLOWS FOR GRAVESEND AND NORTHFLEET FAMILIES.

Shakespeare never wrote a truer line than "Troubles come not as single spies, but in battalions," and he might have had this terrible war in his vision when he perceived the truth, for it has brought trouble and anxiety, suffering and bereavement to nearly every home in the land. There are two cases to be recorded in which double blows have been dealt by fate. The first is to the Gravesend family of Mr. William Elkin, of 8, William-street. His daughter-in-law, who lives at 45, Lynton-road, has received news that her husband, Pte. Arthur Walter Elkin, A.S.C., has been killed in France, and the day after the date of his death his mother passed away. The deceased was well-known in the town, and for 10 years was a driver for Mr. Harry Legg, after which he was head porter and motor driver for Messrs. Bryant and Rackstraw. He joined the Army on the 25th July, 1916, and was sent to France straight away for service in the Motor Transport. His wife never saw him in khaki. While his mother lay ill, several telegrams were sent to him asking him to return, as she wanted to see him before she died, and the last was sent on the very day he was killed. He was 33 years of age, and he leaves one child, aged 14 months. From Second-Lieut. B. Noel Middleton, Mrs. Elkin has received a letter stating that her husband was seriously wounded by a shell on the night of the 28th July, and died immediately without recovering consciousness. At the time he was delivering ammunition to a battery, and the shell killed one of his comrades and wounded two others. "His loss will be most keenly felt not only by us personally, but by all the men in this column," Lieut. Middleton adds. "He was a willing worker and always had a cheery smile for everyone. . . It was unfortunate that I was unable to obtain leave for your husband in view of his mother's illness, and your registered letters arrived after his death." The information is also given that deceased was buried with his comrade, Pte. Clough, near the spot where he was hit, and on behalf of the column, Lieut. Middleton sends the deepest sympathy, adding "Remember that he died gallantly in action doing his duty to his country."

GR 18/8/17 [Andrew Marshall]

GR 18/8/17 [Andrew Marshall]

ELKIN. — On July 28th, 1917, Arthur Walter, son of William Elkin, of 8, William-street, beloved husband of Isabelle Elkin, of 45, Lynton-road, aged 33 years.

152nd arrived in France on February 28th, 1916. He died of wounds on July 28th, 1917. He is buried at Duhallow A.D.S. Cemetery. Duhallow Advanced Dressing Station, believed to have been named after a southern Irish hunt, was a medical post 1.6 km north of Ypres. The cemetery was begun in July 1917 and in October and November 1918, it was used by the 11th, 36th and 44th Casualty Clearing Stations.

The cemetery contains many graves of the artillery and engineers and 41 men of the 13th Company Labour Corps, killed when a German aircraft dropped a bomb on an ammunition truck in January 1918.

After the Armistice, the cemetery was enlarged when graves were brought into this cemetery from isolated sites and a number of small cemeteries on the battlefields around Ypres. Special memorials commemorate a number of casualties known to have been buried in two of these cemeteries, Malakoff Farm Cemetery, Brielen, and Fusilier Wood Cemetery, Hollebeke, whose graves were destroyed by shellfire.

There are now 1,544 Commonwealth casualties of the First World War buried or commemorated in this cemetery, 231 of the burials unidentified. There are also 57 war graves of other nationalities, mostly German, and one Commonwealth burial of the Second World War, which dates from the Allied withdrawal ahead of the German advance of May 1940.

Arthur Ernest Elley
Australian Field Artillery. 5th Bde
Service No. 7808 - Gunner

Arthur was born in 1887 in Gravesend. His father Alfred was born in 1853 in Northfleet. He worked as an auctioneer's foreman. His wife Elizabeth was a year younger and was from Northfleet. The couple had five children – Clara, born in 1886, Arthur, Ada, born in 1892, Lizzie, born in 1894 and Edith, born in 1898. The family lived at 94 Edwin Street.

Arthur and his wife Daisy lived with their adopted son Cecil Thomas at 54 Trafalgar Street, Annandale, Sydney.

Arthur was a chef at The Ritz in Sydney. Prior to this Arthur was an assistant cook on board the *Ophir* and 3rd cook on the *Zealandia* travelling between London and Sydney over a seven year period from 1906.

Arthur enlisted on August 19th, 1915 in Warwick Farm, New South Wales with the 5th Artillery Brigade. He was 5 feet 2½ inches tall and weighed 112lbs. he was of fair complexion, had blue eyes and brown hair.

In January 1916, Major General A. J. Godley, then commanding the Australian and New Zealand Army Corps, put forward a proposal to use Australian reinforcements then training in Egypt to form two new divisions. The Australian government concurred and the Fifth Division began forming in Egypt in February 1916. The new division included some existing units: the 8th Infantry Brigade, 8th Field Company, 8th Field Ambulance and 10th Army Service Corps Company, but only the 8th Field Company had fought at Gallipoli. The 14th and 15th Infantry Brigades were formed by taking half the personnel of the 1st and 2nd Infantry Brigades.

Arthur was killed in action near Flers on October 16th, 1916. There remains differing accounts of his death whether by sniper or by shrapnel. He is buried in Railway Dugouts Cemetery.

Railway Dugouts Cemetery is 2 km west of Zillebeke village, where the

railway runs on an embankment overlooking a small farmstead, which was known to the troops as Transport Farm. The site of the cemetery was screened by slightly rising ground to the east, and burials began there in April 1915. They continued until the Armistice, especially in 1916 and 1917, when Advanced Dressing Stations were placed in the dugouts and the farm. They were made in small groups, without any definite arrangement and in the summer of 1917 a considerable number were obliterated by shell fire before they could be marked. The names "Railway Dugouts" and "Transport Farm" were both used for the cemetery.

At the time of the Armistice, more than 1,700 graves in the cemetery were known and marked. Other graves were then brought in from the battlefields and small cemeteries in the vicinity, and a number of the known graves destroyed by artillery fire were specially commemorated.

Local Anzac's Sacrifice for the Empire

Mr. and Mrs. Alfred Elley, of Meva Lodge, St. James's-road, Gravesend, have been notified that their youngest son, Gunner Arthur E. Elley, of the Australian Field Artillery, was killed in action on October 17th. He was educated at Wrotham-road Schools, and went out to Australia about 7 years ago. He joined the Australian Forces and saw service in Egypt, after which he was sent to Gallipoli, where he had narrow escapes and was in the withdrawal from the peninsula. Five months ago he came to England and visited his parents, after which he was sent to Belgium, where he met his end. He was 29 years of age, and was married, his wife being in Australia. A friend, Mr. James McLaurin, communicated the fact of his death to his parents, and added:—"After more than a year in the same unit as Tibby, as we all called him I have learned what a stout-hearted sterling fellow he was and know what a terribly sad blow his death will be to you. Tib's death has cast a gloom over us all and our only consolation is that he did not have a lingering death, being killed outright by a large shell bursting just above his head a splinter of the case being driven through the left shoulder blade and penetrating to the heart. All our boys join me in sending you the deepest sympathy in your very sad bereavement." Gunner M. J. McConnell, who signs himself "his sorrowing chum," has also written a fine tribute; "His first and only thoughts were for his own people and his mates. I am sending you what was always his wish for you to have. It was only the night before he was killed that he received your parcel and his sweet little sister's photo, and he was so proud and pleased as he showed them all to me. We would be awake at night and he would read his little mother's letters to me. He was buried the same afternoon and all the battery that could be spared followed him to his grave. We are getting a nice headstone erected over him, and while we are at this position will see that his grave is cared for."

GR 8/11/16 [Andrew Marshall]

ELLEY,—Killed in action, in France, 17th October, Gunner Arthur Elley, Australian Field Artillery, youngest and beloved son of Alfred and Elizabeth Elley, of Meva Lodge, St. James's-road, Gravesend.—Sydney papers, please copy.

GR 8/11/16 [Andrew Marshall]

The cemetery now contains 2,459 Commonwealth burials and commemorations of the First World War. 430 of the burials are unidentified and 261 casualties are represented by special memorials

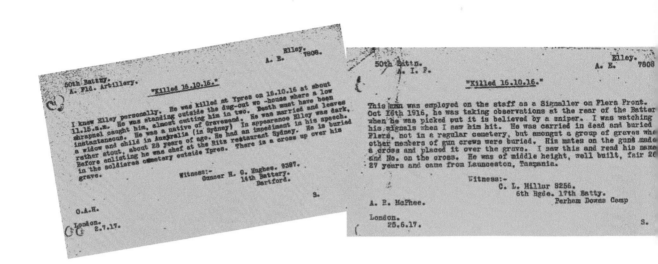

Statements regarding the circumstances of death.

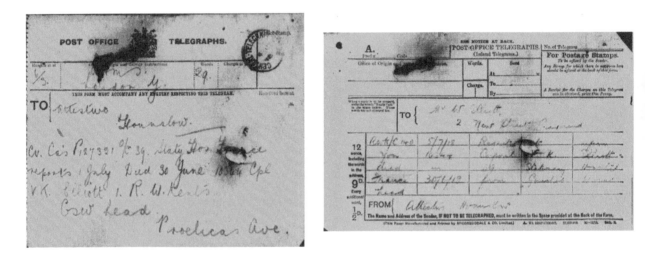

Telegrams notifying of the death, above, and below,
details of personal effects found on the remains.

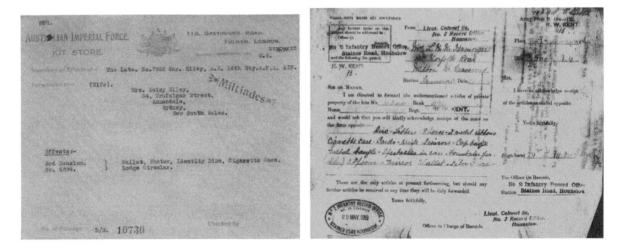

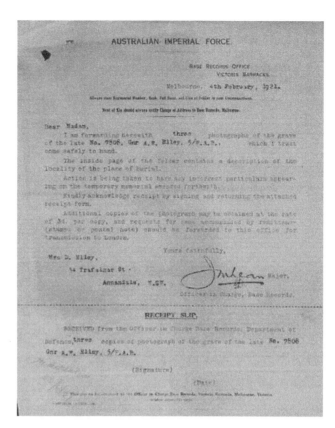

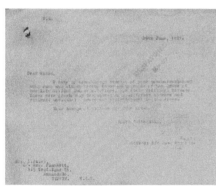

Correspondence in relation
to pension, medals,
location and photograph of
grave.

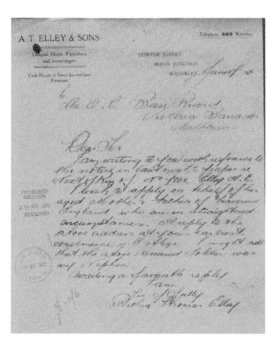

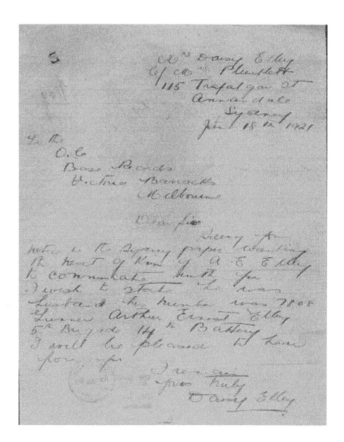

Railway Dugouts
Cemetery, Ypres –
Arthur Elley

Gravesend Cemetery –
Charles Elford

Duhallow A.D.S.
Cemetery,
Ypres – Arthur
Elkin

After the Armistice, the cemetery was enlarged when graves were brought into this cemetery from isolated sites and a number of small cemeteries on the battlefields around Ypres. Special memorials commemorate a number of casualties known to have been buried in two of these cemeteries, Malakoff Farm Cemetery, Brielen, and Fusilier Wood Cemetery, Hollebeke, whose graves were destroyed by shellfire. There are now 1,544 Commonwealth casualties of the First World War buried or commemorated in this cemetery, 231 of the burials unidentified. There are also 57 war graves of other nationalities, mostly German, and one Commonwealth burial of the Second World War, which dates from the Allied withdrawal ahead of the German advance of May 1940.

William Albert Ellingham
Royal Marine Light Infantry

Service No. CH/3830 – Colour Sgt
William was born in Islington on September 13th, 1866. His wife Louisa was born in 1863 in Telegraph Road, Walmer. The couple were married on June 13th, 1892 and had four children – Louisa, born in 1895, Lillian, born in 1896, William, born in 1898, and Leslie, born in 1901. The family home was at 23 Oliver Street, Luton, Chatham at his discharge in 1906 but the family subsequently moved to 55 Raphael Road.

William enlisted in London in August 1885. He re-engaged in February 1897 by which time he had been promoted Corporal, May 1893, Lance-Sergeant, June 1894, and Sergeant, March 1895. He was awarded the RN Long Service and Good Conduct medal on October 8th, 1910.

He was discharged, having completed his term of service, on December 4th,

1906. He had been promoted Colour-Sergeant in October 1905. Eleven days after his discharge, William re-enlisted with the Royal Naval Division, Chatham Battalion.

Following the outbreak of war, a Marine Brigade of four infantry battalions was formed from men of the Marine Light Infantry and Marine Artillery who were not required for service aboard ship. These included both regular active-service Marines as well as those mobilised from the Fleet Reserve. Each battalion was drawn from one of the major naval depot ports - Chatham, Portsmouth, Plymouth, and Deal - and was named accordingly. It was envisaged that this force could be used by the Admiralty to help secure and defend forward ports for naval forces.

Shortly afterwards, it became apparent that there was still a large surplus of mobilised manpower in the Navy itself, and on August 17th a decision was taken by Winston Churchill (then First Lord of the Admiralty) to form eight battalions in two Naval Brigades, which would join with the Marine Brigade to produce a composite Royal Naval Division. While a few petty officers and ratings were transferred from the Navy to provide a cadre, and some officers were provided by the Army, the recruits were almost entirely reservists or men who had volunteered on the outbreak of war. The eight battalions were named after past naval commanders - Drake, Benbow, Hawke, Collingwood, Nelson, Howe, Hood, and Anson - and later numbered 1st to 8th. The division as a whole was not provided with support arms - there were no medical, artillery, or engineer units - and consisted solely of lightly-equipped infantry.

The Marine Brigade began training for overseas service in mid-August, and the naval battalions were assembled in Kent towards the end of the month. Training was slow; most resources were needed for the rapid expansion of the Army, and the ratings had not been issued with field equipment or khaki uniforms before being embarked for overseas service. Rifles were drawn from Royal Navy stockpiles, and only arrived at the end of September; these were older charger-loading Lee Enfields rather than the more modern Short Magazine Lee-Enfields issued to the Army.

Following early defeats in the German invasion of Belgium, and cut off from the rest of the Allies by the German advance, the majority of the Belgian army fell back towards the fortified port of Antwerp during late August 1914. In doing so, Belgian troops were withdrawn from a number of smaller ports along the Belgian coast; the Admiralty was concerned that if these were occupied by Germany, they could provide a base for naval forces to harass ships bringing reinforcements and supplies from England. On August 24th, German cavalry patrols were reported near Ostend, and the decision was taken to land a small naval detachment from the fleet to secure the town.

Further south, the main French and British force was retreating into France, with the German Army driving south-west after them and leaving very few units to guard the lines of communication. Admiralty planners realised that this offered the opportunity of using the Channel ports as a base to attack German supply routes on land, and decided to use the recently formed Royal Marine Brigade as the basis for a landing force. Three battalions (Chatham, Portsmouth and Plymouth) were sent to Flanders; two landed on the early morning of August 27th and the other the following day. They were ordered to hold the town until Belgian troops who had retreated into France could be shipped in; 4,000 men duly arrived on August 30th. The Marines were re-embarked on September 31st, and returned to their ports.

The division also participated in the defence of Antwerp. A German bombardment of the Belgian fortif-ications began on September 28th. The Belgian garrison had no hope of victory without relief and despite the arrival of the Royal Naval Division beginning on October 3rd, the Germans penetrated the outer ring of forts. When the German advance began to compress a corridor from the west of the city along the Dutch border to the coast, through which the Belgians at Antwerp had maintained contact with the rest of unoccupied Belgium, the Belgian field army commenced a withdrawal westwards towards the coast. On October 9th, the remaining garrison surrendered. William was with the Chatham Division at Dunkirk and the defence of Antwerp in 1914.

ELLINGHAM.—On March 4th, 1915, at R.M. Hospital, Walmer, Colour-S William Albert Ellingham, Royal Mar in his 49th year. "A devoted Hus and loving father."—R.I.P.

GR 13/3/15 [Andrew Marshall]

On February 2nd, 1915 he was discharged to Chatham Head Quarters. It was at the Royal Marine Depot in Deal that William died on March 4th, 1916. He is buried in Deal Cemetery.

William Albert Ellingham

Royal Marine Light Infantry

Service No. CH/17902 - Bugler

William was the eldest son of Colour Sergeant William and Louisa Ellingham. He was born on April 28th, 1898 in Eastry.

Bugler Ellingham was killed in action on *H.M.S. Cressy* on September 22nd, 1914.

HMS *Cressy* was a *Cressy*-class armoured cruiser built for the Royal Navy around 1900. Upon completion she was assigned to the China Station. In 1907 she was transferred to the North America and West Indies Station before being placed in reserve in 1909. Re-commissioned at the start of World War I, she played a minor role in the Battle of Heligoland Bight a few weeks after the beginning of the war. *Cressy*, together with two of her sister ships,, was torpedoed and sunk by the German submarine *U-9* on September 22nd, 1914 with the loss of 560 of her crew.

He has no known grave and is commemorated on the Chatham Naval Memorial.

Gravesend Men on Sunken Warships.

WAITING FOR NEWS.

Once more we are brought face to face with the grim realities of the War of the Nations. While the sinking by German submarines of three ships of His Majesty's Navy has plunged Chatham in mourning, Gravesend is tensely awaiting news of what has happened to its several townsmen who were aboard those vessels. By the time these lines are in print probably their fate will be known. Happily we have heard of some Gravesend survivors. A. Bailey, 28, Allington-road, who was aboard the "Cressy," and Reservists named Stevens, of Lower Range-road, and Petts, of Canterbury-road, are reported saved, and the wife of Robert Everett, a Naval Reservist, of Railway-street, Northfleet, who was aboard the "Aboukir," yesterday received a wire from a town in Holland, the one word "Saved," indicating that her husband is interned in that country. Other men of whom at the time of writing news is being awaited are:—

F. J. Dann, Royal Fleet Reserve, of 71, Havelock-road ("Hogue").

W. Lovatt, Park Cottage, Milton-road ("Cressy").

Harry Sams, proprietor of the Public Hall Restaurant ("Aboukir").

George Bennett, of Newman-road, Perry Street ("Cressy").

— Ellingham, 55, Raphael-road ("Cressy").

We understand several other Gravesend and district men are involved.

GR 26/9/14 [Andrew Marshall]

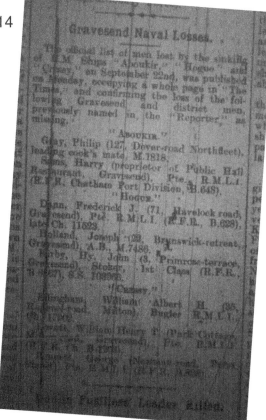

BELENGER, RICHARD STANLEY, Leading Seaman, 239356, H.M.S. Hawke; lost when that ship was torpedoed in the North Sea, 15 Oct. 1914.

ELLINGHAM, WILLIAM ALBERT HENRY, Bugler, R.M.L.I., Ch./17902, H.M.S. Cressy; lost in action in the North Sea, 22 Sept. 1914.

ELLIOT, JAMES, Carpenter's Mate (Pensioner, 3700), 133049, H.M.S. Hogue, lost in action in the North Sea, 22 Sept. 1914.

Father and son;
William Albert Ellingham buried in Deal Cemetery, above, and William Albert Henry Ellingham commemorated on the Chatham Naval Memorial, Panel 7, right and below and the De Ruvigny entry, above right.

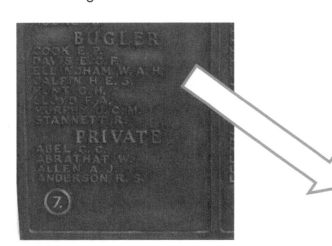

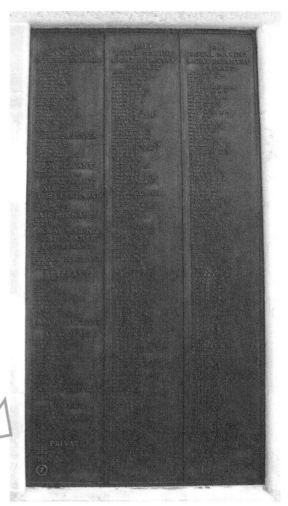

374

Vincent Kenneth Elliott, M.M.
Royal West Kent, 1st Battalion
Service No. L/10344 - Corporal

Vincent was born in 1896 in Gravesend. His father William Joseph was born in 1857 in Plumstead. He was an engine driver at the Gas Works. His wife was Harriett who was born in 1863 and came from Northfleet. The couple were married in 1884 and there were five children in the family – Adeline, born in 1888, Joseph, born in 1890, Stanley, born in 1895, Vincent and Dorothy, born in 1902. The family lived at 83 Raphael Road.

Vincent was a plumber by profession before enlisting with the Royal Engineers on April 4th, 1914 at Gravesend. He was posted 42 days later to the 3rd Battalion. He was 5 foot 5½ inches tall and weighed 115lbs. he had greyish blue eyes, brown hair and had a fresh complexion. He was described, in his attestation papers, *as being of smart appearance and intelligent looking, suitable for the aim of the service in which he desires to be enlisted.*

He arrived in France on December 12th, 1914 and was wounded in the left leg on January 26th, 1915. He was in Gravesend convalescing until early September. He returned to France on September 8th. He was awarded 10 days Field Punishment No. 2 on April 26th, 1916 for a misdemeanour not recorded on his records. Vincent was awarded the Military Medal for bravery in the field on August 22nd, 1916.

On October 9th, 1916 he was badly wounded in the right ankle, the result of a shell explosion. He was back in Gravesend from the 14th until March 15th, 1917. On the 14th, 1916 he was transferred to the 6th Battalion.

He was back to the 3rd Battalion in January 1917 and finally transferred to the 1st Battalion on March 23rd. he was appointed Lance Corporal on October 6th and Corporal on the 27th. The previous day he was wounded in the left arm, gunshot wound.

Corporal Elliott was seriously wounded in action on June 30th, 1918. He died from his wounds at 39th Stationary Hospital at Aire the following day. He is buried in Aire Communal Cemetery. Aire is 14 kms south-south-east of St. Omer. From March 1915 to February 1918, Aire was a busy but peaceful centre used by Commonwealth forces as corps headquarters. The Highland Casualty Clearing Station was based there as was the 39th Stationary Hospital (from May 1917) and other medical units. The cemetery now contains 894 Commonwealth burials of the First World War. There are also 21 Second War burials, mostly dating from the withdrawal to Dunkirk in May 1940.

83 Raphael Road, above – Vincent Elliott and 4 Northcote Road, below – Albert and Henry Elston.

Albert and ***Henry Elston*** whose biographies now follow were brothers.

Albert Edward Elston
Royal West Kent Regiment, 6th Bn
Service No. 12155

Albert was born in Colchester in 1891. His father Samuel came from Crediton, Devonshire and was born in 1854. He was a blacksmith and farrier and worked for a company manufacturing carriages. His wife Julia was born in 1857 and came from Southwold, Suffolk. The couple had nine children – Charlotte, born in 1878, Thomas, born in 1880, William, born in 1882, Clara, born in 1885, Alice, born in 1887, Henry, born in 1889, Albert, Ernest, born in 1893 and Florence, born in 1897. The family lived at 4 Garden Road before moving to 4 Northcote Road.

Albert was a milkman initially before securing employment as an assistant in a print works before enlisting on December 12th, 1915 being mobilised with the 3rd Battalion on February 10th, 1916. He was 5 feet 11 inches tall and weighed 159lbs.

He was posted to the 6th Battalion on September 12th. On the 19th of January they began a period of training in Open Warfare at Busnes, then moved back into the front line at Loos on the 12th of February 1916. In June they moved to Flesselles and carried out a training exercise. They moved to Baizieux on the 30th June and went into the reserve at Hencourt and Millencourt by mid-morning on July 1st. They relieved the 8th Division at Ovillers-la-Boisselle that night and attacked at 3.15 the following morning with mixed success. On the 7th they attacked again and despite suffering heavy casualties in the area of Mash Valley, they succeeded in capturing and holding the first and second lines close to Ovillers. They were withdrawn to Contay on July 9th. They were in action in The Battle of Pozieres on August 3rd with a successful attack capturing 4th Avenue Trench and were engaged in heavy fighting until they were withdrawn on the 9th.

Albert was posted to the 6th as part of the reinforcements.

He was wounded in action on October 7th, 1916 and died of these wounds on the 12th. He is buried in Heilly Station Cemetery, Mericourt-L'Abbe.

Mericourt-l'Abbe is 19 kms north-east of Amiens and 10 kms south-west of Albert.

The 36th Casualty Clearing Station was at Heilly from April 1916. It was joined in May by the 38th, and in July by the 2/2nd London, but these hospitals had all moved on by early June 1917.

The cemetery was begun in May 1916 and was used by the three medical units until April 1917. From March to May 1918, it was used by Australian units and in the early autumn for further hospital burials when the 20th Casualty Clearing Station was there briefly in August and September 1918. The last burial was made in May 1919.

There are now 2,890 Commonwealth servicemen of the First World War buried or commemorated in this cemetery. Only 12 of the burials are unidentified and special memorials are erected to 21 casualties whose graves in the cemetery could not be exactly located. The cemetery also contains 83 German graves.

The burials in this cemetery were carried out under extreme pressure and many of the graves are either too close together to be marked individually, or they contain multiple burials. Some headstones carry as many as three sets of casualty details,

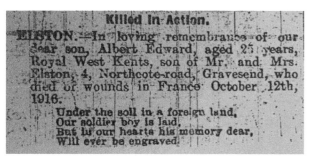

GR 9/12/16 [Andrew Marshall]

and in these cases, regimental badges have had to be omitted. Instead, these badges, 117 in all, have been carved on a cloister wall on the north side of the cemetery.

> The above is a photograph of Pte. A. E. Elston, Royal West Kent Regiment, son of Mr. and Mrs. Elston, 4, Northcote-road, Gravesend, who died of wounds in France on October 12th. The deceased, who was employed at the Amalgamated Press before enlisting, only sailed for France on the 13th September. He lost one brother at Gheluvelt on October, 1914, and has another at present in France, serving in the R.H.A., and a third brother in the A.S.C. Private Elston was a member of the Gravesend 1st Police Reserve.

GR 9/12/16 [Andrew Marshall]

Henry Charles Elston
Worcestershire Regiment, 2nd Bn
Service No. 11344 - Private

Henry was born in Maidstone in 1889, the younger brother of Albert Elston.

He enlisted with the Worcestershire Regiment in 1906 and was a career soldier.

2nd Battalion, Worcestershire Regiment were based at Aldershot with 5th Brigade, 2nd Division when war broke out in August 1914. They proceeded to France with the BEF, landing at Boulogne on August 14th, 1914.

They were in action in The Battle of Mons and the subsequent retreat, The Battle of the Marne, The Battle of the Aisne, the Actions on the Aisne heights and First Battle of Ypres.

The crisis of the Battle of Ypres hinged around the village of Gheluvelt. Lying on a forward spur of the low ridge that covers the town of Ypres, Gheluvelt was the last point retained in British hands from which the enemy's line could be dominated.

By noon on October 31st, 1914, the Queens, the Royal Scots Fusiliers, the Welsh and the Kings Royal Rifles had been overwhelmed, while on the right the South Wales Borderers had been rolled back.

Gheluvelt had been lost and a serious gap had been made in the line. So serious was the situation that unless the gap could be closed, a breakthrough could not be avoided. Indeed orders had already been prepared for artillery to move back in preparation for a general retreat. On the evening of October 30th the Second Battalion The Worcestershire Regiment remained uncommitted, all other units having been sent to reinforce the line. Located in Polygon Wood, the Battalion, was commanded by Major E. B. Hankey and the Adjutant was Captain B. C. Senhouse-Clarke. At 13.00 hours on October 31st, the Battalion received an order to attack and retake Gheluvelt.

Captain A. F. Thorne of the Grenadier Guards was to act as a guide. From Polygon Wood, the chateau which dominated the village could not be seen but the nearby church tower rising amidst the smoke was visible. All around were wounded and stragglers coming to the rear and batteries could be seen limbering up and moving back.

The Worcestershires alone were moving towards the enemy. The ridge was littered with dead and wounded, and along the crest, German shells were falling fast. Hankey decided that the only way to cross this dangerous area was at the double.

As the leading men reached the ridge, they came in view of the German guns whose high explosive shells were quickly directed on the charging soldiers. Over 100 of the Battalion were killed or wounded but the rest pushed on and, increasing their speed as they came to the downward slope in sight of Gheluvelt, made the final charge through hedges and on to the Chateau grounds. Here they met the remnants of the South Wales Bord-

erers who had made a heroic stand. The meeting was unexpected, for the Worcestershires had believed no soldiers were left. The 2nd Worcestershires had gone into this action with about 370 men of whom 187 were killed or wounded. Gheluvelt had been saved and the line restored. It is rare that the action of one unit can exert such a profound influence as did this now famous counter attack.

As a result of the capture of Gheluvelt against terrific odds, and the consequent closing of the gap in the British Lines, Ypres was held and the Channel Ports were saved.

Daybreak of October 31st was calm and clear. The 2nd Worcestershire, in their reserve position west of the Polygon Wood, were roused early by the crash of gun-fire. The troops turned out, breakfasts were cooked and eaten and weapons were cleaned and inspected. Then for several hours the companies lay idle about their billets, listening to the ever-increasing bombardment and watching the German shrapnel bursting in black puffs of smoke above the tree-tops. The 2nd Worcestershire were almost the last available reserve of the British defence. Nearly every other unit had been drawn into the battle-line or had been broken beyond recovery; and to an onlooker that last reserve would not have seemed very formidable. The Battalion could muster not more than five hundred men. Ten days of battle had left all ranks haggard, unshaven and unwashed: their uniforms had been soaked in the mud of the Langemarck trenches and torn by the brambles of Polygon Wood: many had lost their puttees or their caps. But their weapons were clean and in good order, they had plenty of ammunition, and three months of war had given them confidence in their fighting power. The short period in reserve had allowed them sleep and food. That crowd of ragged soldiers was still a fighting battalion, officers and men bound together by that proud and willing discipline which is the soul of the Regiment.

Hour by hour the thunder of the guns grew more intense. Stragglers and wounded from beyond the wood brought news that a great German attack was in progress. The enemy's infantry were coming on in overwhelming numbers against the remnants of the five British battalions, together mustering barely a thousand men, which were holding the trenches about the Menin Road.

Before midday weight of numbers had told. The Queen's and the Royal Scots Fusiliers had fought to the last, the Welsh and the K.R.R.C. had been overwhelmed, the right flank of the South Wales Borderers had been rolled back. Gheluvelt had been lost, and a great gap had been broken in the British line. Unless that gap could be closed the British army was doomed to disaster.

So serious was the situation caused by the loss of Gheluvelt that orders were issued for the British artillery to move back, in preparation for a general retreat, At the same time it was decided that a counter-attack against the lost position should be made by the 2nd Worcestershire. Brigadier-General C. FitzClarence, V.C. (*Commanding the 1st (Guards) Brigade. Technically the 2nd Worcestershire, belonging to the 2nd Division, were not under his orders. General Lomax, commanding the 1st Division, had directed General FitzClarence to order the Worcestershire into the fight*) was in command of the front about the Menin Road. Soon after midday he sent for an officer of the 2nd Worcestershire to take orders. Major Hankey sent his Adjutant, Captain B. C. Senhouse Clarke.

Twenty minutes later Captain Senhouse Clarke returned, bringing word that the Battalion would probably be wanted for a counter-attack, and that meanwhile one company was to be detached to prevent the enemy from advancing up the Menin Road. "A" Company was detailed for the latter duty. Led by Captain P. S. G. Wainman, the company advanced at 12.45 p.m. (*the other officers of " A " Coy. were Lieut. E. C. R. Hudson and 2/Lieut. G. A. Sheppard*) to a position on the embankment of the light railway northwest of Gheluvelt. The company held the embankment during the following two hours, firing rapidly at such of the enemy as attempted to advance beyond the houses.

About 1 p.m., Major Hankey was summoned by General FitzClarence, and was given definite orders. The 2nd Worcestershire were to make a counter-attack to regain the lost British positions around Gheluvelt. General FitzClarence pointed out the Church in Gheluvelt as a landmark for the advance, explained that the situation was desperate and that speed was essential, and ordered his Staff Captain, Captain A. F. Thorne of the Grenadier Guards, to guide the Battalion on its way.

At 1.45 p.m. Major Hankey sent off the Battalion scouts, under Lieutenant E. A. Haskett-Smith, to cut any wire fences across the line of advance. Extra ammunition was issued, and all kit was lightened as much as possible, packs being left behind. Then bayonets were fixed, and at 2 p.m. the Battalion moved off in file, led by Major Hankey and Captain Thorne, along under cover of the trees to the south-west corner of Polygon Wood (*Afterwards known as "Black Watch Corner"*).

From that corner of the wood the ground to the south-eastward is clear and open, falling to the little valley of the Reutelbeek and rising again to the bare ridge above Polderhoek. That ridge hid from view the Chateau of Gheluvelt, and the exact situation there was unknown; but further to the right could be seen the Church tower rising amid the smoke of the burning village.

The open ground was dotted with wounded and stragglers coming back from the front. In every direction German shells were bursting. British batteries could be seen limbering up and moving to the rear. Everywhere there were signs of retreat. The Worcestershire alone were moving towards the enemy. But the three companies tramped grimly forward, down into the valley of the Reutelbeek. Beyond a little wood the Battalion deployed, "C" and "D" Companies in front line, with "B" Company in second line behind - about 370 all told (Including eight officers - Major E. B. Hankey (commanding), Captain B. C. Senhouse Clarke (Adjutant), Captain E. L. Bowring, Captain H. C. Grimley, 2/Lieut. F. C. F. Biscoe ("C" Coy.), Captain R. J. Ford ("D" Coy.), Captain E. G. Williams ("B" Coy.) and 2/Lieut. C. H. Ralston. Lieut. E. A. Haskett-Smith, the Battalion Scout Officer, had preceded the three companies. In front of them rose the bare slope of the Polderhoek Ridge. The ridge was littered with dead and wounded, and along its crest the enemy's shells were bursting in rapid succession. Major Hankey decided that the only way of crossing that deadly stretch of ground was by one long rush. The companies extended into line and advanced. The ground underfoot was rank grass or rough stubble. The two leading companies broke into a steady double and swept forward across the open, the officers leading on in front, and behind them their men with fixed bayonets in one long irregular line. As they reached the crest, the rushing wave of bayonets was sighted by the hostile artillery beyond. A storm of shells burst along the ridge. Shrapnel bullets rained down and high-explosive shells crashed into the charging line. Men fell at every pace: over a hundred of the Battalion were killed or wounded: the rest dashed on. The speed of the rush increased as on the downward slope the troops came in sight of Gheluvelt Chateau close in front. The platoons scrambled across the light railway, through some hedges and wire fences, and then in the grounds of the Chateau they closed with the enemy.

The enemy were ill-prepared to meet the charge. The German infantry were crowded in disorder among the trees of the park, their attention divided between exploring the out-houses and surrounding the remnant of the British defenders; for the musketry of the defence still swept the lawn in front of the Chateau. The enemy's disorder was increased by a sharp and accurate fire of shrapnel from British batteries behind Polygon Wood.

The Germans were young troops of newly-formed units (The 244th and 245th Reserve Regiments and the 16th Bavarian Reserve Regiment). Probably they had lost their best leaders earlier in the day, for they made no great attempt to stand their ground and face the counter-attack. They gave way at once before the onslaught of the British battalion and crowded back out of the grounds of the Chateau into the hedgerows beyond. Shooting and stabbing, "C" Company of the Worcestershire charged across the lawn and came up into line with the gallant remnant of the South Wales Borderers.

The South Wales Borderers had made a wonderful stand. All day they had held their ground at the Chateau and they were still stubbornly fighting although almost surrounded by the enemy. Their resistance had delayed and diverted the German advance, and the success of the counter-attack was largely due to their brave defence. The meeting of the two battalions was unexpected. The Worcestershires had not known that any of the South Wales Borderers were still holding out. Major Hankey went over to their commander and found him to be Colonel H. E. Burleigh Leach, an old friend. With him was their second-in-command Major A. J. Reddie, brother of Major J. M. Reddie of the Worcestershire. "My God, fancy meeting you here," said Major Hankey, and Colonel Burleigh Leach replied quietly "Thank God you have come."

The routed enemy were hunted out of the hedges (Among those specially distinguished for gallantry in that fighting were Sergts. G. Ellis and A. E. Kemp : both received the D.C.M.) and across the open fields beyond the Chateau. "C" and "D" Companies of the Worcestershire took up position in the sunken road, which runs past the grounds. "B" Company was brought up and prolonged the line to the right.

But the village of Gheluvelt, on the slope above the right flank, was still in the enemy's hands. Most of the German troops in the village seem to have been drawn northwards by the fighting around the Chateau; but a certain number of Saxons of the 242nd Regiment had remained in the village, whence they opened a fire which took the sunken road in enfilade. To silence that fire Major Hankey sent fighting patrols from the front line into the village. Those patrols drove back the German snipers and took some prisoners (In that fighting Sergt. P. Sutton showed great bravery. Attacking a German machine-gun single-handed he captured one of its team and put the gun out of action.

Sergt. Sutton was subsequently awarded the D.C.M. During that patrol fighting in the village, Lieut. Haskett-Smith was severely wounded and Sergt. G. F. Poole was killed): but it became clear that the position in the sunken road would be unsafe until the village was secured. Accordingly Major Hankey sent orders to Captain Wainman that "A" Company were to advance from their defensive position and occupy the village. Captain Wainman led forward his company and, after some sharp fighting among burning buildings and bursting shells, occupied a new line with his left flank in touch with the right of the position in the sunken road and his right flank in the village, holding the church and churchyard. Thence he sent forward patrols to clear the village. Those patrols, led by a tall young subaltern, 2nd Lieutenant G. A. Sheppard,

Gheluvelt – the Memorials.

worked forward from house to house until they reached the cross-roads at the eastern end of Gheluvelt. It was not possible permanently to occupy the centre of the village, for it was being bombarded by both the German and the British artillery. On all sides houses were burning, roofs falling and walls collapsing. The stubborn Saxons still held some small posts in the scattered houses on the south-eastern outskirts. Nevertheless the enemy's main force had been driven out, and the peril of a collapse of the British defence about the Menin Road had been averted.

The German forces made no further effort that day to retake Gheluvelt. The reason for the enemy's inaction is not clear. It is possible that the very boldness of the counter-attack may have given the impression that the Battalion was but the first wave of a stronger force, and possibly the enemy may have stood on the defensive to meet that imagined attack.

Furthermore the British artillery maintained throughout the afternoon a heavy fire on the low ground east of Gheluvelt, a fire which may have disorganised the enemy and which probably hampered the transmission of information and orders: indeed the vagueness of most German accounts of the fighting at Gheluvelt suggests that the position in the village was not ascertained. In such circumstances, with the situation obscure, young troops discouraged and hostile shellfire unsubdued, it is no easy matter to organise a fresh attack. Perhaps some commander of importance was disabled or some vital line of communication severed. Whatever the reason, the result was that the enemy's action during the rest of the day was limited to a violent bombardment, which fortunately caused but little loss. The 2nd Worcestershire held firm on the ground they had won, 'while behind them General FitzClarence reorganised his troops and made preparations for further resistance.

Evening came on. From his position in the village Captain Wainman sent out patrols to the right to gain touch with any troops who might be there. But no communication with any other unit could be established, nor did any other British troops come forward to the position held by the Battalion.

About 6 p.m. came fresh orders from General FitzClarence. The General had decided to withdraw his defensive line from the forward slope of the ridge at Gheluvelt to a new position further back at Veldhoek where the trenches would be sheltered from direct observation of the German artillery.

The order was sent along the line. Arrangements were made in conjunction with the South Wales Borderers and the retirement was begun. One by one, at intervals of ten minutes, the companies withdrew from their positions. In the darkness they assembled under cover and then tramped back along the Menin Road to Veldhoek. The withdrawal was not realised by the enemy, and was carried out without interference, save for the intermittent bombardment which continued throughout that night (The evacuation of Gheluvelt was not discovered by the enemy until dawn next morning, November 1st). Then the village and the Chateau were occupied by the 242nd Reserve Regiment, who drove out a few remaining British stragglers). As the last company of the 2nd Worcestershire marched back out of the village, several of the houses were still burning, and the darkness was torn at intervals by the blaze of bursting shells. Four long years were to pass before the bayonets of the Regiment were again to sweep through the ruins of Gheluvelt.

At Veklhoek the Battalion halted in the darkness, deployed facing east and began to entrench the new position. Presently troops of the 1st Brigade relieved the Worcestershire, and the Battalion drew back into reserve. Officers and men lay down where they halted, and slept the sleep of exhaustion.

The day's fighting had cost the 2nd Worcestershire a third of the Battalion's remaining strength, for 187 of all ranks (including three officers wounded—Captain E. G. Williams, Lieut. E. C. R. Hudson, Lieut. E. A. Haskett-Smith.) had been killed or wounded; but their achievement had been worthy of that sacrifice. Their counter-attack had thrown back the enemy at a moment, which the British Commander-in-Chief afterwards called "the worst half-hour of my life." In all probability that counter-attack had saved Ypres from capture and the British army from defeat. It had been a desperate measure to retrieve a desperate situation; and no one could have foretold its extraordinary success in paralysing the German advance.

Gravesend Soldier Killed.

PTE. H. C. ELSTON.

The death at the front is announced of Pte. Henry Charles Elston, of the 2nd Battalion Worcestershire Regiment. He was reported missing at the end of October, but the War Office now notify his death as taking place on October 31st. He was 26 years of age, and his home was at 4 Northcote-road, Gravesend, where he resided with his parents. Deceased had been very well-known at Gravesend, where he had always resided until he joined the army some years ago. He served in India for five years, and came home to England about a year before the outbreak of war. He took part with his regiment in the great retreat from Mons, and also in the battles of the Marne and Aisne. At the end of October he was reported missing at Ghuleveldt; the last time he wrote home was on the 19th October. Deceased has two brother serving in the army. One is at the front at the present time with the R.H.A., and the other has been invalided home after being there seven months with the 3rd Division Ammunition Column, A.S.C.

GR 22/5/15 [Andre Marshall]

That success was not achieved by the 2nd Worcestershire alone. Success would hardly have been possible but for the brave defence of the South Wales Borderers and the supporting fire of the artillery. Nevertheless it stands to the perpetual credit of the Regiment that at the darkest hour of that great battle, when all others around them were in retreat, our war-worn officers and men went forward unflinching to meet unknown odds, and by their devotion saved the day.Harry was killed in action on October 31st, 1914. He has no known grave and is commemorated on the Menin Gate, Ypres.

Thomas Samuel Elston
Royal Horse Artillery,
Q Battery, 16th Brigade
Service No. 1778 - Gunner

Thomas was born in 1880 in Canterbury, the eldest son of Samuel and Julia Elston and the older brother of Albert and Henry.

Thomas was a career soldier, enlisting with the Royal Horse Artillery in 1898. He had left the army prior to the Great War and was employed as a floor hand in a print works. He re-enlisted with the Royal Horse Artillery on the declaration of war.

The RHA was responsible for light, mobile guns that provided firepower in support of the cavalry. It was the senior arm of the artillery, but the one that developed and grew least during the Great War. In 1914 the establishment of the RHA was one battery to each brigade of cavalry. A battery had six 13-pounder field guns and included 5 officers and 200 men. Motive power was supplied by the battery's 228 horses.

Thomas was killed in action on April 4th, 1918. He has no known grave and is commemorated on the Pozieres Memorial.

Gunner T. S. Elston (Gravesend),
Royal Horse Artillery.
KILLED IN ACTION.

Gunner Thomas Samuel Elston, R.H.A., reported killed in action on the 4th inst. (as announced in the "Kent Messenger" last week), was the third son of Mr. and Mrs. S. Elston, of 4, Northcote Road, Gravesend, to make the great sacrifice in France. Definite confirmation of his death is, unfortunately, now forthcoming, in the shape of a letter received by his parents from the Major of his battery, who writes: "It is my painful duty to have to inform you that your son was killed upon the 'Field of Honour' on April 4th. His death, I am glad to be able to say, was painless. You will also be pleased to know that your son had been doing splendid work during the recent heavy fighting. He is a great loss to the battery. He lost his life in helping others. He had been posted as sentry in a rather exposed spot, where shells were falling. I sent to have him called in, and on his way he was sent out to call some other men under cover. He went back and did so, but before he could get under cover, the shell landed by him and he was killed instantaneously. We buried him on the spot and turfed his grave and erected a little cross. You have the profound sympathy of the whole battery in your sad loss." Gunner Elston, who was in his 39th year, had fought in France from the commencement.

GM 27/4/18 [AndrewMarshall]

Harry Elvidge
A.I.F., 1st Battalion
Service No. 3311

Harry was born in Gravesend in 1894, the son of Harry and Elizabeth Elvidge of 41 Victoria Road, Perry Street. Harry was born in Gravesend in 1871 and was a carpenter. Elizabeth was also born in 1871 and came from Grays. They had just the two children – Harry and Kate Ethel, born in 1896. The two children attended Wrotham Road Board School.

Harry was a motor and cycle repairer. He emigrated to Australia in 1915

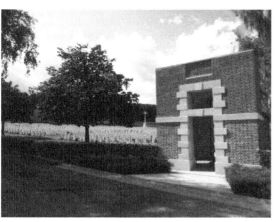

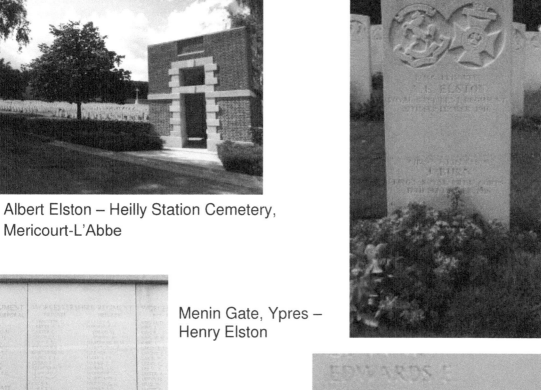

Albert Elston – Heilly Station Cemetery,
Mericourt-L'Abbe

Menin Gate, Ypres –
Henry Elston

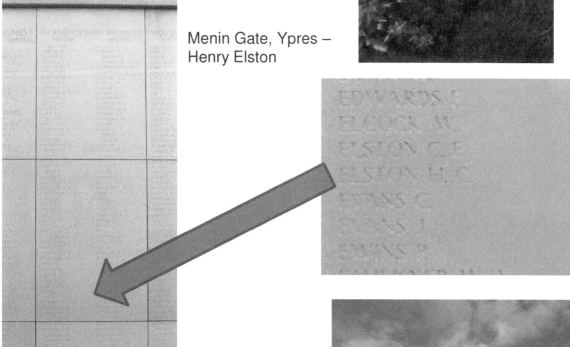

Thomas Elston
– Pozieres
Memorial.

working his passage as a ship steward. He enlisted [11th Reinforcements] on July 15th, 1915. He was 5 feet 7 inches tall and weighed 132lbs. he had fair hair, blue eyes and had a fair complexion. He arrived at Tel-el-Kebir on February 16th, 1916 and embarked from Alexandria on board the *Ivernia* on March 22nd, arriving in Marseilles six days later.

On June 6th he was absent from his billet at stand to arms between 9pm and 9.30pm; he was awarded a sentence of seven days confinement to Barracks.

The 1st Battalion was the first infantry unit recruited for the AIF in New South Wales during the First World War.

The battalion was raised within a fortnight of the declaration of war in August 1914 and embarked just two months later. After a brief stop in Albany, Western Australia, the Battalion proceeded to Egypt, arriving on December 2nd. The battalion took part in the Anzac landing on April 25th, 1915 as part of the second and third waves, and served there until the evacuation in December. Its most notable engagement at Gallipoli was the battle of Lone Pine in August. Two members of the battalion, Captain A. J. Shout and Lieutenant L.M. Keysor were awarded Victoria Crosses for their valour at Lone Pine, Captain Shout posthumously.

After the withdrawal from Gallipoli in December 1915, the battalion returned to Egypt. In March 1916, it sailed for France and the Western Front. From then until 1918 the battalion took part in operations against the German Army, principally in the Somme Valley in France and around Ypres in Belgium.

The Battle of the Somme commenced on July 1st, 1916. British attacks on the Somme had brought the front line close to the village of Pozières. There, in darkness on July 23rd, the 1st Australian Division made an assault supported by heavy artillery fire. The ruined village was taken in hard and intense fighting and enemy counter-attacks were repelled. The Germans responded by pounding the area with their artillery. The capture of Pozières was a significant achievement, but within five days the 1st Division had lost 5,000 men.

The 1st Division was replaced by the 2nd, whose first attack met with disastrous losses. In further fighting the division captured some ground but suffered more casualties – overall, almost 7,000 in twelve days. The 4th Division was the next to take part, pressing its attacks towards the adjoining Mouquet Farm. With this move, the Australians were trying to threaten the enemy positions at Thiepval, where the British had been stuck for weeks. However, in attacking on a narrow front they became increasingly exposed to murderous shell-fire and yet more counter-attacks. The three Australian divisions took their turn at Pozières and all suffered heavily. Then, with their numbers built up to only two-thirds strength, each was sent into the inferno for a second tour. Over a period of 42 days the Australians made 19 attacks, 16 of them at night; as a consequence, the casualties finally totalled a staggering 23,000 men, of whom 6,800 were killed.

For men thrown into the fighting at Pozières the experience was simply hell. The battlefield had become the focus of artillery fire from both sides. Attacks went in, some ground was taken, and then the enemy would counter-attack. Throughout this action the fighting was wild, and all the time the shelling tore up the ground, folded the trenches in, and blew away any protection.

Australian infantrymen who were once taught that "the bullet and bayonet are

Gravesend Cemetery –

DEAREST LOVED

KILLED IN ACTION AT POZIERES
JULY 22 – 25. 1916. AGED 22

[Photograph – Andy White]

Harry Elvidge

Villers-Bretonneux; war damage dating to the Second World War.

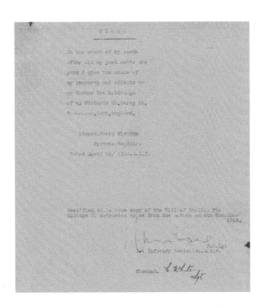

Harry's last will and testament.

the deciding factors in fighting" saw at Pozières that the destructive power of artillery now dominated the battlefield. Shrapnel tore men to pieces, high explosive blew them to bits and destroyed trenches, smoke covered the turned-up, stinking ground. Added to this were gas shells. It was the worst artillery shelling that the Australians experienced in the entire war.

Finally, in early September the Australian divisions were taken out of the main battle and sent back to Flanders to recover and rebuild their strength. During this time the New Zealanders went into action on the Somme, fighting an important battle near Flers, a few kilometres from Pozières, an action in which tanks were used in combat for the first time.

Harry was killed in action between July 22nd and 25th, 1916. He was originally buried in Pozières but his grave was subsequently lost. He has, therefore now, no known grave and is commemorated on the Villers-Bretonneux Memorial.

Villers-Bretonneux is 16 km east of Amiens. Villers-Bretonneux became famous in 1918, when the German advance on Amiens ended in the capture of the village by their tanks and infantry on April 23rd. On the following day, the 4th and 5th Australian Divisions, with units of the 8th and 18th Divisions, recaptured the whole of the village and on August 8th, 1918, the 2nd and 5th Australian Divisions advanced from its eastern outskirts in the Battle of Amiens.

We regret to announce the death of Pte. Harry Elvidge, of 41, Victoria-road, Perry Street, son of Mr. and Mrs. H. Elvidge, a portrait of whom is given above. He was born in February, 1894, and from fourteen to seventeen was telegraph messenger, after which he emigrated to Australia. He joined the Australian Forces in Sydney 12 months ago, and went to Egypt with the Australian Expeditionary Force in December last. From there he was sent to France. Pte. A. S. Barclay, who is in Frensham Hill Hospital, Farnham, Surrey, in a letter to Mrs. Elvidge on the 4th August, says:—"I am writing to express my sympathy in your bereavement. I was with your son when he was killed, and I got a couple of mates to carry him away, and give him as good a funeral as was possible. I myself am now in hospital with wounds in the knee." In a subsequent letter, Pte. Barclay says that Pte. Elvidge was killed on July 27th at Pozières. "I have forwarded to you his only personal possession—his birth certificate." This shows that deceased was born at 2, Salisbury-road, Gravesend, and that his father was an electrician in the employ of the Electric Light Company.

Killed in Action.

ELVIDGE.—Killed in action at Poizières, July 27th, 1916, Pte. Harry Elvidge, 1st Infantry Brigade, Australian Imperial Forces, dearly-loved only son of the late Harry and Elizabeth Elvidge; aged 22.

GR 26/8/16 [Andrew Marshall]

GR 2/9/16 [Andrew Marshall]

388

The memorial is the Australian National Memorial erected to commemorate all Australian soldiers who fought in France and Belgium during the First World War, to their dead, and especially to name those whose graves are not known. The Australian servicemen died in the battlefields of the Somme, Arras, the German advance of 1918 and the Advance to Victory. The memorial stands within Villers-Bretonneux Military Cemetery, which was made after the Armistice when graves were brought in from other burial grounds in the area. There are 10,762 Australian servicemen officially commemorated by this memorial.

John Archibald Evans

Royal Naval Reserve, Lieutenant

John was born in Gravesend in 1885, the son of Nicholas and Charlotte Evans. Nicholas was from Glamorgan and was born in 1861. Charlotte was also from Glamorgan being born in 1862. Nicholas was a Customs' Officer with the Coastguard. There were six children in the family – John, born in 1885, Elizabeth, born in 1886, Sidney, born in 1889, Herbert, born in 1892, Annete, born in 1894 and Kathleen, born in 1897.

John married Elizabeth Smith at St. Bartholomew's Church, Bethnal Green on September 22nd, 1915. At the time he was living at Shipwell Road. He was, by then, a Lieutenant in the Royal Naval Reserve. John was a sea faring man having acquired his Second Mate qualification on January 15th, 1907, his First Mate Certificate on February 26th, 1911 and his Certificate of Competency as Master on October 18th, 1912.

John served on board *H.M. Yacht Conqueror II.* Built by Russell & Co. Port Glasgow and launched on Feb-

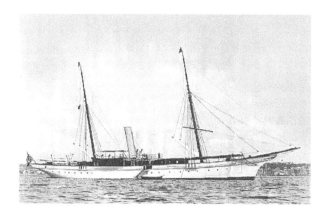

ruary 20th, 1889 as the *Lady Aline* she was renamed *Conqueror II* in 1913. She was 188 feet in length with a breadth of 24½ feet. Prior to being requisitioned in 1915 she was bought by the Duke of Manchester in 1913 from F.W. Vanderbilt.

On September 26th, 1916 Conqueror was sunk by a German submarine off Fair Island. The armed Trawler *Sarah Alice* was in company with the *Conqueror* off the Shetlands searching for what was reported as an unidentified steamer when a submarine fired three torpedoes. The first struck the *Sarah Alice*, the second passed *Conquerer*'s the third struck the *Conqueror* in the magazine forward of the bridge. There were no survivors from *Sarah Alice*. The next morning 17 officers and men were rescued from Carley rafts.

Locals reported the presence of two submarines, apparently U52 and U48 in coordinated attacks, the survivors of *Conqueror* reported that the Germans surfaced and asked for Admiralty papers and when told they were thrown overboard were, not surprisingly, quite angry.

At night the submarines fired white flares to aid the lifeboats but there was no immediate British response. The survivors took it that the very lights were to draw other victims, with one voice saying it was possibly for rescue. *U52* was attempting to signal a fishing trawler it had observed at a distance to come rescue survivors

[Courtesy Mike Young, B.S.C., North East Medals]

U 52's war diary describes the sinkings somewhat differently. The first torpedo was actually fired at *Conquerer II*, missing but striking *Sarah Alice* instead. The U-boat's commanding officer had noticed this overlap before firing. A second torpedo then hit and sank *Conquerer II*. A third torpedo, fired about 19 minutes after the first torpedo was launched, accounted for the steamer *St. Gothard*.

There's no mention of a second submarine by *U 52*. *U 52's* commander at the time, Hans Walther, was awarded the Pour le Mérite in early 1917.

John was among the casualties of the *Conqueror*. He has no known grave and is commemorated on the Portsmouth Naval Memorial.

A **_G H Eves_** is listed on the Windmill Hill Memorial but no such name appears in the service records. **_George Henry Eve_** is listed in Army Records and no doubt is the soldier commemorated, albeit with an incorrect spelling of the surname.

George Henry Eve
Middlesex Regiment, 1st Battalion
Service No. 24480

Harry was born in Gravesend in 1885 the son of George and Charlotte Eve of 5 Bridge House, Higham. Although christened George after his father, the family opted for Harry to distinguish him from his father. George was born in 1864 in Gravesend. He was a plate layer working on the railway. Charlotte was born in 1866 in Shorne. The couple married in 1884 and there were eight children in the family – Harry, Mabel, born 1888, Bertie, born in 1891, Albert, born in 1893, Thomas, born in 1885, Arthur, born in 1898, Archibald, born in 1900 and Emily in 1905. The family home was at 8 Minerva Cottage, Shorne.

George became a bricklayer's apprentice on leaving school. He subsequently found employment as a factory hand at the Uralite Works, Higham and was a boarder with Frederick and Susan Stirling in Shorne. Frederick was also a plate layer with the railway as was Harry's father, George.

The Uralite Works opened at the turn of the century making pipes. The factory had its own railway siding from the branch line to Grain and Allhallows. It had its own station, Uralte Halt, which opened in 1906. It was a public station but was primarily intended to be used by the workforce.

Although long since closed most of the original buildings are still standing. Several are in a poor condition. The site is now part of the Canal Road Industrial Estate. On the opposite side of the line there is a large EWS marshalling yard and permanent way depot.

Harry was with D Company, 1st Battalion, Middlesex Regiment. 1st Battalion, The Middlesex Regiment (Duke of Cambridge's Own) was at Woolwich when war was declared in August 1914. They proceeded to France on August 11th landing at Rouen and taking on duties as Lines of Communication troops. On the 22nd they became attached to 19th Infantry Brigade, which was an independent command at this time, not attached to any division.

In 1916 they were in action on The Somme. The 1st Middlesex had arrived at Méaulte on July 13th, but the following morning the Battalion moved to Bécordel and bivouacked for some two or three hours. The 33rd Division had been ordered to attack between High Wood and the railway, and later the 1st Battalion moved forward and, after various halts and stops, reached the southern edge of Mametz Wood, finally bivouacking on the western lip of the valley just north of Fricourt.

The Battalion was now involved in The Battle of Bazentin Ridge, July 14th to the 17th which started with the Capture of Trônes Wood. From here the Brigade was again ordered to attack, and the 1st Middlesex set out for Bazentin-le-Petit, from which village the assault of the enemy's position was to be made. The advance was made through a gas cloud, which made everyone feel most uncomfortable, though apparently none of the troops were actually gassed. On reaching the church at Bazentin-le-Petit, B and C Companies worked round the northern side of the village, whilst A and D Companies went straight through it. Just beyond the eastern edge of the village there was a road running north and south; here the Companies deployed for the attack. B and D formed the front line, with C and A in support. The Battalion attacked on a frontage of 800 yards.

The Battalion had scarcely deployed for action when a party of the enemy in the Northern corner of Bazentin Le Petit Wood fired into the left flank of the advancing Middlesex men, with machine gun and rifle. Machine-gun fire now began to take heavy toll of the advancing Companies, which were finally brought to a standstill on the crest of a slight ridge east of the village. Shelled unmercifully and machine-gunned from both flanks, the Middlesex, attempting to "dig in" on the position gained, were eventually compelled to fall back to the road running north and south on the eastern outskirts of Bazentin-le-Petit from which they had started.

On August 13th the Battalion again moved back to the line, first in reserve in Mametz Wood and then to the front line on 14th in High Wood.

The Battalion moved back to Mametz Wood on the 19th, after a terrible time forward. The tour had cost the Die-Hards 1 officer wounded, 25 other ranks killed, 96 wounded, and 9 missing. On the 25th the Battalion was back again in the front line just north of Delville Wood. When relief came on 30th the Battalion had lost during the tour 2 officers killed and 3 wounded, 34 other ranks killed, 77 wounded, and 7 missing. From September 1st to the 20th, the Battalion was out of the line resting and training, but on the latter date moved into the Hebuterne trenches-an uneventful tour. The first three weeks of October were similarly uneventful until, on the 23rd, the Middlesex moved to Trônes Wood via Mametz and Montauban. On the 24th the Battalion went into the line east of Les Boeufs. The enemy was attacked on October 28th, the objective of the Brigade being the German positions in front of Le Transloy, known as Rainy Trench and Dewdrop Trench, and the dug-outs and points north-east of the latter. A and C Companies led the attack of the 1st Middlesex and by 9.30am the whole objective was in their hands and handed over to a relieving battalion (4th Suffolk Regt.) that night. That success was dearly bought, for one officer was killed and seven officers were wounded; 35 other ranks were killed, 136 wounded. On relief the Battalion moved back to the Flers line.

Harry was among those wounded and was evacuated from the Front. He succumbed to his wounds on November 8th, 1916. He is buried in Etaples Military Cemetery.

Sidney Thomas Eves
Royal West Kent, 8th Battalion
Service No. G/1087 - Private

Sidney was born in Gravesend in 1896, the son of Thomas and Rosina Eves of 94 All Saints Road, Perry Street. There were six children in the family – Rose, born in 1894, Sidney, Ernest, born in 1898, Frederick, born in 1900, Ada, born in 1902 and Maud, born in 1908.

Sidney was a gardener by profession and prior to enlisting lived as a boarder with David and Elizabeth Smythe. David ran his own business, that of a market garden. They lived at Longwalk Cottage, Downs Road, Northfleet.

He enlisted with the Royal West Kent Regiment on September 3rd, 1914 in Gravesend. He was 5 feet 5 inches tall and weighed 112lbs. he had brown hair and brown eyes and had a fresh complexion. Initially with the 3rd Battalion he was posted to the 9th Battalion on October 24th and a year later, on October 11th, he was off to war with the 8th Battalion.

In between his sole indiscretion which was not obeying a direct order, on May 22nd, 1915, resulted in he being confined to Barracks for three days. On July 3rd 1916 he sprained his left ankle playing football in Calais.

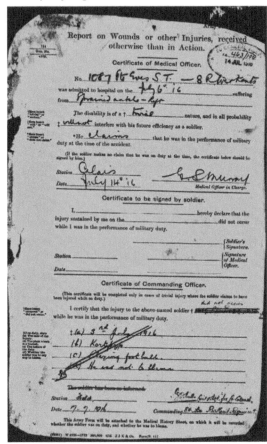

The 8th (Service) Battalion, The Royal West Kent Regiment was raised at Maidstone on September 12th, 1914 as part of Kitchener's Third New Army and joined 72nd Brigade, 24th Division. They trained at Shoreham and moved to billets in Worthing for the winter in December, returning to Shoreham in April 1915. They moved to Blackdown in July for final training and proceeded to France on August 30th, 1915, landing at Boulogne. The Division concentrated in the area between Etaples and St Pol on September 4th and a few days later marched across France into the reserve for the British assault at Loos, going into action on the 26th of September and suffering heavy losses. In 1916 they suffered in the German gas attack at Wulverghem and then moved to The Somme seeing action in The Battle of Delville Wood and The Battle of Guillemont.

Sidney was killed in action on November 23rd, 1916. He is buried in Philosophe Cemetery, Mazingarbe.

EVES.—Killed in action, in France, on November 23rd, 1916, Private Sidney Thomas Eves of Royal West Kents, the beloved son of Mr. and Mrs. Thomas Eves, 94, All Saints'-road, Northfleet, aged 21.

God gave us strength to part with you,
Courage to let you go,
But all that it means to lose you,
Only our sad hearts know.

—From Mother, Dad, Brothers and Sisters.

Philosophe lies between Bethune and Lens. The cemetery was started in August 1915. In 1916 it was taken over by the 16th (Irish) Division, who held the Loos Salient at the time, and many of their dead were brought back to the cemetery from the front line. Succeeding divisions used the cemetery until October 1918, and men of the same Division, and often the same battalion, were buried side by side.

After the Armistice, this cemetery was one of those used for the concentration of isolated graves from the Loos battlefield. The bodies of 41 men of the 9th Black Watch were brought from positions a little West of Loos, and those of 340 officers and men of other Regiments from different points in the communes of Cambrin, Auchy, Vermelles, Halluch and Loos.

The R.W.K.'s have lost another brave lad in Pte. Sidney Thomas Eves, son of Mr. and Mrs. Thomas Eves, of 94, All Saints-road, Northfleet, at the age of 21. Pte. Eves joined the county regiment in September, 1914, went to France in 1915, and was killed by a trench mortar bomb on November 23rd. Sec.-Lieut. C. R. H. Allworth, writing to his parents states that the bomb fell in the trench and killed him instantly. Sending the sympathy of all, he says that Pte. Eves was a good soldier, always cheerful, and very much liked by everybody, and his loss was greatly felt. This is also borne out in letters from the Rev. S. D. B. Poole (chaplain) and Lance-Corpl. Winton. He was buried with military honours in a grave behind the line, and his last resting place will be marked with a cross. Pte. Eves belonged to a patriotic family. His brothers serving are Sergt. J. Eves, R.E., Pte. H. Eves, R.W. Surrey's, and E. Eves, R.N. Division, all in France; Pte. Ed. Eves, R.N.R., Chatham; his brother-in-law is Pte. T. Allen, R.W.K., France; his uncles are Ptes. H. Worlidge, Grenadier Guards, France; and C. Worlidge, A.S.C., Aldershot; and his cousin is also in the Army.

GR 16/12/16 [Andrew Marshall]

GR 16/12/16 [Andrew Marshall]

Samuel Evett
Yorkshire Regiment, 5th Battalion
Service No. 1921 - Lance Corp

Samuel was born in Jersey in 1888, the son of Emmanuel George and Mary Everett. Samuel enlisted with the 5th Battalion Alexandra, Princes of Wales's Own [Yorkshire Regiment] in Bridlington.

Lance Corporal Evett was killed in action on April 28th, 1915.

The 5th Battalion War Diary for April, 1915 relates the fate of Samuel –

15th - Advance Party of Transport and details left Newcastle on Tyne, 35 strong, under Captain JAR Thomson. Other Officers were Lt GA Maxwell. Lt JS Wadsworth [TO] and 2nd Lt GB Purvis [MGO].

16th - This party arrived at Southampton 6.00 am and sailed 7.30.am.

George Eve –
Etaples Military Cemetery

Sidney Eves – Philosophe Cemetery, Mazingarbe

17th - This party arrived Le Havre in the forenoon and marched at night to camp.

18th - Left Le Havre 11.30 by train and formed juncture with Battalion en route and de-trained Cassels 6.00 am on the 19th.

17th - Battalion left Newcastle on Tyne 11.0 am at full strength [less advance party],
The Battalion arrived at Folkestone at 10.00 pm and embarked on HM Transport "Onward".

18th - Battalion arrived at Boulogne 1.50 am and proceeded to Camp at St Martins. Left by train at night.
19th - Arrived at Cassels at 6.00 am and marched to Steenvoorde twelve 'hot and very tiring' miles to billets outside the village of Steenvoorde, where they had finally rested, for three whole days.
20th to 22nd - In billets at Steenvoorde. At midnight on the 22nd ordered to be ready at 2 hours' notice.
23rd - Battalion [less QM, QMS, Sgt.Dr.5 men and guard of 6 NCOs and men of A Company] proceeded by Motor Buses to Vlamertinghe and from thence marched to A Huts at Ypres. Transport and M Guns followed.
Informed we were to be held in Corps Reserve and ready to move at ten minutes notice. Received orders and fell in 1.15 am.
24th - Proceeded [less Machine Guns] to the banks of the Yser Canal in support of 2nd Zouaves.

The Battalion lined the Canal banks under the shelter of a ridge before daylight, the men shortly afterwards digging themselves into shelter holes. B Company, which was somewhat exposed, suffered minor casualties from over dropping bullets. Had first experience of shell fire in forenoon, but sustained no injury. Attached 2nd Lt Craig and MG Section of 7th Northumberland Fus to us. Shortly in the afternoon the Battalion was ordered to cross the Canal and support the Canadians at Chateau, where it reported at 3.00 pm being subject to rifle and shell fire en route. From Chateau it was ordered to proceed to Saint Jean to the support of the 3rd Canadian Infantry Brigade.
This village was soon afterwards in flames and the Battalion skirting its rear, skirmished across open country under heavy shelling to the 3rd Canadian Infantry Brigade HQ. Attempted repeatedly to get into touch with the York and Durham Brigade, but could obtain no reply. Taken over by a Canadian General. Re-inforced one of his trenches and received the following order:-
"You will take up a position and entrench in rear of our present line in C.16.C. You will be ready to counter attack when necessary." signed G B Hughes, Lt Col. 3rd Canadian Inf Brigade.
Constant rain all night. Several men wounded and one killed.
25th - At 3.00 am received orders to proceed to Fortuin. En route passed a number of detached bodies of troops in retreat.
Arrived at rendezvous about 5.00 am in company with 5th Durham Light Infantry and met the General Officer in Command of the Yorks and Durham Brigade.
With daylight shelling commenced. B and C Companies occupied line of reserve trenches on the Right of the

road to the Left of the DLI, but no shelter available for the A and D Companies except the hedge bottom on roadside.

About 6.00 am these latter Companies advanced to support of Royal Irish across open field and were met with heavy shrapnel fire.
Leading parties obtained the objective when the order was given to retire as Royal Irish were falling back.
In this movement A and D Companies suffered severely, losing 8 killed and about 40 wounded [the latter including the Adjutant].
A and D Coys then dug themselves in the hedge bottom of a field to the left of the road. D Coy in line with B and C and with A at right angles on the left of D Coy.
The 7th Northumberland Fusiliers Machine Gun Section was placed on A Coy line.
Alternating bursts of the shell and rifle fire continued throughout the day. About noon the DLI, who had been ordered to search a farmhouse requested assistance and a party of 25 of D Company under Capt GC Barber and Lt H Brown was sent out. It was met by the fire of a Machine Gun concealed in the house and Capt Barber and a L/Cpl [Dell] were instantly killed.
Capt Purvis reported small parties of Germans due North in trenches. Orderlies were sent to Brigade stating that "Enemy was inclined to press" and asking "Have you any orders ?". No reply could be obtained. Other casualties occurred from shell and rifle fire, which died down at nightfall, when the dead were collected and buried.
The wounded had all been attended to under fire and conveyed to the advanced dressing station. trenches were improved and preparations to hold the line for the night at all costs.

Among the wounded was Lance Corporal Evett.

26th - Same position. Reported position again to Brigade. Ordered to remain. 2 Lt E Majolier, Acting Adjutant. Heavy shelling as on previous day with much sniping.
Closely adjacent farmhouse destroyed by enemy's incendiary shells. Slight relief in local area when Lahore Division went into action during afternoon on the slopes to West of our position.
Trenches further improved. Further casualties. At night advanced and occupied line of trenches in relief of London Regiment in Horseshoe.
27th - In these trenches. Shelled, but replied vigourously to rifle fire.
28th - In trenches. Relieved midnight by 4th East Yorks Regt.
Casualties for tour. Killed 1 Officer and 23 Other Ranks.
Wounded 1 Officer and 106 OR. Of these 6 subsequently died of their wounds.
The Annals of Bridlington noted that - News has reached Bridlington that Private Samuel Evett has died of wounds received in action near Ypres, on the 25th April. He was formerly in the employ of Mr J. J. Wardill, dentist, on Prospect Street, Bridlington, and was held in high esteem by all who knew him.
It appears that he was wounded on Sunday, April 25, but news of his death did not reach Bridlington until early this week.
The following extract from a letter written by Lance-Sergeant Saltonstall to his mother tells how bravely Private Evett met his death:
"My dearest Mother. You ask how Sammy is. Well, dear, I have not told you before, as I thought it would upset you, but he was hit badly last Sunday week, the 25th, when we were in a very hot corner. He was next to me, dear, at

the time, and I did all in my power for him. I bandaged him up, and talked to him to keep him cheerful. I saw him removed on a stretcher, and the last I saw of the poor little chap. We had stuck together throughout it all until then and his last goodbye to me was: 'So long, old boy, and thank you; we have been pals, haven't we?' Since then, yesterday to be exact, I heard in the orderly room that he was dead. Of course, it may not be that but I am afraid it is. Still, even if it is, he died like a man, and was in war. But I do miss him."

Samuel succumbed to his wounds on the 28th.

He is buried in Hazebrouck Communal Cemetery. Hazebrouck is 56 km southeast of Calais. From October 1914 to September 1917, casualty clearing stations were posted at Hazebrouck. The Germans shelled and bombed the town between September 1917 and September 1918 making it unsafe for hospitals, but in September and October 1918, No.9 British Red Cross Hospital was stationed there.

Commonwealth burials began in the communal cemetery in October 1914 and continued until July 1918. At first, they were made among the civilian graves, but after the Armistice these earlier burials were moved into the main Commonwealth enclosure.

Sam Evett –

Hazebrouck Communal Cemetery

The cemetery is unusual in that French soldiers are buried with headstones – in the bottom image these are to the right with the Commonwealth casualties to the left.

The memorial, below, is to the mid left of the image at the bottom of the page with the town Memorial facing opposite.

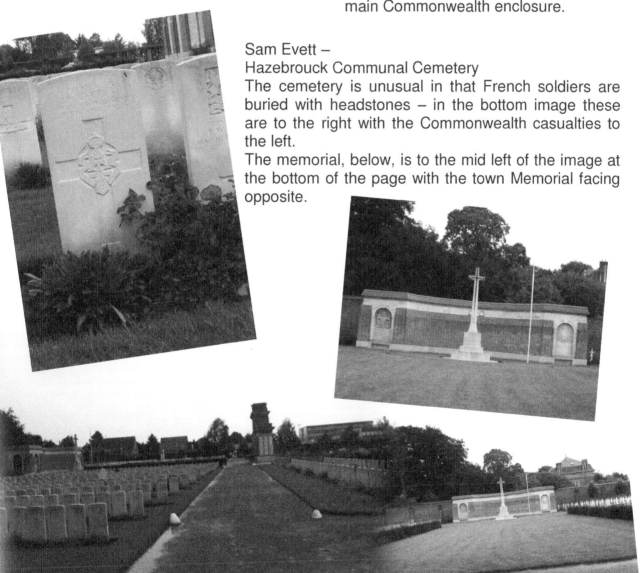

397

MILTON CHURCH, GRAVESEND.   No. 5006

The excitement of war!

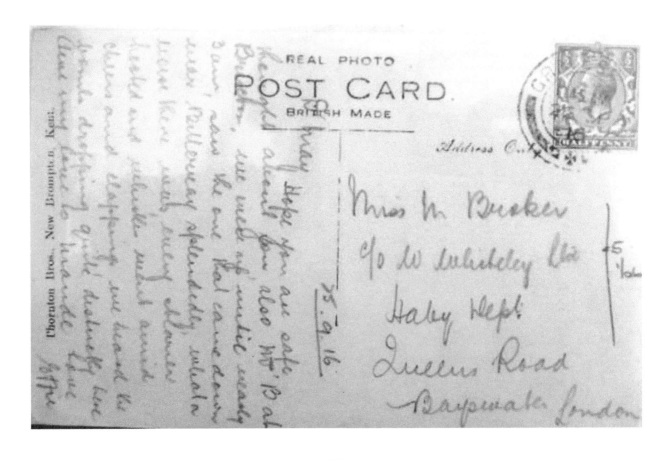

BIBLIOGRAPHY

- A PARISH GOES TO WAR, Friends of St George's, Northfleet Press, 2014

- AN ILLUSTRATED HISTORY OF THE SECOND YEAR OF THE GREAT WAR 1915, Britain At War Magazine, 2014

- CEMETERIES & MEMORIALS IN BELGIUM & NORTHERN FRANCE, CWGC / Michelin, Clermont-Ferrand, 2008

- IGHTHAM MOTE, National Trust, Rotherham, 2013

- PEACE SOUVENIR AND CONCISE HISTORY OF THE WAR 1914 – 1918, Gravesend & Dartford Reporter, 1919.

Arnold, Georg M., GRAVESEND IN THE VERY TIMES OF OLD, Caddel & Son, Gravesend, 1896

Atkinson, Captain C.T., THE QUEEN'S OWN ROYAL WEST KENT REGIMENT 1914-1919, Simpkin, Marshall, Hamilton, Kent & Co., Ltd, 1924

Benson, James [revised and edited by Hiscock, Robert H.], HISTORY OF GRAVESEND, Phillimore, 1976

De Ruvigny's ROLL OF HONOUR 1914-18, Part 1, Naval & Military Press, Uckfield, East Sussex

De Ruvigny's ROLL OF HONOUR 1914-18, Part 2, Naval & Military Press, Uckfield, East Sussex

De Ruvigny's ROLL OF HONOUR 1914-18, Part 3, Naval & Military Press, Uckfield, East Sussex

De Ruvigny's ROLL OF HONOUR 1914-18, Part 4, Naval & Military Press, Uckfield, East Sussex

De Ruvigny's ROLL OF HONOUR 1914-18, Part 5, Naval & Military Press, Uckfield, East Sussex

Foster, Paul, IN CONTINUING AND GRATEFUL MEMORY – THE MONS SECTOR 1914, Minutecircle, Sittingbourne, 2014

Foster, Paul, IN CONTINUING & GRATEFUL MEMORY THE MENIN GATE, Volume 2, Minutecircle, Sittingbourne, 2014

Foster, Paul, IN CONTINUING & GRATEFUL MEMORY THE MENIN GATE, Volume 3, Minutecircle, Sittingbourne, 2014

Foster, Paul, IN CONTINUING & GRATEFUL MEMORY - THE PLOEGSTEERT SECTOR, Minutecircle, Sittingbourne, 2014

Hammerton, J.A., THE WAR ILLUSTRATED, Volumes 1-8, Amalgamated Press, London

Legg, Philip, THE QUEEN'S OWN ROYAL WEST KENT REGIMENT, Colourplan, Ipswich, 2004

Mansfield, F.A., HISTORY OF GRAVESEND IN THE COUNTY OF KENT, Gravesend & Dartford Reporter, Gravesend, 1922

Mitchell, Gardiner, THREE CHEERS FOR THE DERRYS! YES! Publications, Derry/Londonderry, 2008

Moody, Colonel R.S.H., HISTORICAL RECORDS OF THE BUFFS EAST KENT REGIMENT 1914-1919, Medici Society, London, 1922

Nicholls, Jonathan, CHEERFUL SACRIFICE, THE BATTLE OF ARRAS 1917, Pen & Sword, Barnsley, 1995

Park-Pirie, Steph [editor], TOGETHER THEY STOOD, AN ANTHOLOGY OF POETIC VERSE, Poetry Now, Peterborough, 2004

Rowe, Verna, THEY ALSO SERVED WHO DID NOT FIGHT: ONE MAN'S WORLD WAR 1 EXPERIENCE, in Historic Gravesham 2014, Number 60, The Gravesend Historical Society, Gravesend 2014

Sheffield, Gary, THE WESTERN FRONT, Carlton Books, London, 2014

ACKNOWLEDGEMENTS

This project - the study of those listed on the many Memorials in Gravesham – has developed into one of much co-operation between students at the school and the Community. We quickly realised that it will take five volumes, the first of which is this one, to cover the complete study.

Students studying for the Local History G.C.S.E. course in conjunction with those students in the History Society undertook research into the many names listed on local Memorials. A variety of sources were utilised to create the biographies, some a couple of paragraphs long, others more than twenty pages. Information, to include images, came from books, the Internet, resources at the local Library in Gravesend and in the field. Where available relevant images were added; as many photographs of the individuals were found and photographs of headstones or names on Memorials [if 'missing'] added. In this respect former students of the school gave valuable assistance; Victoria Syrett in helping research and Maria Peters, assisting with the extension of the project the creation of the internet site.

Once the initial research was completed the expertise of researchers and historians in the Community was sought. In this we were ably assisted by Andrew Marshall and Andy White in particular. The former offered his massive collection of material both primary and secondary sources and here is no doubt that the equal of his research and collection could not be bettered anywhere. The latter provided many photographs of those buried in Gravesend Cemetery and are remembered on family headstones (in the Cemetery).

Tony Larkin provided much assistance and advice on local history, characters and individuals of the time of the Great War. Karen Syrett added her expertise in researching, developing the biographies and adding further information. Christoph Bull was equally as helpful offering his expertise and knowledge. It was good to receive material from relatives and in particular we need to mention Hugh Mackrell who provided much of the material on Robert Drennan and the Drennan family. Betty McNerlin and Alistair Harper, Limavady, also supported us through providing guidance, advice and photographs for the Drennan biography. The Mayor of Gravesham, John Càller offered the services of his office, there being much material held in the Mayor's Office. Nicola Tubbs of Gravesend Library gave support and the use of the Library for the launch of the book.

Lyndsey Thompson advised us on several matters – from funding through to providing assistance with the 'Memorial Book' at the Woodville Halls. Neil Fisher, Church Warden, provided photographs of the several Memorials within St. George's Church. Stephen Thompson and Dean Nelson ensured we had photographs of the 1917 Memorial 'Boards'.

Further afield we are fully supported in Cambrai by Cécile and Jean Horent; visiting cemeteries with Jean revealed many exciting facets of information we would not otherwise be aware of. Paul Foster ensured similar in the Ypres area. Paul not alone provided the inspiration for our series of books but also assisted us enormously with the lay out, the covers and the printing and publishing work.

A huge thank you to Catherine Murphy for the support given, for the driving but in particular the proof reading which was continuous and relentless. We also need to thank Councillor Tanmanjeet Singh Dhesi and Jackie Denton for their support and to the GRAVESHAM CAN funding which has ensured publication of this book through providing the necessary funding.

This work would not be possible without the support of the leadership team at St. John's and we thank Tom Cahill, Sean Maher and Matthew Barron for their ongoing support, good humour, guidance and advice. Our thanks too to Sid Harris whose poignant poem makes us reflect on Remembrance.

We apologise for anyone not mentioned – the book is the result of much work by many individuals. Our thanks to everyone.

History Society, St John's Catholic School

Lightning Source UK Ltd.
Milton Keynes UK
UKOW07f0801120315

247758UK00004B/11/P